Virago!

The authors: Marion B. Dunlevy (left) and Alice S. Maxwell

Virago!

The Story of Anne Newport Royall
(1769–1854)

Alice S. Maxwell
Marion B. Dunlevy

McFarland & Company, Inc., Publishers
Jefferson, North Carolina, and London

Library of Congress Cataloging in Publication Data

Maxwell, Alice S., 1924–
*Virago! The story of Anne Newport Royall (1769–
1854).*

Bibliography : p.
Includes index.
1. Royall, Anne Newport, 1769–1854. 2. Travelers –
United States – Biography. 3. Journalists – United
States – Biography. I. Dunlevy, Marion B. II. Title.
E340.R88M39 1985   917.3′045   84-42731

ISBN 0-89950-133-8 (alk. paper)

Printed in the United States of America.

McFarland   Box 611   Jefferson NC 28640

To Marion, Mary and Max
without whom this book
would not have been written

Table of Contents

An Historical Mystery

Anne Newport Royall, 1769-1854, dared to be the first American writer on our national affairs, the first of our Washington commentators, columnists, muckrakers, and was punished because she was born a woman of reason in a world which too many wanted only for men and God.

Alice S. Maxwell
Marion B. Dunlevy

A Word About a Word

"Virago" is the word used in the Vulgate Bible rendering of the story of Adam and Eve. It was the first name for the being made from man, taken from him like a clone, to be his mate and match him in his life. "Virago" was woman, mirroring man in her vigor, her boldness, her ability to speak. It has been a lost word but its time has come again.

In an age when women striving for equality have at last found it, this word regains its meaning against the corruptions of men who have misused it. If ever a name could define the extraordinary woman of any time, her ability to move the world with her presence, VIRAGO is it.

Introduction

In the archives of our nation and in many universities, small books sit in closed cases like treasures to be shielded from view. These are rare books, being among the first produced by American citizens in the new nation, the United States of America. Their titles? *Sketches of History, Life and Manners in the United States, The Tennessean*, three volumes of *Black Book, Travels in Pennsylvania* in two volumes, *Letters from Alabama* and *A Southern Tour*. The period they cover is one of the most important in American history—1823 to 1833 —when our government child was becoming our government parent.

The books sit on library shelves, receive mention in catalogs and bibliographies, and all who need them are glad they are there. But no one ever seems to think twice about the person who wrote them. This is an odd omission in the literary and scholarly world, which celebrates every other writer of such memorable and mentionable work with tome after tome illuminating authors' lives and thoughts. It is even more peculiar when we consider that the author of these books about that maturing period in our history was one of the first writers America produced. It is even more amazing because this writer is credited with the first use of quotation marks in news stories, and in fact invented the kind of writing which is still stamped uniquely American, *muckraking*. In so doing, the author established the information industry we call "journalism," a word this writer popularized. But the real blockbuster is that the writer of these books was a woman—a most remarkable woman!

Her name was Anne Newport Royall. How she achieved her status, what she did, and why she was stripped of the historical celebration she deserves is what *Virago!* is all about. Her story is a fascinating commentary on the history, manners, and customs of our nation. How her story began for us is part of Anne Royall.

Virago! came into being because one of us experienced the same treatment in a court of law in 1972 that Anne Newport Royall suffered in another court of law in 1829. The researchers for that brush with "justice" brought to light the 1829 story and with it, an extraordinary woman, her work, and her life. The visits to four states and countless libraries, necessary to tracking down the woman and her times, produced a tale so bizarre as to make any fiction pale by comparison. Anne Newport Royall was erased from history by the actions of a United States' Court of Law: these same actions were used against another woman in 1972.

In September of 1971, Marion B. Dunlevy, the researcher for this book, was arrested as a "common scold," held on $1,000 bail, indicted on said charge, arraigned, and then brought to trial in Monmouth County Court, Freehold, New Jersey, on April 10, 1972. Her eight months of distress and the oddity of the charge sent her to law libraries to learn what it was all about. The result? Anne Newport Royall came to light again, for Mrs. Royall was the first and only woman to be tried on such a charge in a federal court. The history of that case was important to Marion B. Dunlevy. Mrs. Royall's indictment and trial as a "com-

1

mon scold" is what had made Marion B. Dunlevy's indictment and trial possible. Marion Dunlevy, like Anne Royall, was tried before judge and jury. Before the first word could be uttered on the 1972 charge, presiding judge Patrick McGann severed that charge from the indictment and "common scold" was held for further study. In a year in which the equal rights amendment to the U.S. Constitution had received affirmative study and action from the Congress of the United States, such an archaic charge was inappropriate, or so Judge McGann declared in July, 1972. That moment of jeopardy for a woman called into a 20th-century court for an ancient "crime," relegated to the invalid file by English Common Law in the 16th century, produced the same emotional experience and response that characterized the 1829 moment of jeopardy for Anne Royall. That feeling, that sense of helplessness and revulsion, and then the compulsion to prove the horror for what it was, gave form to *Virago!*

Alice Maxwell, a newspaperwoman and columnist for a weekly newspaper in New Jersey, researched with Marion Dunlevy. So this book was born, carried through, and a strange court story told. Marion Dunlevy had the 20th century for her defense and she was exonerated. It seemed only right that Anne Royall should have our century for her defense too, and for her exoneration.

Virago! has one purpose. The world has lost Anne Royall long enough and her work deserves better.

Alice S. Maxwell
Marion B. Dunlevy
Middletown, N.J.

Chapter 1

Two Washington Homes

It was January 23rd, 1829, when a small carriage rolled through the Maryland swamps vying with a steady stream of outbound traffic for the narrow road to Washington, the capital of the United States of America. The busy road foretold a momentous change in America's history.

The sixth president of the United States, John Quincy Adams, was preparing to depart the White House for his home in Massachusetts while an old soldier, Andrew Jackson, was enroute from his Tennessee plantation to take his place. On the surface, it appeared to be one more customary transfer of office from an American leader to his successor, but this time there was a difference.

John Quincy Adams had served just four years as the chief executive of the Republic. Unlike his predecessors Jefferson, Madison, and Monroe, he did not enjoy eight years in office. As the son of a former president who also had been denied a second term, Adams the younger had striven for reelection to prove that he could accomplish what his father had not; but he had failed. Overwhelmed by the fickleness of his constituency, by rejection from the people he had served all of his life, he did not understand his defeat. Neither did his followers, but the Jackson forces did. It was a result for which they had worked ten years, a reward for a man with a strange hold on the popular will and a punishment for those whom that majority loathed. This matter was much in the mind of the passenger in the carriage bound for Washington, for Anne Newport Royall, writer, was returning to the American capital to record the changes she knew were about to take place.

The arduous journey was almost over, and Mrs. Royall was glad. Her trip to Harrisburg, Pennsylvania, had been difficult, and it could not end soon enough. She parted the curtains again and again, looking for the city she knew was before her. A black bag sat by her side, and she patted it reassuringly. It held her notes for the third and last volume of her *Black Book* series and 2,100 subscribers were waiting. With this trek she had added another 250 supporters and was two weeks behind schedule but with so much more money available for day-to-day necessities, she would have more leisure to pursue her real purpose.

The carriage made slow progress, stopping often for others to pass on the single-land road. Mrs. Royall frowned; this road was a scandal. Her friend, old Governor DeWitt Clinton of New York, was right: Clinton's canals, so assailed by his opposition, were better than these dirt tracks. As she mused, the old post house was passed and she was in Washington City at last.

A cold damp had calmed the dust of the city streets, but the wide ruts were deep in the noon-softened dirt. The weight of the vehicle accentuated every jolt. Passers-by could note the passenger's discomfort by the jerks of her bonneted

3

head and the evening gales were moving in with freezing shadows to harden the road ridges into back-breaking patterns of disarray. Mrs. Royall saw few sights to relish, for the city had not yet awakened to its position as the heart of a nation; its buildings, like the streets, were unfinished. The reconstruction after the destruction of the 1814 British raid was producing beauty, but it was haphazard and the city's inhabitants could not have cared less. On the capital's perimeter, debris was everywhere. Much of it was indistinguishable from the dwellings of the poor and the shanties of those who had recently arrived.

Washington City was a part-time government headquarters. The nation had inaugurated six presidents and was readying itself for the seventh, but Congress met only a few months of the year and the government was foundering in a welter of unfinished details. Lodging houses and inns outnumbered well-built homes and most public buildings were tenuous structures thrown up to meet pressing needs. The only two imposing edifices were the houses of the new "people's government": the Capitol for the legislature and the White House for the president. These crowned the city's center like jewels and were surrounded by offices and churches overseeing the people below.[1] Washington was an old campground for those who awaited better days, searching out government posts to carry on the business of governing for a Congress and president more absent than present. But temporary headquarters or not, Washington City was to become, for many, a permanent home. One of these was Mrs. Royall, returning on that cold January evening.

Bank Street was the carriage's destination, and as the house in the shadow of the new dome of the Capitol was reached, night had come. As Mrs. Royall disembarked from the stiff landark, other houses about began to show the soft radiance of whale-oil lamps. While the driver unloaded her baggage, she climbed the stairs to her door, tugged at the bellstring, and stood patiently awaiting her things. The door did not open, even to repeated knocks and calls; finally, in exasperation, she raised her cane to summon someone within the walls before her with hard whacks. Unable to gain entrance, Mrs. Royall descended to the street once more to try a side door. There were other residents in this rambling brick structure, and once again she used her cane. Finally a door was opened.

This was not the kind of homecoming Mrs. Royall had expected: "I had written to Washington that I would arrive on that day and sent money to purchase wood and gave instructions to have a fire laid in my parlour and everything in readiness, for the moment I arrived I must go to writing."[2] That note had been sent to inform Mrs. Royall's maidservant, but it had been to no avail. Her apartment was empty, and there was a coldness in its rooms that only days without warmth could produce. Signs of neglect were everywhere as she went about her rooms; Mrs. Royall became angry. She had left Washington City on September 18 to answer summons from friends in Pennsylvania and had given her notes for work in progress to her girl, and where was that girl? Mrs. Royall had promised to send her book to her printers before the end of February.

Mrs. Royall knew she had to make the best of her situation. After traveling 1,500 miles on terrible roads, she could take the empty house in stride, and in one hour would set to writing, with or without a fire or supper. Black Book, Volume III, had to be resumed; she had candles in her luggage for light and for warmth she could gather her traveling rug about her legs.

Mrs. Royall had been ten years traveling the country, the last five as a writer describing the land as it prospered. She had built a large following by careful attention to detail, facts, people, and by personally selling subscriptions, contracting printing, promoting, and delivering her finished work. She boasted 2,000 subscribers and by locating her own booksellers had increased the demand for her work to over 3,500, sometimes going into another printing. She supported herself from these literary efforts, and each new book brought her greater audiences and more renown. When she entered a city or town on her travels, she was a celebrity accepted by local commerce journals and newspapers in search of new ideas with which to leaven their provinciality. She was "Mrs. Royall" and that name carried all the weight implied, borne as it was by a woman strong in physical definition whose wide regard had been duly noted in the capital. Anne Newport Royall was recognized by senators, congressmen, the White House, cabinet members, and accredited embassies; but this was cold comfort as she surveyed her problems on a cold night in a dark room.

Work was her answer, and arranging her notes before her, Mrs. Royall took pen in hand. Even as she did, she was frustrated. The ink, the life blood of her thought for paper, was ice. She dipped her pen again and again, but it would not respond. She looked about her, and the candle burning bright was her solution. It could warm the ink, return its true black character; so with numb hands, she steadied the bottle above the flame, twisting it to and fro as she thought on her situation.

She had come to the capital in early 1824, on her first visit, after a long trip from Huntsville, Alabama, to petition the Congress to repay money due her husband for services in the Revolution. How naive she had been! She had learned much since then, and she smiled as she stared at the blackness about her. A sudden flow of memories engulfed her; she put aside the miseries of the moment, talking to herself to dispel the silence about her.

Memories are good friends when one is alone, and it did no harm to return in fantasy to places one had known, resurrect people part of an old life. It was a diversion she could use, and she indulged it by thinking back on her childhood in Hannahstown, Pennsylvania. She took herself back to the old stockade, and suddenly she was running with others seeking shelter behind the stout wooden walls from Indian and English marauders. She shuddered as she recalled the flight and felt a shot of pain—she had scorched her cuff! Still lost in reveries, she changed the ink bottle to her other hand and let her mind wander more.

The Revolution! Poor Hannahstown was dead by the time it began. The fort, that small community which only came to life when threatened, had disappeared in flames in an Indian raid.[3] Mrs. Royall shivered as she remembered the event. The women, men, and children of her youth had disappeared with that first town she had known. She could thank a merciful God that Hannahstown had not been her last; she had come a long way to this Washington City, capital of a nation with more than 12 million people.[4]

The ink bottle was wearisome to hold. Mrs. Royall set it down. She stood and went to her window. The street below was deserted. There were people about her in all the houses along the street: Americans. What a lot of history was in that word, "American."

Anne Newport Royall had not been born an American; she had come into the world as a Marylander, an English citizen born in an English crown colony in 1769. Her parents had taken her from Baltimore when she was two as they trekked west to escape the political strife beginning to engulf their lives.[5] Her father had led them across the plains of Pennsylvania and settled them in a small cabin, so different from the fine house left behind. She never knew what he did, but she could recall that he came and went on long journeys. He had not been a farmer, and he was not a soldier; he had been with them one day, and then he was gone. She could remember no grief at his loss and his place was not taken for two years. Then there was Butler, her stepfather. Try as she could, she could not recall either man's face, only the face of her mother. The recollection of those gone made her shudder.

Even as she threw off the past, a shout in the street stunned her. Indians!

She laughed. There were no Indians in Washington City, but the thought of them reminded her of the black forest of her youth. Once again she was in reverie.

1775! Hannahstown had been burnt that year, but she had not been in it. Her mother, pushing Anne before her, had escaped the Indians to begin a search for surviving relatives that took two years. Anne had been just six years old, but she could remember those 1,200 miles through the mountain frontiers. The discomfort of this Washington room could never match the horrors on that long flight to survival.

Another shout in the street and Indians came again to mind. Mrs. Royall went back to her desk. Strange how such memoreies could still evoke fear after all these years. The Indians had been monsters at Hannahstown, but women of that race had later aided two white sisters in catastrophe; Mrs. Royall still gave thanks to those benefactors.[6]

If an American was to be defined in 1829, it was a woman sitting at her desk, remembering her past and then putting it aside as she prepared to write about the present. She had known no formal schooling, had educated herself, and was in the process of educating others. The active curiosity she represented was that of a whole nation, a people's intelligence, the insurance for its continuance. Mrs. Royall was ready to summon it to the defense of its origins. A nation had been created in spite of a million bad experiences, and the men and women who had surmounted them had built a new world; she would keep faith with them all by never forgetting how hard it had been. Mrs. Royall remembered the present, put the past from her, and tried the ink once more. Ice still imprisoned its power.

She twirled the bottle closer to the flame. The sight of her gloved hand gave her a start. Such gnarled and misshapen talons! At 60 years of age, her beautiful hands had been ruined long ago; these ugly things made her what she was. She took up her steel quill, and it shone in the candlelight. This small instrument was the master of her being, enslaved her to its needs. She went on warming its life blood, the ink with which it must write.

The calendar of her years was in her hands, but her mind was revealed in what she wrote; together they told her story. In 1829, few women lived to Mrs. Royall's age, and even fewer mustered a talent with which to make their own mark. Recognized as the writer on American affairs, she was a phenomenon in an era accustomed to the extraordinary but not always ready to accept it. Mrs. Royall had to earn her audience and never more so than now. The past had its place, since memories were clues to present ill, but if too much time was spent in such tracings, what must be done would not be done. Mrs. Royall put her trance from her and tried the ink again. This time it gave to her pen, and she started to write. Outside the Bank Street house, most of Washington City slept on. But others also were burning candles well into the morning hours.

The President-elect of the United States, General Andrew Jackson, was making a triumphal tour enroute from his home, the Hermitage, to the capital, showing Americans the face of their new leader as he rode to assume his post. His aides from the election campaign had preceded him to Washington to prepare for his inauguration, and his assumption of power. Jackson's staff had taken over an inn, the Indian Queen, and in its rooms they were plotting the steps with which their leader would bring his campaign into being as national policy. They had come from the many states carried in the last election, and they were busy assessing their positions in Congress and government offices. As Washington City slept, these men were planning on its new awakening. For the first time in American history, long lists of government offices and their employees were being compiled to implement a new venture, a departure unknown to the fitfully sleeping opposition. The birth of a new politics was being scratched out in the lengthening lists of a dozen pens, and no one was expecting its advent, not even those who wrote.[7]

Andrew Jackson had presented his aides with a difficult problem: every government office was to be evaluated, along with all the clerks and officials. The general believed that their allegiance was suspect, for they were working heaven and had worked hell to close door after door to him; he was determined to open those doors with his own people. They who had assumed they were the government were no longer; Jackson was, but he had to prove it just as he had proven himself so many times past on the field of battle. He would take his enemies by surprise, and his staff was charged with setting up the operation. It was a monumental chore.

Washington City slept on, never dreaming it was in the throes of shaking changes. John Quincy Adams was in the White House still, and all was well with his world for a few more weeks. Adams believed that what he had inherited from his predecessors he was about to bestow upon his successor, and the outgoing President took consolation in this fact. If the natural intransigeance in the government bureaus had undone him, it would work to undo Jackson too. Adams had long-term experience with Washington's offices. Government was in the hands of those who held its seats and no newcomer, not even a general, could change it; John Quincy Adams was very sure of that. Four years as chief executive of the United States of America had taught him how illusory power was. Congress ruled, and all the president had was the White House and a tenuous overseeing of the operations of a capital city, the inhabitants of which were the real U.S. government. Adams had found that national office was not expected to touch the nation's life except in foreign affairs. He was sure that Jackson would not find it otherwise. He slept soundly in the White House.[8]

The American capital called itself Washington City in a conscious effort to make itself a city when it wasn't. An overgrown town, the capital came to life only when Congress convened, and it found national spirit only once every four years when a president was about to be inaugurated. The rest of its days, it was a sleepy way-station on the road to more important places, commercial centers like Philadelphia, New York, and Boston, even Baltimore. Congress accepted this and did not stay long in Washington's precincts. Its titular leaders spent most of the year elsewhere, most often back home. The entire town, like a resort, geared itself to the law-making season and, when that was over, most in the city retired to better climes to wait for the season to begin again the next year.

The population of the town mirrored this quality. Most of Washington City's people were blacks, freed slaves picking up a living serving the hordes of visitors accompanying the return of Congress and searching for sinecures to keep government and its houses in custody until Congress met again. These blacks were joined by whites who sensed the need for administrative talent to keep the ignorant and haphazard at their tasks; whites who were careful not to publish their intent for fear that Washington City would become another frontier and attract a stampede of talent to compete with them for the few worthwhile positions.[9]

And so Washington City existed, a capital in name only, directed by its natives and undiscovered by the rest of the nation. It was a sleeping giant unaware of its real potential, fearful of discovery, and extremely wary of any who would prod it toward national glory. It was so insulated that it was not unlike a large plantation where the outbuildings are filled with workers but the main mansion is empty most of the year because the master must spend his time seeking a better livelihood elsewhere. The Washington City workers liked it that way; they had bent other president-masters to their will and now awaited another to pass through them and go about his business elsewhere. To them Andrew Jackson was no threat. They believed he was an old man tired of battle, ready to settle for new honor before death. They did not know what was happening in the night hours in the Indian Queen, but across town, one woman did. Mrs. Royall burned her candles through the night. She had much to put on paper. Like the president-elect, she too had been traveling the country, and she was well prepared for what was to come. While Jackson's aides powwowed in their tavern wigwam, listing friends and foes, Mrs. Royall busied herself writing the definition of both

Mrs. Royall had produced three books in three years and was at work on her fourth. Her best year had been 1828, and she was determined to make 1829 better. She had a message for people hungry for information about the national drama beginning to affect their lives. It had been a long time coming, this national focus on what was happening in Washington City, for the people had left the capital to its own devices as they looked to their old colonial capitals for guidance. For the first time, the nation's citizens were beginning to realize that the United States of America took precedence over Virginia, Massachusetts, New York, and Pennsylvania as national problems reached into those states and the states found themselves powerless to act without Washington. It was a situation she had anticipated long before others, that Washington would supplant the old colonial capitals just to get the country in proper order. Everywhere she had been this year, she had met more people who understood the ultimate destiny of the United States. Washington had to take full direction of American affairs: it could not leave each state to itself, to the mercy of a few cities and, the commerce which controlled them. Too many enemies were working against the United States of America and these divisions among states were weaknesses easily exploited by those skilled in the use of fractional power against the people. Americans had to learn that Washington was their heart, their protection, their direction; they had to make their capital their own.

Mrs. Royall was writing to put her philosophy to work. She had pioneered the idea that Americans had to pool information to find their unity. She had set out to convert and she had. Editors accepted her letters and articles on a regular basis and published them.[10] The mail she received grew with her renown. Letters from publishers like Major Mordecai Noah in New York, Wilfred Palfry in Massachusetts, and dear Mr. Butler in Pennsylvania praised her for her talent. They knew the value of her facts and figures, the charting of directions divined from them as she moved about the country and then returned to Washington to test them out. Mrs. Royall was America's first roving correspondent,[11] and she gave her editors and their readers what they wanted in a simple, straightforward manner. She was the first American writer to travel the United States with the purpose of listing its growing accomplishments, new industries, and developing economies, commenting as she went on the divers subjects of a diverse breed. As she grew in her talents, she added descriptive articles about personalities. These "pen portraits," both acid and kind, defined the men and women pacing the nation; since no pictures were available, they were welcome informative sketches to readers who knew how to use their imaginations.[12] The data she compiled and the vignettes she drew aided investment, spread progressive ideas, and informed Congress and its offices of changes before they occurred. The public she had created appreciated her work and waited for her series on Jackson. She had predicted his victory and she would predict his actions.

Mrs. Royall arranged her papers for this task. Notes were piled neatly for reference and the pamphlets she had written enroute were there for inclusion. It was serious business but she had a sense of humor which she put to use whenever possible. She kept her perspective by indulging this talent, having her fun. She spent enough paper on diatribe, the fashion of the day, and exhortation, the oration of the times. Although both had their place, the nation was not just a mass of problems. It was people in action, and Mrs. Royall did not confine herself to the great and near great. There were others to be chronicled too, people seeking the nation for themselves and trying to explain it to others. As they came to mind, she could laugh. They had to be mentioned because they existed, and the world needed to know who had passed by. Their voices were loud and their contributions small, but their personalities gave them prominence. Mrs. Royall treated them with wit, and she knew how to equivocate. She understood her function to her subscribers.

People were finally realizing that posterity required some kind of record, that mortality could be beaten in part with a mention in cold, hard print. The growth in printing in the country was phenomenal; every town boasted a press, and the people supported it. A name in print beside an action made a man or woman better known among neighbors than word of mouth. Printers did their jobs well, but their local sheets had short memories and even shorter lives.

Mrs. Royall patted her books. These were different—treasured possessions in the meanest of homes, well on their way to becoming national treasures as well. The Congress had declared them so when it had established the Library of Congress, funded and charged with documenting and cataloging the early and continuing steps of the Republic. American communities took the hint. Records and histories in hard covers insured shelf life in the new government buildings springing up everywhere. Someone or something could be put on file for eternity, or at least as long as men cherished information about other men and government insisted upon keeping it. This aspect Mrs. Royall knew better than other writers of her time, for she had popularized placing the first copy of any work with the Library of Congress[13] to give every writer the protection of that imprimatur, that catalogue for posterity. She was watchful of her own words, for the printing press led to plagiarism and corruption of thought. She who made her living with the pen did not want to bestow her profits on her enemies.

Mrs. Royall knew she had pioneered a new form of writing, but she was not jealous of imitators. She believed that American writers had to emerge in numbers to meet the nation's demand for detailed information about itself. She was the new writers' best booster so long as they promoted progress in America, a subject she knew people would read because it was about them, their egos, and it would spur the national momentum. She wrote from a series of journals kept faithfully as she traveled and the nature of those notes gave her a name for her work. She was writing "journalism," a creation mirroring the manner in which she deduced details and opinion influencing others. Journals had been kept by others, and had been published before, but hers were different, broader and wider in scope. She shared her notes in growing correspondence with publishers and editors of commercial papers in her effort to inform. Painting the national picture with daily brush strokes, she placed day-to-day occurrences in the context of country, people, invention, and industry in the towns as she passed and in Washington City on her return. She was pleased with her innovation and worked hard to make it come to life for her editors and for her readers.[14]

As the dawn hour passed, the candles and lamps were snuffed in the Indian Queen's rooms and in Mrs. Royall's room. Those who had worked by waxen and oil light looked at what they had done. Mrs. Royall glanced at her pages then at her subscription ledgers. Jackson's aides looked at their longer lists. These workers shared a common thought: They were about to summon new intelligence for the nation and its problems. They were charting national directions and new policies were being born. None knew, as they laid their pens to rest, but two Washington homes, the poor brick one of Mrs. Royall and the great White House awaiting Andrew Jackson, would change America. And so the dark night of January 23, 1829, became the bright day of January 24.

Chapter 2

The Culprits

It was a cold, sparkling day, and Mrs. Royall rose late in the morning. The night's activities had exhausted her, but she could not let the day go without asking about her housegirl's whereabouts. The girl had been faithful before, and there was no reason to suppose she was not now. Mrs. Royall canvassed the neighborhood for information.

No neighbor could tell her what had become of the black maidservant. The new tenants in the Bank Street house were impudent when asked about it. Another black was missing, but that was the way with such; besides, they had more to worry about than another's servant. They did not care for Mrs. Royall's predicament and said so; she cared less for them as a result. She had not asked for charity, only information. Her new fellow tenants were a loud, low, questionable lot, and she was uncomfortable sharing the premises with them. She had to have someone to stay with her until she found the girl.

Mrs. Royall did not have to look hard for a companion. She was fortunate in that a friend of five years was accustomed to her call for assistance and would ready herself for any task. Mrs. Royall went to see Sally Dorrett Stackpool.

Mrs. Stackpool and Mrs. Royall had become friends shortly after Mrs. Royall arrived in Washington. The writer had taken bed and board at the Old Capitol, a brick building which had been the temporary Congress of the United States after the burning of Washington by the British.[1] Here she had joined such fellow residents as Henry Clay, John Randolph, and many members of Congress, but such luminaries were no recompense for the appalling lack of sanitary facilities from which the Old Capitol suffered. Mrs. Royall had stayed just long enough in those brick walls to meet the nation's leaders and know them by their opinion, and then she had looked about for more suitable quarters.

Conducting a house-to-house search for decent lodging, preferably with a family, Mrs. Royall had stopped to take rest on the step of a modest dwelling. The front door had opened and a cheerful young woman had come forth to offer the tired old woman a glass of water. This act of generosity began the friendship with Sally Dorrett, who took pleasure in serving others. A single woman, she was raising the orphaned sons of her sister. She had an extra room and welcomed the company of another woman in the world of men about them. The friendship continued even after Sally's later marriage, the births of her own children, and separate homes.

Sally Dorrett Stackpool came to Mrs. Royall's assistance immediately. She had no knowledge of Mrs. Royall's black girl, but said she would be very pleased to attend to her friend, preparing her food and seeing to the small conveniences necessary to Mrs. Royall's continuing her writing uninterrupted. Sally's hus-

10

band, John Stackpool, a purser in the U.S. Navy, was away on duty, and Mrs. Royall's needs would fill Sally's dull days. It would be a pleasure for both, for the women had shared so much that they were family. Mrs. Royall accepted Sally's offer and went back to work.[2]

Washington City was in a frenetic state. The last week in January saw the first mobs of visitors descend upon the capital. Jackson's supporters were flooding in by stage, horse, and foot, and the outskirts of the city had become a gigantic *bivouac* for every manner of farmer, backwoodsman, and veteran of the general's many campaigns. They had come to see their hero made president and Adams booted out. Among them were thousands who hoped their allegiance to Jackson would be rewarded with government positions. The impudence of such outspoken aspirations was not lost on the Washingtonians, and for the first time the coming presidential transition instilled fear in those who held government offices. The heralded arrival February 15 of Andrew Jackson began to assume the face of revolution, and old Washington did not sleep well.[3]

Andrew Jackson was a man to be feared. The rumors about the general's vindictiveness crept into daily conversations. Adams and his *coterie* were to be the targets of his wrath, the result of the curious alignment of forces which had ignored Jackson, keeping Washington's offices a private club to reward those who had denied the presidency to Jackson in 1824. The sitting Congress did not like this prospect and was at work strengthening its defenses against retribution.

Andrew Jackson had been elected president in November but would not take office until March 4. Many prayed openly that the "hero" would not make it; he was an old man and his enemies' hopes were buoyed by the death of Rachel Jackson. There was open talk that this tragedy could break the man, even as it was said that scandal had killed his wife.[4] These thoughts went the rounds, and with them, Washingtonians found both fear and elation. As the days passed and the general came closer, however, others had more sense.

Mrs. Royall watched as this confusion and cabal circulated about her. *Black Book, Volume III*, had to be completed, so she kept to her desk. She was well aware of everything; she was recording it as she wrote. There was rising political chaos in the capital, but she was not afraid. The new faces in the streets of Washington were not strangers to her but friends, and Mrs. Royall saluted these invaders. Her pen was plumbing muddy waters to assist them in their quest. She was the advocate of a frontal attack in a strange conflict with an enemy Americans were only beginning to know existed. She was the *agent provocateur* of new politics, awaiting the advent of Andrew Jackson with pleasure; but she soon learned that her new neighbors were not.

The year before, Bank Street had gained many new residents, including the new tenants in her building. The firemen of the Columbia Engine House, a public facility a few doors removed from Mrs. Royall's, had leased their hall to one of the new evangelical sects spouting new religious doctrines. This particular group was an offshoot of the Presbyterian Church in Scotland and Northern Ireland, and had embraced the immediate second coming of Christ. With this center established, followers had moved into the available lodgings close to their religious heart. Among them were those who had been so rude in reply to Mrs. Royall's queries about her servant.

The Engine House Congregation was an enthusiastic one, holding daily services with loud preaching and song. The sermons were in broad Scotch-Irish accents and, as the hullabaloo rose each evening, Mrs. Royal could not help but wonder about this new kind of Christian. With a few questions to the right people, she discovered that most held government positions bestowed upon them by the Adams regime. Pressed by time, noting that these "aliens" sat in government office, she went on with her writing.

The evening hours were most important to the writer, for the busy street usually quieted with night. Now, however, the new congregation promoted its mission in loud voice. Time and again she put down her pen, and the more she did, the less tolerant she became. Who were these fools that they shouted up such a storm, stealing the peace of evening from all the others on the street? She found herself listening to their preachings, searching for sense in the words poured forth. As the cries of "Christ comes now, will ye be ready?" continued unabated, she would curse the assembly and wait for the services to end before completing her page.

The Engine House Congregation was preparing for the end of the world and the beginning of Heaven,[5] and as Easter approached, the wailing and services increased. The preaching was now exhortation to give, give until it hurt, for the glory of Jesus. The congregation was sent forth to sell penny pamphlets to all they met, so each time Mrs. Royall set foot from her house, she was accosted in the street by women and children peddling these calls to Christ and asking for donations. Women who should have been attending to home and children were standing dirty before her, bawling out, "Christ is coming tomorrow!"

Mrs. Royall studied these strange people, recent arrivals from Scotland and Northern Ireland, and some from the English midlands. They were fanatics, converts who had traded whiskied pub cries for the new hosannahs with which they assaulted their listeners. Drunk with new-found goodness, as they had once been drunk with alcoholic spirits, they reeled from the spirit of religious grace. Calling upon God to save, they would cry out for the forgiveness of their own sins and then alight upon another sinner. Mrs. Royall found herself a target of their acts of salvation, her conversion a sign of their redemption, and she resented it. She knew that religion could be a release for these new arrivals in a new land, but why did they not keep it to themselves?

The cold air of February amplified the congregation's goings-on, penetrating the old houses on Bank Street. As she set down her pen again and again, Mrs. Royall found herself describing them. She coined a name for these religious pests: holy rollers.[6] The humor in her invention almost made her evening tolerable, but the continued intrusions soured even that. She found herself counterattacking with her pen.

For two years Mrs. Royall had been encountering this new religion in her travels, alien missionaries had appeared everywhere, promoting the second coming and the end of the world, disrupting communities with their demands for obedience to God's word as they preached it. Mrs. Royall suffered yet from one encounter with such a preacher in Vermont. Calling upon him to keep the peace, she had been set upon and pushed down a flight of stairs. The fall had broken her leg;[7] it had cost her months of work. She knew all about the religious literature they peddled, for she had those handbills containing scurrilous attacks on General Jackson in her *portmanteau*. There had been a political motivation to the preaching of the second coming in Vermont and elsewhere in the North. These people had led the attacks on Jackson and they were now enjoying office in the government. How many citizens had been displaced by these immigrants? she knew of many business offices where they were, too, particularly the Bank of the United States. She began to listen more closely to the preachings.[8]

The Engine House Congregation did not need to be on Bank Street. There was a good American Presbyterian Church in Washington; in fact, two. Why was this group of aliens establishing a competing unit under her windows? If it was to meet with their own kind, why were they sponsoring a black group, too? Royall found herself investigating her neighbors, and as she heard the constant calls for money, the exhortations to peddle tracts for donations, she guessed the real reason for the congregation. Men and women, convinced that the end of the world was near, were being gulled to beg in the streets and turn all that they had or earned into this new church, to its leaders. Satisfied with this discovery, she turned to her writing with a new subject and new vigor.

It would have remained a passive affair, but an unseasonably mild mid-February morning found the congregation's children reporting for Sunday instruction to a hall locked against them and not an adult in sight. This sudden reprieve from Bible discipline sent them chasing about Bank Street in wild abandon. Their own noise fired their enthusiasm for more inventive pursuits, and they soon took large stones from the street and began throwing them at any target, testing their accuracy. Mrs. Royall woke to hear her windows shatter. She had finished a full night's writing to escape the constant celebration in the Engine House and lost her sense of humor. She dressed and went to District Magistrate Young, demanding that the congregation replace her windows at once.

Days passed with no restitution and broken panes still unrepaired. Mrs. Royall could stand the cold no longer. She went to the U.S. Marshal's office, and this time she raised a more serious question. What was a religious group doing in a hall owned by the government?[9] What had been the magistrate's simple act of inaction was made into a serious matter which could cost the Engine House more than the repair of her windows.

Two of the leaders of the congregation held important posts in the United States government. John Coyle, Sr., was the head clerk in the U.S. Auditor's office and John Dunn was sergeant-at-arms in the House of representatives.[10] Both decided to test their influence against Mrs. Royall and enlist protection for their group. They set the children to more harassment to force the writer to move from Bank Street.

Mrs. Royall accepted this war. She enjoyed her lodgings thanks to the largess of old family friends, Charles Carroll and his son, Daniel.[11] She had no intention of giving up a comfortable and free home. She demanded action from the U.S. Marshal and waited. It appeared to be a standoff, with Mrs. Royall's windows still unrepaired, but something was about to happen which would put the matter on the desks of Congress.

Late one evening, as the February gusts blew harder, Mrs. Royall was summoned to her door by incessant knocking. Answering and expecting to see another child bent on harassment, she was startled to see before her the errant housegirl missing these past weeks. Throwing the door wide, Mrs. Royall welcomed her with pleasure. As the girl entered, Mrs. Royall saw that the girl was not alone; she held a small babe in her arms.

Mrs. Royall asked, "Where have you been these many weeks?"

The girl gave no answer. Turning her attention to the babe, Mrs. Royall asked, "Whose child is this?"

The black girl stood staring at the floor. Mrs. Royall waited for reply. When the girl found her voice, her words were lost in garble. Mrs. Royall demanded that the girl speak out and pulled her to the light to look more closely at her and the child. The light and warmth relaxed the black girl, and she straightened. She was very nervous, so Mrs. Royall did not press her. Finally the girl began to talk, and Mrs. Royall could not believe what she heard.

The housegirl said that she had been entrusted with the care of the small babe by the mother, who came of great family but had encountered scandal. The whole affair was to be kept secret. Mrs. Royall stared at her servant in disbelief. The girl must have read the latest of the penny dreadfuls, religious tracts with stories of great ladies gone astray. She started to laugh. She had taught the girl to read, but not for this!

Mrs. Royall took the child from the girl's arms. It was obviously the girl's own, but who was the father? It was not her usual boyfriend, for the babe was light in color. Mrs. Royall considered the situation and decided to make the best of it; the girl was welcome, and so was the babe.[12]

The maidservant had come back at just the right time. John Stackpool had returned, and Sally had her own household to attend to. *Black Book, Volume III*, was ready for the printer, and Mrs. Royall had much to do to promote it. She had penned the last pages that very day and had a surprise in store for the noisy Engine House Congregation.

In January, just as Mrs. Royall had become aware of her new neighbors, Senator Richard Johnson of Kentucky had taken the Senate floor to give a farewell address. An American hero, this tall man was a legend because he had killed Tecumseh, the Indian chief, in hand-to-hand combat. With this dispatch of a powerful British ally in the War of 1812, Richard Johnson had joined Andrew Jackson in the hearts and minds of the American people.

Johnson had labored mightily to elect Andrew Jackson president in 1824, losing his state to Henry Clay; but in 1828 he had taken it back for Jackson. Henry Clay had retaliated by having the Kentucky Legislature strip Richard Johnson of his Senate seat. In 1829, U.S. senators were selected by state assemblies, not by popular ballot. To accomplish this, Clay had sided with the "Sabbatarians," religious groups demanding the Sunday closing of all business and government offices, a practice that was not in force in 1829. Richard Johnson found himself leaving Washington even as his friend Andrew Jackson was arriving.[13]

The man who had killed Tecumseh was not the kind to take his defeat quietly, and he was in a position to affront Clay and his allies. As chairman of the Senate committee charged with considering Sabbatarian demands as a national policy, he presented his committee's final report. Richard Johnson announced that the Senate had found against Sunday closings and, for his argument, had drawn upon words penned by Mrs. Royall. His appreciation was expressed to her by the gift of his personal copy of his remarks to the Senate. Sensing that the Sabbatarians had much in common with her Engine House oppressors, Mrs. Royall appended the full text of Richard Johnson's speech to her new book. If the Engine House Congregation and its leaders wanted a fight, Mrs. Royall would see that they got it. She would print the first statement of the new Jackson administration[14] in the Congress as her answer to her harassment.

The servant girl settled into her old routine, and the child posed no problem. Sally Stackpool came and went, keeping a close eye on things, and it was she who first noticed something was amiss with the young girl. Did Mrs. Royall know the girl was pregnant again?, Sally asked.

Mrs. Royall was stunned. One child was tolerable in her small lodgings, but two! This time the father would have to assume responsibility and both women set themselves to discover him. It did not take them long.

One leader of the Engine House Congregation showed more interest in the girl than any desire to convert allowed. This man waited for her and her infant every evening and on Sunday. He was obvious in his attention, hiding at the back door. The black girl had been injected by him with more than religion. Mrs. Royall welcomed this knowledge, for this was the stuff of satire with which to arouse men in Congress. Richard Johnson's speech could treat the religious menace seriously, but a good story would open more ears.

Mrs. Royall wrote, enjoying every word. Righteous indignation produced drama, and she built on it in her own way.

Holy Willy, moved for compassion for my lost state, would often be seen under my window with his hands and eyes raised to heaven in silent prayer for the conversion of my soul. In this, however, I might be mistaken, for there was another lost sinner under my roof. She had strayed from the path of rectitude and had two douce children and whether the holy man's prayers were designed for her or me, I am not able to say. But it is clear that he could have nothing but the good of our souls in view. What else would bring such a pious man there?[15]

Holy Willy was a synonym coined for John Coyle, Sr., for he was the man who stood awaiting the servant. Coyle was not only the leader of the alien congregation, but he had used his position in the government to obtain employment for his followers; they had burrowed deep into government office. They had veneered their true intent too long with piety, and Mrs. Royall had the means to strip one of them of his sham.

Congress was a man's world, and Mrs. Royall knew it. She lost no time in taking to the Capitol and the effect was as she had hoped: Holy Willy found himself the center of unwanted attention. Even as she had penned the first description of John Coyle, Sr., she described his friends in terms which caused titters in congressional offices.

Capital . . . . a den of blackcoats. Old Holy Willy, young Holy Willy, Old Habakuk, Mucklewrath, Hallelujah Holdforth . . .[16]

As she walked the halls of the Capitol, doors opened and she was invited to tell the latest installment of her faintly disguised attacks on her religious neighbors.

Laughter is a powerful weapon, particularly against the pompous. Mrs. Royall used it well. She told the story of the fatal assignation between old Coyle and another servant woman. Coyle loved his ladies, and some of them did not survive it

Holy Willy is commander-in-chief. Strange stories are told about him and an aged sister, black sister in Christ. It is said he used to instruct her in the gospel, gave her wholesome lessons in the salvation of her soul. She being a hardened sinner, he was forced to caustic specifics, even to the wounding of her flesh, and I believe this report says she died in her sins under the operation. This however, was not his fault (she had no business to die) as he was influenced by pure and holy motives.[17]

Mrs. Royall's attack on Holy Willy and those associated with him had a double purpose. Congress knew that Senators John Calhoun, Henry Clay, and Daniel Webster had turned over their offices to John Coyle and his black-suited associates. A line was forming which had greater implications than laughter, and Mrs. Royall was daring to draw it. The congressmen took Mrs. Royall's titillations as intended; they had suffered from the newly pious, and it was refreshing to hear these different tales.

John Coyle found himself the object of growing ridicule and retaliated. Holy Willy marshalled his congregation and marched them to Mrs. Royall's doorstop. He conducted prayer meetings before her house, calling upon Heaven to relieve him of the oppressor. When she was about to leave her house, he had a group there to harass her. He set his clerks upon her in the halls of Congress, and the impromptu debates attracted crowds.

Mrs. Royall came to enjoy these encounters. In good voice she would answer her opponents, heap scorn on their bowdlerized scriptures, then parody their tracts and send them running with her cane or umbrella. Her friends urged her on. She would meet strident appeal with mock demeanor, and then tell them their religious services resembled Christ's discourses as witches in their covens resembled the truly Godly.

Mrs. Royall's efforts carried in the Congress halls, but the Engine House Congregation struck back on Bank Street. They took to sending odd persons into her house asking for all manner of obscene services from her and moved black prostitutes into the rooms beneath her. She had to spend precious days contacting Daniel Carroll to effect their removal. The children were sent against her again with stones, and young men mounted her stairs in the dead of night to frighten her. Mrs. Royall took the harassment in calm but remembered the months of torture from her leg broken in Vermont. She kept her equanimity by remembering that the small conflict on Bank Street was just a prelude to a larger struggle. As the evangelicals became more insistent and then blocked her departure and arrival, she met this physical problem with indignant anger and forceful words.

In 1829, Anglo-Saxon vulgarisms were part of America's language and everyone used them, from the lowliest clerk to the highest official.[18] The false modesty yet to be effected with the rising tide of evangelism and the reign of Victoria in England was still years away, and Mrs. Royall knew how to use epithets to put an opponent in his place. For her ailing husband, she had managed a plantation for twenty years and gained and retained a firm command of language. One spirited encounter with Holy Willy in sight and sound of his followers, and she sent them packing back to the Engine House crying louder than ever for her "salvation."

All Washington City watched and took sides. Mrs. Royall's protagonists thought her better than ever; her antagonists thought her worse.

The Engine House Congregation and its leaders knew too late that Mrs. Royall was not a sinner to be converted; she was a deadly foe putting the godly to ridicule in the street and then committing the events to paper. People read what she wrote. She had termed the evangelists "religious imposters" and was against not only their spiritual pretensions but working to end their government positions as well. They did not know what she would do next, but she knew.

Always thorough and astute, Mrs. Royall recognized that her maidservant had given her a course of action against the religious freaks who sat in government offices, against the hypocrisy of Coyle and his friends. The maidservant had been "saved," was with child, and had no pious husband to care for her.

My girl came in with a thumping young missionary under her cloak, a fine boy, the very image of Holy Willy.[19]

Mrs. Royall's barbs encouraged congressmen to look more closely at the "evangelicals" about them, to use backwoods reason against fanatical religion, and it began to take effect.

The practice of employing Scots-Irish immigrants for bookkeeping and record making had given these aliens employment in overwhelming numbers in Washington. In government offices, their religious mania carried over into their work. Men of free thought, even those who held the elective posts of the land, found themselves intimidated by this pious crew, this advance guard of a new order. Men elected to represent civil authority could not rail against this unwanted intrusion of religious intent upon the legislature without incurring cries of "religious suppression," but they could relieve their anxiety in laughter. Holy Willy not so holy after all, nor were Mucklewrath and Holdforth. These comedic characters became a safety valve, and many made the most of it. Senator Thomas Hart Benton, the big Missourian, was one of Mrs. Royall's most appreciative listeners. He not only enjoyed her stories but would tell and retell her tales. Mrs. Royall put her appreciation in print:

. . . the Hon. Senator Benton . . . his towering height, and interesting person, was very striking, as he sat behind the other members . . . his height may be six feet at least. His figure is noble and commanding; he is quite a young-looking man; his face remarkably fair and beautiful, his eyes large bright blue, his countenance open, gay and intelligent, with light hair; his manner like his person, is at once engaging and dignified.[20]

Her final comment, "In short, I would say that Mr. B. has few equals," was in direct contrast to her pen sketch of Benton's colleague from Vermont, who was in league with the black-coated missionaries:

One of the snags come next, Senator Chase, of Vermont. His presence was not necessary to remind me of his state, as I was at that moment in infinite pain . . . having no place to rest my foot. Mr. C. is a very stout man with a large handsome face, fair complexion, and dark hair, but as grim as the Green Mountains. One would have thought he would come forward (as I was pointed out to him by several) and have condoled with me, or in some manner have apologized for the barbarous usage I met with in his state, but he had too much of the missionary and too little of the gentleman in him for that.[21]

And Mrs. Royall really took off after a Senate clerk:

I was really pained however, at the sight of a gloomy Presbyterian, who looked as though his face was made of the lava of Mount Aetna. It is astonishing that the religion of these people effectually conquers nature, and changes the features of the human countenance into terrible savageness . . .

and why men so dangerous to our liberty . . . are retained in such high offices is unaccountable, while many able and patriotic men can be found to fill the office better. This man's countenance is quite appalling. Nature or art, one, has lavished the dismals upon him with a bountiful hand. He looks like nothing Human, though he is a tall good figure in human shape. His visage is long and black, and his forehead narrow, and vengeance and bloodshed are in his countenance. He is exactly the monster he would make his God.[22]

These pungent paragraphs were potent weapons to men who understood issues they would have to face as they prepared for the inauguration of Andrew Jackson as president. Mrs. Royall had marked them with mockery.

John Coyle and his Engine House friends sat in disbelief. Who was this old hag who pitted her blasphemous wit against their godly selves and threatened the whole fabric of their existence? Who was she to call them culprits, to single them out for their employment, and what gave her the power to speak to the most important men in the country? The search was begun for answers and what would surface would make the self-employed writer and her antagonistic neighbors instruments of history in a way no one could anticipate. Mrs. Royall and those foes who proposed to know her better would together define the real culprits, who would never recover from that discovery.

Chapter 3

Taking Measure

Neighbors can live side by side in friendship without knowledge of one another's background but in enmity, never. John Coyle, Sr., had to know about Mrs. Royall and soon. The writer's appeals to authorities for action against his Engine House Congregation had been troublesome, but her new attack on his religious friends and their government employment was frightening. Coyle's position as the first clerk in the office of the U.S. auditor was a prestigious one, and he intended to keep it. He knew he needed allies if he and his kind were to survive. He set out to find them, going first to those who were beholden to him for information, seeking help against Mrs. Royall.

His first queries confirmed his need. Mrs. Royall was involved in the growing American repugnance to the "new religion" which placed such emphasis on giving money to God and her polemics in the recent Jackson campaign had made her famous. Worse, he learned that Mrs. Royall was not an itinerant writer but a close confidante to those who would make policy in the new Jackson regime. Not a friend wanted to offer open assistance against her. Instead he was advised to take the measure of his new opponent carefully, for Mrs. Royall not only possessed a dangerous mouth, but her hand guided a pen far more poisonous in corrupting his Garden of Eden. The first clerk was told to obtain Mrs. Royall's *Black Books* and anything else she had written to learn what he must defend against; he would need to know why she wrote. Further, he might gain clues as to who paid her to do so. It was a difficult task for a man who read the Bible only.

In 1829, there were few books on popular subjects, for the novelist's craft scarcely had begun, and the few lighthearted pensmen about gave service to religion or politics as paid servants gave to controlling masters.[1] Mrs. Royall was different. The woman who pained John Coyle lived to write and wrote to live for herself. She had no known master. She had arrived in Washington within the last five years, was old and experienced, and eschewed all worldly goods. It was said that she lived for the present; each day could well be the only future she would know.[2]

Mrs. Royall had come to the nation's capital alone and had kept her solitude. To those who boasted an acquaintance, she was Mrs. Royall with no family and no visible responsibilities. She was not interested in success and accepted a bare minimum in her day-to-day needs. She appeared to care only for the intellectual stimulation which she found in traveling about America, writing about her discoveries. American cause and effect was her subject, and she put everything into it. She fed it her comfort, her pleasures, even her friendships, and it rewarded her with identity. Mrs. Royall was America's own author, the first of a

18

new kind of writer, and she celebrated her work with a constant stream of books.

John Coyle did not understand Mrs. Royall or her work. To him, she was a woman and a small one at that, slightly under five feet, uneasy in her gait, plump but not fat, and he could not fathom why leaders in Congress allowed her to walk with them, why they would step aside for her. He recognized her overpowering aura of energy, the obstinacy with which she braced herself against immediate fate, for he shuddered when he thought about her. He did not recognize that determination which most people of character desired and admired, nor the lovely smile she could display to win people to her side. He did not share her civil purpose, the intimidating strength with which she served it, or the sense of humor with which she tempered her cause.[3] He had no ability to appreciate the talent she had to put all this on paper.

John Coyle knew as little about Mrs. Royall two weeks after his inquiries began as he did before. Her books meant nothing to him, for they seemed only attacks on his personal position. He only knew the woman was his mortal enemy, and he had to find a way to stop her.

Mrs. Royall had been busy since her January return. Not only was she involved with the Engine House Congregation and John Coyle, but she had stumbled upon another incident of inordinate religious intrusion in government affairs.

As the Engine House Congregation had interfered more with her life, Mrs. Royall had sought refuge in the inner precincts of the Library of Congress. Here she planned to do her writing in the comfort and seclusion she was denied in her own home. On her first visit, she came across a shocking discovery: In plain view, on tables scattered about the reading room, Mrs. Royall found countless numbers of tract society and Bible society pamphlets neatly stacked, inviting public distribution! These were rehashings of the theocratic and biblical nonsense she faced daily on Bank Street. She took herself immediately to George Watterston, the Librarian of Congress, to inquire as to why such pamphlets were there.

George Watterston was a man of great importance in the capital. A lawyer turned writer, with several novels to his credit, he had received Mrs. Royall warmly on previous visits. He received her so this time. Mrs. Royall raised her point. What was Bible and tract society nonsense doing in the Library of Congress, why was so much of it stacked on tables and for what reason had Mr. Watterson, the trusted librarian, allowed such trash, in this most prestigious of all libraries, to defile his library shelves?

George Watterston was taken by surprise. He could not take such a complaint seriously; he saw nothing wrong in a few religious tracts being displayed in the congressional library. Mrs. Royall was indignant. The nonsense was not a few tracts at all, but stacks of them obviously put out for public distribution. That was in direct contravention to the purposes of the Library. She demanded that George Watterston remove the offending piles immediately.

The librarian refused. He admitted that the tracts were there inviting public acceptance but after all, they were for a good cause—Christianity—and he would not continue the discussion.

"Good cause." That phrase destroyed a friendship even as it was uttered.[4] The Librarian of Congress had taken leave of his senses and knew those stacked printed mulings were sitting on his library tables in grievous error. George Watterston would admit no such thing. Mrs. Royall was making too much of simple writings, he thought, and they would stay where they were.

Mrs. Royall left the Library of Congress in a state of agitation. George Watterston was not doing his duty. Worse, he refused to recognize his error and he had been rude in turning aside her complaint as not worthy of consideration. She would deal with this in her own way and she did, in a remarkable display of one woman's determination to see things done properly.

George Watterston had accepted the objectionable pamphlets on what were, to him, firm grounds. A congressional committee, charged with overseeing the operations of the prestigious Library of Congress, had made a special appropriation to purchase the tracts and pamphlets. The committee chairman, Edward Everett, Representative from Massachusetts, had directed Mr. Watterston to place the tracts in the library and oversee their distribution to other government offices. Accordingly, beginning in January, 1829, Mr. Watterston had purchased the publications, kept some for the library, and sent others to various government departments for general distribution. Among the offices to receive them was that of the first auditor; the man chosen to distribute them for that office was none other than John Coyle, Sr. This had happened a week before Mrs. Royall had discovered it.[5]

After Mrs. Royall's visit, George Watterston went on with his affairs, secure that he had dispatched another problem. John Coyle continued to distribute the tract pamphlets assigned to him. Neither man knew the other very well, but they were destined to become fast friends in a few short weeks.

Mrs. Royall hastened from her discovery at the Library of Congress to her friends in Congress. She had stumbled on not just a free distribution of religious matter to the library and other government offices, but also what amounted to a forbidden raid on the U.S. Treasury by certain religious groups, the very religious culprits she had confronted in the halls of Congress. The practice was unconstitutional.

Mrs. Royall pressed her point in personal confrontations with congressmen, testified to it before hastily convened committees, and then wrote about it to her editors and in *Black Book, Volume III*:

> But my friend Watterston ought to be hauled over the coals about his duties; being a man of sense and learning, he is the more dangerous. He tells me, "That he is not in favor of the missionary scheme." If he is not, why did he suffer (if he did not buy them) the books of the Sunday School Union to be put in the Congress Library?[6]

Mrs. Royall had looked at her former friend carefully and had made other discoveries, revelations that would shake Washington:

> Why does he go to the blackcoat church? Why does he entertain shoals of these missionaries? Pass his house when you will, you will find it enveloped in a flock of blackcoats, like ravens around carrion. Why is this? I judge altogether by the facts, I do not care what any man says, I attend to what he does. These Sunday School books are lying useless in the Library, as I would suppose no member of Congress reads them. Let Mr. W. sell them and give the amount to the suffering poor—if he is so pious, let him show it that way.[7]

George Watterston was not Mrs. Royall's only target: Representative Edward Everett came in for his share of attention too. What was this avowed Unitarian minister doing in the blackcoat missionary camp? Had he quietly joined the new religionists? Mrs. Royall expressed her displeasure:

> Nor am I satisfied with my neat, quiet Mr. Everett, for not attending better to his part of the business. I shall not be at peace while the dignity of our country is insulted in this manner.[8]

But Mrs. Royall's search of the congressional halls for support against the distribution of the religious tracts centered on one man, he who had raised her wrath in the first place:

As for Mr. W., were it not for the suspicion that clings to him, and his openly associating with these traitors, no worthier man could be selected as librarian . . . but no further evidence is necessary to prove him a dangerous man to our government and he ought to be dismissed as soon as possible, even if he were my brother.[9]

Washington City was agog. A lone woman had taken on the congressional establishment and spoken aloud of treason.

What was going to happen? Mrs. Royall surely had overstepped herself and everyone waited for the congressional reply.

John Coyle, Sr., found himself in another adversary position to Mrs. Royall. As he hurried to finish the distribution of the tracts within his department, he was sure she would be put down. He congratulated his blackcoat friends and allies as he gave them their tracts.

The entire contingent employed in the government felt very secure; they had powerful friends in Mr. Everett and George Watterston. Representative Everett was a distinguished theologian, albeit a heretical Unitarian, but he had been responsible for this latest triumph of their God. He was a powerful man with powerful friends, and Coyle and his associates waited for the pounce upon Mrs. Royall.

They waited in vain. Mrs. Royall kept to the Capitol halls through February and as she marched, she wrote. The passages quoted were read the week before inauguration, and Congress, alerted by this exposition, took public notice of the controversy at last. Mrs. Royall had raised a very pertinent question, one that required an answer, especially before Andrew Jackson took over the helm of the nation. Why had the congressional library committee sanctioned the use of public money to purchase religious tracts and then suffered them to be placed in the Library of Congress and government offices for distribution; It was a question put squarely to Edward Everett; he could provide no rational answer. Mr. Everett was about to run for governor of Massachusetts, and he had a problem with his Unitarian constituency. In no time at all, that most respected of New England's leaders, John Quincy Adams's own good friend, stood before his colleagues and publicly recanted his error in approving the use of public funds to purchase tracts promoting a particular religion. Representative Everett, as outgoing chairman of the library committee, directed that every piece of religious matter purchased be removed not only from the Library of Congress but from every government office to which it had been sent.[10] John Coyle, Sr., found himself gathering the very same tracts he had distributed and turning them in for refunding. He knew that he was out of his depth with the old woman, for her power was indisputable. She had done the unthinkable, the impossible, and he still did not understand how, for the clerk had not indulged in a proper reading of the U.S. Constitution.

Mrs. Royall's victory over the religious tract societies had more far-reaching effects than John Coyle knew. The writer had presented Andrew Jackson with the position of the Librarian of Congress for distribution. Mrs. Royall had set Watterston up for Jacksonian retribution, given the perfect argument to effect the coup. Further, the recanting of Edward Everett had stilled the opposition. This was obvious, even to Andrew Jackson's enemies.

This new development was stunning to John Coyle and his alien followers in American offices. Not only was their religious fanaticism frustrated, but methods were being explored which could lead to their removal from office. It was more important than ever to locate and join Mrs. Royall's enemies in efforts against her.

Mrs. Royall was not preoccupied with the Engine House Congregation now. Her battle with Watterston was not over, although Edward Everett had capitulated. The confrontation was grist for her correspondence with editors, and her new book would sell better than ever with it. She did not intend to dissipate this new advantage. She did not care that John Coyle preached that she was in league with the devil and was openly searching for allies to work against her. She had a brand new world open to her pen. She had graduated from meetings with small town and city groups to increase grassroot political activity and had propelled herself into the national legislature itself. This new ascent to the heights of power she had not anticipated, and she felt an exhilaration which flowed into her work. Her pen became her wonder, for everything she had heard about the power of that small instrument to effect change was true. An observer armed with it could make men reverse direction and a woman who used it was the match for any man. Mrs. Royall wondered what end this beginning would forge. Her friends and her enemies did too.

It is taken for granted in our time that all a writer needs is an overriding interest in something to take pen in hand and make a life with it. In 1829, it was not so simple. The times did not recognize writing as a profession; it was a pastime for minds unoccupied with more important pursuits. The craft was not a business and less an industry. Books in existence were labors of love, created by authors who not only stole the moments to write them, but in most cases had to print them at their own expense, peddle them in their own spheres of influence, and keep their own accounts. All this had to be accomplished while earning a living in another way.[11]

There were not too many who could take such risks. Times were hard and capital was scarce. Printers lived by printing pamphlets or reprinting "classics" to meet the demand for "education." These classics were words from thinkers long dead, or theses and sermons from theologians promised support from their various religious groups. Most writers were wealthy dilettantes, and the few who were not had to find rich men and women to sponsor them. In America, it was particularly difficult. A new nation had more important commitments for scarce capital than the promotion of literature.

American book publishers were few in number and lacking in organization. The only advantage in the craft was the number of booksellers in most of the cities and towns, by-products of the new commercialism and its trade centers. The bookseller was the stationer, the printing contractor for bills of lading and so on, and his books were mainly reprints, used tomes from estates and, with the introduction of tract pamphlets, the more popular of these semi-religious promotions. Booksellers did offer a possibility of growth, and with the explosion of words on paper made possible by the invention of new English steam printing presses, they had begun to add to their numbers throughout the country.[12]

These new book merchants, cognizant that education was a new "status symbol" in the growing society about them, maintained a semblance of quality in this transition by offering "accepted" knowledge to the masses. The effect was to promote what was already in print, to sell English authors and books, and by-pass American ones. Americans were just too busy to take time to put to paper American thoughts, and with this peculiar rationale even American statesmen and the formerly popular revolutionary pamphleteers were shunted aside.

Books were becoming a very marketable quantity, as proliferating booksellers in American cities proved, but still American authors received little consideration. The argument was moot; an author had to be known to sell, and what

American was known? The implication was not lost. If an American wanted renown, he had to go to England and make his reputation there, for American booksellers dealt primarily in British products. From Socrates as explained by an Oxford theologian to the latest speeches from Parliament, British writers held a virtual monopoly in the American market. Few booksellers could buck this tide, and as a result there were few to aid an American writer. There was such an all-encompassing commercial tie with Britain, with all the attendant subtleties, that such Americans as Washington Irving, James Fenimore Cooper, and even Noah Webster had to make long pilgrimages to London before they could find acceptance in America.[13] It is to Mrs. Royall's credit that she solved this problem without embarking on that journey, but she was in love with the United States, not intrigued by Europe. She was aided by writing at the right time in the right place, and the right people helped her to escape that first step. She also engaged in the right kind of writing.

Just five years before, in the middle of the 1820s, after a decade of inattention, everything American suddenly had become a passion again. The constant trade problems with Great Britain, the growing pains of the new American mercantile communities, and the restless press of the population against the nation's ill-defined borders had served to heighten an interest in the national character, to prepare for an explosion of the national spirit.

In 1826, the United States of America had survived half a century, reaching a milestone to be noted. Accordingly, Americans began to prepare for the hoopla and parades such an occasion required. As the preparations mounted, Americans naturally became curious as to their beginnings, their achievements, and their future in the next half century to come. Everyone reacted to this historical event, even the booksellers. By sheer chance, this was the time Mrs. Royall began her career. The Golden Jubilee was a tidal wave for a woman who regarded the American Revolution, the reason for celebration, as the most important event in world history to date.

Mrs. Royall was dedicated to the United States as the refuge for reasonable men from the irrationalities of past history. Only the United States had given birth to a nation which promised so much to men and women. She was so close to the nation's beginning that the words with which it had been initiated were not just words, but promises. They had rescued her generation from futility, and now, fifty years later, offered a continuing philosophy to a world still suffering the inequities of history.

Mrs. Royall's accent on all things American coincided with the rebirth of the American spirit. Hers was a reassuring voice from another generation to a younger one just assessing its chances. She made a special appeal to youth with her acclaim of the American future and her careful survey of what had been accomplished and what had yet to be done. Anne Royall's first book, *Sketches of History, Life and Manners in the United States*, was not so much a critique of the country as a blueprint for its future. It was a long-overdue look at America, and it was received very well. It had been published anonymously, but its success focused national attention upon its author and soon Anne Royall came forward. She was an instant celebrity and thus produced a biography, short and terse, one as American in character as the first book she had written.

Anne Newport Royall was born in 1769 to parents not among those who desired or sought a war for independence. Her father was a Marylander who had ties to the Royalist cause. When the clouds of dissension finally threatened the Royal Colony of Maryland, he had taken his wife and daughter to a far frontier to wait out the conflict. Anne, born seven years before the Revolution, was brought up on that Pennsylvania frontier.

Mrs. Royall's own stories about her beginnings hint that her father, William

Newport, had been a conscious agent of the British forces. Other sources suggest that he was part of the complicated plots to arouse the Indians against the American border settlements, but no mention of his name has been found in any of the journals of the men who did England's duty with the Indians. What Royalist stamp Newport had was in the income he had received in Maryland from Crown sources, an income that ceased as rebellion grew. All we know is that William Newport one day disappeared from his young daughter's life, before his background or philosophy could mark hers, but he did teach her to read at an early age. For this gift she revered him, but her real development had been in another man's hands.[14]

Mrs. Royall confessed that she owed everything to her association with William Royall, a 40-year-old veteran of the Revolution. She met him on the western Virginia frontier when she was eighteen. This encounter with the middle-aged scion of a Virginia first family, a self-professed radical follower of Rousseau, Voltaire, and Thomas Paine, changed her life. The young girl had a rare asset for her times, perfect white teeth used well in winning smile, and was taken by an old bachelor in a manner to which she gave few words. Mrs. Royall told her world that a Tidewater aristocrat, craving love and discourse, had rescued a mother and daughter, taken both into service upon his estate and Anne had become Mrs. Royall.[15] It was a story often heard in early America.

These were the facts that John Coyle, Sr., learned: The woman who made a mockery of his life and his morals had been a frontier derelict, a harlot, and she admitted it. She had lived with Major Royall before marriage, openly consorted with him before his friends. This hag, this heretic who made a joke of him and questioned his God, was a heinous sinner.

John Coyle counterattacked with this knowledge. His friends heard him with great interest, but others did not. Mrs. Royall's story was well known; she told it herself and she was now no frontier derelict, no harlot. She was the legal wife of Major William Royall and used his name properly. It was obvious that John Coyle's small mind was not able to deal with the sophisticated attack Mrs. Royall had launched. His prattle of scandal would not return Anne Newport Royall, Washington writer, the capital's new power broker, to Anne Newport, an eighteen-year-old vagrant with questionable morals.

John Coyle had a goal, and he was determined to meet it: He would take that old woman and break her yet. His friends cheered while others smiled. He made his oath. He had taken the old woman's measure, and he would punish her with it. It was a sobering thought, and his friends wished him well. They were under attack: Mrs. Royall was working her own measures against them, and her success or failure would be the real measure of them all.

Chapter 4

Friends or Enemies?

John Coyle had involved the Engine House Congregation in one problem only to generate another: His vendetta with Mrs. Royal had focused attention on his breed. They stood apart from Americans and did so by choice; now that voluntary alienation could haunt them. Enjoying employment in American government, many of them were not citizens, and those who were had begun to note it. The congregation had not been guilty of an oversight; it simply had not been necessary to join the nation to work for it and profit by it. The United States had not legislated any stricture against foreign skills and talent in its national administration.[1] The Scots-Irish had arrived, found a need, and filled it. That logical reaction to the realities of the new American existence was in jeopardy now; the self-proclaimed aliens were sitting ducks for any who wished to supplant them. With the coming of Andrew Jackson, there was no law against them, but there was no law for them.

Americans, prior to 1829, thought little of nationality. Being an American was a passion just developing. Prior to the Revolution, all colonists had been citizens of their colonies by virtue of being there. The act of rebellion had forged a nation, but that nation's nationals would be a long time in the making. With this in mind, any attempts to close government employment lists to all but the native born had been fought successfully in every administration. The few attempts to exclude aliens had been directed at non-English elements during the upheavals of the French Revolution, and even those had not met with the acceptance of a nation dedicated to the Age of Reason. Americans had not raised any singular national outcry against aliens in their midst because most could remember their own alien origins. The sons of English colonists and the new British immigrants worked side by side in most of the offices of the land. It was an amity many cherished, particularly the new immigrants.

This was before 1829 and before Mrs. Royall. This was before the advent of Andrew Jackson. This was before the new British accents began to submerge the American. In 1829, a new assessment was in progress and Mrs. Royall had taken the lead, building on her experience of two years, fueled by her new confrontation with the Engine House Congregation, John Coyle, and his friends.

Mrs. Royall's travels had alerted her to many curious situations regarding the growing British direction of American life. Apart from the heritage the nation had received, there were those British-controlled booksellers, a subtle influence which was subjugating emerging American attitudes. Then came the black-garbed missionaries peddling an admittedly foreign concept and openly involved with the British press, which was committed to their new doctrine. These elements had alarmed her in her travels, but back in Washington, Mrs. Royall was

25

face-to-face with a more serious matter. The national government itself had been infiltrated by those who shared this curious affiliation. She had to become interested in that religion and its followers, and since they were one and the same with her personal enemies in the Bank Street Engine House Congregation, they only spurred her efforts to discover more.

Mrs. Royall walked Capitol Hill and the government offices, wittily making her points. As she marched, however, she also catalogued the new breed holding office and those who employed them. While she was structuring a new attack, Mrs. Royall knew she had many watching and cheering her. She threw all caution aside. The Jackson landslide had brought to Washington hordes of hopefuls and to the Congress itself many new faces, among them the Pennsylvanians who had aided her before against insidious influence in their state legislature. Mrs. Royall knew they would support her in her new determination to erase a religious influence in the national government, particularly an alien religious influence. As she marched, she added to her enlistments in this new crusade.

The rumors about Mrs. Royall's new efforts and new direction went before her. John Coyle and his friends were frightened. The she-devil was among them, worming herself into the councils of the Congress with one avowed purpose: to destroy their influence in public office. John Coyle had forced the issue but he could not counter it alone; he had to move beyond his immediate circle.

Coyle's Engine House Congregation did maintain contact with a more established Presbyterian Church, members of which were in the government too. He appealed to them for assistance, and one responded. Lewis Machen, clerk to John C. Calhoun, heard him out and recognized an opportunity to settle a personal score with Mrs. Royall and help another friend, John Dunn.

Lewis Machen was the man who had pained Mrs. Royall with his face like "the lava of Mount Aetna." Like Coyle, he was Scots-Irish, but he came from older stock which had emigrated to the United States in the first decade of the century. He had arrived in Washington to clerk for the First Bank of the United States and, with that institution's demise, had moved to his position with Calhoun. Machen was a citizen but still had a native accent. For years he had insinuated himself into the American Scots community and among the Free Presbyterians, but of late he had been swept into the new revivalist movement swelling the influence of his more newly arrived countrymen. The circumstances of such conversions as Machen's was a Washington phenomenon.[2]

Prior to 1818, the capital had been served by one Presbyterian church, the First as it was called. In that year, the New Life movement within that body had gathered enough adherents to divide the congregation and organize the Second Church, built in 1820. One of those involved in this enterprise was the Secretary of State, John Quincy Adams, and by 1823, the Second Presbyterian Church had become the most prestigious, supplanting the First. Secretary Adams was a trustee, a position which he continued to hold during his term as president. This was a signal to the Scots-Irish contingent in the capital. If Adams, a former Unitarian, accepted the new Presbyterian doctrines, others as ambitious would too.[3] Lewis Machen and John Dunn always watched the movements about them for personal gain.

The leaders of the new Congress had not been selected yet. The schisms and factions produced in the last two presidential battles had created a many-headed power block on both sides, with no seeming allegiance to any one movement. To the casual and uninformed observer, all might appear to be political, but to the astute there was a definite religious bent to be considered. Machen knew all about it, for the growing presence of "missionaries" on powerful congressional staffs was a fact.[4] If Mrs. Royall's detested "dominion of God" was a real influence, Machen and his confrere Dunn saw no reason why one should not clerk for a church-state while the other opined he was willing to open doors to either church or state. Both were interested only in holding on to their positions and did not intend to be swept aside for any Jackson appointee.

John Coyle had found his first allies: Machen and Dunn. Machen took the lead. Unimpressed with Coyle's religious problem, he was interested in the Engine House preoccupation with Mrs. Royall's character and her past. Dunn agreed to assist Machen in whatever he planned in the Congress.

Mrs. Royall was aware of Machen and Dunn and their activities,[5] even as they began. They were searching out those who sponsored her, trying to counteract her assault. As they worked, many more became interested in the writer.

The American capital, like any capital, was a mass of important personalities. Most were judged or known by their positions in the hierarchy of government, but Mrs. Royall was an exception. She held no government post and had asked for none. This lack of official connection made it difficult to pinpoint who promoted her, sustained her, and enlarged her prerogatives. Each person assigned to her his own concepts based on his own experience. The result was confusion. Mrs. Royall was an enigma, and the only fact anyone had was that she was the widow of Major William Royall and had been introduced to Washington through him. All letters of introduction to her contacts in the capital were in his name or in those of his former friends and associates. Mrs. Royall had been welcomed into the finest homes, was assisted by the best people, enjoyed support from the wealthiest, and yet remained unknown. It was a curious situation, and it bothered Lewis Machen and his friends.

Knowledge of William Royall had one origin in Washington—Mrs. Royall. It was her tale that everyone told. By her own words, William Royall had been a very different man. Born the scion of wealth to a first family of Virginia,[6] William Royall had eschewed inherited position and at 40 years of age organized his own contingent of the Virginia Militia, spent his own funds to equip it, and played his own part in the great rebellion. Patrick Henry had been an enrollee in Royall's forces, and Mrs. Royall boasted that her husband had known all the Revolutionary greats, among them Marquis de Lafayette, and she could produce a letter from that august Frenchman to prove it.[7]

Mrs. Royall did not rely alone upon the major's service; she celebrated his selflessness. Her man of Virginia had committed his entire estate to the revolutionary cause, pledging his lands to raise his militia. After victory, he had chosen to turn from the life of an aristocrat to join the remnants of his patriotic band on the Western Virginia frontier to carve out a new life. Major Royall had ignored acclaim, financial gain from his contribution to the nation's birth, and left the remainder of his Tidewater properties to his brother and family while he moved to settle among his hardy veterans. He had chosen to drop from old Virginia's sight five years after the Revolution.[8]

Machen and Dunn could not believe what they learned. No one really knew Major Royall when pressed for details about him, but everyone seemed to know all about him. The stories of this remarkable patriot all came from Mrs. Royall. The tales of his vision, his dedication, and his adoption of the men who served him as the only family he needed had intrigued everyone, and the writer's addition of her own tales of suffering only enhanced the legend. Major Royall had saved a young woman not by cries to God, but by taking her aging mother in as a housekeeper and noting the keen mind of the daughter he had then taken the maiden to him, teaching her from his library as well as his life. It was a story to rival any Bible society tract in circulation, and it found ready listeners in Washington circles.

Lewis Machen and John Dunn were appalled. This clever woman had satirized the many preachings and mouthings of the evangelicals and their publications in her own way for her own purposes, employing their well-tested story technique.

Mrs. Royall had provided an excellent background for her entrance into Washington's life. She was always frank about details when anyone asked. Her openness about her past and her knowledge about life had made her a welcome addition to many a gathering in the city. Her seeming unconcern about politics and her insistence upon the greatness of the United States and any who served it added to her ranks of admirers. The fact that she had talent and could write made her that much more acceptable, and even that talent had been exploited in its explanation.

Mrs. Royall was frank about her lack of schooling. She explained her ability with the pen as the result of her own natural curiosity and a lot of hard work, guided by the well-educated William Royall. The major boasted the finest collection of books beyond the Tidewater Country and she had learned from them all.[9]

Necessity had been her instructor. Promoted to serve as William Royall's hostess, in the free ways of the frontier, she had been accepted by his many guests. William Royall, as a former leader in the Revolution, had a constant stream of visitors from both home and abroad, and many came to renew their acquaintances, joined by others. Meeting with such men of stature became courses in history and philosophy, and Anne Newport read widely in the major's library to meet such minds equally,[10] to become an educated woman by any standard applied in 1829.

How Anne Newport became Mrs. Royall was covered nicely too. With no detailed explanation, Mrs. Royall, casually asserted that she had done the major's bidding for ten years before she married him. Her marriage had come when she was 28 years of age, when the 57-year-old veteran summoned her to him. She had gone, as so many times before, but this time he married her. Anne Newport became Mrs. Royall on November 17, 1797, in a ceremony conducted by the Reverend William P. Martin, recorded after the winter circuit on May 4, 1798, in the Botencourt County records in Virginia. When the snows had melted, the Reverend Martin had crossed the mountains to Fincastle, and then Anne Newport had been certified as Mrs. William Royall. That lapse of six months in certification was to cost her dearly.[11]

Nevertheless, it was a circumstance accepted by the times, and by it Mrs. Royall obtained a background which none but the most narrow Tidewater aristocrat could dispute. William Royall had given Anne Newport a name and respectability, but more important, he gave her his friends who were now duty-bound to assist her. That assistance was the information Lewis Machen and John Dunn sought.

Sixteen years of marriage made Mrs. Royall a part of her husband's enthusiasms. Major Royall, like Thomas Jefferson, was a revolutionary in the French stamp. A student, then a follower of those philosophies which had mounted the first attack upon aristocracy, upon the men who claimed they had been ordained by an omnipotent God to rule and abuse other men in His name, Major Royall had deserted his patrimony to prove the validity of his beliefs. His library of revolutionary works had instilled respect for them in his new consort. A new world was being born and they were watching it happen. The Major had been present at its first birth pangs and was too old to watch its full term, but he knew his young wife would. He had prepared her for association with those who would accomplish the lasting miracle, and to that end, he had made her an extension of himself, initiated her into his circles. This fact made the most impression upon Lewis Machen. He knew what that fraternity was, and at last he understood how Mrs. Royall had achieved her position and from what arose her hidden power.

Mrs. Royall had not gained entrance to Washington and its councils because William Royall had bequeathed her his name. The man had prepared her entry to a most important community of men and it was that community which welcomed Mrs. Royall and promoted her. Lewis Machen knew many members of that community and feared them. He understood why so many in Washington knew of William Royall who did not know him personally. This knowledge made Mrs. Royall more important than ever to the men against her.

William Royall was a member of that remarkable order of men who in the 18th and 19th centuries made the Age of Reason a political crusade: Masons.[12] This fraternity of men, born in an ancient camaraderie, had become an international group dedicated to new assumptions, and had joined hands across national borders in an awesome endeavor to promote these new interests. In common cause, men in England, France, Germany, Poland, Italy, Spain, and the American colonies worked to depose the old order of kings and "divine right" as archaic remnants of a system designed to keep savages in check, not for men reaching for knowledge. They sought to replace that system with leadership from educated men who would write mankind's rights into constitutions as the governing authority for a new world rising against the ignorance of ages. These Masonic groups, building on past associations, provided the vehicle for solidification and communication of the ideas, techniques, and strategies with which the new order, the Age of Reason, would come to pass. Men in France had led the march, but it was the men in the United States who had carried the ideal to its logical conclusion. The Masons in the United States had been successful and had invited their brethren to come and see what they had done. The rest of the world was being readied for revolt.[13]

The visiting brethren had come from all parts of Europe. Many of these visitors had stayed with the Royalls in Sweet Springs, Virginia, and, like William Royall, they had shared their enthusiasms with those who shared their dedication. In this way, William Royall's Masonic commitments were made Mrs. Royall's. The woman found herself an equal with men involved in larger purpose.

The Masonic involvement with the American Revolution was a fact of life in 1829. Five of the nation's first seven presidents had been members of its orders. That it was an extension of a worldwide movement was known: The leaders of the French Revolution, then aborted, had been Masonic pamphleteers. In England, the extension of the basic rights movement in Parliament was spearheaded by known Masonic brethren, while in Germany and Italy, the princes seeking to transform feudal fiefs into new nations were professed Masons, together with the most famous philosophers and new writers of the day. Even tyrants paid lip service to the Masonic fraternity. Emperor Napoleon celebrated the orders in his heraldry and Louis Napoleon, about to begin his career, would continue it. It was the intellectual fraternity to join if a man had any pretense to new political thoughts and ideas for the new world emerging in the 19th century.[14]

Such thoughts were not limited to men. The Masons early understood the role and power of women in such efforts. Women seeking liberation from ancient strictures were welcome into the ranks of men working to achieve it; this was true of the French orders in particular. Most of the women who did emerge from obscurity to make contributions to art, the new literature, and even politics and science received their initial support from the orders. In France and in the French-inspired American lodges, women were adoptive members of the Masons.[15] This circumstance was an important factor to Mrs. Royall.

The Masonic orders of the 18th and 19th centuries were the ideological left of the times. The Masons were professed deists and theists; God was the creator but each man had been set down in that creation to do what he could do, and in such men's ability to lead their brethren to that end was the real power of government. Like the cathedrals which the Masons had built to house the religions of Europe, God had created a house in which man lived. Each man, however, had to seek for himself God and his life. No one man's God was better than another's.

Hence the Masons of 1829 still celebrated all expressions of God by examining all men's beliefs in Him, discarding that which perverted their premise. Such investigations were a logical extension of the human desire to seek perfection, a goal all reasonable men had to search out, and the Masons conducted that search. They were not Christian, but they did not deny Christianity nor its roots in Judaism. They merely asked that Man exercise Reason as his true celebration of his God. Man was to go about his world doing his best to develop himself, but always with his fellow man in mind. To this end, Masons screened their brethren carefully and in those perilous times of religious and political persecution, they met in secret to carry out their reasoned conclusions.

Every Mason pledged his assistance to other Masons in solemn bonds of brotherhood, a brotherhood which knew no limitations. On this, the chain of rebellion was forged which transformed their world. In 1829, most American churches accepted Masonry, encouraged by the need to cope with new ideas beyond their restricted dogmas in a new world on a new continent. Even the Catholic Church included the Masonic orders, with many of its hierarchical officers as members. Father Matthews, later Bishop of Washington, and famous laity such as Charles Carroll were active participants in Masonic endeavors, despite papal bulls to the contrary. Jewish synagogues and Protestant churches cooperated with the Masonic movement as they involved themselves with the new world. There was no religious call for approbation against men seeking knowledge, dedicated to making a new society, only forbearance as the experiment continued.[16] For fifty years, American Masonic orders directed American affairs. It was a simple case of those who had effected the Revolution being allowed to direct its course.

Lewis Machen had identified Mrs. Royall's Washington base. The Masons had been her education and her substance, and they helped provide the showcase for her talent. Mrs. Royall, in turn, equated the Masonic movement with the Republic, and the fact that most of the nation's leaders, in Washington and without, were members of its orders only reinforced her position. Mrs. Royall was at last understood, but before any action could be successfully initiated against her, more work had to be done. Lewis Machen knew what work to do.

Mrs. Royall was secure in her Masonic base, but times were changing. The Masons were celebrating power patterns now fifty years from their source, and although sustaining the direction of American affairs through their tenuous compact, other virile groups were reaching for that control.

There was a rising religious tide directed towards the acceptance of a particular God, and this was working against Masonry. In New York, Pennsylvania, and Vermont, anti-Masonic leagues had been formed under the direction of the same religious groups John Coyle represented. With the assistance of the tract-society publishing companies, Masons were being assailed, and Masons in those states were no longer the heroes they had been.[17] There were anti-Masonic groups in Washington, and their members could be contacted, particularly the former Attorney General, William Wirt.[18] Surely he would know what to do with Mrs. Royall.

John Coyle was jubilant with Lewis Machen's suggestion, but John Dunn was not so sure. It was no secret on Capitol Hill that Mrs. Royall was a Masonic enthusiast, for she had written extensively about it, but so was most of Washington City. It was wise to remember that Andrew Jackson was a Mason, and with him in the White House, the other half of Washington could go Mason too. After all, they still had their jobs and an anti-Masonic move at this time could jeopardize them. If any work was to be done, it had to be done quietly, directing no attention to them.

John Dunn knew of what he counseled. He had invested heavily in a publishing venture with his brother James, but changes in political directions and his espousal of them had submerged it more than once.[19] Masonic persuasions were not a crime, despite the cries of such evangelicals as John Coyle, and the House sergeant-at-arms was not anxious to build any more congressional opposition to himself than he already had. Mrs. Royall's beliefs were dangerous, but her actions were the real issue. That was where they should center their attack. If the woman was to be stopped, it was not wise to launch an attack on her supporters. It would be better to learn who provided her living, who paid her to write, who sustained her in her travels, who clothed her with their power. Then they could move in a logical fashion against the most vulnerable and turn them against her. John Dunn did have a better idea.

Lewis Machen assumed the responsibility for searching out Mrs. Royall's immediate backers. He had the Senate to work with, men who had been in Washington a long time, and he had the mind and the time to read her work for clues to what others might now know. He undertook the task immediately.

Mrs. Royall had provided her own open book. She had written frankly of herself, her friends, her finances, and her past and present. It was all there for the diligent reader.

Mrs. Royall's past had intrigued John Coyle. Lewis Machen decided to begin with it and a very different Mrs. Royall emerged. A wealthy widow and inheritor of all the estates of William Royall, for ten years that lady had enjoyed her position. She had traveled the frontier, tracing her holdings and investing in new ventures, and she had enjoyed considerable success. She had been an early investor in the salt-mining boom in Huntsville, Alabama, and had increased her wealth immeasurably as a result. During the Huntsville foray she had met Andrew Jackson, who was investing too, a circumstance to be remembered.[20] This activity had laid the groundwork for her ability to assess an area and its potential for development, and Lewis Machen had to salute her for that. Her present penury was no result of her inability to recognize a good property; rather it was *because* she knew how to make money.

Mrs. Royall had been reduced from a wealthy widow, the owner of a considerable estate, and its income, by a protracted court action initiated by relatives, both her own and her husband's. In each case, the desire to remove the woman from control of wealth had been the motivation, and the long battle had begun after her Huntsville, Alabama, success.[21]

Major William Royall had made his wife his sole heir one week before his death in a will witnessed by Mary Butler, Anne Royall's mother, and James Wiley, a neighbor whose plantation abutted the Royall land. In a series of complicated sale actions to settle the estate and provide cash for investment, the Royall land had been sold to James Wiley. This sale to a witness of Major Royall's will became the circumstance Elizabeth Royall Roan, the major's niece, and her husband, James Roan, used to attempt to break the major's will. They alleged that the female interloper, Anne Newport, a woman of ill repute, had entered into an unholy bargain with James Wiley, attested to by her mother, to unduly influence the aged William Royall to disinherit his only kin. They cited as proof the preferential sale of the Royall home and lands to Wiley and asserted that the major had lost his competence. On this basis they sued to recover what they declared was theirs by birthright. This court battle began immediately and dragged on for years.

Huntsville and its success involved Mrs. Royall's niece and her husband in another action against the wealthy widow. It sought to gain control for the young husband of those properties managed by aunt for niece, now Mrs. Royall's inheritor. This new action encouraged the old action, and both young couples joined against Mrs. Royall. For ten years, she fought them, first the Roans and then the Gardners, but in the end the battle turned against her. The Huntsville properties, encumbered by the costs of such litigation, were sold. The boom disappeared and with it, Mrs. Royall's own niece and nephew, but the attacks on her estate continued. Mrs. Royall's aristocratic nephew-in-law, James Roan, losing in the courts of the new frontier, had the case transferred to the unreformed Tory courts of Richmond, Virginia. There Mrs. Royall was stripped of everything she had in a raw exercise of the forbidden English laws of blood possession at the expense of the widow. Even her dowry was taken from her, together with her inheritance, for the court had demanded that she account for all income produced during the decade she had been the inheritor and she was ordered to surrender all properties. The excuse for this legal thievery was that she had lived with William Royall without benefit of clergy prior to her marriage, and therefore she was without repute, guilty as James Roan accused her. The sixteen years of marriage, the bonds forged between man and wife, meant nothing to the Tidewater aristocracy fighting a continuing battle against the rise of people of no known lineage.

At 53 years of age, Mrs. Royall was forced by an old English law, cited in a Tidewater court, to repay what could not be repaid, mortgaging what little future she had. Reduced to an indigent, a constant debtor with fines to pay, she was sent to a debtors' prison in Alabama as hostage for properties to be sold. There she sat for seven months until her Masonic friends could free her. For the first time, Mrs. Royall learned what the Masonic commitment could mean, that her husband's life touched her still.[22]

The Masons in Huntsville obtained Mrs. Royall's release by citing the fact that Mrs. Royall was entitled to remuneration from the federal government for Major Royall's contributions to the War of Independence. His widow was to be released to apply to Washington for repayment of the large sums expended by her late husband in behalf of the government's birth. Further, as the wife of a Revolutionary veteran, Mrs. Royall was entitled to a widow's pension and both these financial entitlements would assist her to repay all debts levied against her. The Alabama courts assented to her release. She was remanded to Masonic custody until the debt was paid, and Mrs. Royall was on her way to Washington. The Masonic brethren handed her from one to the other as she sought what was hers to satisfy the courts and her debts.[23]

Machen, Dunn, and Coyle were jubilant with this discovery. Mrs. Royall had been in prison and was still under legal impressment for debt, for her pension and the money due William Royall, had not been granted by Congress. The widow's pension was tied up in technicalities. Congress had decreed that a Revolutionary widow was one who was wife to a Revolutionary veteran before 1798, with all documents recorded before that date. Mrs. Royall had been married in 1797, but the marriage had not been recorded until 1798. A special act of Congress was required to hurdle this impasse. The money due her husband was even more complicated in process.[24]

Major Royall had never made personal application for the refund of money he had expended for the Virginia militia he had formed; therefore, he had not substantiated his costs. Mrs. Royall alone faced the labor to prove the money spent, and having met that condition, she had to spur Congress to enact special legislation again. Certain congressional leaders promised annual enabling writs, but no action had been taken. At last Mrs. Royall's enemies had a definite course of action they could follow. They would have to move quietly; they did not want to alert her friends before they had allied her enemies.

Lewis Machen went to work listing Mrs. Royall's friends. The Masons who had been so kind to her were all in print, put there by Mrs. Royall's own hand. The men who had expedited her papers in Richmond, the man who had given her lodging in Alexandria, and the men who kept her going in Washington were all named. Mrs. Royall had been proud of her association with the Masonic brethren who had kept faith with William Royall through his widow, and Charles Carroll headed her list. The richest man in the nation, a signer of the Declaration of Independence, and a hero even in 1829, he was Mrs. Royall's chief sponsor. Lewis Machen and John Dunn had to find lesser figures for their aims; Charles Carroll was too powerful.

Mrs. Royall heaped much praise upon M.E. Clagget, the first man in the Washington area to assist her. Clagget had taken her in, given her the best room in his hostelry for six months, and provided a personal maid to nurse her through her recovery from the rigors of imprisonment. Clagget was a hotel keeper, not a power figure.[25]

Mrs. Royall had made no secret of her great affection for M.E. Clagget. She acknowledged that he was the one who had encouraged her to write for a living and had opened the doors of Washington to help her do so. She averred she had been writing for years, keeping journals of travels and the people she met, and occasionally trying poetry and even a novel. She had tried to publish and had been refused, but had continued to play with the craft for her friends and her personal satisfaction. Always she hoped for a publisher.

Mrs. Royall also cited as her mainstay during this time Matthew Dunbar, her lawyer. Her journals had been important additions to her communications with him, and she had started making in-depth notations about innovations and discoveries in 1818.

These notations had begun as an afterthought, not a conscious effort. She was alone, moving about to oversee her investments, and her need to keep in touch with young Matt Dunbar made informative letters imperative.[26] As she wrote, she could not dwell on business detail alone; she needed to confide many more things. It became a written conversation between two people who enjoyed one another's confidence, an intensely private communication. One day a book came into Mrs. Royall's hands, one book among the many she read as she went.

It was a small volume, *The Journal of Lady Sydney Morgan*, a diary of an Englishwoman writing extensively on the turmoil of revolution in France and its aftermath. Mrs. Royall could not put the book down once she had started it, and she wrote Matt her delight with its discovery.

> Oh Matt, have you seen Lady Morgan's France? You will be so pleased with it. For a woman she is a fine writer. This work will long remain a standing evidence of that towering genius which knows no sex. Her delineations of men and manners are well drawn. Her style is classical, nervous, glowing, and pure, and she discovers a perfect knowledge of mankind. She is the best portrayer I have met with, except Voltaire. She descends to the bottom, and searches the lowest depths of society. She reascends amongst the nobility and gentry, and unlocks the cabinet of kings and ministers. She examines for herself. She bursts the chains of prejudice, and comes forth arrayed in the brightest ornament of literature, was once, it seems, an actress and on the stage![27]

Mrs. Royall had stumbled upon the work of a woman who would more than delight her; she would point the way for Mrs. Royall to follow.

Lady Sydney Morgan was more than a writer; she was an adoptive Mason. Even as Mrs. Royall wrote about her to Matt Dunbar, Lady Morgan had been received into the orders of the Marchioness de Villette, a favorite of Voltaire and Grand Mistress of the Paris Lodge, *La Belle et Bonne*, a title then gaining fame in European literature for sponsoring a "school" of writing.28 Mrs. Royall could not know it, but the very pen which struck fire within her was sponsored by those who would someday sponsor her. Lady Morgan's journal opened a door through which Anne Newport Royall walked. The book about France was so timely that an American woman of like sympathies, caught up in a similar transition in another country, could not put it away from her. Someone had to do this for the new America! Mrs. Royall decided it was what she wanted to do. Mrs. Royall, writer, was born.

Publishing was another matter. Within the week of the Lady Morgan discovery, Mrs. Royall, browsing in a bookstore in Huntsville, found *Salmagundi*, a compilation by American authors Paulding and Irving. American authors were few, and asking about the new work, she learned that booksellers in America were prejudiced against American writers. *Salmagundi* had been in the store trashpile; the bookseller did his best to dissuade her from buying it, pressing upon her his idea of a really good book. The sight of that offering would stay with her the rest of her life. It was Robert Russell's *Seven Sermons*, an English cleric's effort published sometime around 1750 and reprinted by a Philadelphia press in its 65th edition. It was being thrust upon American readers in 1818! A whole new world had been born, and yet this relic of the old world was still being presented as "something to read." The man had to be mad; Mrs. Royall bought *Salmagundi.* 29

The incident had been peculiar. Mrs. Royall could not put it out of her mind. How many thoughtless people bought a book of sermons and not *Salmagundi?* She was to learn it was no isolated incident; the excuse would always be the same, that there were no good American authors. She determined that she would prove these book merchants wrong.

It was this incident which had sparked the first discussion of Mrs. Royall's writing during her stay with M.E. Claggett. The evenings had been long in Alexandria, and Mrs. Royall had little with which to express her appreciation to her host. She did have a facile tongue and a wealth of information about places she had been and seen. These after-hours talks had been pleasant for them both, and for the people who dropped in to meet this woman from so far away. From time to time, Mrs. Royall would refer to her journals to refresh her memory or produce a pertinent fact. Her listeners were entranced. Mrs. Royall wrote! They liked what she had produced. The effect was not lost upon M.E. Claggett.

Mrs. Royall had a long wait for action on her many claims against the government. Why didn't she write and publish what she wrote? There were many who were hungry for the knowledge she had. The effect on friends and neighbors in Alexandria had been remarkable; Claggett was sure there were many more who would appreciate information about American places they would never see, from an American point of view. Mrs. Royall agreed with his premise, but she had tried. American authors could not be published; she had letters in hand from prestigious presses in Philadelphia to prove it.

M.E. Claggett suggested that if a writer needed support, someone to buy, someone to help sell, the Philadelphia presses were not important. Mrs. Royall already was sponsored by the Masonic brethren, and he saw no reason why they would not extend help for this worthy project too. He would subscribe, and he was sure he could find others to do so too.

It was such a simple solution, it took Mrs. Royall's breath away. If M.E. Claggett and other Masons believed she could write and had something to contribute, she would be delighted to do so. The nation did need to know what its many parts were doing; she had a good start at such a catalogue in her travels to date. She decided she would embark on the project at once.[30]

Mrs. Royall wrote to Matt Dunbar and asked him to forward all the letters and manuscripts he had in his possession, all the writings she had produced from 1816 to 1824. She was going to turn them into a book.

Matt Dunbar gathered up her letters and sent them on, but he reminded her to work harder at her task than before. His friend was 54 years of age, and such discipline could be very tiring. Matt Dunbar posed the right kind of challenge for Mrs. Royall.

Matt Dunbar was not just her lawyer; he was her confidante and surrogate son. William Royall had educated him and enabled him to become a man of the law. Mrs. Royall was very dear to him, and he worried about her and this new project. He knew about her interest in writing, for during the long months of her imprisonment it was he who saw to it that she had paper to keep her occupied with her journal. He had received what she had written, sent her finished work to the Philadelphia publishers, and received the rejections. No one bought Americans; Matt did not want her to be disheartened again. What Matt did not know was that M.E. Claggett had evolved a new plan for Mrs. Royall, and he had done something about it.[31]

Claggett was the Grand Master of the Alexandria Lodge, and he knew many important people in the surrounding lodges. If Mrs. Royall was willing, he would give her letters to Washington City's better-known citizens, to those who could offer more help and more influence in this project. The nation's capital would be a good starting point. Surely the nation's leaders would see, as he did, that Americans needed to see themselves through American eyes, not just through the biased squints of Europeans who would not and did not understand the country. M.E. Claggett was sure that Masons would subscribe to her books in advance and the money received would finance her venture. It was a capital idea.

Mrs. Royall went to Washington armed with M.E. Claggett's letters of introduction and a few of her own from past encounters. Claggett, Grand Master Mason, opened wide the capital's doors and almost everyone of importance responded to his call. In one short month, Mrs. Royall had in hand her first list of subscribers. They included John Quincy Adams, John Randolph, Charles Carroll, William Brent, the Van Ness family, Catholic priest Father Matthews, Baptist preacher Obadiah Brown, John Eaton and Daniel Webster.[32]

Women helped Mrs. Royall, too. Mrs. William Prout, Mrs. John Van Ness, and Louisa Adams opened homes to her and presented her. It was a pleasure to sponsor a woman so well read, so skilled in conversation beyond the home.

This was Mrs. Royall's Washington source, and it gave pause to her enemies. Machen, Dunn, Coyle, and the entire Engine House Congregation could not match the caliber of Mrs. Royall's known supporters. It was a difficult situation, but many things had changed since Mrs. Royall had come to Washington. The capital had before it the shifting of alliances and allegiances, and Mrs. Royall was involved in those changing loyalties. Friends who had supported her were among those suffering from the victory of Jackson; among these were John Quincy Adams and his wife, Louisa. Using Mrs. Royall's own words, Lewis Machen promised action: "Friends or enemies today, there are many who can be enlisted to our side tomorrow."

Chapter 5

Points of View

Lewis Machen sat in the Senate close to John Calhoun, the vice president of the United States, who also served as the president of the Senate. He was well aware of the stress in that august chamber. Andrew Jackson had fought hard for his victory in 1828 and had left the congressional aisles strewn with broken friendships. Men who had cooperated with each other for years were at each other's throats, for the Jackson forces had submerged the politics of the half century before. The most prestigious men in both houses were adrift, seeking new bases and constituencies, and issues with which to promote themselves.[1]

Lewis Machen had not made an idle boast to his comrades. He knew many men with faces like the lava of Aetna who served on congressional staffs who would like to discuss Mrs. Royall, particularly those in Daniel Webster's and Henry Clay's offices. Lewis Machen had in hand Mrs. Royall's last book; it was all the introduction he would need. He was spurred on by the words Mrs. Royall had used against him:

I was attacked in a hostile manner by one of the clerks of the Senate, another Presbyterian, for the honor of our wise government . . . I believe firmly that had it not been for the presence of one or two of the messengers, who witnessed the whole affair, he would have laid violent hands on me.[2]

Lewis Machen did not intend to use that passage. He preferred another:

Now tell me why this man, and every man of them, receives such extravagant wages, and why they are suffered, paid by the quarter, to leave their business?

It is very clear that something is rotten in our government, or these enemies to its vitals would not be cherished in its bosom. "But these men have been in a long time" it will be said. And for this reason alone they ought to be turned out and let others of equal right at least share a little of the loaves and fishes. It is their being in so long that has rendered them so dangerous. So many of them being already in office had induced fellows out of office to unite with them to establish their religion, and have at length came out boldly for that purpose. I hope the dignity of our country may no longer be prostituted in this manner.[3]

If these words did not produce the allies he needed, Lewis Machen would indeed be in greater difficulty than he was now. He didn't realize it, but he was about to plumb political depths much deeper than his purpose; he was braving winds raised five years before.

36

The year Mrs. Royall had come to Washington, 1824, had posed a new problem to the American Republic. James Monroe, the last of the "original" revolutionaries to serve as president, was leaving office, having completed his second term. The nation had outlived its founding fathers and there were no more revolutionary "greats" to accept the mantle of leadership. Washington, Adams, Jefferson, Madison, and Monroe—who would receive the presidency from these? Franklin and Hamilton were long dead, Aaron Burr hounded from the scene. Who was left? The lesser men who had marched with these were too old, and even if their age had been no consideration, none had the luster with which to direct the work remaining. America had reached her first crisis in leadership, and it was a formidable one.

The wrong man in the presidency at the wrong time could wreck the small ship of state so artfully contrived to weather the heavy seas of the emerging 19th century. Yet the time had come to turn to a new generation for leadership. What men with vitality could carry the nation through continuing peril?

The first inclination of the existing leadership charged with finding a new leader had been to look at the sons the past presidents had produced. It was well within custom that when pleased with the father, a nation looked to his blood. However, only one of America's presidents had a son connected with its national life. John Adams's John Quincy Adams was well known and admired in many circles. He had accompanied his father through the evolution of American nationhood and power and was well qualified. In 1824, he sat as James Monroe's secretary of state, a position which had produced several presidents to date. But he posed a problem. John Quincy Adams had specialized in foreign affairs to the detriment of domestic concerns; his labors had kept him abroad most of his adult life. Many suspected he was less American for that experience. Coming home to counteract his critics, his ardent advocacy in Congress for his home state of Massachusetts had added the charge of sectionalism to narrow his support further.[4]

The wise men in Washington wrestled with Adams the Younger's problems and as they did so, a surprising contender emerged for the nation's leadership. Andrew Jackson was presented not as an heir to revolutionary acclaim, but as a self-made hero. The claims put forward for him were impressive.

Andrew Jackson was a revolutionary great, his supporters claimed. He was not of the stamp of 1776—he had been too young—but he had equaled his elders by the simple act of behaving like a hero when America needed it again, in the War of 1812. He alone of America's leaders in that conflict, that second War for Independence, had fought the enemy and produced a stunning victory. The defeat he had visited upon the British forces at New Orleans in 1815, saving the nation from the ignominy of constant entreaty for survival, now put him into contention for the presidency.

The Congress did not welcome this new aspirant or his popular support. They ignored both, hoping the suggestion would die, but it did not. James Monroe, packing in the White House, watched the Jackson movement with dismay. The fragile union was not ready to affront its enemies, particularly Great Britain, but he could not select John Quincy Adams as his successor without precipitating political disaster. Instead, he prevailed upon his fellow Virginians to promote William Harris Crawford, his secretary of the treasury from Georgia, and draw all the Jackson fire in his direction. He urged the congressional establishment to run as they pleased: John Calhoun of South Carolina, Henry Clay of Kentucky and of course, John Quincy Adams of Massachusetts. In this manner, the election of 1824 had five candidates, and yet only one could be chosen to lead the nation.[5]

James Monroe had no doubt as to who would win in this overcrowded race.

William Crawford would keep Virginia and Georgia bottled up and Jackson's popular support would be no match for Adams's hold on the Congress. The capital breathed easier with Monroe. Andrew Jackson was not of their stripe, and his claim to fame, his brutish victory over the British at New Orleans, made him an impossible leader for a nation being quietly wed to British interests by John Quincy Adams as secretary of state.[6] James Monroe believed he had insured the continuation of his well-publicized Era of Good Feeling.

In effect, Washington had been beguiled by the brilliance of young Adams. Despite continued English intransigeance and interference in American affairs, the British impressment of American sailors, suppression of trade, and even interference with American currency, Secretary Adams had convinced Monroe that the United States could treat themselves out of all these problems by adopting a positive and friendly attitude to the mother country. Adams had gone so far as to accept and proclaim as American policy the doctrine suggested by Lord Canning, enunciating an American warning to all nations but Great Britain about involvements in the Western Hemisphere. The Monroe Doctrine, using Canning's own words to Adams, saved Britain the necessity of placing armed forces in North and South America to protect its empire flank, and the Monroe Administration even created a new United States Navy to do it for them.[7] It had become James Monroe's historical design and the Anglophobe, Andrew Jackson, was not to be allowed to thwart it.

This was the scene into which Mrs. Royall walked in 1824, propelled by M.E. Claggett and her own ambition. It was a year of fantastic intrigue and deception.

General Andrew Jackson was the man Washington City mobilized to defeat. In 1824, his name was never out of mind in the nation's capital. The citizens of the federal town hated him, for Jackson had shamed them all by achieving victory in New Orleans even after Washington had been burned. Worse, the Federalists had formed other plans for the nation, plans revealed by the extraordinary convention in Hartford, Connecticut, during which certain clerics and financiers from New England demanded capitulation and negotiation for whatever they could get from a triumphant British government.[8] Jackson had surprised them with an unwanted success at the very moment they had signed their capitulation into treaty. Like men at Bladensburg, Maryland, who ran before the British, these men ran again, hiding their action in confusion. The rout at Bladensburg, which had sent Virginia's finest and President James Madison running before 4,000 British troops, was a poor show beside the monumental destruction of 5,000 British troops by the hero of New Orleans.[9] These stains, Bladensburg and the Hartford Convention, were made deeper and more ugly every time Jackson's name was mentioned. Washington City and its government hated that man with a vengeance.

But there was a reason. Those who had been routed, those who had conspired, and those who had sued for less than an honorable peace had retained their positions in Congress and the government by simple strategem. They simply put the War of 1812 out of their minds. They never discussed it, and they not only "forgot" it but spent ten years punishing Andrew Jackson by keeping him in virtual exile.

James Monroe had seen to that. Andrew Jackson had been gifted with the worst duty possible, from actions against the Creek Indians to assignment in Florida. These were actions in which success was never planned, actions which Washington City hoped would produce his defeat. It didn't happen. Andrew Jackson produced victory in every assignment, and his reward was yet one more attempt to blacken his name and stain him with personal slander. It was that circumstance that made him more of a threat.

Andrew Jackson had not finished with the British at New Orleans. He had found them involved with the Creeks and in Florida too. General Andrew Jackson had the impudence to discover English conspirators behind the troubles wherever he went, and he routed them. With each rout, more fame accumulated about his name. Washington City and its Anglophiles hated him even more.[10] By 1824, it was out in the open and the people, confused by their national leaders, responded by promoting Andrew Jackson to president, putting an end to his exile.

The Congress was the last bastion against Andrew Jackson. It mobilized silently about John Quincy Adams, with a "son" of the Hartford Convention, Daniel Webster, leading.[11] Under Webster's auspices, the wheeling and dealing was conducted for the Adams presidency. Congress had no need for a renegade general in command; it had men of quality in its midst. Lesser men were promoted to argue in the national lists and as they did, Adams was promoted more and more. Adams, keeping to his gentlemanly pose, would gain in stature and after the electioneering. Congress, in its wisdom, would select the man to whom the ship of state could be entrusted for the next four years. Leave the countryside to Jackson and his bands, Congress had the real mandate and would use it.[12]

It was into this maze of congressional manipulation and machination that Mrs. Royall marched with her pen in 1824. Like an American Everyman, armed with introductions from men of importance beyond the legislature's narrow precincts, she excited men searching for clues in the confusion at hand. Mrs. Royall was a woman of mature intelligence, well connected, and from Virginia, but born of Maryland, raised in Pennsylvania, and newly arrived from Alabama and Tennessee.

Her sponsors had presented her as a known observer of the American scene, one competent to report on the American mind. How would such as she react to the choices at hand? Leaders in the Congress who might have brushed aside such a woman months before now took time to sit and discuss their problems with her. She displayed the knowledge and background to understand the unique position they shared. Men who were participants in the national story were eager to talk to a woman who was purported to be writing its history.

Lewis Machen did not find any instant allies for his project against Mrs. Royall. Many agreed with his contention that she was a menace, but no one wanted to draw attention to his own position. Mrs. Royall was known to be well aware of Machen's activities, and Dunn's and Coyle's too. She was their problem. The woman knew many important people and perhaps Lewis Machen should go to some of them looking for help. It was good advice and just about all that was left to Machen. He decided to try it.

William Brent, clerk of the Federal District Court, was one of Mrs. Royall's friends. A militia colonel, he held great position in the capital based on the fact that he was nephew to Charles Carroll and the steward of the Carroll properties in Washington City. His connection with the writer was rumored to go back to Mrs. Royall's own family beginnings.[13] All this was interesting to Lewis Machen, but what really sent him to William Brent was the fact that the Colonel had been a great supporter of John Quincy Adams.[14]

William Brent received Lewis Machen. As an admirer of the writer, Colonel Brent liked to talk about her. He had been privileged to assist her in her extraordinary work, to follow his uncle's directions, and provide lodgings for her whenever she required them as well as giving her letters of introduction. It was a responsibility he still attended to, at her request.

The lady had first come to his attention in the year of the 1824 election. He remembered the circumstances well. It had been a pleasure to sit with Mrs. Royall and discuss those exciting days, for the lady held views similar to his own.

The country was tired of revolution and had outgrown it, and the time had come to celebrate it as past history only. The nation had to be built from the vast country it held. Colonel Brent had preferred Adams, and Mrs. Royall had too. The Adamses and their circles had received her and appreciated her for the well-traveled and considered observations she brought to them all. Mrs. Royall had known Andrew Jackson for years, and yet in 1824 she had chosen to support Adams because she thought him to be the better choice for the times. Like Colonel Brent, Mrs. Royall believed that a statesman's experience was preferable to the successful but precipitous military talents of Andrew Jackson for the advent of the second half century of life for America. Naturally it had solidified the Adamses' affection for her, as it did for their other supporters. Surely Mr. Machen knew about Louisa Adams and her gesture of appreciation to Mrs. Royall, her presentation of her own shawl to the writer when she left Washington on that first tour for her first book.[15]

Colonel Brent was not displeased with Mrs. Royall's change of heart about the Adams presidency. Adams had been a great disappointment and Mrs. Royall was not alone in her desertion of his cause. Things were not going well for the nation, and it was time for an Andrew Jackson. The shipping and trading mess grew, and the Cherokee Indians were problems, as were the recent spate of bankruptcies in road companies; something had to be done and a strong hand could help.[16] As for Jackson and the English, the nation needed someone to stand up to them; Adams had achieved nothing with his temporizing. Colonel Brent saluted Mrs. Royall for her ability to recognize facts. The nation needed such talents. More open minds should be in Washington, and perhaps Jackson would bring more like her to the capital.

Lewis Machen beat a fast retreat from Colonel Brent. The legacy of 1824, despite John Quincy Adams and Louisa, was still a strong foundation for the aged writer.

Mrs. Royall's debut in Washington had been a traumatic experience for a woman not so long removed from an Alabama debtor's prison. She had known enormous changes before, but she had been young then. At 54 years of age, it was not so easy to move from the quiet affairs of the frontier into the midst of the sophisticated matters of a nation's capital. That she had accomplished it at all was a tribute to her powers.

Mrs. Royall had kept herself afloat in that sea of confusion by a simple device. She had selected one basis with which to judge the events about her: The United States was all that mattered, and what served the nation best would determine her direction. She did not even include herself in this basic. This gave her the courage to sit as an observer amid the currents swirling about her in the capital. Keeping to the narrow confines of national interest, disregarding personal matters, she escaped the pitfalls of states' rivalries, and it was easy for her to converse with everyone in Washington City, especially the Adamses.

In those early days in the capital, Mrs. Royall came to know both John and Louisa Adams well. His office was open to her always, and his wife opened their home as well. Mrs. Royall was encouraged to come and go with her tales and her comments, and she had reciprocated with a growing affection for the quiet man and his lovely wife, neither of whom were ever too busy to see her. In Adams's gentleness with her, his ability to lay aside the affairs of state for a moment of plain talk, Mrs. Royall thought she glimpsed the greatness of a son born to a great father. John Quincy Adams to Mrs. Royall was more than an extension of his father; he had his own commitment to the nation, a dedication it sorely needed.[17] The fact that her new friends shared this sympathy for the man and the constant reminder that Jackson was grounded only in militarism firmed her enthusiasm for Adams. Walking the halls of the Congress and government offices presented Mrs. Royall with new perspectives, and she followed them to logical conclusions. National affairs were problems of the mind, not emotion. Adams was of the mind, and Jackson was of the emotion. Mrs. Royall had supported the mind, John Quincy Adams.

These considerations were ruling Congress too. Jackson had many friends in the body he had served and some, like Mrs. Royall, had reservations about the man's ability to cope with the problems they recognized. The United States had wrested a bare victory from the British, albeit with Jackson's help, and no one really wanted to try it again. The need was for some peaceful accommodation with the former enemy, not more confrontation. The nation simply could not afford any more war and whole sections had shown their distaste for the military marshaling of forces in the late Indian and Florida campaigns.[18]

The Monroe Doctrine, although questioned, had opened the door to continual mediation of problems with England and the best president in 1824 would be the man who could promote a peaceful extension of that promise. It was not hard to accept the basic reason that England would accept an Adams but never a Jackson; the English press and its associates in the United States proclaimed the fact every day.[19] Mrs. Royall, a newcomer, had common cause with her new friends and they extended the encouragement she needed to put her pen to work.

In 1824, the Washington Masons were keeping their usual stance. Officially, they did not indulge in political affairs, but there was no doubt that members did. Most of the Washington lodge were in the Adams camp. It was a singular departure for them, since Adams was no known Mason, although it was rumored he had joined in Europe.[20] Andrew Jackson, however, was a practitioner and a past Grand Master.[21] This posed no problem in Washington City. The Masons there believed they held a more universal view, and Adams was the better man. They were anxious to inform brethren elsewhere of this extraordinary decision, at variance with usual Masonic practice, and Mrs. Royall was Heaven-sent to help them accomplish that purpose.

The Jackson movements in Pennsylvania and New York had been very disturbing to Monroe's and Adams's plans. Brother Masons were flocking to the general, shunting aside any consideration of Adams.[22] Mrs. Royall, as an observer under Washington's Masonic sponsorship, could be most useful in carrying tidings to certain Masons in both states still not committed in the campaign. Her tour could be arranged, and it would be appreciated if she would carry their good faith to others and apprise them of what was really happening in the capital. She did not have to speak against Jackson, but rather she was to emphasize the sweet reason of Adams, a quality all Masons celebrated. Those Masons contacted would secure in turn for her the interviews and introductions she required to carry out her own purpose. Mrs. Royall would be on her own but as she had learned, Masons did respond. They would do so wherever she went.[23]

The proposition was more than Mrs. Royall had expected. Frankly, it was all she had. Her application for her widow's pension had failed because her certification could not meet the arbitrary deadline enacted by Congress, and a special bill would have to be framed for her relief. That would take time. She had but one resource left, her pen, and she had to make the best of it. The Masonic offer, her friends' sponsorship, was the key to a new career. Mrs. Royall accepted. She was sent on her way by none other than John Quincy Adams himself, wearing the shawl Colonel Brent still remembered, a lovely garment which Louisa Adams took off her own shoulders to clothe her new friend.

The United States was about to be rediscovered in a most surprising way. Mrs. Royall had undertaken a difficult and arduous task. Most women did not take to the road in 1824, and the few who did found every disadvantage riding with them. Public inns and accommodations were terrible, geared as they were to the rough and ready demands of men inured to hardships. The only way to assure a decent reception in a strange town or city was to travel with personal introductions in hand and hope that accommodations would be forthcoming upon the presentation of same.[24] However, finding someone who knew someone where one wanted to go was not easy. Nothing was national in character despite the network of human interests implied, but Mrs. Royall was fortunate. There was one organization which prided itself on the practical application of brotherhood, the kind of contact which could be used to provide communication as well as accommodation. The Masons took over the direction of it. They scheduled her arrivals and departures. Lodges which had sat quietly in the backwash of more recent events were approached, their members alerted, support solicited, and doors opened for a woman no one knew but so many were destined to help.[25].

Mrs. Royall produced her first book from that journey, which began October 1, 1824, one month before the crucial election. Its title was *Sketches of History, Life and Manners in the United States*. It was an instant success, for it delivered on the promise the writer had made. The United States had been described, dissected, and encouraged as it had never been before. Mrs. Royall's sponsors were happy with their creation. It was a straightforward presentation of the nation, and all could read it without controversy. In fact, the only mention of politics in the whole volume was casual comment about actual encounters. There was Adams bias, but Mrs. Royall did not claim it as her own; she was careful to put it in another's mind and mouth.

> The Georgetown man was in favor of Mr. Crawford and the yankee in favor of Mr. Adams. The Georgetown man was of pleasing manners, but the other, though a perfect boor, had the best of the argument. The first praised the talents, the long and faithful service of Mr. Crawford; the yankee opposed with sound judgment, the head to contrive, the skill to direct, the tried experience of Mr. Adams, and gained complete victory over his opponent.[26]

This is an example of the kind of argument Mrs. Royall undoubtedly engaged in herself as she talked to the Masons enroute. She did mention the election again, but passed it off with a small reference as she was traveling New Jersey enroute to New York. The first results had Jackson carrying New Jersey, and the passengers attributed this extraordinary fact to the fact that John Quincy Adams, Unitarian, did not believe in God. Adams the ungodly one and Jackson the anointed. 1824 indeed was a far cry from 1829.

John Quincy Adams became president in 1824. The year of intrigue in Congress did produce the parliamentary victory for which he had worked. Mrs. Royall made no mention of it in her *Sketches*, published fifteen months later, but her comments on visiting with John Adams, the former president, left no doubt where her sentiments lay. The Congress of the United States had shunted aside the popular vote for General Jackson, but he had not received the majority of the votes cast and Congress did have the right to choose. It was good enough for Mrs. Royall.

Mrs. Royall's first book became a subject of interest to Lewis Machen. Colonel Brent's reaction needed to be clarified. Whatever charm the old woman had was in that *Sketches* and Machen went looking for it. Somewhere he had to find a clue to the people he could contact to help him and his friends remove her from their world.

Lewis Machen could find no fault with *Sketches*. The book was a popular survey of America, city by city, town by town, connected by experiences on the road. Mrs. Royall had reported faithfully the stories and histories she had gathered as she went, describing changes going on about her. Everything she was known for was there: people, places, even the statistics. Business, hospitals, prisons, schools and colleges, museums and new developments were described in a most interesting fashion. Her sections on churches startled him. Mrs. Royall appeared to be a willing visitor to those edifices, and she gave them their due. Lewis Machen perused those passages carefully. He could find little hint as to her dislike for Presbyterianism in the volume. The only bias he detected was her outburst against English theater promoters in Baltimore who would not review dramatic material she had brought to them for consideration. The Englishmen had told her that American theater works did not sell and she had become incensed. Her comments were well within reason on civil servants in Washington too, although John Coyle and John Dunn would not think so.

Lewis Machen could not find anything in *Sketches* to use against her. Mrs. Royall was an able writer telling her reaction to America in her own way. Her format was free and easy and her stories interesting, and he could understand why Mrs. Royall had gained such popularity with *Sketches*.

Lewis Machen had noticed one oddity about *Sketches*. Mrs. Royall had published her book without her name. Why had she done so? The best information he could find concerning this strange situation was that Mrs. Royall's friends had suggested that she use "by a Traveller" to prove her merit. It was said that *Sketches* had struck such a responsive chord and had been so well received that John Quincy Adams himself had hailed Mrs. Royall's book as the long-awaited American publication which would tell all Americans what the country was about.[27]

The simple act of a woman not putting her name to her work had not prejudiced it with men. The anonymity had not lasted long; *Sketches* had opened the literary door wide. "A Traveller" had achieved a name and a cause and a host of friends to help her.

Sketches filled a void in 1826. As of this date, the United States had displayed little information-gathering ability with which to review itself.[28] Its citizens appeared too busy meeting the everyday demands of their existence to put hopes and aspirations, let alone achievements, to paper and then distribute it throughout the country. The few networks carrying such communications were private ones solely for the use of those who sponsored them. Mrs. Royall's popular book was not. It provided facts and figures and commentary long overdue for the average American. For the first time, Americans could read about developments in places far from their own towns, not in the stereotyped style of their penny journals, but in the chatty prose of an experienced traveler. The fact that Mrs. Royall went to such trouble to catalog facts, figures, plans, and directions roused the people's interest in the nation. Overnight, people in Boston learned that other cities were advancing faster than their fair metropolis, and it had its desired effect. The older towns, even states, were put on notice that there were fierce new competitors for attention from the national legislature. In one small volume, Mrs. Royall had not only supplied information but had emphasized the necessity of acquiring such information in order to lead the nation properly. It was time those who directed Washington took a good look at what was out there in the great stretch of land.

Mrs. Royall had catalogued the changes in America; the nation's leaders in Washington had not. Her journals were keys to knowledge and carried influence far beyond the writer's original expectation. She had acquired knowledge her friends did not have; that was what she was selling.

Anne Royall had seen and noted what others had missed. It had brought about a change in her, and Lewis Machen found it immediately. Mrs. Royall had begun to preach! She had found another church, her own. The seeds of dissension were there. Mrs. Royall had changed her mind and her point of view was what he needed to make his own point of view carry the weight needed to end it.

Chapter 6

Beware the Blackcoats

Mrs. Royall *had* changed. The penniless arrival in 1824 to the capital's circles was an accepted commentator on national affairs by 1829, and it was not due to her writing alone.

Following *Sketches*, Mrs. Royall had published what she had written before. She, who had created her own market, became her own publisher and set to work to prove her versatility. With printers in Connecticut and New York and critical praise from editors in many cities and towns, she launched a play and resurrected a novel.

The play *The Cabinet* was a peek into the inner workings of the federal administration. It opened in a blizzard and closed before its thaw.[1] The novel, *The Tennessean*, drawn from her early attempts at writing, was more fortunate, for it went to her subscribers. It was a rambling story about characters more traveled than herself, facing problems on a road which extended through foreign countries. It was an imitation of the writings just emerging from English presses, and it dealt with people too far removed from the American political scene to appeal to her public. Mrs. Royall knew at once she had made a mistake. One of her friends, with great tact, congratulated her upon the excellent biography she had produced about William Wirt, a politician from Tennessee for whom she had little regard.[2] This "acclaim" reminded her that she was not a writer of fiction, and that her public would not accept her as one. The United States abounded in cheap tract romances, each more maudlin than the last. Her friends wanted no more. Mrs. Royall's strength lay in translating fact to print, telling about the real changes taking place in the nation.

Sketches had opened doors that the poor novel, *The Tennessean*, could not close, and Mrs. Royall learned to keep with her real talent. She was in no position to alienate her subscribers. Despite her initial success with printing and selling her work, Mrs. Royall had little money and as yet no congressional action on the money due her husband's estate. Her poverty propelled her into her next venture. She had to take to the road again for a new edition, a sequel to *Sketches*.

Mrs. Royall was on her own in this second national survey. Adams, firmly in his White House, had no interest in current trends, and his friends offered no assistance. To insure that her subscribers supported her, she announced her plans to catalog the changes she found everywhere as a result of Adams's two years in office. Her public responded with cash, and once again her timing was right.

John Quincy Adams held the presidency, but the means by which he had achieved it had set loose a cloud of suspicion and innuendo. The defeated Jack-

45

son forces made the most of the intricate congressional maneuvering which had produced Adams's minority victory.[3] Adams found himself suffering a tenuous alliance which, although it had given him the White House, did not provide support in Congress for those policies with which he hoped to make his mark. For two years the nation drifted, and as it did, James Monroe's Era of Good Feeling became the Era of Ill Feeling. Special interests had a field day, and temporary alliances were formed and fueled by financial combines to gain harvests at the expense of the general citizenry. There was a feeling of desperation taking hold of the people, and it had to be abated.

In 1826, the American Revolution had reached its full maturity. For fifty years it had been the spirit of the land and national celebration was an obvious opportunity for leadership to cover any deficiencies. John Quincy Adams had full charge of the planning for the events which would welcome the Golden Anniversary, having received it as Monroe's secretary of state.[4]

The nation was expecting a great party with which to kick off the second century of life for the United States of America. Adams and his *coterie*, however, saw the event in a different light. The American anniversary was not to be a nostalgic recreation of the Revolution, but a summons to the nation's new arrivals to join with its older ones. The men and women who had fought the birth battles of the new democracy faced a growing number of hostile newcomers with no attachment to the glorious American past. To Adams, 1826 was not an occasion for rejoicing; it was a difficult situation which had to be handled carefully.

Washington's leaders did not want to see war passions restored or memories of conflict with England evoked. Such a move could work against them politically, and Adams made it his special mission to plan for 1826 without conflict. The Revolution would be celebrated, but its dead passions would not.

It was a labor which called for great cleverness, and Adams thought he had it. Only two of the original American Revolution heroes still lived: Adams's own father and Thomas Jefferson. Both men were in their eighties. No celebration could be built around them or with them. A living hero was crucial to his plan, however, for that person was needed to receive salutation and be acclaimed as the ultimate symbol of what the United States had achieved.

There was another living Revolutionary hero, but he was a Frenchman, not an American. The Marquis de Lafayette was the man to represent the Revolution fifty years later, and with him Adams hoped to achieve his purpose. The Marquis would be sent for, restored to his former glory, and presented as the surrogate for all that America represented not only to Americans but to the newcomers amongst them.

It was a bold design. Adams planned to glorify an old revolutionary, a foreigner who would parade that fact and then return to live with the growing aristocracy reaching again for power in Europe, a potent symbol for the new industrial aristocracy seeking its power in the United States. It was hoped that Lafayette could be brought from France as a reminder of what had been, and then returned to live in peace with what was now to be achieved. Adams planned to structure a new era in diplomacy on this, as well as to build his political fortunes at home. He, as an American leader, would prove his ability to produce a new position in world affairs and world commerce for the United States.

John Quincy Adams's world was England and France. The rest of Europe was too far removed from American considerations for inclusion in his thinking. England and France were an American preoccupation because these two nations had been at war with one another for over fifty years. The United States had been a constant pawn in that conflict. Adams hoped that his selection of a discard of France, Lafayette, used as the symbol of American progress, would impart a subtle hint to both nations. The United States was neither's enemy; it was its own entity, and it wished to be considered as a fully vested partner in the coming century's developments. The United States wanted to restore respectability, replace the contentions of the past with cooperation, and become a worthwhile member of a growing Atlantic community. Lafayette was to prove that aim. The design was typical of Adams and his quiet diplomacy.[5]

The Golden Jubilee was celebrated in the American states as John Quincy Adams had envisioned. The Marquis de Lafayette toured the nation in 1824, two years before the 1826 birthday. That fact was not lost on Adams's opponents. Most of them were unable to do a thing about it, but the men about Andrew Jackson knew how to counter it. Among the Americans who waited for the Marquis de Lafayette were the Masonic entourages, emblazoned in uniforms and medals, and as the old gentleman passed, so did the Masons in review. The old hero took on a meaning not intended by Adams as he traveled the United States. The Revolution did come to life again, with all of its passions, and low-key diplomacy was lost in its resurgence.

Mrs. Royall was in Boston when the Marquis de Lafayette arrived. She described the event and as she did so, the lines forming became very apparent:

I was likewise present at the celebration of Bunker Hill; the greatest procession probably that ever took place in the history of America. This procession had been so generally diffused in the newspapers, and if it had not, it so far exceeds not only the limits of this work, but my powers of description, that I should only sully a subject which I hold too sacred to profane. I collected the newspapers the following day, and intended to give the order of procession, but upon reflection I thought it would be dry . . From a window in School-street, I viewed the procession from beginning to end . . . The music of all New England was there, and all the Masons, which are numerous in those states; the bands were divided, and every lodge by itself, each leaving a small vacancy, with a splendid banner, on which was the name and number of the lodge, and the state to which it belonged. The Knights all in black, with lofty black plumes waving in their hats, their black pointed aprons, Gen. Lafayette in an open carriage, the soldiers of the Revolution in open carriages, (a venerable band), drove by young gentlemen of the first distinction in the city. It was a moving scene! But while our extasy was wrought up to the highest pitch, a dear old man, dressed in an old coat, and an old hat, passed under us; he was sitting in the front of the carriage, with his right arm extended and in his hand he held an old continental shot bag, with the same bullets in it which he had used at the Battle of Bunker Hill. He gently waved it backwards and forwards from one side to the other, so that people on each side might have a chance to see it; and continued to do so throughout the procession. The coat he had on, and the hat, were likewise those he wore in the battle; we saw distinctly several bullet holes in each—the solemn motion of the carriage! the effect cannot be described! Gen. Lafayette, and even the Knights, all glorious as they shone, shrunk into nothing beside this war-worn soldier! It transported us fifty years back, and we in imagination were fighting the Battle of Bunker Hill; the sacred relic he bore in his hand seemed endued with speech; its effect, like an electric shock, flew through the lines, and held each heart in fond delusion. Not a word was uttered for several minutes! till, "did you see that?" whispered one to the other, whilst every cheek was wet! The music was ravishing, the masons looked divine, and the Knights Templar like supernatural beings! The whole was not only grand, it was sublime! but our language is too poor for such occasions. The procession was about an hour and a half passing through the streets, and supposed to consist of eighty thousand persons, while we were favored throughout with one of the most brilliant suns.[6]

Mrs. Royall had perceived that the Marquis de Lafayette's visit was a triumph of staging, enveloped in great parade and attention, thronged by thousands. The show, however, had not overshadowed what was being celebrated. July 4, 1825, began the American tradition of fireworks in magnificent panorama displays, bought and paid for by a government anxious to lay revolutionary passions to rest as it re-established a partnership with former antagonists; but the shots and flares accented the fraud. The crowds turned out, the silver tongues of Daniel Webster, John Calhoun and Henry Clay sermonized greatly, and Lafayette passed, but the celebration had a hollow ring. The old man and his bullet-holed cloak had stolen the show. It held a portent of things to come.

The Marquis de Lafayette's tour was a commercial success. The New England textile factories made money as they never had before, and the bunting draped over the small town buildings hung long after the hoopla passed. As it faded, it became the symbol of a dismal aftermath. John Quincy Adams's celebration of the American Revolution one year before its fiftieth birthday would mark the nation with such dissension that American politics would never be the same.[7]

John Quincy Adams had miscalculated the American mind and the British one too. The Marquis de Lafayette was the worst Revolutionary symbol Adams could have promoted. The honors heaped upon a Frenchman only heightened the new immigrants' confusion, and the nation's enemies were emboldened by the chaos engendered by his tour.

The Marquis de Lafayette became a symbol in a manner in which Adams and his *coterie* never intended. The nobleman had received French sanction to attend the American celebration, but he was an inherent affront to Great Britain, despite Adams's attempt to redefine his position.[8] The Marquis had received American homage dressed in the trappings of the French Masonic lodges and the badges he wore as Grand Master of the Freemasons of France, the same emblems once worn by Washington and Franklin, were the new emblems of France. The jewels of these pendants caught the native-born Americans' imaginations, but the new immigrants from Britain did not appreciate them. Lafayette's emblems, emblazoned as the symbols of the independent spirit of free men joined together, were seen by the newly arrived sons of Scotland, Ireland, Wales, and England as symbols of France. The reaction among them was immediate. They did not applaud Lafayette, especially those who had fought against Napoleon, and there were many of those veterans among the dour Scots-Irish faces as Lafayette's parade passed them by. To them, the whole event was a sinful travesty. They had no understanding of the Age of Reason and no allegiance to the United States; they had assumed a higher one: God's dominion over man.

The government of Great Britain watched the jubilee end with great interest; it had not accepted Adams's implied reassurance. The parading of Lafayette had been a poor show, and the English moved to exploit it immediately, even as a ship carried Lafayette back to France. The Grand Master Mason, the last living Revolutionary who had served in the councils of George Washington, left the United States even as an outcry against Masonry was raised in Scots-Irish accents in the new evangelical pulpits along the seaboard while he was still in sight.[9] The few overtures in progress in diplomatic negotiations between Britain and the United States were abruptly terminated.[10]

John Quincy Adams had been affronted, and he did not know why. The same forces with which he had cooperated since 1812 deserted him and would not let him lead them. Bitter in his inability to charm Great Britain into open partnership with its former colony with his known Anglophilism, he took immediate refuge in blaming his failure upon Andrew Jackson, the man Congress had put aside for him.[11] John Quincy Adams continued to entreat his British brethren to reach accommodation, but the English believed that the United States was falling apart and that they had only to wait until the whole would fall back into British hands. Surreptitiously, Britain had placed an army within its old colony, an army which was just about reveal its face.

Mrs. Royall had not stayed in Boston after the jubilee, but had gone on to other places. That travel exposed the strange paradox taking place as the Revolution's celebration ended. The appearance of religious vituperation against American tradition in alien accents was the reason for her first break with her dear friend, John Quincy Adams.

To the traveler on the American road in 1826, it was apparent that President Adams had failed. The great diplomat had been unable to get American ships back on the seas, had been rebuffed in opening British and Caribbean ports to American trade, and now endured growing cries from the pulpits that everything American was a new alarum. The United States were in dangerous drift, and Adams had no policy with which to salve the old American, let alone the new American. His paper hero had gone back across the sea, and the miracle he was to have wrought aborted. The American flags hung limp and American tongues were strangely silent, while other tongues were not.

Americans were settling into dangerous apathy. The old political attitudes, that impetus born of revolution, no longer affected them. The gradual civilization of the entire country had dulled the sense of injustice which had bred and fed its origins. The very success of reasonable government was sapping the vitality of the movement which had produced it. The new freedom had amassed wealth, and with it, a large middle class which, in seeking to ape the achievements of those who had founded the country, talked about commitment with no sense of it. People were busy building a nation, not making it. The sum total of their attachment to anything was being read in dollars, not sense. They were not alone: Even their late visiting hero, Lafayette, had joined them in this new interest. Congress had voted the Marquis the nation's appreciation with $200,000, and that aged hero, the last of the Revolutionaries, had rushed home to France to use those dollars to recreate the life of the aristocrat he had enjoyed before the Revolution.[12]

The American experiment was in danger of becoming an exercise in semantics easily corrupted as to its meaning. Words had taken the place of deeds, and such wordmasters as Daniel Webster were now being promoted as the nation's heroes. It was only logical that Mrs. Royall use her words too.

The Age of Reason had asserted that men could and should improve themselves. The instrument of such improvement was rebellion or revolution, but both were first steps in the long process to the realization of Reason. The real work took more commitment, harder discipline; it made men use their minds.

The promotion of that ideal was simple to the early, wealthy educated fathers of the American Age: give all men the means to learn, and they would do so. Men, beggars or kings, had the same potential, and the United States of America set out to prove it. Give men the ability to read what other men had done, and they could do it too. Accordingly, the first business of the new nation became education. What had produced the miracle of the Revolution, the right of Everyman to aspire to heights never before assessed, had to be supported. Everyone was for education, even the uneducated, but there were problems. What would be read, and how was it to be made available and distributed?[13]

The Masonic lodges had been centers of study. Discussion groups investigated the problems and presented papers and books for the initiate, and these men were among the first to promote the need for education. Mrs. Royall's support by the orders came under this category, as did others like her in more provincial matters.

Books had always been the symbols of education, but books were expensive. The government had no funds to print them, and by its concept of freedom could not promote them, but education-conscious people demanded them. It was an impasse, for only the dedicated bought their own, while others averred they would buy them too, for a price, and so the vacuum existed. People were hungry for the status of literacy, but most were unwilling or unable to pay for this advantage. The first cheap solution would be most welcome.

Shortly after 1815, tract societies had begun to make their appearance in the American coastal cities. Beginning in Philadelphia, they spread rapidly to New York, New Haven, Hartford, and Boston. These tract societies were religious publishing groups or Bible groups. They began producing cheap paper pamphlets extolling the ways of righteousness with "true to life" vignettes about people "saved" from lives of sin by the new evangelism for the living Christ. They had the flavor of the accents and customs of the new immigrants from Scotland, Ireland, the English midland, and Wales.[14]

To a nation free from established discipline other than what they had assumed with their own manmade laws, it was a new subject. The advent of these pamphlets, "true" stories at first low keyed but then growing in lurid detail about fallen women, sinning men, young girls and boys entrapped in youthful desires, all enjoying but then forsaking evil ways to find God and live, or die happily under the Cross, created a new fashion. Men and women, hungry for excitement and free to read what they liked took to the scandal inherent in these tales. Turned out by the thousands on presses lately imported from England, tracts flooded the country. Where books cost dollars, these paper tracts cost mere cents, and both proved the owner could read. The American Tract Society, the Sunday School Union, and a host of imitators ground out "true confessions" and "life" stories. The women of the times took to them like their sisters in the 20th century would take to soap operas. Scandal became a national mania in the guise of religious teachings, and by 1827 women who should have been preparing their minds to stand equally beside men in the business of living and governing were swooning at the vicarious evils and redemptions peddled by self-appointed messengers of God who claimed they had been called to spread His Word in the new American nation, distributing tracts to prove it.[15]

Mrs. Royall had noted the emergent evangelical movements in *Sketches*, which dealt with the years 1823 through 1825. She witnessed the remarkable growth of these groups just by cataloging the numbers of churches and halls committed to each religious sect, established and evangelist, in each town as she went. She was cognizant of the appeal of the new religious doctrines, but like all free thinkers, she had dismissed the tawdry implications of such efforts and taken refuge in admitting the right of others to practice their religion as they pleased. Mrs. Royall's only reservation had been her belief that residence and education among Americans would change the new religionists' direction. It was a tenet of the nation, and Mrs. Royall accepted it, that all could and should follow their own religious intent without fear of repression. She was as free as they were to express her beliefs, and her opinions of their wisdom, and did it in strong language with friends. She had not, however, written it, and she might never have done so but for a strange set of circumstances.

The Golden Jubilee of the United States had produced a banner year for Mrs. Royall, but her personal success had not blinded her to the quiet which followed the celebration. Americans should have been roused to great patriotic heights by their accomplishment in establishing their Republic, but the public was strangely apathetic. This reaction attracted Mrs. Royall's attention, and she went looking for the reason. She had good contacts and she turned to them, her favorite editors and booksellers, to find out what was happening in their areas.

The booksellers gave Mrs. Royall her first hint. The writer was familiar with all the problems of these merchants. She had watched them grow as the American printing industry grew, and she knew that the new presses flooding the country with books and pamphlets were a mixed blessing. Americans had the opportunity to read, but the bias against American writers had not been eliminated. She had rationalized this situation because there had been so few American printing houses, and one could not fault a bookseller for selling books he could get in quantity from English presses instead of those in short supply from American ones. She had condemned such preference for foreign writers but believed it would correct itself as Americans like herself took the lead.

Mrs. Royall, setting forth to write about America for Americans, had been assured cooperation by bookseller after bookseller as she traveled in preparation for her first work. However, when the time came to distribute what she published, she had to go far afield from the major booksellers in New York and Philadelphia to get her work to the public. The personal consequences had been horrendous, but Mrs. Royall discovered she was not alone. Men more renowned than she had been cut off in the midst of their writing lives in a far more insidious manner, and it was not difficult to find out why.[16]

It was during her visit to Philadelphia that Mrs. Royall learned about the true facts and operations of the new publishing ventures she celebrated. The bookstore to which she had consigned her books would not account for them to her. Further inquiries turned up the fact that her books had not been available for those who had asked for them. Mrs. Royall soon ascertained the presence of alien missionaries in the store buying hundreds of dollars worth of books and commenting on those they did not like. Carey and Lea, her booksellers, listening to the new religionists, were selling only missionary products, and British ones at that! This personal experience was disheartening, but a meeting with one of the great early American writers was the final straw.

Mrs. Royall visited the famous William Duane, renowned pamphleteer of the Revolution. What she found upset her more:

> Having made sundry attempts in my various visits to Philadelphia to see the celebrated Mr. Duane, former editor of the Aurora, without success, I now determined not to leave the city without seeing him. Almost since I can remember to have read a newspaper, this gentleman interested me.[17]

Mrs. Royall eventually saw William Duane. He was younger than she supposed, and that made the circumstances of their meeting more poignant:

> His heart, his genius, and his principles, were depicted in his fine open countenance . . . . With strong mental powers, and the most dignified person, had this man been properly encouraged and supported by his country, he would not now be, as he told me, a poor police magistrate. After fighting with his pen gratis most of his life in defence of the freedom of his country, he is now in his old age forgotten and left to struggle with poverty.[18]

This man, this last of the great American revolutionary writers, had been reduced to serving as a pamphleteer for whatever sponsor could pay him, and he did not hesitate to pinpoint the oppressor. The new religion and its promoters had gained control of every book merchant of worth in the cities of Philadelphia and New York and were marching northward into that last citadel of free thought, Boston. His experiences and those of his friends matched Mrs. Royall's, and the two writers knew they had happened upon a coincidence too great to be ignored. William Duane could do nothing, but Mrs. Royall could.[19]

From that meeting, Mrs. Royall made it her business to look carefully at all booksellers and publishers as she continued her travels. What she found confirmed her worst fears. America's writers were being shunted aside for the new religious breed; there was a physical presence, suited in black British cloth, standing in the aisleways of every bookshop refusing to stock American books. This not-so-subtle influence to promote English authors had been a petty annoyance before, but now it took on a far more serious aspect. The oft-repeated excuse that no one would buy American authors did not make sense when in every public place, black-coated men and their women were pressing unknown books by unknown writers upon an unwary public.

Self-interest is a tremendous spur, and Mrs. Royall had lots of it. Not only was her own personal position at stake, but the philosophy she followed was at variance with what was happening. The presses printing the flood of material swamping the country made no secrets of their English affiliations and the peculiar imprimatur of Bible tract societies and Sunday school unions on publications whose content was less religious than it should have been was even more grist for her consideration. Dwelling upon sin to extoll virtue was pandering, and exhorting a populace to find God within lurid tracts was an abomination. Such ulterior actions meant ulterior motives, and Mrs. Royall went to work to find them.

The growth of the new religion was very evident along the routes Mrs. Royall traveled. In the northeastern states, the new missionary preachers were feeding upon growing prosperity and commerce and its handmaiden, sophistication. The nation's life was no longer hard. Men and women of all classes were enjoying leisure hours for the first time in history. Merchants' wives and daughters did not have to work as their pioneer mothers once had, and the merchants themselves found the ledger book a part-time replacement for the adze, hoe, and plow. Even workers in the mills found life easier in exchanging labor for case and cash for goods than they found the round-the-clock effort for existence on the farms they had left behind. Days passed with office and householding chores at a minimum. Women socialized more and more; the upper classes discovered the English fashion of teatime, and the lower classes found ladies' aid activities sponsored by the new religions. Men found their own social clubs; the upper classes invested in their private rooms while the lower patronized their public ones. As they went their own ways, the only men available to women for the new afternoon and evening socializing were preachers. Missionaries came to tea, led the ladies' aid groups, and left tracts; women went wild for the new religion and especially for the stories about sin. Wherever Mrs. Royall went, women talked of nothing else, and their men began to follow them into movements sparked by this national mania.

Mrs. Royall visited town after town and renewed her contacts and acquaintances. Invited to homes and meetings, she was in a good position to assess the impact of the new religionists. She did not accept the premise that America needed to be "saved"; that act had been accomplished in 1776, and she was not intrigued with the new accent on "sin." She made no secret of her skepticism of those who dispensed salvation in penny tracts or in the ridiculous prose vignettes with which they peddled their wares. She did not hesitate to ridicule those who accepted such nonsense. She was well aware of the commercial aspects of the ventures, for their activities paralleled her own. The tract societies had become big businesses, and they had created an enormous pool of capital with which to further their efforts.[20]

Time after time, Mrs. Royall reminded her friends of these facts. It was obvious that America was being flooded with British propaganda aimed at changing American attitudes, and the vehicle was a messianic movement evident in its very intent. Divine right was being set up in opposition to the Age of Reason and

Man. The churches in America and their roles in its public life were being subverted once more by aliens. It was an argument easily proven by pointing to the facts of life about her wherever the black-coated men and their women were. Wherever Mrs. Royall went, she called on people to note what was happening about them, and she did so in terms well calculated to rouse reasonable men and women to the defense of the American experiment in civil leadership. Mrs. Royall found herself crusading to counter the new religionists.

It appeared to be an unequal battle. The tract publishing groups had gone national. They had hundreds of salesmen on the road and every evangelical minister was a merchant for their works. Alone, Mrs. Royall would come into town, rally the local Masons, visit the newspapers, and then press the old American element to stand firm against the tide of the new religion. The disparity in the odds never fazed Mrs. Royall. Rather, it amused her, but the Bible societies did not view her with such equanimity. Her fame spread largely through their fearful words as she progressed from state to state.

The impetus of the new religion was dependent upon the recent Scots-Irish immigrants who were inundating the American establishments. These new parishioners were nothing like the brethren who had preceded them to American shores one hundred years before. These new arrivals were born of a new schism in the English churches in the early 19th century, a strife precipitated by evangelical leaders who arose to challenge the more moderate hierarchy who reflected the rationalism and tolerance born of the Age of Reason in church affairs.[21] These new evangelists believed that man's salvation lay in wedding the potent power of a living God to existing politics to change the world. In the creation of this new Divine Right, they had reverted to the hardline religious philosophies of Thomas Cartwright and John Knox.[22] All who refused to accept their thesis that God ruled men by preselecting other men to represent Him found themselves accused of heresy and subjected to punishments reasonable men had discarded long ago. In pursuit of this joint church-state society, these new religionists had promoted murder and mayhem to effect their end. They had visited upon Scotland and Northern Ireland and the English midlands civil war and physical upheavals as they sought to inflict their beliefs upon others of different persuasions. In time, many of them had become criminals, terrorists, and finally fugitives. England would not tolerate them within her borders, but she did export them to the United States and other "colonies" where the climates of religious tolerance were prime for the importation of zealous creeds of intolerance.[23]

Thousands of these religious fanatics entered the United States from 1818 forward. Capitalizing upon the good repute of the Scots-Irish from a century before, they became willing pawns of the vestigial Tory influence of the Hartford Convention clerics seeking full command of the American Congregationalists and the General Assembly of the American Presbyterian Church. Committed to Knoxonian and Cartwrighter attitudes, they cooperated to exploit the divine right of God and self-appointed representatives against American civil authority. Heresy was their weapon, and it took a heretic to mount the attack against them.

Mrs. Royall was that heretic. Her considerable reputation as a nondoctrinaire and unaffiliated "Christian," along with her Masonic sympathies, enhanced her free-thinking fame. The lack of commitment to an established church or religion magnified her influence. As a writer with a national following, she was lionized above the itinerant or seated minister, particularly those with Scots or Irish brogues. Further, she knew the lines of American civil power and that the real leaders of the American communities were still Americans; the newcomers only thought they had made their mark. Mrs. Royall mounted her appeal to those in power to note the challenges to that power, to identify those who had laid the challenge first in the churches, and she then sought to transfer it to town, county and state halls. She knew how to contact her audience and set forth her argument, and she determined to take the offensive against those who supported these new theocrats and their intrusion into civil affairs. To do so she coined new words and phrases with which to arouse the public. She would use the good American vocabulary, evoke good American imagery, and with them assail the prattlers who marched upon the nation.

Mrs. Royal launched a crusade. No longer did she just write; she spoke in towns, Masonic halls, legislative chambers, and friendly churches, seeking to stem invasion. She kept up a constant stream of letters to editors all over the country. Mrs. Royall poured ridicule upon the new religious fanatics. Watching them descend upon people in public places, pamphlets waving and crying out the threats from their God, "Save or be damned," demeaning freemen and free thought, Mrs. Royall saw them as big black crows and their women as so many magpies, cawing and chirping away at Reason and the government it represented. Their leaders she saw as morticians in black hats and coats hoping to preside at the death of the United States Constitution.

Mrs. Royall led a one-woman counterattack and called upon fellow Americans to meet the black-coated missionaries infecting their lives. Her battle cry raised the spectre of former oppressors, and all those who remembered rallied to her crusade. The old revolutionary spirit once called to action with "The Redcoats are coming!" awoke to Mrs. Royall's new call, "Beware the blackcoats," and a national confrontation began.

Chapter 7

The Holy Terror

Mrs. Royall had launched her first full-scale attack on the blackcoats in February, 1828, with the release of *The Black Book, Continuation of Travels, Volume I.* Mrs. Royall's promised survey of things American was a clearly enunciated attack on the problems she perceived in the northeastern states. Her thesis was so unexpected and controversial that it propelled her into the national limelight of politics. Her small book appeared at the same time that General Andrew Jackson's supporters regrouped for his second ballot assault upon Washington and the White House.

The peripatetic traveler announced that she had discovered something that America's leaders had missed:

> Foreigners are not the only enemies of native genius, our own countrymen, to their shame, are equally guilty; who, hired by British gold, have entered into a confederacy with the trade over the water; and between them and the missionaries, as they have most of the capital in the country, have a whole hand in the pie, they have gibbetted American genius.[1]

Mrs. Royall charged that there was a conscious effort to submerge the United States and that the new presses and the new religionists were the advance guard in the action. This was just the kind of information the Jackson forces had been seeking to prove that a conspiracy had deprived their hero of his rightful election in 1824 and was at work against them in 1828. Mrs. Royall's call to action to her fellow Americans was translated into the Jacksonian battle plan, and as the followers of Andrew Jackson moved across the country, Mrs. Royall's *Black Book* went with them.

Mrs. Royall told her readers that a holy terror was upon the land and that it had initiated a war against the nation. It was supported and abetted by traitors, many of whom used government position as a shield for their actions. Mrs. Royall called for the removal from public office of any who supported religious leaders who sought to mingle church with state. She took dead aim on those who led the particular movements and among them were some extraordinary people indeed. They were the same people whom the Jacksonians were drawing their own bead upon, but Mrs. Royall had produced new reasons for counteraction and a new blueprint to effect it.

Mrs. Royall cited a series of recent events which, although seemingly unconnected, when linked one to the other gave rise to a movement so bizarre that if the United States of America continued to overlook it, the consequence would be the nation's destruction. Further, she not only pinpointed the problem, she proclaimed its dire imminence and presented facts and figures to prove her assertions. Those facts and figures had been tested in public argument and before state legislatures.

Mrs. Royall outlined for her readers the emergence of a religious conspiracy to undermine and destroy freedom in the United States. This conspiracy was not confined to the church halls wherein it was spawned, but had spilled forth in a conscious and well-executed effort to interfere in the political processes of the nation. It had infiltrated government on all levels, in all offices. She pointed her finger to those who cooperated with the menace and promoted its growth, and the implication was plain. Those who were in office, enjoying the public support of the new evangelicals, had to go. Mrs. Royall's list of these new enemies of the nation matched the names the Jacksonians already knew, but her complaints were new.

Mrs. Royall provided in one small book all the ammunition which Andrew Jackson and his men needed to reveal the conspirators that Jackson had long insisted worked against him.[2] Mrs. Royall was no longer a benign travel writer riding the roads and crossing the streams of the nation. She was cataloging actual happenings, and her reading of those events was explosive enough to generate political inquiry.

Mrs. Royall's series of events, as outlined for her readers, began with the appearance in Philadelphia, that city of brotherly love, of a new kind of religious leader, an American effete turned evangelical. Mrs. Royall named him: He was the Reverend Ezra Stiles Ely, and he was not just another minister hammering out his slogans on the wood of the pulpit before him; he was a leader of the General Assembly of the American Presbyterian Church. Dr. Ely had attracted Mrs. Royall's attention with actions which were at variance with accepted conduct in the Presbyterian Church in the United States to date, actions which were spilling controversy and schism into other churches and invading civil government. The time had come for the American public to take another look at this man, at any others like him.

There are many who achieve great renown and great prominence without the general public knowing anything about them. These people arrive by walking upon a stage and not leaving it. Such was the case with Ezra Stiles Ely. He appeared one Sunday to mount the pulpit of an established Presbyterian church, and that church was never the same again.

It was in 1813, in the midst of the nation's second war with England. The Third Presbyterian Church, known as the Old Pine in Philadelphia, was in need of a new preacher and applied to its Sessions and the Presbytery for a nominee. The church was famous, for it had contributed the flag to the cause of American liberty. The Old Pine received its candidate, a young man from mission duty in New York, but the congregation was not pleased with the Presbytery choice. The leader presented to them was a former Congregationalist turned Presbyterian, and the Old Pine was not in sympathy with anything Congregational, not in 1813.

A lengthy examination followed, and young Dr. Ely's views were found to be unacceptable; the Presbytery was so informed. However, one Old Pine family, the Biddles, supported the young man, for their son Nicholas had been a student associate of young Ely at Princeton. The Presbytery insisted the nominee take the pulpit. A lengthy controversy ensued from November 16, 1813, to September 7, 1814.[3]

Ezra Stiles Ely had been called from New York where he had served as a missionary to the jails and whorehouses of the city, specializing in the needs of fallen women, their evils, and redemptions. It was an experience he had exploited in a series of books about whores and streetwalkers published in England under the imprimatur of the new English tract societies. This profitable venture about the scum of society did not sit well with the cream of society of the Old Pine, but they had better reason not to want this new preacher.

Dr. Ely had been born in Connecticut to a family high in Congregational circles. In the midst of the war with England, his father and uncles were leaders in a Sabbath movement which had become a national scandal. Congregational clerics had been banding together followers to interdict all travel and commerce on Sunday, an obsession not received well in Philadelphia. Further, these Sabbaticals had been involving themselves in peculiar and treasonous actions exciting the American public. The Sunday enthusiasts would sally forth on the Lord's Day and seize caravans of supplies bound for American troops placed along the coast to forestall British landings. These seizures were made with the excuse that any transport on Sunday was an affront to God, and the goods and those who carried them were held for action before ecclesiastical courts hastily convened for the purpose. These rump courts declared such supplies forfeited to God, and those who moved them were fined or jailed; so the needed supplies did not reach their destinations.

The incidence of such happenings had become so widespread that New England's capacity to muster proper military action in its defense against British raids was seriously in question. Further, these same ecclesiasticals were associated with others who had been sounding out the old Federalist leaders for a peace convention to phrase separate overtures to England, bypassing the Congress of the United States.[4] All this was known to Americans of different philosophy sitting in the pews of Old Pine. Ely was an affront to their patriotism, and the fact that the Biddles, accepted patriots, commended the young man carried no weight; they did not want him.

For ten months young Ely sat out the fracas, communing with his old roommate from Princeton, Nicholas Biddle. This did not improve his reception, for young Biddle had not pleased many of the Old Pine. He had the reputation of being a dandy who made no secret of his preference for things European, and such sentiments were not appreciated by old Philadelphia, particularly those in the Old Pine Church. The fact that Nicholas Biddle had acquired his European flair in service in American foreign affairs posts abroad was no excuse, for unlike Benjamin Franklin, young Biddle had not attempted to cloak his wider interests with the American flag. Nicholas Biddle was no asset for Ezra Stiles Ely in 1813.

But Preacher Ely did mount his pulpit despite the objections to him, even as the Hartford Convention issued its call to meeting of December 14, 1814. He had not achieved his post with the approval of the Old Pine's congregation. The ten months of controversy surrounding him had witnessed a systematic flooding of the benches and pews of the old church with new Scots-Irish communicants and they carried the day for young Ely. It was an event the Old Pine would long remember, for it became the incubator for an alien missionary movement in the United States, the blackcoat mission.

For the next ten years, Ezra Stiles Ely used his pulpit and his growing position to organize the eastern Pennsylvania Presbytery to his liking, in his family's mold. The Sabbatical influence became paramount, and with it he forged links to other captured Presbyterian units in western Pennsylvania. He cofounded a number of publishing ventures, among them the Sunday School Union and the American Tract Society, both of which rewarded him by publishing American editions of his New York mission days.[5] Ezra Stiles Ely was a master organizer, but behind him stood his old friend Nicholas Biddle.

As Philadelphia's Presbyterianism was remolded, a new image was presented. Dr. Ely promoted dozens of societies to appeal to every segment and any problem in the general citizenry and, thanks to the proliferation of these groups, the preacher was not only in command of his church but controlled many other voices. He also had the key to a constant money infusion, money which enabled him to enjoy and exert an influence in the community far beyond that of ordinary church leaders. Dr. Ely not only promoted tithing, that old biblical allocation of a tenth of a man's earnings, he promoted sales of his tracts and books with an assiduity that blanketed the city squares with hawkers of his wares.

Ezra Stiles Ely created church-owned and -dominated saving societies which became the envy of the hard-pressed banks of Philadelphia. He had them for every conceivable purpose: for widows, for children, for working men. All the funds were paid into his church for safekeeping. His movement was such a success that it spread to Pittsburgh, New York, and of course, Hartford, the Congregational center. Preachers came to see and went home to copy. With this widespread acceptance, Ely's influence became pervasive, not only in religion but in civil affairs. At a time when the pressing need in America was a constant infusion of capital, such accumulations of savings were enticing indeed to other Americans who knew how to put them to work. Dr. Ely and his followers found they had more friends than their preachings brought to their side and the Elyites took full advantage of their new power position. As the need for money grew, so did their cooperative efforts with others. Evangelical sects of all persuasions were contacted and their members alerted and solicited. Ely's Presbyterian Church found itself with another best-selling crusade on its hands.

Preaching and capital became powerful sermons for conversion. Monies consecrated to God and His work went into accounts and did not come out unless God and His representative permitted it. In ten years, Ezra Stiles Ely had become a very important person; he lived in a great mansion and rode like a king.[6]

Mrs. Royall had learned about Dr. Ely on her initial visit to Philadelphia in 1825. The Ingersolls, a prominent free-thinking family late of New England, were residing in the City of Brotherly Love. Asked to extend a helping hand to the visitor from Washington, they became Mrs. Royall's sponsors. These sophisticated people were much amused by the travails of the Presbyterians in Philadelphia, especially those of the Old Pine Church with the Biddles and Ely, and they acquainted their guest with the facts. Philadelphia did not know a dull moment with Ely in pulpit. He was America's new Cotton Mather, and those who were not Presbyterians could laugh long and loud at his antics. The old revolutionaries thought him a crackpot, one his new parishioners deserved.

Mrs. Royall did not; the tales of Ely and his tract societies interested the budding writer. Her experience with American booksellers gave her a background her informers lacked. In 1825, Ely was just reaching for control of the Philadelphia book merchants and to businessmen in the city his move was proof of the preacher's growing business acumen. To Mrs. Royall, it was quite another matter. There was a growing censorship aimed against American writers and the efforts of Ely promoted it. She tucked the information in her head and went about her business, producing Sketches.

After the publication of Sketches, Mrs. Royall returned to Philadelphia to promote her book. Once again she met with the Ingersolls. This time there was no laughter about Ely and his actions. The preacher had reintroduced the Sabbatical issue to the city; he had directed his congregation to use chains to seal off the public streets near the Old Pine on Sunday "in observance of the Lord's Day." Half of Philadelphia had been out to see the sight, and the local press had something new to write about. Such bold actions from a man of the black cloth were the talk of Philadelphia, and the city loved it.[7]

Mrs. Royall did not, nor did her friends the Ingersolls. They were watching another Ely event with consternation. The Ingersolls, father and son, well-known constitutional lawyers,[8] knew a structured attack on freedom when they saw it.

Convinced that Philadelphia held many more sinners than he had reached, Dr. Ely decided to invade the civil affairs of the city by employing the Scottish immigrants to wed state and church within his own congregation. He planned to exercise absolute control over his parishioners.[9]

An elderly female in the Old Pine congregation, accustomed to the more liberal precedents of her church, openly opposed Dr. Ely. News of her courage reached the churchman, and one Sunday morning the lady found herself accused by Dr. Ely from the pulpit in stentorian tones:

> Common fame accused you of being a notorious scold, of ungovernable temper . . . . and peculiarly abusive to your husband . . . . The Session of the Church require you to abstain from participating in the communion of the Lord's Supper, until further notice.[10]

With these words, the long-time communicant of the Old Pine found herself excluded from her church, denied the friendship of many, and ostracized by her fellows because Ely had ordered it. This strange occurrence in a church spawned a series of reckless legal experiments in the City of Brotherly Love, one of which was a case in which the Ingersolls, father and son, became involved.

In 1824, another woman named Nancy James had found herself indicted as "a common scold."[11] The term was an archaic remnant of the old Presbyterian law as practiced in Scotland and Northern Ireland before English law had declared it obsolete. This curious charge was processed in Philadelphia's General Session Court, and Mrs. James found herself indicted for a crime which the United States Constitution had declared null and void after 1789. The constitutional mandates about laws and cruel and unusual punishment had been put aside. Mrs. James stood trial on both counts and heard herself declared to be guilty by a jury drawn largely from Ely's church.

Then the Ingersolls had stepped in. Coming on the heels of Ely's action against his elderly parishioner, the connection to Mrs. James's case was too obvious to be ignored. Ely was retrieving from the dustbins of his own church ecclesiastical mementos of a dark age. He had to be stopped. The Ingersolls took Mrs. James's case to the Pennsylvania Court of Appeals and that body, cognizant of the constitutional strictures against such legal convolutions, examined the curious circumstances of the case. The court found for Mrs. James, and Charles Jared Ingersoll was still scandalized regarding the matter and the fact that Philadelphia had processed this comic opera. This was all Mrs. Royall needed to take another good look at Ezra Stiles Ely.

Unlike the Ingersolls and the bulk of Philadelphia society, Mrs. Royall did not believe that Ely and his affairs were just a Philadelphia aberration. These black-coats had a design; they were not Presbyterian jokes, but evil clues to worse things to come. Dr. Ely controlled a vast publishing empire, and he was promoting a strange continuity in these silly affairs. There were motives and new directions involved that wise men like the Ingersolls should investigate, and she told her friends so.

Mrs. Royall had one advantage many of her listeners did not: She was far more traveled than they. What they could consider as a purely local phenomenon, she could persuade them was a movement much more pervasive; they accepted the fact that she was more informed.

Mrs. Royall knew that the old-line Presbyterians in Pennsylvania, New York, Vermont, and Connecticut did not know what was happening to them. Accustomed as most were to the pious invocation of God, the Sunday worshippers slept their way through their pastors' sermons, but the new Scots-Irish among them did not. The dominie, the preacher who took the law unto himself in Scotland and Northern Ireland and could inflict civil penalty upon those not heeding his dictates, was the pattern for Ely and others like him. True sons of the Hartford Convention, these preachers, building on this Scots-Irish custom, were out to transform the Presbyterian Church in America into a church-state in the image of Scotland's old traditions. The implications in such a move did not escape Mrs. Royall. She had seen enough of these blackcoats and their actions to know where they were going, and now she knew who their leaders were.

As Mrs. Royall assessed this situation, Ezra Stiles Ely had gathered new associates in his ventures. Lyman Beecher from Connecticut, Gardiner Spring in New York, Dr. Black in Pittsburgh, and Moses Waddell in Georgia had joined together to promote the new religion.[12] The street closings spread to other cities, and the suspension of the right of congregation members to take issue with their leaders passed to other churches. Suddenly a raging cry for all government to cease and desist on the Sabbath was upon the land. Dr. Ely and his associates attacked the movement of the United States mails on Sunday. It came as a surprise to the nation's leaders, but not to Mrs. Royall.

In 1827, government was a daily affair in the United States. The mails moved every day, and citizens expected government action from government appointees, employees, or elected officials when they needed it, day or night. This concept was a natural extension of the belief that government was an agency of Man, derived from his consent and in existence to serve him. The people were ruled in the name of the people. This sudden Sabbath assault, a replay of the nonsense suffered in the War of 1812 in New England, was an unwelcome intrusion into American life. Mrs. Royall decided to treat it as such.

Ely and his brethren had entered the national arena, and they were on Mrs. Royall's ground. The zealots expounded their doctrinal philosophy without regard to public reaction, and Mrs. Royall decided to test that public reaction. Dr. Ely gave her the perfect example to use.

Ely was determined to intrude upon government and make his God supreme over Man. To this end, he had fastened upon another member of his congregation, the master of a Delaware River steamboat which carried the U.S. mails from Washington to Philadelphia. As a contracted service, this steamboat moved seven days a week to meet its commitments. Dr. Ely demanded that the captain cease and desist his services on the Sabbath and lay up his steamboat on the Lord's Day.

The captain refused to heed Ely's demand. Ely mounted the pulpit once again and denounced the captain. The fellowship was told to refuse the sinner communication until he repented of his sinfulness and he complied with Dr. Ely's dictum. It was a significant confrontation.[13]

The fellowship of the church had more meaning in 1827. The captain faced ostracism from his Presbyterian fellows, but he was also threatened with the loss of credit privileges from bank officials under Ely's influence. The implications were enormous. Dr. Ely, through his parishioner, was moving to effect direction of the government by using his powers to counter civil authority and policy. Dr. Ely could not stop the steamer from running the mail on Sunday, but he could effect the same end by removing its captain from its bridge.

The exercise of such ecclesiastical direction in contravention to the prevailing custom of government had the expected results. The voice from the Philadelphia pulpit found its echoes in the Pennsylvania Legislature and further reverberations in the Congress of the United States itself.

Mrs. Royall was right. The warnings she had spoken had come to pass. As the stated champion of a people's government against dominion by God, this attempt by Ely was put to good use immediately by the writer. With Ely's own printed words in hand, she traveled Pennsylvania seeking supporters against him. Dr. Ely's intrusion into public matters should gain him public attention but not the sort of attention he wanted. Mrs. Royall called upon her reasonable friends to do battle with a mounting holy terror.

Mrs. Royall had two things going for her in her quest. The first was Ely himself, but the second was a growing controversy quite apart from what was in everyone's mind. They were both trumps that she played to win.

Mrs. Royall's influence with leaders in Pennsylvania was not alone the product of her writings, it was also a result of her Masonic affiliation. The officials of the Commonwealth, including the Governor, gloried in their Masonry. Most were supporters of General Jackson, had delivered the state for him in 1824, and were regrouping in their lodges to support him again in 1828. A counterattack had been launched against them, but its leadership had not been discovered. An issue was being made of the institution of Masonry, a controversy begun in New York and spilling over the border into Pennsylvania.[14] Mrs. Royall knew all about that matter, and she used her knowledge to good advantage.

The issue, anti-Masonry, had begun with an incident in Genessee County, Upper New York, in September 1826.[15] Even as the Masonic contingents marched in the last of the parades celebrating the Golden Jubilee of the nation, a man named William Morgan announced in the religious press of the area that he was writing a book to expose the secrets and designs of Masonry and its followers. This pronouncement, coming on the heels of the hoopla and frankly Masonic pageantry of the fiftieth birthday of the nation, had an electric effect on the upstate New York communities. This area had seen a tremendous immigration of Scots-Irish into normally Dutch areas, and relations were not good between the groups. Further, the Dutch were great Masonic enthusiasts, thanks to the influence of DeWitt Clinton and the Van Schuylers, and such an announcement was like a red flag to many bulls. It had an incendiary result for yet another reason.

Andrew Jackson was a popular figure among the Dutch. The English were not loved by the men who had settled New York, and one hundred years later they still were resented. Jackson's Anglophobia was shared by New York's Anglophobes, and his expected candidacy was welcome among them. As in Pennsylvania, the Jackson effort was being promoted in the Masonic lodges and the recent jubilee had rallied more than ever to Jackson's banner. A sudden move against Masonry had all the overtones of a political maneuver.

Morgan's collaborator, David Miller, a small newspaper publishers, enlarged the impact with editorials assaulting the Masonic orders in the most lurid prose. For the first time in the United States, Masons who enjoyed public acceptance to such an extent that membership in their lodges had been a silent prerequisite for public office found themselves reeling from attack. A movement had begun which was to have far-reaching consequences.

William Morgan was the epitome of the kind of man the Dutch burghers disliked. Born in Culpepper, Virginia, in 1775, he had missed the first American War for Independence only to taste the second as a private in the War of 1812. Then, serving with raw recruits at Bladensburg, Maryland, he had been among those who broke and ran from the British troops before the burning of Washington. Nothing more was known of him until 1819, when at 44 years of age he married the 16-year-old daughter of a new Methodist evangelical minister committed to the Second Coming of Christ Now. Morgan moved with his wife to Canada where he plied the trade of stonemason and later became a worker in a Canadian brewery.[16]

In 1824, he made his first appearance in Le Roy, a small upstate New York town. There William Morgan, stonemason, became William Morgan, Freemason by transfer, a member of the secret orders with all the rights, privileges, and duties thereof.

In time, William Morgan attained the high degrees of his lodge and when the Knights Templar in his district planned to erect a temple, Brother Morgan bid on the contract for the new building. Before the contract was awarded, Morgan's bid was returned abruptly and the contract went to another. Morgan became irate. He left his home lodge and attempted to join a new one then in the process of forming, but was denied membership. Blackballed and humiliated, he joined with another outcast from the local Masonic fraternity, David Miller, the editor of a religiously oriented weekly. Together with a hired writer, these men prepared the book which Morgan announced would expose Masonry in discreditable terms. David Miller fanned the ensuing controversy by headlining the event in his own paper, coupling it with a call for Sunday closures and proclaiming his allegiance to the Sabbaticals.

The local Masons reacted. The oath of allegiance to the Masonic orders was such that it was not and could not be abrogated by resignation or expulsion, and the Masons moved to protect and enforce that compact. Miller's paper was burned and his presses wrecked, and William Morgan was arrested for debt. In Canandaigua, New York, on September 11, 1827, he spent the night in jail.

The next day William Morgan was released to two men, apparent friends, upon the payment of his debt and legal costs, and entered a carriage with them to depart. Mrs. Hall, the jailor's wife, standing at the window watching the carriage depart, heard cries of "Murder, murder" and, rushing to the door, saw four men and Morgan struggling in the carriage as it sped away.

Fanned by the religious presses, this "kidnaping" of an American citizen under such conditions was heavily publicized, spreading from New York into the surrounding states, particularly Vermont. From the moment of Morgan's disappearance, the innuendo was one of murder and the implied culprits were the Masons. The outcry became so widespread that New York's Governor DeWitt Clinton, himself a Masonic leader, in order to protect himself from political attack, took the lead in condemning the suggested outrage and thereby gave credence to the story as published. Rewards far in excess of any previously offered brought no trace or news of Morgan. The story went on, intensely religious and increasingly political. The Masons, followers of the devil, were doing Satan's work and should be ostracized, particularly those in public office, cried the new religionists. Another witch hunt was on.[17]

In Albany and New York City, a new breed was reaching for political ascendancy: men far removed from American Revolution beginnings. Thurlow Weed, printer, editor and Tory descendant, was its leader.[18] Nominally on Adams's side, and seeking any issue with which to assault the rising Jackson forces, he took the Morgan affair and made it his own. He sought the discovery of Morgan's body and offered payment in an extraordinary newspaper promotion. The ploy was good; as headlines were produced, one body after another was found.

Morgan's *exposé* of Masonry became a best seller and was followed by pamphlets illustrating the Masonic rituals in a most scurrilous manner. It was a natural for the anti-Jackson forces, and they joined common cause with the anti-Masons. General Jackson, the hero of New Orleans, was not only a fervent Mason but also Grand Master of the southern lodges and their counterparts in the Northern states. His candidacy was relying on that fact in 1827, as it had in 1824. John Quincy Adams, never publicly a Mason and only rumored to have been initiated into its orders in his youth, gave unacknowledged support to Weed. His friends let it be known that whatever Masonic connection Adams ever had was intended only to further his career, for the President was practicing its rituals no longer. In this strange manner did Weed develop an issue between the two major contestants for the presidency in 1828, an issue which had not existed in 1824. It did not have the effect Weed had planned.

Mrs. Royall had taken no political position prior to the Morgan affair. She had happened on the incident because she had traveled through the very towns involved with the event. At the time, she had been preoccupied with the insistent evangelical bias of the local press in the area, not the summer prominence of New York City religious leaders in these small upstate New York towns.[19] She had encountered increasing difficulty in not only selling her *Sketches* but in meeting community leaders and gaining their cooperation to produce her next book. Before she intimated any displeasure concerning the blackcoats to old friends or gave her opinion concerning their intolerance, she found that her reputation as their opponent had gone before her. She herself had not credited her potential as a counterforce to their activities but they had recognized it even before she published her opinions.

To a well-traveled writer, the Morgan controversy had all the elements of a clever book promotion directed by clerics. The promise of an *exposé* of "secrets," the intimation of "devilish" rituals, the sudden difficulties of the author, his strange disappearance, and the headlines produced were just too pat. As the forces behind the Morgan affair attacked her more, she spoke out for the Masons, and as she did, she found herself on Jackson's side.

The Jacksonians in New York were some time in counterattacking the anti-Masons. Finally rallying reason, they reached into the courts to protect themselves. As the cry "criminals" mounted against them, they demanded it be proven. All Masons were summoned to the general's side since his reputation and theirs faced a broadside of epic proportions. The Adams forces, led by Weed, pushed the anti-Mason outcries and found themselves with ecclesiastical allies speaking in Scots and Irish accents from the Protestant pulpits.

The President of the United States, John Quincy Adams, had been embroiled in a controversy over which it was believed he exercised no control. The man in Washington appeared to be too far removed from New York to exercise any influence, but more of his friends, particularly the old Federalists who had supported his father, joined the outcry. Thurlow Weed was building a campaign organization. "The King of the Lobby," the man who had directed press assaults on Governor Clinton and the New York State Legislature, had a free hand in developing this. Weed wanted to move nationally, and William Morgan had found for him allies in other states against the old "Revolutionaries" who still directed the nation. Thurlow Weed had one aim: to ally New York with the new forces in Philadelphia.

The Masons in New York watched the growth of the Morgan affair with disbelief and then despair. At first they could not tell who was supporting the scandal, for it was a quixotic affair, alternating first from the pulpit and then from the associated religious press. It was having a devastating effect. All Masonry and Masons were being taken to task for a murder without a body or a shred of evidence, and Masons and their orders were being castigated for their involvement with unknown men as instigators of a crime unproven. There was only the jailor's wife, a woman in the throes of religious ecstacy, her story, and the fact that William Morgan was no longer in Genessee County. Worse, as the attack went on, it was carried into the Masons' own churches by evangelical preachers using the pulpit to condemn and excoriate such "sin."

The scandal continued. The constant allusion to Masonic involvement with the Morgan "murder" took a strange and ominous direction. Preachings against the Masons now spread to missions in other states, especially Pennsylvania. The established churches were being exhorted to join the pack. Religious condemnations were being uttered against the many ministers who were members of the Masonic orders. Hierarchical meetings were called and thrown into uproars as evangelicals hurled charges of "heresy" and accusations of "followers of Satan" at ministers who remained Masons. That most of these charges were thrown in British accents at ministers using the old American ones was a fact lost in the conflict and confusion. Not content with denunciations of church leaders standing fast, the evangelicals attacked the laity too. Church members were ordered to resign from the Masonic orders by rump groups asserting their control of the churches involved. Sunday after Sunday, the new religionists would mount pulpits, often forcibly seized, and preach against Masonry. In New York, Vermont, Connecticut, and Pennsylvania, where the new Presbyterians held sway, resignations from the Masonic lodges became epidemic. An American institution was in rout in four states and was on the brink of national rout too.[20]

On July 4, 1827, exactly one year after the United States of America's golden anniversary, Dr. Ely celebrated his new power standing confidently in the pulpit of the Seventh Presbyterian Church in Philadelphia. There, looking over the "Old Scots" and into the faces of his new Scots-Irish supporters, this preacher vowed to replace the American idea of government by men with a new government by God. God's Kingdom on Earth was to come with an assault on the Constitution of the United States and the freedom it assured to all men.

Dr. Ely began with an attack upon the nation's leaders:

> None of our rulers have the consent of their maker, that they should be Pagans, Socinians, Mussulmen, Deists, the opponents of Christianity; and a religious people should never think of giving them permission, as public officers, to be and do, what they might not lawfully be and do, as private individuals.

> . . . . our Presidents, Secretaries of the Government, Senators and other Representatives in Congress, Governors of States, Judges, State Legislators, Justices of the Peace, and City Magistrates, are just as much bound as any other persons in the United States, to be orthodox in their faith, and virtuous and religious in their whole deportment.

> God, my hearers, requires a Christian faith, a Christian profession and a Christian practice of all our public men; and we as Christian citizens ought, by the publication of our opinions, to require the same.[21]

These words were salvos directed at every president of the United States to date, words that cited them as opponents of Christianity by coupling pagans, Socinians, and Deists in a direct thrust at Unitarians and Freemasons. And Dr. Ely did not limit his attack to those who had gone before:

> I propose, fellow citizens, a new union, or, if you please, a Christian party in politics which I am exceeding desirous all good men in our country should join: not by subscribing a constitution and the formation of a new society, to be added to the scores that now exist; but by adopting, avowing, and determining to act upon truly religious principles in all civil matters.[22]

"Not by subscribing a constitution and the formation of a new society," words that described the United States of America, "but by adopting, avowing, and determining to act upon truly religious principles in all civil matters," words setting forth a return to divine right and divine rule:

> We will not pretend to search the heart; but surely all sects of Christians may agree in opinion, that it is more desirable to have a Christian than a Jew, Mohammedan, or Pagan, in any civil office; and they may accordingly settle it in their minds, that they will never vote for any one to fill any office in the nation or state, who does not profess to receive the Bible as the rule of his faith. If three or four of the most numerous denominations

of Christians in the United States, the Presbyterians, the Baptists, the Methodists and the Congregationalists for instance, should act upon this principle, our country would never be dishonored with an avowed infidel in her national cabinet or capitol.[23]

Dr. Ely had a plan and he proceeded to outline it:

The Presbyterians alone could bring "half a million electors" into the field, in opposition to any known advocate of Deism, Socinianism or any species of avowed hostility to the truth of Christianity. If to the denominations above named we add the members of the Protestant Episcopal Church in our Country, the electors of these five classes of true Christians . . . could govern every public election in our country, without infringing the least upon the charter of our civil liberties. To these might be added, in this State and Ohio, the numerous German Christians, and in New York and New Jersey, the members of the Reformed Dutch Church, who are all zealous for the fundamental truths of Christianity. What should prevent us from cooperating in such a union as this?[24]

Dr. Ely had anticipated the division of the political spoils before his hearers raised the issue; he knew exactly how to arrange the nation's leadership:

At one time he will be a Baptist, at another an Episcopalian, at another a Methodist, at another a Presbyterian of the American, Scotch, Irish, Dutch or German stamp, and always a friend to our common Christianity. Why should we suffer an enemy, an open and known enemy of the true religion of Christ to enact our laws or fill the executive chair? Our Christian rules will not oppress Jews or Infidels; they will kiss the Son and serve the Lord; while we have the best security for their fidelity to our republican, and I may say scriptural forms of government.[25]

Even as these words were spoken, Dr. Ely's Sunday School Union and the American Tract Society had his blackcoats out on the streets peddling his call to action in Philadelphia, Pittsburgh, New York, Hartford and Boston. Dr. Ely, as moderator of the General Assembly of the Presbyterian Church, had called upon Christians to join together to establish a new nation governed by his God in place of the nation governed by men. Even as his sermon was applauded and hailed by those at his feet, their brethren were preparing to translate it into action in government halls in the states and then in Washington itself.

Dr. Ely's discourse was adopted by the General Assembly of the Presbyterian Church meeting in Philadelphia as a program for action, effectively declaring war on the constitutional government of the United States. The citizens of the United States were not sure what to make of it, but the leaders of its governments knew what a new political party—a religious one—had been born. It had begun with Sunday closure, intruded upon the local courts, and spearheaded the drive against Masonry, but its open aim was the disestablishment of the American state and its substitution with a church state. Divine right was being asserted openly as a new political movement from mouths speaking with British and Scots-Irish accents.

The nation was thrown into confusion. The Adams forces were surprised by the open assault by their allies, the Jacksonians stupefied by such iniquity, the religionists jubilant, and their Anglicized brethren triumphant.

Mrs. Royall had what she sought: positive proof that she was right in her analysis. The stage was set for the campaign to come. Those who invoked their God and His power against their fellow men had unwittingly unleashed Reason from the bondage of American apathy, and her small black book would produce its own holy terror to put Dr. Ely and his holy terror in its place.

Chapter 8

The Strange Alliance

The Pennsylvania Legislature was the first test of Ezra Stiles Ely's July 4 "Call to Arms." The assault on civil government had been timed to produce an outpouring of Elyite support to be directed at the Harrisburg legislature's meeting to begin in September. Confident that a stampede upon the legislators would effect the triumph he had decreed for his God, Ely and his followers set aside petitions and requests and instituted demands and threats to gain action on their terms.

Mrs. Royall had traveled to Harrisburg to be on hand when this operation began. While Ely and his Philadelphians and Dr. Black and his followers from Pittsburgh assailed the legislature, she gathered together all the information she had and produced her own pamphlet laced with opinions and comments. These Royall writings were placed on every desk in the Harrisburg legislature and the intrusion drove Ely and his friends to fury. Mrs. Royall was mobbed in the streets when she arrived in Harrisburg to give personal testimony, an invitation which recognized her contribution to the controversy. An army in black coats attempted to hobble their small enemy, but with her cane raised against them, she led her own small army of facts and figures to begin the battle. Mrs. Royall had been traveling the state, summoning Masons, old-line churchmen and patriots to fight this new religious mania. Even as the legislature met, she saw success.[1]

The woman from Washington knew what Ely and his blackcoats were after. Their meetings in towns and cities had been window dressing for this, the real action, but they had overestimated their influence. The Harrisburg government was the precinct of Masonry still, and the blackcoats had placed all Masonry under pogrom. This was their mistake. As the Elyites assailed the Masons, Mrs. Royall exhorted the brethren. At stake was the control of government, the civil authority which men had established to escape the tyranny of the God now being advanced by Ely and his cohorts.

Mrs. Royall knew that although God was the excuse for the action demanded by her opponents, the real motive was money, lots of it. She knew how that money had been made and what it was destined to do, and her knowledge of the blackcoat operations became the keystone of her counterattack:

The missionaries have crept in! Can no part of our fair country escape the gripping fangs of these ferocious marauders? From Maine to Georgia— from the Atlantic to the Missouri—they swarm like locusts; and under the name of *foreign* missions, *home* missions, *Bible* societies, *tract* societies, the gospel, *pincushion* societies, *cent* societies, *mite* societies, *widow's* societies, *children's* societies, *rag bag* societies, and Sunday School socie-

66

ties, they have laid the whole country under contribution! Figures cannot calculate the amount collected by those public and private robbers: it
is more than would liberate every slave in the United States; it would pay
the British debt![2]

Money was the root of the blackcoat evil, and she reminded the lawmakers
who controlled that blackcoat money. These fanatics and their forced savings
groups had been joined by others. In New York, Lyman Beecher had mounted a
growing crusade against slavery which netted him pledges of $100,000 in a single
night.[3] A movement was abroad in the land, cloaked in religion, which sought
to invade the civil affairs of the nation by gathering vast sums with which to increase its power. The elected representatives of the people could not continue
to sit idly by while these self-anointed leaders took the nation.

Mrs. Royall warned civil authorities that the enemy not only had the money
to enlarge influence, but the method to do so.

These orthodox have at least half of the booksellers in the United States in
their pay, with a view to establishing a national religion; the British have
nearly the balance in theirs, with a view to crushing the genius of our
country, and by trick and cunning, are gradually sapping the foundation of
that structure which cost us so much blood and treasure; so that, by one
or both, we are to be choused out of our liberties.[4]

Mrs. Royall could turn a phrase. "Choused" was not a common word, but it
had a wealth of meaning. Duped, tricked, cheated, or swindled would not suf-
fice; only "choused" would do for it had originated with a Turk who used the
cover of his diplomatic immunity to dupe English merchants out of 4,000
pounds sterling in the 17th century. There were different kinds of Turks at
work in America in 1828, but the result was the same:

If we patronize foreign literature, exclusively, the result is plain; those
foreigners must ultimately govern us.[5]

Mrs. Royall alerted the nation to the plans and directions of the blackcoats:

This money is not designated to spread the gospel, nor is it appropriated to
that end, if indeed the true gospel of Christ could be bought and sold for a
price: no, it is piled up in banks to buy up presses, to overturn our liberties, to make slaves of one part of the community, to maintain the other.
True a few Missionaries are sent off for a blind to keep up appearances;
but the principle part is secreted in Boston, Philadelphia and New York; to
buy up and put in operation, presses and bookstores, and to hire men, as
unprincipled as themselves, to conduct them. This fact is too obvious to
be denied for there are presses, and there are the booksellers, both of
which have increased to an alarming number. The plan has been well laid,
and pursued by cool and deliberate steps, these artful imposters well know
the importance of presses to effect their purpose and the necessity of having them under their control. Were these palladiums of our liberties free
to combat their black designs, they would be exposed and defeated: with
money they get presses, and by presses they get money, and by both they
get power.[6]

These words meant much to men assailed in pamphlets and books, especially
the Morgan book, all bearing the new marks of the religious presses. Mrs. Royall
took full advantage of the situation, and her contributions to it:

I could not forbear smiling at the Hon. Dana, a soldier of the revolution
and formerly a member of Congress from Connecticut, showing him a

blasphemous sermon preached in Pittsburg, by one of the canting hypocrites, on the propriety and blessings of a national religion, he rushed into
an adjoining room, and running out with a double barrelled rusty pistol in
his hand, red with rage, he exclaimed: "By this, madam, I achieved my liberty, and with this I will defend it." I fancy those fellows will meet with
too many Danas to put their treacherous designs into effect.[7]

Passions were high in early 1828, and with them Jackson's forces gathered
strength. It was a bruising confrontation for the Pennsylvania Legislature. Ely
had coupled his own demands with others, and the lawmakers were assailed
from so many directions that they reeled from his attack. The Elyites promoted
a tax revolt in Lancaster County.[8] Using the primitive religious sects rife in that
region, they incited fears that the expansion of the canal system into Pennsylvania would pollute Pennsylvania with sin. The Mennonites and Amish responded; Man was not to build what God, in his infinite wisdom, did not provide. These farmers, raising crops from land which did not provide without
Man's assistance, took Ely's irrational bait and ran with it. Dr. Ely had not only
mounted a clever religious assault upon Reason, but he had also pleased the toll
road bondholders in Pennsylvania which feared the canal companies' competition. Money indeed was upon his mind as was education.
      People were demanding public schools, and the Pennsylvania Legislature was
in the vanguard of the movement. It was trying to establish ways to fund a uniform system without establishing control of the young minds being prepared for
citizenship. The blackcoats had lent their apparent approval, but with certain
restrictions to that support. All they wanted was money from the legislature for
their own schools and the certification of teachers, a certification they would
control. It was a quiet demand, but there was no doubt that they wanted to intrude upon the civil schools, superintend the money spent, and provide the
"trained" teachers. It was apparent that their aim was to prepare Pennsylvania's
children to serve their God. These issues were only preludes to Ely's goal.[9]
      As a casual afterthought, Dr. Ely and his friends requested the Pennsylvania
Legislature to allow them to incorporate the Sunday School Union and the
many tract and saving societies and thus establish these religious offshoots as
bona fide businesses.[10] On the surface, it appeared to be a reasonable request,
but an act of incorporation would cloak these enterprises with a mantle of anonymity and remove them from member congregation control. The afterthought
did not match the frontal assault of the other Elyite demands, and that fact
alerted the legislature. This measure would require protracted debate and careful consideration; Mrs. Royall had prepared the opposition well.
      Dr. Ely and his followers had planned their march on civil government to co-
incide with the coming 1828 national election. They expected to corner members of the legislature with anti-Masonry and a slowing of tax money, and defuse
the movement toward public schools until they were assured they could gain
control. They sought to align themselves with the growing business world by
initiating their own corporations and using that influence to bolster their demands. They were out to prove that they, God's anointed, were the match for
every civil responsibility. They had successfully mounted the same attack in
Connecticut and Vermont.[11] Ely was out to prove he could take his own state,
for Pennsylvania was the key to his planned assault on the national legislature.
If Ezra Stiles Ely succeeded in Harrisburg, Andrew Jackson could not become
president, for Pennsylvania was the heart of the Jacksonian movement.
      Mrs. Royall attacked Ely and his supporters with the very issues Ely thought
would bring him victory. The Elyites had excited the tax revolts in Lancaster
County, and their own words indicted them. They did not want the canal system because God had not created it. Balderdash! These blackcoats didn't want

the canals because those waterways would create a larger commercial network than their own and put both commerce and communication beyond their tenacious control. Those who promoted the idiocy that men should not build what God had not provided insulted all reason. How did they explain the activities they were engaged in: the churches, the presses, the societies they established? What nonsense would these blackboats yet visit upon men elected to exercise reason? These men represented no God; they incited rebellion against the people, and they should be put in their place at once.

Mrs. Royall was in rare form in this counterattack. Public education was no concern of these religious fanatics; the Constitution of the United States had established that fact. They didn't even know what education meant. She had visited their schools and colleges, and they were mockeries. They did not produce graduates to advance Reason. They did not have students thinking and using talent and inventiveness; they had slaves on their knees groveling before a mental idol so terrible it made Satan look like a saint. Mrs. Royall pointed to the blackcoat invasion of West Point, the national military academy. In one year, they had taken men being trained to protect the nation and instead of arming them with knowledge, had put them on their knees, spouting Bible tracts.[12] She informed her listeners and readers that they did not have to travel to West Point to see what the blackcoat influence was: the Presbyterian colleges in Pennsylvania were in the same condition. She suggested that the legislature mount a board of inquiry and that professors at those institutions would corroborate the facts of this deplorable condition.[13]

Ely and his followers were in an uproar. They cried out that the state had no right to intrude upon their affairs. The legislators did not agree, for many were grateful graduates of these institutions and curious about the rumored changes; and most of them were Masons.

Mrs. Royall saved her last salvo for her best effect. So Dr. Ely wanted incorporation for the Sunday School Union, the American Tract Society, and their related activities, did he? Of course he did, and it was dear to that churchman's heart. The Sunday School Union had promoted tithing in its allied churches and collected large sums of money in its printing activities, all in God's name. So had the hundred different charities the Elyites had established, and Dr. Ely and his friends had used those many funds for their own purposes. They now sought to escape accounting for those funds and their curious uses, and the anonymity that an act of incorporation would bestow would aid them in this "Christian" effort. The Pennsylvania Legislature was being stampeded to give God's monies to a group of men. If the people's representatives fell for this newest ruse, they would legislate themselves out of power forever. They would establish a propaganda juggernaut against themselves for which no one could be brought to account.

Mrs. Royall held one other argument in her arsenal. It was the history of the Morgan affair. Dr. Ely's printing presses, his allied booksellers, and the religious press had promoted that affair. Even as Pennsylvania's legislators, many Masons among them, met to consider Ely, his followers, and their demands, their henchmen in New York had been caught at this lying game. Thurlow Weed's reward offer had produced a body, but it had not been William Morgan's after all. His coconspirators had fled across the New York border into Vermont to escape the wrath of the courts. Ely and his friends had counted upon this last caper of the anti-Masons, the discovery of Morgan's body, to stampede the opposition, destroy the Masons, and leave the state legislatures to them.

Mrs. Royall's counterattack turned back the Elyite tide in Harrisburg. The canal system was wanted by most of Pennsylvania, and the cry for public education was real. Both helped swell the opposition to those who sought to submerge both. In a final assault upon her religious enemies, Mrs. Royall collected Dr. Ely's own printed renditions of his July 4 "Call to Arms," the sermon which had called for the abandonment of the U.S. Constitution and its replacement with his theology. She placed it as she had placed her own writing, on every legislative desk in Harrisburg. She did not have to rely upon her own pamphlets any longer. What fools the men in Harrisburg would be to give anything to men who mouthed and wrote such words as Ely's.[14]

Dr. Ely's own publication sealed the argument. To the men sitting in the Harrisburg legislature, the sound of the Scots-Irish accents crying for their God's recognition outside the hall only reinforced what the old woman had placed before them. They would not be forced into any action even though the legislature was surrounded by blackcoated missionaries seeking to force legislative action.

Mrs. Royall had done her work. She had written, she had lectured, she had contacted her editors across the state, had faced mobs of her opponents, and walked boldly into their power dens. In the end, she had made men think. She had no illusions about her power, two hundred years of American history had been her strength. The descendants of those early colonists who had fought the inquisitions and the Mathers had remembered those ancient battles. The holy devils who had visited upon the nation's history the abominations in Salem, the curious communes in Vermont, and the religious enslavement of the first settlers were not figures from the past; they had come again to haunt the American experiment. The United States had to be ever vigilant against them. Just fourteen years before, in 1814, these same fanatics, in the Hartford Convention, had tried to restore their ecclesiastical control of the American nation by treating separately with England for dismemberment of the country. Mrs. Royall sent the spirit of that convention wafting over the Harrisburg body as the Pennsylvania Legislature made its decision. Dr. Ely himself appeared before it to try to dispel her attack. His words, "Let us all be Christian politicians," proved her truth and his fate. The Pennsylvania Legislature refused the Elyite demands, including the incorporation of their societies.[15]

Ezra Stiles Ely could not accept his defeat. He had gone to the Pennsylvania Legislature with his God and his followers, but he also had presented the best wishes of the most powerful man in the nation. Nicholas Biddle, by then the president of the Second Bank of the United States and the man who stewarded the money of the nation, had recommended that the act of incorporation be granted his friends. Mrs. Royall, he thought, could not prevail over Nicholas Biddle. Dr. Ely appealed to his friend and awaited an answer that never came.

The back rooms of the Pennsylvania capital buzzed with Masonic activity in response to the exhortations of Mrs. Royall. The Jackson forces seized their opportunity through that door opened by her and the planned blackcoat rout of Andrew Jackson became the springboard for his victory. The plea for incorporation of Ely's many societies roused not only the Masons and the democrats, but those of the old-line churches themselves. The fanatics were assailed for what they were, in Mrs. Royall's words:

> No government that has ever existed, can please a Presbyterian; monarchy cannot please them; they beheaded their king, and drenched the country in blood. Democracy does not please them. When they had the power in their own hands, they devoured each other like wild beasts. Republicanism, our present government, does not please them; every other sect is pleased with it. They seem to possess an inbred hostility to peace, and an unconquerable thirst for human blood; and all their aim is to get into power, to spill it . . . See the pains they are taking to raise an army of fanatics, altering the school books . . . .[16]

These words were punctuated by daily confrontations with the Elyites, and Jackson's men in Pennsylvania found themselves with a growing army recruited by Mrs. Royall. Mrs. Royall knew why Dr. Ely and his cohorts wanted their societies incorporated, but why was the nation's most important banker, Nicholas Biddle, recommending such approval? Why would the man who had absolute control of the nation's financial interests ally himself to those who proclaimed their intentions to destroy that nation? What did Nicholas Biddle, president of the Second Bank of the United States, have in common with Ezra Stiles Ely and his crew?

Mrs. Royall never got the chance to ask her questions of Banker Biddle in Harrisburg, for the famous man decamped, deserting Ely. The Pennsylvania Legislature not only refused incorporation to the Sunday School Union and its related enterprises, it tossed the rest of the blackcoat issues in its legislative dustbin, closing its doors to take its part in the presidential and congressional elections of 1828.

But Mrs. Royall's questions remained. Indeed, what was the connection between Ely and Biddle? It was a strange alliance, and now more than Mrs. Royall wanted an answer.

Chapter 9

The Black Gauntlets

The campaign of 1828 was a bitter one. Vile invective was heaped upon both major candidates, but the main target was Andrew Jackson. The hero of New Orleans was portrayed as Satan, credited not with a victory but with a chain of murders, assailed as an incompetent, a man of such vindictiveness that he would put his enemies to the sword if he gained the White House. Not content with attacks upon the man, Jackson's enemies had taken after his wife, who sat apart from the campaign in her home in Tennessee. In their tales, Rachel Jackson became a 'fallen woman" and the circumstances of the first divorce involving a candidate for the presidency were presented to the American public in the worst possible light. John Quincy Adams suffered assaults too, but the attack on his "dynasty," his aristocratic ways, and his extravagance was a poor show beside the personal scandal heaped upon Andrew and Rachel Jackson.[1]

The broadsides and pamphlets directed at Andrew Jackson and Rachel had a familiar look. The type and the paper looked like the penny tracts the black-coats sold, and the spearhead of the attack was centered in Philadelphia. The famous coffin handbills and the lurid "fallen woman" descriptions had a familiar ring to them. Like the missionary solicitations, the anti-Jackson literature, printed on imported presses and bordered in black like funeral notices, were distributed on every street corner, in every conveyance, and in taverns, meeting halls, and churches.

The religious attack on Masonry also grew. In New York and Philadelphia, anti-Masonic conventions were held with the expressed purpose of escalating anti-Masonry into a national issue and a national party.[2] The blackcoat aim used a tried and true military tactic, division. Religion was being used to woo from Jackson the Scots and Irish, especially the Catholics among them. Anti-Masonry was tailored to meet the new papal admonition against the men who had spurred so much revolution and to enlist the Roman Catholics, those the New Presbyterians sought to murder in Northern Ireland.[3] Popes Leo XII and Pious VII found their words reprinted in American Tract Society publications by men who were their confirmed enemies in all other religious matters. The campaign against Masonry and Andrew Jackson took precedence over Elyite-preferred "Christians." This new explosion of religious "love and tolerance" joined the scandalous "lay" tracts designed to bring together all those who hated Jackson.

The tactic did not work. John Quincy Adams, an incumbent president with the nation's bureaucracy and God on his side, was defeated in a massive avalanche of votes for a man called Satan in a half a million pieces of penny tract literature. Andrew Jackson had prevailed.

72

Andrew Jackson, from the moment of his election, loomed larger than ever after the invective heaped upon him. The dire predictions, the promised calamities, the insidious calumnies used against him, his wife, Masonry, and his military exploits had proved to be of no avail. The blackcoat effort had been resoundingly defeated, and Andrew Jackson became the American champion, the second to be so acclaimed in the nation's history. The nation originated by George Washington had found Andrew Jackson to continue it.

The November victory of the Jackson forces brought Mrs. Royall more national attention. Jackson's victory had been due to the massing of the Masons behind his colors, and Mrs. Royall's role in that enlistment was acknowledged. She had been the first to identify the forces against Jackson. Her *Black Book, Volume I*, had been followed by *Black Book Volume II*, published in September, 1828, outlining the enemies the nation faced. Entwined with the Jackson campaign, it cited in detail the problems to be met. A debt of gratitude was owed to the woman who had braved attack to lead the assault against those who would have denied Jackson the presidency. She had breathed courage into legislators to stand fast against the Elys of the world.

The Pennsylvanians initiated that appreciation. Mrs. Royall was summoned to Harrisburg to receive the first of her honors. She was feted by the Pennsylvania Legislature at its opening session in January, 1829.[4] A special coach was prepared for her journey, and for the first time in her life, Mrs. Royall found herself traveling like a queen. It was a thrill for the lady used to all manner of rude conveyance, but, alas, it was not to last. In an ominous omen for the year to come, Mrs. Royall and her coach had a strange accident. Passing under a bridge too low for the height of the carriage, the famous lady was showered with broken wood and, for a moment, broken dreams:

> The coach had been neatly painted, stuffed and lined anew, the stage lanterns were shining, the horses were the best in the line, and the driver no way behind.[5]

Mrs. Royall arrived in Harrisburg not in her special coach, but in a sleigh provided for her trip across the ice of the Susquehannah.

The Pennsylvanians gave Mrs. Royall a grand reception. She was given the freedom of the legislature, and she addressed a joint session convened for the purpose. The governor rode with her in a great parade and she was entertained for two days. Mrs. Royall was overwhelmed; it made the miseries of the last year disappear. All was right with her world at last and never more so than when she heard the final toast of her visit. She had laid aside her cry "Beware the blackcoats," but one of her supporters had decided it was time for a new crusade. Raising his glass in homage to Madame Royall, Editor Stambaugh of *The Reporter* cried out, "I will pledge you, Mrs. Royall, blueskins, may all their throats be cut!"[6] This new affront to John Quincy Adams and his supporters gave the writer pause, but she lifted her glass in acceptance of the toast. The accident and the loss of the new carriage forgotten, Mrs. Royall returned to Washington on that cold January 23, 1829, warm from her applause in Harrisburg.

The Jackson regime was to take office on Inauguration Day, March 4, 1829. It was one thing to be elected, but quite another to take the power that election conferred. Andrew Jackson, unlike his predecessors, had few friends awaiting him in Washington. The government was in the hands of his outspoken enemies; they ruled the Congress and held the offices.

Andrew Jackson was aware of his problem and had been seeking the best maneuvers to place his men where he would need them to govern. The selection of the attorney general and secretaries to oversee the Department of State, the

Treasury, the War Department and the Navy was his by law, but the hiring of workers to serve under them was a different matter. He had to find a way to put his own men in place and remove his opponents. The general had turned this matter over to his most trusted aide, Senator John Eaton from Tennessee.

Senator Eaton had served Andrew Jackson as adjutant and confidant through war and peace for sixteen years. A much younger man, he was held in great affection by his mentor and had been in charge of Jackson's Washington affairs for a decade. He had come to the capital in 1818 not only as a senator, but also to organize and manage Jackson's march to the presidency.[7] He was the chief Jackson strategist and credited with the successful national political campaign, the Jackson foes watched him closely, seeking clues to their own futures. He was involved in a situation which titillated his opponents.

John Eaton, a widower, had been for many years a boarder at a singular Washington establishment, the home of William O'Neal. It also catered to other congressmen and senators attached to the Jackson fortunes. The O'Neals, despite their lowly occupation as innkeepers, came from old American stock of good repute. Mrs. O'Neal was the sister of a former governor of New Jersey, Richard Howell, and her husband had been close to Thomas Jefferson. As a consequence, every member of the family lived and breathed politics, including the youngest daughter, Margaret "Peg" O'Neal.[8]

Peg was a capital attraction. She was a lovely, vivacious redhead who had a way with men, as many of the lonely men attending Congress could attest. Further, she was known to be a particular favorite of Andrew Jackson and his wife Rachel, for they too stayed at O'Neal's when in the capital. Rachel had confided to friends that in Peg she had found a daughter, a substitute for the child she never had.[9] All this enhanced Peg's reputation.

In time, Peg O'Neal married. Her husband was a young Navy officer, Purser John Timberlake, a career man who was away for extended duty while his beautiful wife filled her time helping her parents in their enterprise. Many in Washington considered such activity on the part of a young married woman unseemly, but Peg did not care. She loved the political atmosphere of her parents' establishment, meeting with new congressmen, secretaries, and emissaries from Jackson. This was much more interesting than attending "lecture" with the New School Presbyterians now flooding Washington's Presbyterian churches, which was a preoccupation of other young wives. While her friends lent their ears to the blackcoats and read the penny tracts from the Sunday School Union and the American Tract Society, Peg O'Neal Timberlake added to her knowledge of the real America by conversing with her family's guests.[10]

The continuing association of Peg Timberlake with her parents' business, the fact that she was the friend, confidante, and surrogate family to those close to Andrew Jackson, as well as the general's and his wife's particular favorite, was known not only to friends but to enemies. She became an important figure with influence far beyond her position. Her beauty only added to the attention paid her. In 1827, it also had added to the attention paid her young husband.

For nine years, Purser John Timberlake had carried through his naval duties admirably. Suddenly, in the heat of the renewed Jackson campaign for the presidency, John Timberlake found himself accused of falsifying records of payments for the requisitions of his ship. It was a trying experience for the young officer, for he was not sure of what he stood accused; the records so questioned had been his precedessor's.[11]

It was natural that the Jacksonians take a hand in this matter. John Eaton came forward with the necessary funds with which Purser Timberlake made good the tangled accounts, and the Navy officer set out to sea for another tour abroad, this time to the Mediterranean.

In early 1828, Purser Timberlake was announced as having taken his own life in that foreign clime. The reason? The Navy said it was another embezzlement of accounts.[12] The tragedy marked the O'Neal household. John Eaton could not bail out young Timberlake, but he showed the widow and her family tender sympathy. This circumstance began an extraordinary set of events for the Jacksonians.

In 1828, John Eaton spent more time than ever in the capital, drawing together the many operations designed to make Andrew Jackson the president of the United States. Long nights working with staff at the Indian Queen meant long mornings at the O'Neal boarding house. Beautiful Peg was there to discuss the current activities and make her own well-known political asides. The affection Eaton had felt for the child, the concern for the young bride, now became an obsession with the attractive widow. By November, his chores done for Jackson and victory won, John Eaton wanted to take Peg O'Neal Timberlake as his second wife. He wrote to his mentor about it, and Andrew Jackson and Rachel sent their approval posthaste; two of those whom they loved were to become one! Rachel was particularly enthusiastic. She would like to have this wedding in the White House; it would be a significant first social assembly for the Jackson administration.[13]

It was not to be. On December 22, 1828, Rachel Jackson died. Her unexpected and tragic death cast a pall over the nation. The news traveled fast, broadcast by the animosities still inflamed from the campaign. Those who mourned Rachel's passing blamed the attacks upon the innocent woman for her death. Those who were against her celebrated this sign from their God that indeed the iniquitous would be destroyed.[14] All Washington preparations for the general were halted. The Jacksonians respected their leader's grief; their enemies exhalted and, rejoicing in this sudden reprieve, looked about for other Jacksonians to assault.

John Eaton seemed a prime target. As the acknowledged leader in preparing for Jackson's new regime, he was now standing for the general in the nation's capital, with Peg O'Neal Timberlake at his side. The temptation was too much for minds well experienced with sin and the profits of its redemption. John Eaton and his bride-to-be became the logical target of the anti-Jackson forces grouping to protect themselves. As a major with a distinguished war record and a senator of accepted ability, John Eaton had presented no easy mark for calumny. Criticism of his "bargains" with the press and his manipulations of the campaign had been to no avail. Now, Eaton was a man in love who had set no date for the marriage. He spent part of every day with a woman; the blackcoats planned a replay of the scandal directed to Rachel Jackson, an embarrassment to the new regime. "The Innkeeper's Daughter and the Senator" was a title with many possibilities, and the blackcoat rumors began.[15]

John Eaton did not wait for this assault to take form. He moved to protect Peg, and on January 1, 1829, Mrs. Timberlake became Mrs. John Eaton with all the Jacksonians in Washington in attendance, including Vice President John Calhoun. It was a happy party closing ranks against imminent scandal,[16] and the Eatons settled in to enter the life of the capital as Jackson's presidency approached.

The death of Rachel Jackson had plunged her husband into deep mourning. Even his close constituency was not prepared for the depth of the widower's feeling. Rachel's demise had not only deprived Jackson of his beloved wife but of his chance to make amends for the ordeal his ambition had visited upon her. Andrew Jackson had wanted to lead his gentle Rachel into the White House to give her that stage from which to face her detractors and the libels they had flung at her. Now it could not be, and Jackson grieved by her graveside in Tennessee, too bereft to take command in the capital. Eaton stood alone for him in the interim. To bolster his aide, Jackson gave him full responsibilities for the preparations for the new government, thus bypassing Vice President John Calhoun.[17]

Official Washington had learned about Eaton and his group and their growing lists of positions sought for appointment. The Senator from Tennessee was the acknowledged logistical genius in Jackson's successful campaign, and outgoing President John Quincy Adams moved to thwart him. Like his father before him, Adams and his *coterie* made their own midnight lists and lame duck appointments. New battle lines had been drawn to welcome President-elect Jackson and his chief aide.

Andrew Jackson arrived in the nation's capital on February 16, 1829. He came as the conqueror, the hero of New Orleans, in an open carriage, dressed in full uniform as he led his army in parade through the streets of Washington. Terror descended upon the holdovers as they barricaded themselves behind closed doors while Jackson and his army passed. Sixteen days remained until inauguration.[18]

The defeated John Quincy Adams sat through this Jackson invasion in abject silence, his White House like a morgue. Those who had supported him were not to be seen, not even his last-minute appointees. His large family and his "connections" tried to bolster his spirits but although many in terms of plush appointments and assignments, they were a small crowd indeed when summoned to a White House social.[19] They were smaller yet when set on the streets among the Jacksonians.

March 4, Inauguration Day, came. It was the moment Andrew Jackson would take Washington. The crowds which had followed the great carriage of the man from Tennessee in February gathered to follow it again. Andrew Jackson emerged from his hotel, but this time he strode at the head of his troops, on foot, right to the Capitol. There was no decorum and no parade. The President-elect had arrived in Washington in full military uniform, but now he wore the simple gray cloth of the masses, relieved only by a wide black band upon his sleeve and upon his hat.[20] The effect was stunning to his enemies and detractors.

The President-elect entered the Capitol Building, and the crowd broke. John Quincy Adams was not there. He had deserted Washington to escape the day.[21] The Jacksonian mob spilled into every available place. Andrew Jackson appeared in the East Portico and the crowd quieted.

Andrew Jackson's words were few. Without mentioning religion once, its intrusion into public affairs was covered succinctly:

> Internal improvements, and the diffusion of knowledge, so far as they can be promoted by the constitutional acts of the federal government, are of high importance.[22]

That brief statement held much for its hearers. Canals and railroads would be built but church-schools would not. The man who commanded no army, only bands of citizens fighting for life and liberty, declared that standing armies were "dangerous to free governments in time of peace" and promised to keep the patriotic militia "the bulwark of our defense" and "the impenetrable aegis" of American liberties. [23] The statement drew huzzahs from his crowd. It was for the office holders sitting in the capital's offices, however, that Jackson reserved his real blast:

> The recent demonstration of public sentiment inscribes on the list of executive duties, in characters too legible to be overlooked, the task of

reform, which will require particularly, the correction of those abuses that
have brought the patronage of the federal government into conflict with
the freedom of elections, and the counteraction of those causes which
have disturbed the rightful course of appointment and have placed or continued power in *unfaithful* or incompetent hands.[24]

President Andrew Jackson had reserved to himself the right to remove those
who had been found to be working against the best interests of the United
States. His entire address was a simple statement of the Jacksonian position and
those who opposed him would have cause to remember it well in the ensuing
months.

The Jacksonians were invited to move from the Capitol to the White House,
and the new president led the way.

The executive mansion was the pride of the Adams administration. After the
destruction of Washington by the British in 1814, the national government had
spared no expense to reconstruct the symbolic home for the president, so as to
erase the stain of capitulation of the American leaders from their very seats. The
new furnishings for the White House had been chosen to emphasize grandeur,
and the Adams family had spent lavishly to create a setting for the chief executive second to none. Years of residence abroad had given John Quincy and
Louisa an appreciation of European elegance, and this was seen in every room of
the White House. Exquisite draperies of damask, fine English furniture, china,
and silver had bestowed a new air upon the executive mansion well received by
urbane Washingtonians but not by Jacksonians.[25] Andrew Jackson was said to
carry his dislike of England to such lengths that his beloved Rachel had to indulge her tastes for fine furnishings by settling for French products when American ones were not available. If she had been allowed some English pieces, they,
like her Spanish ones, had been war booty, and that condition mollified her
exacting husband.[26] The new White House did not.

The Jackson forces had made the most of Adams's penchant for things English in the campaign. Adams had carried his interest in English fads to such an
extent that he had brought into the presidential home two billiard tables hand-
crafted in London at a cost of over a thousand dollars.[27] That extravagance had
cost him more than election pains; it had cost Adams congressional support. His
best friends had found it difficult to sustain that purchase, and the Jacksonians
had used that singular buying misadventure to tarnish Adams's refurbishing of
the nation's "home." The national abhorrence had become so great that a boycott was visited upon the Adamses in the last few months of his administration,
a condition duly noted by Adams's good friend, Justice Story of the U.S. Supreme Court:

> Mr. Adams had no more favors to bestow and he is now passed by with
> indifference by all the fair weather friends. They are all ready to hail the
> rising sun. Never have I felt so forcibly the emptiness of public honors and
> public favor.[28]

This remembrance was on the occasion of the annual celebration of George
Washington's birthday, February 22, 1829, at the White House. The John
Quincy Adamses had planned to have this last gala, but less than half the guests
invited came. The out-going President of the United States, cognizant of the
insult, left his own party early and retired in anguish.[29] It was obvious that
Jackson's campaign had not abated with his victory at the polls.

The Adams *coterie* wondered what Andrew Jackson would do when he came
to live in the presidential mansion among the treasures accumulated by Monroe
and Adams. Many of them enjoyed the prospect of the old Anglophobe taking

his morning repast at an English table, served on English china and linen from English silver and glass; others were angry that this detractor should enjoy what he had excoriated others for having.[30] No one thought for a moment that the old general would clear the White House out, not after the campaign his aides had waged concerning the cost of its refurbishing.

President Jackson, man of the people, held an inaugural reception in the White House, the likes of which that building has not seen since. By his personal direction, the doors of the executive mansion were opened to all who wished to enter, and on the day he became president he led them in. The stampede is recorded in history. Like a back country hoedown and barbecue, all protocol, service, and manners were thrown to the winds. Punch, well spiked, was ladled from barrels, wheels of cheese placed on table surfaces, and fine china was mingled with other necessary vessels for serving. The people had themselves a ball. When the affair was over, the White House was in shambles. The joyous celebration of Americans had eliminated what Jackson did not enjoy. The English furniture, china, glass, silver, linens, and even the new billiard table were destroyed. Congress could say nothing to its constituents, and Jackson's adversaries were speechless. President Andrew Jackson directed that the White House be refurbished with all things American.[31] It was a magnificent affront to his enemies, one they would long remember and misconstrue for history.

Andrew Jackson had taken the capital and set loose a new force to sweep the land. That force wore a distinct badge of commitment, the mourning band for Rachel Jackson. The general's lady had not lived to enter the White House, but because she had not, her spirit lay as a pall over the future, evident in the gaunt and worn face of President Andrew Jackson.

Anne Newport Royall recorded the events of the inauguration. She watched the Jacksonians take the Capitol and the White House, and she applauded. She noted that Jackson's enemies had deserted the American capital once again and she described that desertion in plain words:

> The officials at Washington, who were friends of Mr. Adams, had agreed not to participate in the inaugural ceremonies, and the only uniformed company of light infantry commanded by Colonel Seaton, of the National Intelligencer, had declined to offer its services as an escort. (The day before the Adams family had quit the White House to visit friends in the suburbs, thus avoiding any show of hospitality to the new President) A number of Revolutionary officers, however, had hastily organized themselves, and walked with General Jackson from Gadsby's Hotel to the Capital.[32]

Mrs. Royall celebrated the inauguration in her own way, by placing a copy of her finished *Black Book, Volume III*, on every congressional desk. To make sure that her friends understood they had work ahead to win the government, she had opened each book to the inclosure of Richard Johnson's final speech to the Senate. The tall man from Kentucky had begun the first national legislative confrontation with Jackson's enemies, and Mrs. Royall meant to see that the new Congress continued it, especially her friends from Pennsylvania sitting for the first time in Washington.

Richard Johnson's speech, as reprinted by Mrs. Royall, was read by the newcomers to Congress:

> Extensive religious combinations, to effect political object, are always dangerous . . . All religious despotism commences by combination and influence; and when that influence begins to operate upon the political institutions of a country, the civil power soon bends under it; and the catastrophe of other nations furnishes an awful warning of the consequences.[33]

This speech for the committee which rejected the Sabbatical arguments, ending the thrust to shut down the post office and government offices on Sundays, was not a simple statement of action; it was a declaration of policy. Like Mrs. Royall's words to the Harrisburg legislature, Senator Johnson asked where such demands would stop:

If the observance of a holiday becomes incorporated in our institutions, shall we forbid the movement of an army; prohibit an assault in the time of war; and lay an injunction upon our naval officers to lie in the wind while on the ocean on that day? Consistency would seem to require it. Nor is it certain that we should stop there. If the principle is once established, that religion or religious observances, shall be interwoven with our legislative acts, we must pursue it to its ultimatum. We shall, if consistent, provide for the erection of edifices for the worship of the Creator, and for the support of Christian ministers, if we believe that such measures will promote the interests of Christianity.[34]

The clarion voice of Richard Johnson raised the Jacksonian banner high, and Mrs. Royall could be heard by both her friends and enemies as his declaration rang to a close:

It is the stated conviction of the committee, that the only method of avoiding these consequences, with their attendant train of evils, is to adhere strictly to the spirit of the constitution, which regards the general government in no other light than that of a civil institution, wholly destitute of religious authority.[35]

Richard Johnson's closing paragraph was the most important:

What other nations call religious toleration, we call religious rights. They are not exercised in virtue of governmental indulgence, but as rights, of which government cannot deprive any portion of citizens however small. Despotic power may invade those rights, but justice still confirms them. Let the national legislature once perform an act which involves the decision of a religious controversy, and it will have passed its legitimate bounds. The precedent will then be established, and the foundation laid for that usurpation of the Divine prerogative in this country, which had been the desolating scourge to the fairest portions of the Old World. Our Constitution recognizes no other power than that of persuasion, for enforcing religious observations. Let the professors of Christianity recommend their religion by deeds of benevolence—by Christian meekness—by lives of temperance and holiness. Let them combine their efforts to instruct the ignorant—to relieve the widow and the orphan—to promulgate to the world the gospel of their saviour, recommending its precepts by their habitual example, government will find its legitimate object in protecting them. It cannot oppose them, and they will not need its aid. Their moral influence will then do infinitely more to advance the true interests of religion, than any measure they can call upon Congress to enact.[36]

The publication of Richard Johnson's words was a reminder from Mrs. Royall that victory for Andrew Jackson had been gained by new forces elected to the Congress. Their policies should be the law of the land, and she pressed her view with the inclusion of her own letter to Congress:

This led me to think that we are not so much in danger from civil or military chieftans, as from the vast clerical collossus which bestrides our land, with its missionaries and its travelling agents, its societies of almost every name and description, which by their various ramifications, are connected with almost every family in the United States. And especially the societies now forming to withdraw all their business and patronage from those who will not submit to their dictation. Their likeness had been drawn by St. John in the Apocalypse, with surprising correctness. To these must be added its princely establishments in our most important cities; its revenue, which now equals that of some nations, and is constantly increasing; its control of our universities, colleges and academies, and last, though not least, the presses, many of whom in its employment and most others afraid to attack that hornets' nest. When I consider that this tremendous machinery is made to center in one point, and is moved by one spring, I fear the time is not far distant, when no man who will not receive the mark of the beast, can be elected into any office. But I have faith that we shall yet be saved from the all devouring jaws of this terrible monster in sheep's clothing. I find, that in some places, they are taking measures to counteract this wide spreading contagion. I hope that you and our other wise men in Congress will take this into consideration with the petitions.[37]

Mrs. Royall's words had defined the mark of the beast and those who conferred it. Rachel Jackson had suffered it, President Jackson damned it, John Eaton had organized the Jackson army against it, and Mrs. Royall's celebration volume on the desks of Congress recollected it. The same black cloth which bound Mrs. Royall's *Black Books* bound the Jacksonians' sleeves like a badge of honor. Those black bands, like the black gauntlets of old, were thrown before their enemies along the route of parade. A declaration of war had been made.

Chapter 10

The Enemy Shows Its Face

Washington was a boiling cauldron of intrigue from the moment of Jackson's inauguration. The infighting in the Congress and in the government offices intensified day by day as those who won sought means to replace those who lost. Invective and vilification from the hard-fought campaign continued against men trying to form a government to exercise the mandate given them by election. Jacksonians found themselves described as "pygmies," their abilities ignored and their pretensions reduced to farce; even those elected to Congress were called pariahs before they set foot in its legislative halls. As victors they were called "failures" before they could put their government in place.[1]

One man in the Jackson administration escaped all this. Like a bridge over muddy waters, John C. Calhoun, vice president of the United States, sat in splendid isolation, his character pristine and unattacked, his office unassailable. John Calhoun had done what John Quincy Adams could not in the campaign of 1828: he had been elected for a second term. As vice president to Adams, he had cleverly maneuvered to become vice president to Andrew Jackson. He had achieved this switching of his horse in midstream because, in 1828, Congress still had the final selection of the president. John C. Calhoun as vice president was the president of the Senate, and his role in assuring what the people voted carried through Congress was crucial to the Jacksonians. They had lost the election of 1824 in the Congress, and they did not want to suffer congressional rebuff again. The Jacksonians were forced to accept John Calhoun to cement the victory for Jackson they had received in the polls.[2]

John Calhoun had engineered a remarkable feat. At 47, he stood in line for the presidency held by a wounded war veteran of 62 years of age. This was not lost on the politically astute. The Jackson opponents, from the moment of defeat, decided their best interests lay in a working relationship with the vice president, and they nestled in behind his mantle. Calhoun's power was enormous. He had spent his adult life in the Congress, and in and out of the cabinets of three presidents. He knew politics like no other man in Washington. His office as president of the Senate gave him an operational base equal to that of the nation's chief executive. His control of patronage was as great as he wished to make it, and his position with the victorious gave him a latitude few men have achieved in Washington since. Any animosities remaining from his "deal" with the Jacksonians in submerging Adams were put aside as the realities of 1829 were accepted. John C. Calhoun sat astride the swirling currents about him, directing the activities of the Senate and the transition of Congress itself. The religious press rallied to him, and suddenly Calhoun was a towering figure, a statesman in the midst of rabble. He took much pleasure in his new fame.[3]

Andrew Jackson had no illusions about Calhoun. The man had been part of a necessary bargain to gain the nation, but Andrew Jackson did not like him, knew his pretensions, and more importantly, knew that enemies would group behind the Vice President and Calhoun would welcome them. Andrew Jackson had to work around him, and for this operation he relied heavily upon John Eaton, who found himself opposed to the Vice President by Jackson's direction.[4]

The Vice President's office was in continual operation. Unlike Andrew Jackson, Calhoun did not have to wait for inauguration to establish himself. A vice president succeeding himself meant no pause in administration, but he had to ingratiate himself with Jackson. To this end, he suffered a working alliance with John Eaton through the campaign. John Eaton was to be endured just long enough to beguile the new president into cabinet choices amenable to John Calhoun's ambitious plans.

The possibility that John Eaton would be a cabinet member did not sit well with the Vice President. Such an astute political manipulator, too close to Jackson, posed a danger; so Calhoun went to work to change things. Through his friends he contacted Hugh White, Jackson's old law partner, in a clumsy attempt to force Eaton from Jackson's side.[5] It did not work; Jackson reaffirmed his intent to place John Eaton as his secretary of war.

John Calhoun could not allow this to happen; he mobilized opposition to Eaton's appointment in the War Department itself, selecting his former aide, Colonel Nathan Towson, to make representations against Eaton's selection as the war chief. Towson, paymaster of the Army and a Calhoun appointee during the Monroe administration, circulated among the Washington officer corps a petition against John Eaton.[6]

Colonel Towson filled his petition from Adams's holdovers and supporters and did present them to Andrew Jackson. The President-elect acted characteristically; he did not announce his appointee for secretary of state first but instead announced his selection of John Eaton as secretary of war.

Washington City was aghast. Calhoun's maneuverings had prepared the capital for Eaton's service apart from the cabinet, as possibly postmaster in charge of the postal services, a fitting place for a political manipulator with lists for patronage. Washington City sat back and waited for Calhoun's explosion, but the Vice President said nothing.

Andrew Jackson announced the rest of his cabinet. John Eaton would be secretary of war, but two of Calhoun's best friends were then selected: John Branch as secretary of navy and John Berrien as attorney general. To compound the growing confusion, Andrew Jackson reached into Pennsylvania and designated Samuel Ingham as secretary of the treasury. The capital could not believe its good fortune; Ingham was Calhoun's man. They eagerly awaited Jackson's nominee for secretary of state. John Calhoun controlled three members of Jackson's cabinet; perhaps he would have four.

Andrew Jackson then threw Washington two curves. He selected Martin Van Buren, newly elected governor of New York, as his secretary of state. Van Buren had opposed him in 1824 but joined him in 1828 and was not a friend to Calhoun.[7] As the capital digested this, Andrew Jackson announced that he would create a new cabinet post, elevating the postal department. For postmaster general, a new title, he designated a complete apostate, William T. Barry, the man who led Henry Clay's campaign for President in 1824, deserting to Jackson in 1828.[8] The cabinet was split three to two, and the Vice President made it four to two. John Calhoun had the power in this new government, and Washington City went to bed and slept easily for the first time in weeks.

Mrs. Royall kept busy reporting on the progress of the new Jackson administration to her editors and subscribers. She was the first to announce Jackson's plans for the Post Office Department, its new cabinet status, and the resultant redistribution of the postmasterships.[9]   She also signaled coming changes in other government offices. John Calhoun may have lulled the Washington office-holders into a sense of security and given them a few nights sleep, but Mrs. Royall knew better. She had been roaming the Capitol halls in pursuit of a personal objective, and she felt it was in her grasp.

Mrs. Royall wanted George Watterston removed as Librarian of Congress. Her discovery of the Bible tracts on the library's tables and the revelation of government money spent to purchase those tracts had invoked a ban on such actions. The tracts were removed, but still she questioned George Watterston's role in the affair and searched to find the answer.

Mrs. Royall concentrated on Watterston's association with the hated blackcoats. Those purveyors of false doctrine were masters of getting men of good sense to do senseless things, but she knew this was not the case with the Librarian of Congress. Representative Everett had admitted his mistake, but George Watterston had not. He still avoided her every time she entered the library. It was possible the man was a willing pawn in the unseemly raid on the American treasury by the Bible-spouting fanatics.

Day after day, Mrs. Royall made it her business to observe George Watterston, his home, and his office. The blackcoats were with him always, and he had come into possession of a fine new home and a most expensive carriage. In a time of great financial press, George Watterston was living very well, better than his government salary allowed.

Mrs. Royall made inquiries among her new friends in Congress and excited considerable interest in her investigation. Watterston's friends heard about the matter and dismissed it with an explanation of their own. Everyone in Washington knew George Watterston was living well because he had become a successful author at last. His books were selling, and his royalties were well on their way to making him a rich man. It was all Mrs. Royall had to hear. The religious bookstores and their related merchants were Watterston's benefactors. The printing press which published him was one and the same with the tract society.[10]

Mrs. Royall knew the game. She had observed the Morgan affair and that of poor John Binns of Philadelphia, the misguided patriot who had produced the infamous coffin bills attacking General Jackson as a murderer and assassin.[11] George Watterston had become a paid servant of the blackcoats, and he had rewarded them with his assistance in the library.

Mrs. Royall put her issue on the desks of Congress: Watterston had used his position to enrich himself. The librarian's friends were aghast at the implications. They sought to soften Mrs. Royall's conclusions, and in so doing resurrected the strange alliance of Ezra Stiles Ely and Nicholas Biddle she had noted in Pennsylvania. George Watterston's friends came to his defense with a commendation from Banker Biddle. Nicholas Biddle, once a youthful editor of the periodical *Forum*, had recommended Watterston's work be published by the tract society press.[12] This affirmation of a link with Ely's blackcoat operations helped Mrs. Royall put it all together at last.

Nicholas Biddle was involved in a partnership with Ezra Stiles Ely. The facts of Ely's rise, the Biddle family's involvement, the promotion of charitable savings societies, the quest for incorporation, and Biddle's own career with the Second Bank of the United States held a peculiar rationale. The tract societies, the grab for booksellers, censorship of American authors, the broadsides, the campaign flyers, assaults on the U.S. Constitution, and the Anti-Masonry leagues presented a clear pattern. The final invasion of civil authority, raids on the public treasury, and on education expenditures fitted together to solve her enigma.[13]

There was a similarity between Ely and his church and Biddle and his bank. Both institutions were managed by the same kind of people: Scots-Irish immigrants lately arrived on American shores. Mrs. Royall was incensed that her own lack of perspective had persisted so long. She had covered the subject two years before in her first *Black Book* after her first encounter with this situation in Baltimore, in Maryland:

> I walked into the United States Branch Bank . . . expecting to see Americans there, at least, if not gentlemen. No, these Baltimoreans are too ignorant of the smallest office, and have to rake all the foreign trash out of the streets, to keep their accounts. Who, could you suppose, I found Cashier and President of this United States Bank? Two more coarse, long toothed, roughest looking bog trotters that ever crossed the Atlantic, particularly the President. Everybody knows him . . . and if any impartial man will say, that a more rough, uncouth, illiberal clown will be found . . . I'll ask the gentleman's pardon. The citizens begged of me to aid them in ousting him.[14]

Mrs. Royall remembered Nicholas Biddle's reply when she went to him directly with this complaint:

> Oh, Mrs. R. we don't care for the shape of a man's face, or his manners; all we are concerned in is, whether he has property enough to indemnify us, should any default occur in the bank![15]

What a fool she had been. Indemnify! What would these Scots-Irish right off the boat, out of the bog, have to indemnity the bank? It was obvious that they had the blackcoat church and its money behind them. The bank and church were a cooperative, even to the men who managed its offices and the accents with which they spoke.

Mrs. Royall held an enormity in her hands, and she had no illusions concerning her personal position in relation to banker Biddle. Although she knew she was right, she had to firm up her foundations before she could proceed against him. She had one advantage: George Watterston. She had to keep up unrelenting pressure on her new congressional allies in the library affair.

Mrs. Royall was becoming an excellent political strategist. The lesson she learned with the Pennsylvania legislators had to be applied. Many new men were in Washington from other states, and each sought to create a new identity in the capital. A congressional inquiry into all the aspects of the Watterston affair was needed to expose the arrangements she knew existed among the anti-Jackson people, Ely, and Biddle and crowd. Andrew Jackson would enjoy a national stage with which to prove the cabal he knew existed against him.

Mrs. Royall visited the halls of Congress, talking to Pennsylvanians and other allies. As she marched, John Eaton was pursuing the means by which he could effect removals of Adams's holdovers for Jackson's replacements. The new war secretary sat in his office unconfirmed by the Senate and surrounded by men who would not cooperate with him. John Calhoun had seen to this; as president of the Senate, he had used procedure to delay approval of Eaton's appointment while seeking a way to oust him from the War Department position.[16]

John Calhoun did not want Eaton to have control of the war office and for a very good reason. Calhoun himself had held the post of secretary of war, serving James Monroe, when Andrew Jackson had suffered most from indirection and charges emanating from that department.[17] The Vice President did not want that past reviewed, and he sensed that Andrew Jackson did.

Since the days of the War of 1812, and 1814, when then Secretary of War John Armstrong had deserted the capital city turning command over to his armchair generals, Andrew Jackson had spoken no kind words for any of the men who staffed the department's offices. These men had allowed the British to burn Washington, delayed Jackson's commission, refused him supplies, and attempted to subvert him. In the end, he had won while they had lost. Thereafter their continued meddling in his Florida command only intensified his disregard of Army bureaucrats.[18]

The "politicians in uniform" not only failed to deliver him proper logistic support, but directed gross personal and political abuse to him from their chairbound stations. They had sought to suspend his military rank, had forced him to contract for his own supplies, and to provide his own monies for his troops as he pursued victory after victory for the nation. Even after he attained success, it was that same group which fabricated charges to tarnish Jackson, the hero, their competitor in the presidential sweepstakes. The scandals hinted at and directed at the hero of New Orleans came right out of the War Department's offices from men allied against him since 1812.[19]

In 1829, the War Department was in a very vulnerable position. Not only did Jackson have a bias against it, but it was admittedly less a military organization than a political one; Monroe and Adams had seen to that. Both presidents had used their budgetary powers to mold it to their political liking. The Army of the United States had become a secondary consideration, and for ten years had been systematically reduced in size until it was the minor service in the defense of the nation.[20] Further, the citizen militia had been discouraged and the available force of 22,000 at the beginning of the decade had been decreased annually until, in 1829, it represented a force of less than 6,000 trained men at a time when the United States had doubled its land mass.[21] Further, officers in the service had been chosen not for their ability to marshal the nation's forces for its best defense, but for their known attachment to whoever was in power, and their antipathy to such as Andrew Jackson.

The Army had become more politicized under Adams, an anomaly that produced more than one *cause célèbre*. Not the least of these was Mrs. Royall's 1827 *exposé* of the black-coated missionary invasion of West Point in 1826-27.[22] John Eaton's anticipated command of the War Department was obviously a calculated maneuver to neutralize these politics.

The Vice President understood his position in the Jackson ranks: He was an Adams man whether he liked it or not. Jackson had brought his personal staff with him and had no working liaison with Calhoun's office. The Vice President accepted this and used it to maintain his old support while he searched out new support. He was ambitious; John Calhoun wanted to be president.

John Calhoun was close to Mrs. Royall's blackcoats. Lewis Machen, her new nemesis was his chief clerk[23] and staffed Calhoun's office with the dour Scots-Irish Mrs. Royall detested, many right off the boat. Calhoun's wife Floride was a leader in the women's circles of the Second Presbyterian Church, the capital blackcoat center, and as the Vice President's wife at a time when there was no First Lady, she planned to reign supreme in the city's salons.

The time had come for a quiet break with the Jackson ranks. The Vice President and his wife had played a very good game with the Jacksonians and especially with John Eaton. They had attended his wedding to Peg O'Neal Timberlake on New Year's Day, but it was time to shed their masks. Accordingly, in early February, when Mrs. John Eaton announced her first "at home" to receive Washington associates, Floride Calhoun did not attend, and neither did any of her group.[24] The excuse for this slight was "mourning for Mrs. Jackson," but as the salons of Washington buzzed with unseemly tales about Peg and her parents, Timberlake's tragedy, and the affair with Eaton, it was obvious something else was afoot.

Because political changes are often announced in the salons of a capital city, the movement against John Eaton and his wife was accepted as such by Washington. Vice President Calhoun and his wife had thrown a silken gauntlet at the man Jackson had chosen to run his show. The Vice President was the only member of the administration to hold his office in transition, and his power play was a strong signal to his supporters past and future.

The inauguration had brought many new faces to Washington, among them Calhoun's own invited guest, Dr. Ezra Stiles Ely. He had been Calhoun's classmate at Yale University, a good friend ever since, and the Calhoun's included him in all their functions for the event. Dr. Ely did not return to Philadelphia but decided to stay on in the capital to assist his old friend.[25]

Mrs. Royall's attack on George Watterston had been two months proceeding and the tract societies involved had kept their distance. George Watterston's defense had been left in the able hands of Henry Clay, Daniel Webster, and John Calhoun, but the last-minute defection of Edward Everett had silenced these famous voices. Dr. Ely was well aware of the situation for his interests were threatened. Years of quiet insinuation into government, assisted by the Vice-President, had to be protected. Voices like Mrs. Royall's calling for removal and investigation had to be quieted before the army Jackson brought to Washington regrouped. Dr. Ely thought he could add a national dimension to the support Watterston needed.

In March, 1829, Dr. Ely was enjoying his second term as the moderator of the General Assembly of the Presbyterian Church in America. It was a prestigious position he had created by midwifing a union of the schismatic elements of the old American and the new Scots-Irish congregations he had captured or organized.[26] He had designed this to gain entry into national affairs, and he was anxious to put it to the test. Dr. Ely was as ambitious as his friend John Calhoun and much more egotistical—he believed he had God on his side and held an exclusive agency from Him. Dr. Ely wished to be presented to President Andrew Jackson with the commendable auspices of the Vice President of the United States.

There is no record of any meeting between Jackson and Ely on Inauguration Day, and Dr. Ely did not gain immediate access to the President of the United States to give him greetings and counsel from God. Rather, the blackcoat leader found himself having to enter the White House in a more round-about way.

Andrew Jackson had closed his White House to all social activity after his inauguration, for Rachel's death still governed his personal life. He had brought what family he had to fill the executive mansion with warmth. Andrew Jackson Donelson and his cousin-wife, Emily, were Rachel's kin, and to them he gave the stewardship of his new house. "Jack" was to serve as secretary for family affairs and Emily as hostess for her uncle, a post equated with that of the First Lady.[27]

John Calhoun had not been able to effect the meeting for his friend Dr. Ely with the President, but his wife Floride did the next best thing. The young Donelsons, like their aunt, were fervent Presbyterians; so they were invited by the Vice President's wife to join her in Sunday worship at the Second Presbyterian Church. Unlike Andrew Jackson, who merely tolerated religion, his young kinfolk were caught up in the New Life movement in the church. Jack Donelson was a graduate of Transylvania College, a school early captured by the blackcoats,[28] and Emily was a young woman enthralled by the new pamphlets of sin and redemption and an attendee at women's circles which promoted them. They readily assented to attend with Floride Calhoun and met the Reverend J.N. Campbell, Ely's follower, who was the pastor of the Second Presbyterian. Ely was to gain access to the White House through the Donelsons.

Dr. Ely, moderator of the General Assembly of the Presbyterian Church in

America, was presented to Mrs. Andrew Jackson Donelson. As a fellow Presbyterian and as leader of the most organized group within that church, he was in a perfect position to offer his unique services as religious advisor. It was a liaison which appealed to the young southern belle completely unprepared for her prestigious assignment. Dr. Ely proffered promises of support for the difficult days ahead, and Emily Donelson, in all innocence, welcomed his offer. Dr. Ely became a constant visitor to the White House, welcomed not by Andrew Jackson, but by his niece and her husband.[29]

It was an audacious move. The man who had helped to direct the campaign of vilification against Jackson, whose tract societies had been responsible for the scurrilous broadsides against Rachel, was the religious advisor, the comforter to her closest kin. The very forces believed to have driven Rachel Jackson to her death now stood ready to profit from it. They had entered the Jackson White House, and they had in hand pliable instruments with which to work their persuasion.

Dr. Ely had not spoken in behalf of George Watterston during the initial difficulties, but he had plans in hand to rectify that situation. Dr. Ely surmised that Andrew Jackson cherished his prerogatives and would take unto himself any decision concerning whom and what office would be vacated or filled. If he, Dr. Ely, could reach the President and implore him to bestow his Christian favor upon a man who had served his country so well, Mrs. Royall could never dislodge the librarian.

Seeking the right time and place to execute his operation, Dr. Ely stayed on in Washington. He had good entry to the White House and he maintained his contact with the Calhouns. As he delved deeper into the problems, he discovered that John Eaton was as important to the matter as Andrew Jackson, since he executed the President's orders. The Calhoun social assault on the Secretary of War-designate and his wife was ripe for Ely's talent.

Dr. Ely knew an opportunity when he had it; young Andrew Jackson Donelson was a marked man from the moment the churchman met him. The young nephew, proud and determined, Andrew Jackson's own namesake, chafed under the great man's shadow. He really held no official position, for Jackson's old friend, Major William Lewis, Eaton's brother-in-law, was the President's official secretary. Dr. Ely reasoned the young man had to be jealous of the influence that the older aides enjoyed. Jack was the young nephew assigned occasional duties, loved but not consulted by his uncle. The churchman knew what to do with such feelings, such sentiments.

It would be no insult to tell Jack Donelson that he was in competition with his uncle's confidants, especially with John Eaton. An aside about Eaton's relationship with Major Lewis, once married to Eaton's first wife's sister,[30] and insinuations about Eaton's second wife, a woman well known to the Donelsons, could help too. The young people had to know the stories about Peg O'Neal as a child from Aunt Rachel, and there could be jealousy. Emily was no match for Peg, and Mrs. Eaton was so close to Andrew Jackson that she could present a problem to Emily. Peg O'Neal Timberlake Eaton was more mature and skilled in political gatherings, and Emily might well fear for her position as White House hostess.

Dr. Ely determined to make excellent capital with these young minds with carefully orchestrated innuendo. He began paying visits to the young Donelsons on a regular basis. The young couple were grateful for his attention, for they were engulfed in the aftermath of the inaugural sweep of the mansion. Restoring order after the chaotic shambles the people had left behind in celebrating Jackson's victory was too much for their inexperience. Dr. Ely assisted them by introducing Colonel Nathan Towson, John Calhoun's friend and appointee, to give aid and financial advice in the matter.[31]

The young Donelsons had been unprepared for the posts assigned them by the President. The duties of running a house had been Aunt Rachel's, and for young Emily to assume them under tragic circumstances made them very onerous. Uncle Andrew mourned for Aunt Rachel, but his young niece wanted to entertain and show off her new position. Emily's growing unhappiness caused Andrew Jackson to relent. Emily would be allowed to hold an open salon for the ladies of the capital. It was not exactly what she wanted, but it was better than sitting alone in a house marked by death. Even her uncle's designation of the women to be entertained did not disturb her. Emily wanted company.

Emily Donelson had a gala. The ladies of Jackson's Washington came to the White House and among them was Mrs. Anne Newport Royall. The aged writer had her first official invitation to the White House. Her friends, the Adamses, had occupied the mansion for four years, but Mrs. Royall had not been included on their invitation lists despite the fact she had been a welcome visitor to the family home in Massachusetts. This recognition from the Jackson family was a bonus from her change in politics, and Mrs. Royall went to the affair to enjoy herself.

Emily Donelson hosted a quiet affair in keeping with the situation of her uncle, but Mrs. Royall did not enjoy it long. Passing among the guests, she glimpsed Dr. Ely standing close to Emily Donelson and, watching his obsequious attentions, she guessed what he was up to before he saw her. Never known for her tact, Mrs. Royall marched up to her young hostess, so bewitched by her premier position among the ladies present; in her forthright manner, Mrs. Royall asked just what such as Dr. Ely was doing in Andrew Jackson's White House.

Emily Donelson was caught by surprise. She did not know the old woman standing before her asking such an impertinent question. Not able to assess the woman's demand as to why she, the niece of Rachel, would receive such as Ezra Stiles Ely, Emily Donelson gave a diffident answer: "Dr. Ely is a very fine man."[32] Mrs. Royall paused. Emily Donelson was young, and with her husband serving as a secretary to the President, they were perfect targets for attempted blackcoat influence. Mrs. Royall did not stay at the White House reception; she marched straight to her Pennsylvania friends in the Congress.

The news that Ely had gained entrance to Jackson's home was a bombshell to the men from Harrisburg. George Kremer was incensed. This new congressman had been Jackson's organizer in Pennsylvania since 1822, and he had no love for Ely and his kind.[33] During the 1824 election, Ely's presses had been busy building the illusion that General Jackson concurred with the Federalists and their philosophy that government was a matter for those God had selected, not the elected. Using Jackson's tenuous affiliation with the Presbyterian Church, certain members of the Monroe cabinet hoped to blunt the growing support for Jackson by presenting him as in favor of the caucus system, which they used to perpetuate themselves in power in order to strip him of the new constituency building against them. It had been George Kremer who had ended this farce. He had addressed an open letter to Jackson asking for his views of those who ruled so with the remnants of the Tories to frustrate the true interests of the people and who claimed he was with them. It was to George Kremer that Jackson had written that had he been in control of the Army, he would have brought the Hartford Conventioneers before courts martial and hung every one of them high on the nearest tree. That letter and its opinion, establishing the Jacksonian position *vis-à-vis* the clerics and those who supported them, had produced the 1824 popular vote for Jackson which the Congress had disregarded in selecting John Quincy Adams. It had also created the landslide for him in

1828 when the people decided to teach Congress a lesson.[34] Mrs. Royall had chosen her contact in the new Congress well: George Kremer had helped her against Ely and his blackcoats in the Pennsylvania Legislature fight. She put the problem to him frankly: Had they misread Andrew Jackson?

George Kremer was appalled at the news of Ely in the White House but he did not believe for a moment that the President sanctioned Ely's presence. The wily churchman had wangled his entrance another way, he was sure. Mrs. Royall had to go at once to John Eaton for an answer, for he was the man most able to do something about this business.[35]

It was good advice, and Mrs. Royall followed it. She was well aware of the growing personal attacks on John Eaton and his wife, and she knew Ely had a hand in it. The Secretary of War would be interested in her news.

John Eaton received Mrs. Royall graciously and she lost no time in telling Eaton of her discovery of Ely at Emily Donelson's White House social. The Secretary was astounded, for Mrs. Royall's news came only a few hours after an incident involving Ely and young Jack Donelson, the President, and the Eatons. John Eaton told Mrs. Royall about it.

He had just come from the White House, having been summoned by Andrew Jackson concerning a most private matter. Jack Donelson had awakened the President early that morning to hand deliver a personal letter from Dr. Ezra Stiles Ely, dated March 17. Coming as it did one day after the President's official birthday celebration,[36] Jackson had opened it expecting one more message of congratulation. What the letter contained had sent the President into a raging temper, and Eaton had been called to handle it.

Dr. Ely had addressed to the President of the United States accusations concerning John Eaton and his wife. The vilifications were similar to those hurled at Jackson and his wife. This affront had roused the General to fury and young Donelson had not escaped his wrath for acting as Ely's delivery boy.

John Eaton's recount of the morning's events did not surprise his visitor. Ely was in the White House and already trouble was upon it; young Donelson deserved to be read out and Emily did too.

John Eaton assured Mrs. Royall that Ely's intrusion would be handled in due time. He had calmed the President and counseled patience. What Mrs. Royall said was true; the young Donelsons had shown lack of judgment in not checking their associates more carefully, but part of the blame lay with Jackson himself. His young relatives had been insulated from the arrows of the last campaign, and when Ely presented himself as a *bona fide* clergyman of their faith, their acceptance of him was understandable. John Eaton did not believe that young Jack knew what was in the letter he carried to his uncle.

Mrs. Royall was skeptical. Surely they had heard the stories going the rounds of the capital. There were enough of the women who carried them in attendance upon young Emily. She did not think Emily kept them from her husband.

John Eaton did not dispute his visitor. He reminded Mrs. Royall that Ely's leadership of a large congregation was a matter to be treated with care. The President had enough problems dealing with the civil authority, and he did not need to incur more controversy in the religious sphere.

Mrs. Royall did not agree. The wily churchman had a history which should interest Mr. Eaton. Ely was a master writer of scandalous stories, and she proceeded to tell Jackson's aide everything she knew about him and his blackcoat press and their role in tarnishing the repute of their opponents. The Ely press made a weapon of gossip and used it too well to be disregarded now.

John Eaton listened carefully to Mrs. Royall's delineation. He already knew some of the details she provided. The Secretary still had those lurid tract societies' products against Andrew Jackson and Rachel in his possession: the coffin hand bills that proclaimed Jackson a murderer, prone to hang young soldiers to satisfy fiendish delight. Eaton had been to see John Binns for an explanation of such obscenities.[36] George Kremer's letter to Jackson and the General's reply had instigated that vile attack, and he knew all about Philadelphia's role in the distribution of that nonsense. Poor John Binns had known poverty so long, watching his children suffer for his services to American independence, that he had capitulated to those who had punished him for that revolutionary success. Mrs. Royall knew about the incident. Being poor was no excuse for such actions, and Dr. Ely was no John Binns.

Mrs. Royall knew more about Ely than John Eaton did. The churchman was not just a spokesman for his religion, the steward of printing and distributing penny tracts and "political" broadsides, but the leader of a curious political movement which shared a strange alliance with Nicholas Biddle and his bank. John Eaton reacted. Mrs. Royall's intimations concerning Biddle's link to Ely was part of a strange chain of command that Eaton, acting as war secretary, had stumbled upon.

To restructure the War Department, Eaton had examined the figures in the ledger books of the war and related departments like the Bureau of Indian Affairs and the Navy Department. It appeared that strange elements were at work in all these offices as well as in the Treasury, and those elements looked very like those described by Mrs. Royall. The writer's blunt assertion that Nicholas Biddle had a financial association with the likes of Ely struck a responsive chord.

Mrs. Royall could hardly contain herself. Was the Secretary interested in Tobias Watkins, or in the Washington Navy Yard as stewarded by Commodore Tingley? Eaton was surprised, for indeed he was. Mrs. Royall expanded on both as well as two other subjects she had been working on.

The Secretary knew about Mrs. Royall's early complaints about the Treasury and her role in forcing Auditor Lee[37] to take a leave of absence the previous year. Adams had filled Lee's chair with Richard Cutts, and Eaton was unraveling that strange circumstance. Mrs. Royall suggested she had information that would interest the Secretary as he expanded his investigation, but she had another more important matter in mind. Had he been following the Watterston affair? John Eaton let her expound.

The Librarian of Congress and his activities were reviewed. Watterston was involved in the tract societies' raids on the public treasury in several ways. Not only had he traded their publishing his books for the library privileges those unworthy Bible pamphlets had received, but he was extending to his benefactors further service which should make him liable for prosecution, or at least removal. John Eaton sat to attention, for Mrs. Royall was telling him something he did not know.

George Watterston had been using his franking privilege, the right of the Librarian of Congress to mail at no cost, to assist his new-found friends. The librarian was distributing tract society publications via the U.S. mails to the entire country, and the United States government was paying for it. Mrs. Royall had been able to have the purchase of the tracts stopped, but she had learned that the franking and free distribution of those publications still continued, aided and abetted by postmasters wedded to the old regime. She hoped that John Eaton would use his auspices to influence new Postmaster General-designate William Barry to stop such illegal use of the mails and to remove those cooperating with this costly raid on the public treasury. She, as a writer-publisher, knew how much money was involved in this scandal, and her anger rose in proportion to the number of tracts mailed at public expense.

John Eaton was amazed. George Kremer had sent Mrs. Royall to see him at just the right time, for she had the information Andrew Jackson needed to reform the Postal Department. Eaton struck a bargain with Mrs. Royall. He did want her help; she was welcome in his office and his home anytime. This invitation began a new friendship, and neither John Eaton nor Mrs. Royall would regret it. Mrs. Royall had shown the Secretary of War the enemy's real face.

Chapter 11

The Eaton Affair

Vice President John Calhoun's procedural maneuvering in the Congress was no secret, nor was his threat to deprive John Eaton the Senate's confirmation of his appointment to the War Department. As the weeks wore on, it became obvious that he would withhold official approval from other appointees of Andrew Jackson as well.

There was a price to be paid for Calhoun's cooperation: Jackson's abandonment of his long-time aide Eaton. The Vice President had planned an audacious assault on the President of the United States.

Andrew Jackson was battle weary, but he was a hard man. He had demanded the replacement of many government workers who opposed his policies, and to suffer such attack from the Vice President was unthinkable. He would not be thwarted by any subordinate, and his appointment of Eaton as his first official adjutant would not be sacrificed.

Official Washington did not believe it. The capital enjoyed the prospect of the confrontation between Eaton and Calhoun and watched the developing strategy of each with intense concentration.

John Eaton was admittedly the weaker. A senator, he had no official position in the administration since his appointment as war secretary had received no confirmation. All knew his strength lay in representing Andrew Jackson, but that surrogation conferred no special powers.

John Eaton had been Andrew Jackson's alter ego for many years. A major in the militia, he had served with Jackson in every campaign the General had undertaken. So trusted was he that in 1815, with the victory over the British at New Orleans, Jackson had selected Eaton as his official biographer, binding both to ever-closer association. As the General swept from Enotochopco through New Orleans, then on to Florida, Eaton never left his side. It was Major Eaton who ordered Jackson's comforts and looked after his finances and land investments, and then was sent forth to blaze the path to national acclaim for the hero. It was Eaton who tasted the intrigue of Congress before Jackson would step foot in it and tramped the eastern states in search of allies for the general's ambition. Last, it was he who returned to Washington to weld the election lines into the resounding Jacksonian victories. [1]

John Calhoun was the stronger but owed his renown to the War of 1812 too. He had not served in any regiment nor fought military battles, but in Congress he had joined with others who espoused the war. These men, not in uniform and far from any battlefield, earned their notoriety with words. After Jackson's victory in New Orleans, John Calhoun was among the new generation acclaimed by the old in Washington. [2]

92

John Calhoun owed his start to his father. South Carolina had sent him to Washington as the youngest man ever elected to the U.S. Congress because he was the son of Patrick Calhoun, its independence leader who, not espousing separation from England, had worked solely for his state, not the country.[3]

Year after year, Calhoun was re-elected to the national legislature. He served James Monroe as secretary of war, a circumstance shrouded in secrecy as Jackson's national fortunes rose. His selection as vice president to John Quincy Adams and then to Jackson was due to complicated politics wherein the old Federalists held the power so the people would not decide and Congress could.[4]

John Caldwell Calhoun in national affairs represented a different constituency from his fellows in the capital. His support in South Carolina was religious and enabled him to treat with Northerners without complaint from his followers. The North in Congress rewarded him with position above that given other Southerners.[5]

John Calhoun had a constant benefactor too: Moses Waddell, Presbyterian preacher who boasted his belief in John Knox.[6]. This man of black cloth and dark forebodings had married John Calhoun's sister and had taken over his young brother-in-law's education. This classic blackcoat first taught the young man at home and then sent him to Yale University for two years to study religion and forensics under Congregationalist tutelage.[7] There, among the men who would frame the Hartford Convention, other clerics molded the young Southerner's mind to Northern needs and interests. In this manner, John Calhoun was taught to walk a well-marked path, and he was assured constant advice as he rose in the national consciousness.

John Calhoun did not directly attack John Eaton. Instead, he turned the task to his wife Floride Colhoun Calhoun, an aging belle from Charleston who had turned her long residence in the nation's capital into personal control of its social life.[8]

Floride Calhoun was a cousin once removed from her husband, and she had brought to the marriage considerable wealth not the product of Calhoun or Colhoun industry, but the result of her father's fortuitous marriage to a wealthy widow. Active in Charleston society, her years in Washington had enhanced her repute as she worked to advance her husband's interests. Known for her piety, she led the capital's Ladies' Tract Society too.[9] Her early February rejection of Peg Eaton's "at home" invitation became full-fledged ostracism as Floride Calhoun took command, allowing her husband to eschew combat in the Senate. Calhoun's friend Ely and a woman were out to make Andrew Jackson choose between affection and support for his friends or the business of the nation. If he insisted upon supporting the Eatons, he would be accused of harboring moral misfits; if he deserted them, he would be deprived of the one man upon whom he depended and would be at the mercy of the Vice President, his intended successor. No matter what the old man in the White House chose, the Calhouns were sure they would win.

The Eaton affair is a matter of recorded history, one of the most bizarre in Washington archives. A cabinet member and his wife were denounced as unfit for social intercourse and denied to their peers in a salon use of libel still curious in tale. The attack on the Eatons, begun by Floride Calhoun in her salons, moved to the records of the nation on March 18, 1829, with the delivery of the letter from Ezra Stiles Ely to Andrew Jackson by the hand of Jack Donelson.[10]

The day had been chosen carefully. Andrew Jackson had allowed his birthday celebration to be moved from March 15, its real date, to March 17 in order to salute his Irish supporters in New York. The Catholic Irish had been celebrating St. Patrick's Day for many years as a deliberate affront to the Roundhead

Protestants from whom they had fled to America.[11] The symbolism in the new Jackson "birthday" was not lost upon the Calhouns or Ezra Stiles Ely.

The Jacksonians planned a gala time. The President put aside his mourning for two hours and raised toasts with his comrades and then retired while the revelry kept Washington awake until the wee hours. Awakening the President early on the morning of March 18, Andrew Jackson Donelson delivered the personal letter from Dr. Ely. In cold, crass malice, the Philadelphia churchman wrote to an Irish President and charged an Irish lass with being unfit to consort with a leader in the American government. Before Andrew Jackson read that letter, the Calhoun cohorts knew the Vice President had carried his combat into the President's bed chamber, for his friend, the most prestigious Presbyterian in Washington, had employed a naked display of his power to summon morality against the chief executive of the United States.

Dr. Ely wrote Andrew Jackson that Peg O'Neal had borne a bad reputation from girlhood, that Mrs. Jackson herself had the worst opinion of her, that Eaton and his wife had enjoyed relations before marriage, and that for the sake of the administration, the credit of the government, and the country, the Eatons could not be countenanced by the good people of Washington nor by Andrew Jackson.[12]

The effect of this letter upon Andrew Jackson can be imagined. It was outrageous that Peg O'Neal, beloved of his wife and himself from her girlhood days, now the wife of John Eaton, was so calumniated, and in the very terms enemies had used against Rachel! As to the man who signed this libel, Jackson knew his stripe well: Ely was one with the fanatics who had intruded upon his life before, attacking Jackson's good friend Pastor Craighead.[13] Ely had dared to invoke his infernal God to threaten the President of the United States and blacken the names of his friends, even as his kind had blackened the sweet Rachel.

Andrew Jackson waited five days to reply to Dr. Ely. Point by point, Jackson refuted the allegations. The President was sure that Calhoun and Clay were behind this base slander and had heard that certain bank personnel and their wives were too. Andrew Jackson would not accept Dr. Ely's insinuations; Rachel had loved Peg and the Jackson White House would be open to her always. John Eaton was his right hand man and would remain so. The President suggested that the preacher get his facts straight, correct his misinformation, and cease his attack. Andrew Jackson put his heart in the final paragraph of his reply. Women were to be protected, not assaulted. "Female virtue is like a tender and delicate flower; let but the breath of suspicion rest upon it, and it withers and perhaps perishes forever." Rachel was on his mind and so was Craighead; in cold calculation Jackson made his final remark, "The Psalmist says, 'The liar's tongue we ever hate, and banish from our sight.' "[14]

Dr. Ely received this letter from the hand of Jack Donelson on the morning of March 24, 1829. That afternoon, Floride Calhoun announced with regret that she could no longer receive Mrs. John Eaton in her home. Since Mrs. Eaton had not visited Mrs. Calhoun, Washington wondered. Mrs. Calhoun kindly cleared the confusion: Dr. Ely had declared Mrs. Eaton to be a fallen woman and the Vice President's lady intended to follow the great churchman's dictates. Floride Calhoun further summoned all women of religious spirit to follow suit. John Calhoun eschewed all responsibility for his wife's actions; the ladies had their own standards, and their religious advisors to sustain them.[15] In truth, however, war had been declared between the Vice President and the President of the United States.

Andrew Jackson kept his silence, but on the first day of April Mrs. John Eaton made the rounds of official Washington and left her card conspicuously displayed in every entry of importance.[16] Capital protocol required that such a visit be returned, and the day chosen for Peg O'Neal Timberlake Eaton's action was significant. If fools some would be, the Jacksonians would know them, and the tally began. Those who stood with Andrew Jackson would return the visit; those who did not would be known for what they were. The battle line had been drawn by the Calhouns and Ely, but the Eatons had crossed it.

The Jackson opponents had not prepared for the open acceptance of their challenge by Peg Eaton. They believed that they had so humbled her that she would be forced into seclusion. Her round of visits astounded them. The woman had not run simpering to her husband, had not hidden behind Andrew Jackson; she had come out into the streets and thrown her gloves and cards at the belle from Charleston. Peg Eaton had taken up the row and blunted Floride's attack. No master stroke of politics here, just another bit of clergymen's and ladies' circle gossip. It was more than Mrs. Calhoun could bear.

Peg Eaton further carried her battle into the confines of Dr. Ely's empire. Mrs. Eaton entered the Second Presbyterian Church, the one ministered by his ally, the Rev. J.N. Cambell, and sat with the President of the United States in a front pew on Sunday. Then, on Monday, she went her rounds again.[17] The hussy had not batted an eye as the blackcoats buzzed with their manufactured scandal about her; a back turned only produced her tinkling laughter. The empty places at her dinner tables were filled with others, mostly men in high places, and Peg Eaton appeared to enjoy it.[18]

Washington City sat paralyzed. John Eaton went every day to the War Department office, more lists ever on his desk. Peg Eaton did not seek succor from the President of the United States; she sat in open defiance with him, unaffected by the disapproval of other, less powerful, women.

The Vice President's wife was beside herself. Floride Calhoun had relied upon Dr. Ely's influence and Emily Donelson had been expected to keep Mrs. Eaton out of the Jackson circle and away from the protecting opinion of Andrew Jackson. Emily Donelson had proved unequal to the task. She had not been able to stand up to her uncle, and any continued intransigence on her part would serve to close the official home to further social functions. Andrew Jackson cared not if his niece entertained; he still mourned Rachel, and if his kin and hers could not respect and honor Rachel's friends, that kin could keep to their silent quarters. If his niece and nephew wished to disregard their uncle's wishes, they were no more than naughty children to a man with far more important affairs at hand. Dr. Ely, as well as Floride Calhoun, found himself powerless in such a situation.

Washington society was shaken. It believed in the Calhouns and their friends, yet Mrs. Calhoun and her social strictures were having no effect, nor was Dr. Ely. Women who had believed in such influences began to doubt them. Mrs. Eaton did not sit at their table and was not a welcome visitor to their homes, but both Eatons still sat with Andrew Jackson in private and in public. It was enough to make a social queen weep with frustration.

Floride's strategy of leaving Peg out of her salons gave Peg the White House. The game became the thing. Peg continued to come and go, leaving her cards, and those who received them knew they were tabulated. Floride Calhoun worked hard to fan her supporters' morale and to keep the innkeeper's daughter in her place, but men appointed to or seeking office had to bow to the beautiful Peg in the White House and then go home to veritable hells with their wives excoriating them for doing so. The strategy backfired. John Eaton was not suffering, but Calhoun's friends were. Andrew Jackson watched them with too much interest. The Calhouns' highly touted battle line had been reduced to a Jacksonian smokescreen.

The Calhoun-Eaton affair had exposed disloyalty in the White House. Andrew Jackson had brought the Donelsons to Washington to augment Jackson solidarity, but the Eaton attack had disclosed that the young Donelsons were not in the Jackson camp. Emily Donelson had joined Mrs. Calhoun and her *clique*, and Jack Donelson was in Dr. Ely's circle. Andrew Jackson had ordered his niece to accept the Eatons and forced the young couple to host events for them, but the child-hostess and the boy-secretary had found their own petulant ways to rebuff the Eatons. Eaton himself had written to Emily Donelson to warn her about heeding certain associates, in particular Ezra Stiles Ely, and Jack Donelson, refusing the hint, had replied for his wife with a rebuff.19 Andrew Jackson's continuing order to receive the Eatons as members of his family only confused the situation more.

All through April, the conflict continued as the capital watched, agog. John Calhoun worked openly with Floride. The mounting tension in the White House began to sap its ability to steward the government, and the Calhouns pressed towards that end. As Mrs. Eaton continued to stand the public assaults alone, criticism began to mount. Andrew Jackson was the President, and what did this nonsense have to do with the more important things at hand? Washington City began to tire of the ridiculous situation.

Floride Calhoun, an elitist from Charleston, could not admit her error; neither could her husband. John Calhoun took little notice of the arguments being raised against his wife's preoccupation. In his mind, Floride had swept Washington society, and Mrs. Eaton was still running about looking for acceptance.

Mrs. Royall was busy with her own affairs during this tempest in the Washington teapot. She noted what was happening, and it confirmed what she had warned against. She knew all about John Calhoun and his associates.

Mrs. Royall had met the Vice President in 1824 while he served as the secretary of war under James Monroe. She had described him in her *Sketches*:

> Mr. Calhoun is quite a young man compared to Mr. Adams and possessed of much personal beauty: he is tall and finely made, neither spare nor robust: his movements are light and graceful, his complexion is dark, his features handsome and animated, with a brilliant black eye: in his countenance all the manly virtues are displayed, overcast with shining benevolence. In his manners, he is frank and courteous. In Washington, as well as elsewhere, Mr. Calhoun is held as a model of perfection.20

By 1828, Mrs. Royall was no longer so complimentary. Vice President Calhoun was involved with some peculiar people and some strange affairs. He had invited a woman blackcoat to preach before a joint session of Congress, and the echoes of that religious tirade in the Capitol's hall still reverberated in Washington.21 That introduction of religion to government had brought about some changes:

> Mr. Calhoun . . . looked much thinner than when I saw him . . . His mind seemed to be turned inward and with placid resignation, without moving a muscle of his face, he kept his eye on the speakers.
>
> I was pained at the sight of his secretary, a gloomy Presbyterian, who looked as though his face was made from the lava of Mt. Aetna!22

Mrs. Royall had little affection for the Vice President now. Lewis Machen was his clerk in the Senate, and she had made complaint about him. The Vice President had not replied.23 The writer had a head for political realities. The Calhouns were riding for a fall, but at the moment, John Branch and his Navy Department interested her more.

The Calhoun-Eaton combat had been a sideshow for Washington society while the Jacksonians had been planning the main event. John Eaton, ringmaster for the administration, had seized upon the lull to accomplish the task demanded by Jackson. He had been busy in his White House office with Jackson while his wife had carried the notice of the city's salons away from the events in the inner circles. The shenanigans concerning the lovely Peg and her acceptability to the elite, as well as Jackson's seeming preoccupation with it, had given Eaton time to set up the administration's next moves.

Chapter 12

Jackson's First Triumph

The Navy Department was of natural interest to those who opposed the old regime in 1829. More money had been poured into that department of government than any other in the federal system, and it did not make much sense. Because American shipping abroad was at its lowest ebb since the Revolution because Britain had denied freedom of traditional Caribbean ports to its former colonists, the phenomenal growth in personnel and funded projects raised many eyebrows. Further, for all the money spent, the United States had few ships upon the seas and few sailors ready for emergency. Even the ships refitted for John Quincy Adams's part in Lord Canning's Western Hemisphere strategy had been allowed to rot for lack of maintenance.[1] The few ships in service had been fitted out not as ships of the line but as ceremonial "couriers" used by ambassadorial retinues, which included officers of the Bank of the United States on the many Adams missions abroad.[2] With Jackson in the White House, these splendiferous vessels were open to review by men who in times of great peril had been made to wait for meager support from Washington while they pursued an active and malevolent enemy attacking the nation within and on its borders.

John Eaton's investigation confirmed Mrs. Royall's observations. The Navy yards were doing no naval work with the funds appropriated. Mrs. Royall had made inquiry of Commodore Tingly in the Washington Navy Yard early in 1827 about the situation, but, as with Watterston, she had been brushed aside. She had included this affront in the *Black Book, Volume III*, with which she had celebrated Jackson's inauguration:

> I did call at the Navy Yard but found little work going on there. A few people only at work in one of the shops and no one to look after them. The Commodore was sick and his wife had to look after him. I sent my name by a servant and this was the answer returned. I asked the servant "if there was any hope of his death" to which he replied with a broad grin.[3]

This comment by Mrs. Royall had been written in early March, but the appointment of John Branch, Calhoun's friend, as Jackson's secretary of the Navy had quieted conjecture. Andrew Jackson apparently was not interested in the Navy or its lack of ships.

The capital circles were wrong. The Navy was a burning consideration, a volcano waiting to explode. John Eaton had done his homework, assisted by an intrepid New Hampshire editor who had been in close communication with

98

Mrs. Royall. Isaac Hill had made good use of the Portsmouth Navy Yard in the 1828 campaign, and Mrs. Royall knew the Washington Navy Yard was going to get the same treatment. Mrs. Royall had taken after the Navy with more than a personal aside about Commodore Tingly:

> But I must go back to my old friend Dr. Watkins . . . he keeps his office in the Navy building . . . . I do not like the company he keeps . . . .

Mrs. Royall had found blackcoats in Dr. Watkins office:

> It is said that he is soon to be hurled to destruction, and that the vessels of wrath are now filling to be poured on his devoted head.[4]

When these words appeared in March, Dr. Watkins, the steward of Navy expenditures at home and abroad, was absent from his post, supposedly visiting other Navy yards and installations in the performance of his duties. But Dr. Watkins was not working out of town, he had taken himself clear out of the country. Washington City knew nothing about this until Jackson sent the name of Amos Kendall, editor, to Congress as his appointment to the post vacated by the fugitive Tobias Watkins.[5]

Watkins' flight was news, but John Calhoun, Henry Clay, and Daniel Webster were strangely silent about it. John Quincy Adams, Watkins's daily riding partner along the Potomac, would not even comment. John Branch, the Navy secretary, moved to take command of Watkins' office but found that Jackson had assigned the mess to Kendall, the proposed appointee. The Jacksonian editor from Kentucky was to replace Watkins, reporting not to the secretary of the Navy nor the Treasury, but to John Eaton and Andrew Jackson. As if this was not enough, Isaac Hill, the Jacksonian anti-bank editor from New Hampshire, arrived in the capital too.[6]

Rumor ran rife in the city, and Mrs. Royall's brief remarks in her inauguration *Black Book* were remembered. The Navy's anonymity for a decade, despite the money at its disposal, was the hot topic in every office and salon. Talk centered on the Washington Navy Yard, the largest employer in the capital. Established to build and repair ships of the fleet, it was a very specialized institution with wood and metal shops, foundries, and all manner of factories needed in ship building and repair. Charges of inefficiency and dispensing favors to sponsors in government and the Congress had been leveled against the yard management in the past, but Congress had a habit of turning a deaf ear to such complaints. The yard was known to enhance congressional offices and homes with fine furniture and brass made by its master craftsmen and had extended these privileges to others too. Accordingly, all complaints were met with a litany of apologies with one main theme: the poor administration of the Washington Navy Yard was a direct result of the necessary rotation of naval officers in charge, an evil to be tolerated since it trained men in the fundamentals of ship work as well as seamanship.

Mrs. Royall, aware of these facts, went on the attack. Rotation of officers! What had this to do with navy yards maintained at such cost, shops without ships to work on? The lady who had exposed George Watterston to view had another *expose*: the wood pews in the Second Presbyterian Church, the blackcoat church, had been made by the navy yard at government expense. It mattered not that it was largess attributed to President John Quincy Adams; Tobias Watkins, the financial steward of the Navy, had no right to approve such illegal expenditures.[7]

Mrs. Royall's charge and the flight of Tobias Watkins unnerved the capital.

The Eatons' morality was nothing compared to this tale. Tobias was in Mexico, and it was rumored that agents of the Bank of England had given him refuge. John Eaton's command of the situation, the selection of Amos Kendall to investigate, and the impossible position of Navy Secretary John Branch only increased the comment. John Calhoun was not in charge, and the pressure mounted against the old regime.

The Jacksonian contingent in the new Congress called for resignations, among them that of Commodore Tingley of the Washington Navy Yard. Calhoun's old cohorts were in panic. Short of the arguments of good repute, they pled for mercy and "Christian charity" while heartbreaking stories of low public salaries suffocated the religious press. It did not matter that few in the United States had salaries at all; no, these public servants had too small salaries, had served the nation for so many years with distinction, and should be allowed lapses. It was Christian to forgive. Was a lifetime of service to be discounted for small derelictions? Men were being prosecuted and persecuted because they had chosen the wrong side in the last election, and if Jackson removed them, he was a man devoid of ideals and heart. Congress rang with speeches from Henry Clay and Daniel Webster to save this man and that, and when such polemics failed, Congress was exhorted to assert its prerogatives against the overweening executive. Congress appropriated money, Congress staffed the government, and Congress should say who would stay and who would go!8

While the old regime in the Congress tried to stay its collapse, Dr. Ely burrowed deeper into the White House. Thanks to the ambition of Jack Donelson and the religious ardor of Emily, the churchman continued to enjoy access to the executive home. The clergyman manufactured his own tales, titillating the women of Floride Calhoun's social circle with excerpts from his letters to the President. Ely intimated that John Eaton had murdered Purser Timberlake by taking Peg as his lover. Timberlake's rejection by his wife and betrayal by his Masonic brother was said to have forced the young man to "commit suicide" in the Mediterranean.9 Ely's newest allegations were trumpeted by that great fellow officer of Jackson, the hero of the Battle of Ft. Erie, Colonel Towson, paymaster of the Army.10 Dr. Ely made it appear that he had enlisted a cohort from the War Department itself—Colonel Towson, an appointee of John Calhoun.

Intimations that Andrew Jackson suffered from mental disorder appeared in the press. The President was neglecting the nation because of family scandal, an abrasion he could end by sending the Eatons packing back to Tennessee. The old man had lost sense of reality when he escorted Mrs. Eaton to church on Sunday with his disapproving family behind him, said reports. Did he not sit without comprehension as the Reverend Campbell extolled those who served the government so well, and then retire to the White House and on Monday serve those same men with notice he wanted their resignations?11 If Jackson had not lost his mind, his opponents were in danger of losing theirs.

Calhoun's friends in the cabinet were in an awkward position. The President pressured them daily for removals to make room for Jacksonians, while John Calhoun exhorted them to stand fast against this. Secretaries Branch and Berrien fell back on their feigned ignorance of offices and duties to deny Jackson what he wanted and to mask direction from the Vice President. They needed expert holdovers to perform tasks, and if the President would not accept that argument, they could complain that certain congressmen would not stand for this one's or that one's dismissal and their departmental appropriations would suffer if they did not heed the desires of Congress.12

John Calhoun took pleasure in the reluctance of the cabinet to accede to Jackson's demands and the Vice President took full credit for it. He led the congressional attack to support his friends in the cabinet. Long oratory was poured forth to salute the very officeholders Jackson wanted out. Those who were not American citizens were saluted for their strong religious and moral sentiments, an attitude more acceptable to government service than citizenship. The religious press expanded this line. Men who served God served the United States of America in better measure than proposed Jackson appointees, backwoodsmen, Masons, followers of the Jackson devil.[13] The hand of Ezra Stiles Ely and the spirits of the Hartford Convention shadowed the Congress. Andrew Jackson's will would be thwarted; his opponents pointed to plans against him directed from meetings said to be in his own White House.

Washington knew all about the young Donelsons. Jack Donelson was a shallow youth, yet it was said that the President allowed him to sit in on the inner circles of the Jackson planning sessions as assistant to Major Lewis.[14] The capital took the view that where there was so much smoke, fire was possible, and more machinations were bred.

John Eaton kept to his purpose: Jackson had demanded Tobias Watkins be brought home. The man had fled to Mexico and exposed his strange alliance. That alliance had a familiar Royall ring to it; Mrs. Royall had written there was a blackcoat presence in Watkins's office, and such import could be the means to break the log jam that Calhoun, Ely, and their blackcoated cohorts had erected against the placement of Jackson's men. The time had come to run rough shod over the opposition, and the elements for surprise were with Eaton. He was not to be deterred by personal attacks.

This was a direct Jackson order. The President had no illusions about familial ties and the young Donelsons, for the arrows slung at beloved Rachel and him had not all come from strange hands. Jackson's cousin, Hugh McGary, had accused him of creeping into another man's bed.[15]

John Eaton moved to get Andrew Jackson what he wanted. Tobias Watkins would be found, brought to Washington, and stand trial in public. The President's anger would be assuaged.

The wrath of Andrew Jackson sears history's pages, for he had a rising passion which left vivid memories of "By the Eternal" thundered out while his face blazed with fire. This was no illusion, but a physical fact, for on the right side of Jackson's face a long, jagged scar, crossed from eye to chin. When Jackson was angered, the scar became red with blood pressure. That scarlet slash reaching into his red hair gave Jackson an aureole that cowed small men with electric effect. The scar was from a saber wielded by a British officer against a boy of fifteen, a prisoner punished because he had refused to black the boots of that British gentleman.[16] Andrew Jackson's youthful agility during the Revolutionary War had saved his head, but he retained an undying hatred of the English which stamped his soul for life.

John Eaton knew how to deal with Jackson's ire, for he had learned from it many times and he made sure he had in hand the means to placate it. Tobias Watkins would arrive in Washington, but the public must be prepared for the revelations to come and what they really meant. It was time for more collaboration with Mrs. Royall.

Andrew Jackson had met Anne Royall ten years before, in 1818, in Melton's Bluff, Tennessee, when he sought the site for the Hermitage.[17] She was evaluating investments as a new widow stewarding her estate. The two began a friendship which had not been destroyed by her support of John Quincy Adams in 1824, but had been renewed by her discoveries, valuable Jackson assets in the campaign of 1828. It was time to forge an open working relationship with the intrepid recorder of all things American. The President agreed to enlist his friend and to aid her as she preached for a cleaning of Washington's Augean stable.[18]

John Eaton summoned Mrs. Royall to do duty and was given the facts. "Uncle Toby" had fled the country not just because of his own tangled accounts but as an agent in foreign transactions which cost the nation millions of dollars and benefited Nicholas Biddle and his bank's foreign connections. Watkins was the perpetrator of a scheme whereby notes against the American treasury found their way into European bank vaults, against American law which prohibited such transfers. The Navy auditor was a financial double-agent serving foreign bankers who snapped up Navy vouchers for "services" to Navy ships in foreign ports, services not justified by the evidence. Vouchers validated by Watkins were converted into escalating calls against the U.S. Treasury, calls used by Nicholas Biddle to effect control of the nation's fiscal policies. [19]

Mrs. Royall understood the mechanics. It was a replay of what she had witnessed in her travels. Mrs. Royall asked only one question. Did the foreign bankers speak in Scots-Irish accents? John Eaton assured her most did, and some spoke in Dutch ones too.

Mrs. Royall took to her usual congressional hustings with more pleasure than ever, and the doors of congressional offices were opened wide for her. Watkins was the password. Everyone wanted to know why Watkins had fled the capital, and Mrs. Royall passed on Secretary Eaton's information. A Pandora's box was opened, and the bottom was about to be exposed. Mrs. Royall did not desert her interest in Watterston in her rounds but coupled his name to Watkins's.

Mrs. Royall was no longer a lunatic in the blackcoat offices, she was a mortal enemy. Her thesis was bearing fruit in the highest circles, and she was asking embarrassing questions not provided by Secretary Eaton. Mrs. Royall had been investigating the peculiar establishment of Watkins's special audit office within the Navy department and his detachment from the treasury; the Navy books were kept separate and apart. This new quest was not yet approached by John Eaton's own review.

Tobias Watkins was the key to Jackson's fortunes. The man had been a Washington fixture for twenty years, the last eight as fourth auditor, but his actual position in the capital was much higher than that. Tobias Watkins was known to be a personal advisor to John Quincy Adams. Further, Navy officers of flag rank paid him respect they paid no one else; some said it was "homage." [20]

Mrs. Royall knew "Uncle Toby" well. She had met him her first year in Washington when her first visits to the Navy department and its yard and shops had been sanctioned and approved by Adams. As a result, Uncle Toby had received her most graciously whenever she entered his precincts, and he had facilitated her accumulation of statistical information for her work. [21] Knowing the difficulties under which she labored and the physical exertion demanded, he would afford her rest and relaxation in his own office. More important than these amenities, Watkins knew about Mrs. Royall's economic difficulties and he did not buy just one book but several, and recommended his friends and subordinates do so too. "Uncle Toby" knew how to make and keep a friend. Mrs. Royall was wooed with appreciation and understanding and given cash as proof of his interest. Perhaps this was insurance for his continued stability.

The election of Andrew Jackson had not ruffled Tobias Watkins. The man had kept a low profile during the campaign, and Mrs. Royall's change in heart towards Adams and her support of Jackson seemingly did not distress the Navy auditor. During 1828 he treated her as always, subscribing to her work, enjoying her visits, and telling her the latest tidbits about the capital. This idyllic arrangement could have continued except for an oversight: Tobias Watkins had employed the son of Mrs. Royall's enemy, John Coyle, and he had not told his friend about it.

For one year John Coyle, Jr., sat in the Navy auditor's office in proper anonymity during Mrs. Royall's visits to "Uncle Toby." The growing controversy concerning the Engine House Congregation and the attacks on John Coyle, Sr., however, suddenly marked Mrs. Royall as the "she devil" for the son too. Young Coyle had to express himself, and in mid-February, 1829, when Mrs. Royall indulged in an impromptu visit with Tobias Watkins, young Coyle found himself face to face with his father's nemesis. Entering the office, Mrs. Royall announced herself to a clerk and expected the clerk to announce her to Auditor Watkins. He ignored her completely.[22]

Mrs. Royall's loud demands to know the young man's name brought Tobias Watkins from his office. Taking her in hand, he led her past the clerk, but Mrs. Royall insisted upon knowing his name. When she heard it, Mrs. Royall looked at her friend with a new interest. "Uncle Toby" could not divert her from that subject even with the best tidbits about Washington. Mrs. Royall demanded an answer as to why he had a blackcoat clerk in his office; how many more did he employ?

Watkins was shaken. With all the charm at his command, he tried to deflect Mrs. Royall's pointed probes. She mentioned West Point, Watterston, and the library affair. Had he forgotten what she had done to Auditor Lee at the Treasury when she had discovered him with those foreign clerks in November? Was "Uncle Toby" enmeshed in strange doings too?[23]

Tobias Watkins never answered Mrs. Royall, for he was involved in a strange financial game. As fourth auditor he did certify invoices for payment, transfers of funds for the entire Navy. The sums were staggering in 1829. American ships spent more money abroad than they spent at home in Navy yards, and that was a fact Watkins did not want exposed. Mrs. Royall, due to a small affront, had stumbled on a forbidden operation.

Tobias Watkins had been busy, under the U.S. Treasury's nose, transferring large batches of Navy vouchers abroad. Covered by seemingly legal bills for ship repairs, inordinate sums were being transferred from treasury vaults to foreign hands. These transfers constituted demands on the United States for payment at any time, and the time could be well chosen to effect or even change policy. Further, the vouchers used in payment for the Navy's "foreign" repairs and maintenance appeared to establish a floating pool of capital beyond the control of the U.S. government but well under the control of the Bank of the United States and Nicholas Biddle. Worse, evidence was at hand that the Bank of the United States had used Navy vouchers, authorized by Tobias Watkins, to facilitate forbidden operations in foreign specie markets in London and Paris, far from the searching eyes of the United States government. It was a cozy operation, a constant procedure, and it had the added advantage to the bank of inflating the amount of money available for foreign purposes, actions forbidden by the bank's charter. Watkins' separate office in the Navy Department and his complete charge of the validation of vouchers for foreign payments had placed those operations beyond Washington's capacity for review. Watkins accounted to the Bank of the United States only, Biddle's bank.[24]

Mrs. Royall left Watkins' office that day with a warning to her old friend. "Uncle Toby" would no longer enjoy her support if he did not answer her complaint. She would take the matter to her new friends in the Congress and demand investigation of his office. She hoped that he was not associated with Ely and Biddle or engaged in another raid on the Treasury, but Watkins's frozen silence sent her forth to do exactly as she had said she would.

The capital learned Mrs. Royall was on the attack again, and her good Pennsylvanians alerted others. John Eaton may have more facts than Mrs. Royall, but rumor attributed Watkins's flight to her visit in February. Mrs. Royall did not deny it.

Watkins' continued absence from his post added to the scandal, and the

Jacksonians found themselves with a great public issue at last. Men in office had been misusing their positions, and Andrew Jackson was correct in demanding resignations. Mrs. Royall had given voice to this fact with Watterston and Watkins, and others recalled Lee. She was becoming the battering ram with which the Jackson mob could beat on the gates of government. Mrs. Royall had become a dangerous reformer who had made her pen into a skewer, piercing her opponents. God only knew how many more unpleasant surprises she had corked in her ink bottle.

Tobias Watkins had few defenders in the capital. Calhoun, Clay, and Webster did not raise their voices in compassion for him and neither did his old friend, John Quincy Adams. Only Dr. Ely tried to assist him in the hushed circles he frequented.

As the Watkins affair grew, John Eaton sat in his War Department office, seemingly unconcerned about it. The secretary of the Navy, John Branch, said nothing, and John Berrien, the attorney general, was the only ally John Calhoun could command. Berrien had to block the removal of Tobias Watkins from Mexico no matter what Andrew Jackson demanded.[25]

Andrew Jackson sat in his White House receiving his daily reports. He had his first triumph in hand, and it would give him the means to take the government and make it his. He was grateful to his adjutant, John Eaton, and regarded Anne Royall with respect. She had been right, and the nation would witness a final battle between those who believed they were ordained to govern and those elected to do so. The American Republic was emerging from behind the sham curtain drawn by the old Virginia aristocracy pursuing their new kind of Divine Right, joined by the old Tories from Philadelphia and Hartford. They were no match for Andrew Jackson, John Eaton, and the aged writer Anne Newport Royall.

Chapter 13

The Collaborators

Although Tobias Watkins was a top priority for the Jackson administration, the capital was unconcerned with the affair. Watkins was beyond reach while the President was not, and new rumors about him excited Washington salons.

Andrew Jackson was a sick man.[1] The excuse of mourning for Rachel had been overdone; the old man was in his bed and not from grief. John Eaton and crowd ran the government because Andrew Jackson could not, and a regency was in the making. Suddenly John Calhoun again was the man of the hour, and John Eaton a growing shadow. It was an anonymity Eaton welcomed.

The President had given the order to repatriate Tobias Watkins, and it had to be a quiet operation. John Calhoun and his friend John Berrien had formed a partnership to prevent it, hiding behind mountainous legalities. The Attorney General could not find a legal rationale to retrieve Watkins to accomplish what the President wanted.

Tobias Watkins's rumored refuge, Mexico, was a haven for a man on the run in 1829. Mexico was a country in upheaval. The spirit which had produced revolution to establish the United States of America was working south of its borders among the *criolles* and Indians. Mexico was in the throes of not one rebellion but a dozen, all going on at once and led by different leaders. There was no single government with which to deal for Watkins. Tobias Watkins could keep going from city to city south of the border forever, protected by the lack of government and supported by those who paid him in exile. Joel Poinsett, the American minister to what constituted the recognized government of Mexico in Mexico City, could not transfer that representation to any other area without jeopardizing his position in Mexico City.[2] John Berrien, Jackson's attorney general, made the most of this argument and John Eaton was powerless to force the issue. It appeared that Tobias Watkins could stay in Mexico forever.

The Secretary of War was a man of action; he knew how to take matters into his own hands. He was no stranger to bureaucratic red tape, road blocks, or extralegal dealings. Florida had been a very good training ground for him, and Eaton could draw upon that experience for this affair.

Mexico and Spain were embroiled in that constant dance of rebellion and pacification which ultimately produces a new nation. The intricacies of such maneuverings occupied both countries, and the United States could consider other measures.

The growing illegal and uncontrollable situation in Mexico itself was an invitation to covert moves from Washington. All that was needed was the dedicated personnel to accomplish them, and John Eaton knew just the personnel to do what had to be done.

American David Porter, an impetuous seaman who had made his heroic mark
in both the War of Independence and the War of 1812, had become the acknowledged master of the Caribbean. Like Andrew Jackson himself, he was no man to
sit out "orders" when the flag of the United States was at stake. The honor of
the nation he loved came first at all times, and, like Jackson, he had chastised
those who scoffed at the United States. In Fajardo, Puerto Rico, he had gone
ashore and forced Spanish authorities to apologize for summarily abusing the
rights and privileges of American seamen in that port. For his act he had received a six-month suspension from his naval assignment ordered by his enemies
in the Navy Department in Washington. Porter had resigned his commission
rather than accept "punishment" from those he held in disrespect. As a consequence of that resignation, he had been offered a post to establish the Mexican
Navy by those who had taken charge of Mexico's revolution. Commodore David
Porter, U.S. Navy, became admiral of the Mexican fleet with all rights and privileges thereof. He was a personal friend and a brother Mason to both Eaton and
Jackson and half of the Mexican revolutionaries.[3]

John Eaton, relying on David Porter, with a great assist from Joel Poinsett,
minister to Mexico, Grand Master of the Mexican Yorkite Lodges of Masonry,
bypassed the attorney general of the United States, the secretary of the navy,
and many Mexican governments, *de jure* and *de facto*, and outwitted his enemies.
What legal representation could not effect, Masonic brotherhood did, and there
were no language barriers. The men who thought they had Tobias Watkins
safely stashed away, supported by an odd collaboration between bank, Bible
society, and foreign partners, woke one Monday morning in mid-April and discovered Tobias Watkins was in Philadelphia on his way to Washington for public
arraignment for crimes committed against the American state and people. Tobias Watkins had been "repatriated" from his haven by a special detachment of
Americans led by David Porter, Jr., and David Porter, Sr., and Joel Poinsett had
each had a hand in it. The news of Watkins's arrival in the United States and the
announcement of his anticipated examination and imprisonment threw capital
offices into an uproar and Philadelphia into a state of muted shock.[4]

John Eaton had delivered for Andrew Jackson again. Tobias Watkins had
been taken out from under the noses of his supporters, sailed back to the United
States in an extralegal action which defied the most astute diplomatic minds,
and there was nothing anyone could do about it. The effect was immediate.

The first reaction was to cry out about the way in which Watkins had been
repatriated, but the man was a fugitive from justice and no manner of law could
erase that fact. Further, the Watkins affair had a far deeper implication to inner
Washington circles. On the surface, Watkins the man was being blamed for setting up a system of voucher payments which enabled him to write checks without proper authorization for all manner of naval needs. These checks, bearing
the legal imprimatur of the United States, had become a fluid device for transferring large sums of money, without cash, both in the United States and abroad.
To raise an issue concerning the manner of Watkins's repatriation would only
raise other questions about those involved with him. The Jacksonians would
raise those questions soon enough, and the wise course dictated no outcry; time
was very important to all concerned.

The United States had Tobias Watkins, and it had a modicum of evidence
with which to try the former fourth auditor. Jackson's government had been
unable to locate the large vouchers circulating in Europe but was endeavoring to
locate those in the branch offices of the United States Bank. It had been unsuc-
cessful so far. Watkins' initial flight had alerted the bank and its managers, and
the records were not available. All the government had were three vouchers
issued under Watkins's direction. Two had found their way into Tobias Wat-

kins' own account: the first one was for the sum of $750 and the second was in the amount of $300. The third one was for $2,000 and had been seized enroute between bank offices, but the bank and the Navy Department were contending that one mistake did not make a crime. John Eaton and Andrew Jackson knew otherwise, and so did their enemies.[5]

Tobias Watkins's arrest and imprisonment cast a pall over Washington. He was a time bomb controlled by the Jacksonians, and the future was unclear. The Jacksonians were on the march against the carefully structured edifices erected against political changes by the remnants of the old and discredited Federalists. The idea that the equality of men could be amended to a cliché that certain men were more equal than others had run its course. Further, the new limiting factor, money, which produced the new aristocrats, nurtured them, organized them, and enabled them to control and manipulate others had to go. That included the new religion, new Presbyterianism, its religious perversion which made a virtue of the accumulation of money and material success and judged man's piety by his ability with both. The unholy triumvirate of politics, religion, and finance was in danger of exposure.[6]

Mrs. Royall sat amidst these swirling currents like a priestess presiding at her own rite. She had recorded the scene like the oracle at Delphi and many came to rejoice with her. Mrs. Royall's defense of Masonry, her assault on the booksellers, her attacks on the blackcoats, and her questions about Biddle and his banks all came together in the cases of George Watterston and Tobias Watkins. Something tremendous was involved and the dimensions were being recorded for the first time.

Tobias Watkins had provided the measure of the real opposition to Andrew Jackson. Watkins, in prison with a grand jury convening, and those who opposed Andrew Jackson found themselves alone. The Jacksonian deluge was upon them. Andrew Jackson had told his supporters to go to the office they wanted and search out the miscreants, for the President was ready to approve any removal for cause.[7] Mrs. Royall had been joined by an army of hopefuls, and every morning as the office holders sat to their work someone would be surveying their work.

Washington City, caught in this game of political chairs, overlooked the main issue: the control of not just the government but the money power of the United States. The Federalists had manufactured a control of the nation's flow of cash insulated from the popular will and masquerading as government authority: the Bank of the United States, in which the money of the nation was deposited and stewarded not by elected officials, but by appointees beholden only to themselves. This bank had been established, dismantled, and then re-established as Federalist fortunes had waxed and waned and waxed again.[8]

The issue was money. The Federalists held that the wealth of the country should be separate from government as a balance against destructive democracy. The Jacksonians, like the Jeffersonians before them, believed that the nation's wealth belonged to the people, who should use it for the public good. Neither side denied that it belonged to the nation; the contention lay in who would command the treasure and how it could be kept inviolate from unreasonable demand and bad investment. The Federalists put their faith in men who had proven their dedication, their protection of such wealth, the Jacksonians preferred those elected to protect the nation. One side believed in the tightening of the Republic, the other in the broadening of democracy; a stalemate had ensued.[9]

Andrew Jackson had won his presidency but not the stewardship of the nation's gold; his foes still held it. The government was run by the transfer of gold and silver, and that exchange was in the hands of men appointed, most of them for life. The Bank of the United States was the legal depository of all the nation's money, as established by Congress, and its charter was still in force.

The growing attack on government officeholders and appointees, signaled an assault upon the bank. Nicholas Biddle could stay in Philadelphia no longer. The situation in the capital and the implications of the Watkins affair pried him loose from his self-designed Greek temple to money power and sent him into the field to captain his troops. He arrived in Washington to use his personal power to counter the stated policies of the President of the United States.[10]

Biddle's arrival caught his friend Ezra Stiles Ely unprepared. The churchman, preoccupied with his White House machinations, had neglected his congregation, and the clerks in the government were in peril. John Eaton had not been deterred by Ely's actions. The clergyman worried about Biddle's reaction.

Dr. Ely was a wily man. He counted his advantages. He had John Calhoun and his wife as support, Colonel Towson as an ally, and had recruited Jack and Emily Donelson. He was in communication with Andrew Jackson. Who else in the great empire wedded to the bank could produce such evidence of earnest activity in behalf of the cause? Biddle would be convinced that Dr. Ely had delivered while others Biddle had trusted had not.

To prepare his report for Biddle, Dr. Ely reviewed his latest actions in regard to the Eatons. He intended to enlarge his accusations, to charge John Eaton with having had Peg O'Neal Timberlake as his mistress for many years, having gotten her with child and then, concurring in an abortion, paying her husband to keep his mouth shut. This would be his next reply to Andrew Jackson's courteous rebuff. Dr. Ely was determined to effect the dismissal of the Eatons from Jackson's council, and he believed Nicholas Biddle could not find fault with that.

The churchman had enlisted Calhoun's trusted aide, Colonel Towson, in his venture, as well as his representative in Washington, the Reverend J.N. Campbell, pastor of the Second Presbyterian Church. Both men would provide testimony, and Colonel Towson had found one man to personally witness Peg's looseness with men. Colonel Towson had enlisted Richard K. Call, an early adjutant to Jackson and John Eaton who had used that position to aid his rise in life.[11] In 1829, he was General Call, a rank which resulted from his previous service in Florida with Andrew Jackson and then as his successor. General Call was no longer a true friend to the Jacksonians, first because of his financial commitments to the Bank of the United States and second, as the new assistant to Colonel Towson in the disbursement of Army funds, and third, because he had been thrashed roundly by John Eaton after an attempt to force his affections upon Peg O'Neal Timberlake during his brief residency in her family's establishment. This enlistment of Richard K. Call forced Jackson to take a sterner view of the Ely correspondence. Accordingly, the President no longer played with Ely in private letters but spoke publicly concerning General Call and the fact that he had never intimated such charges before, despite innumerable opportunities to do so. President Jackson could muster many of Call's former associates to corroborate this fact.[12] Jackson's disavowal of Call came to Nicholas Biddle's attention.

The banker from Philadelphia was a most astute man. It was obvious that his friend, Dr. Ely, was on dangerous ground. The enlistment of Colonel Towson and then General Call was an invitation to more trouble. The Army Paymaster and his assistant were not to be involved, not after the Tobias Watkins affair. Dr. Ely was to cease and desist with his line of attack and turn his attention to other problems.

Nicholas Biddle had heard about Mrs. Royall and her activities, even in Philadelphia. After Harrisburg, he had been watching her carefully. It was time to blunt her attacks and her criticisms. Biddle knew her personally and had dealt with her when she had been curious about the policies and personnel of the bank in Baltimore. Then he had been able to calm her fears.[13] It was time to approach the writer again.

Dr. Ely did not agree with his old friend. That Royall woman was a nasty hag who had a capacity for continually making trouble, and to meet with her would only give her more recognition. She should be ignored and ostracized. He had prevailed upon the young Donelsons to deny her the White House.

Nicholas Biddle could not convince Ely that Mrs. Royall should be wooed, that a helping hand should be extended to ease her poverty and her uncertain situation. The banker decided to try his own hand with the matter.

Mrs. Royall knew about Biddle's arrival in the capital, for the city talked of nothing else. Changes were in the offing. The new treasury secretary, Samuel Ingham, was said to be most unhappy and despairing at his impossible situation in the maneuverings about him. He had failed to gain Jackson's confidence in the Watkins affair. There was talk of his resignation, and wild rumors circulated as to his successor.

Mrs. Royall kept her ears tuned to any news about banker Biddle, and when the story began to circulate that Biddle would propose Ezra Stiles Ely as a replacement for Samuel Ingham,[14] she did not dismiss it but determined to see Biddle himself about it. The idea of the churchman moving to the treasury post was not farfetched to a woman who knew his part in the money power the bank wielded. Ely was now more a financier than a preacher, for his charitable societies had evolved into savings and acceptance groups with large sums of money which he personally controlled.

Mrs. Royall went to see Biddle. As she addressed the nation's first banker, she was well aware of political double dealing and after her experience with Adams, she did not dismiss the possibility for Jackson. The President could have been enticed into a bargain to get his new administration going and his appointments confirmed, and Ely was also John Calhoun's good friend.

The banker and the writer had an in-depth talk about the interests they shared and those they did not. Ezra Stiles Ely was their immediate preoccupation and introduction, but the bank was the real subject. Biddle hoped to impress upon Mrs. Royall the importance of the financial entity he captained and the necessity of its position as a separate and distinct authority apart from the government of the United States. He moved to blunt her opposition, but a wall was between them. Ely the man submerged the bank.

Mrs. Royall recorded the meeting.[15] Even as she spoke with Biddle, she had the notion that he was doing with her what had been done with George Watterston. She was not wrong. Nicholas Biddle sought to influence Mrs. Royall with his charm and the importance of his friendship. It was a good try; never once did Biddle make the mistake of talking down to the perceptive woman before him. The aged writer was a good candidate for what he had in mind, and yet he did not abuse her. Nicholas Biddle, a writer himself, had great compassion for the old woman before him. She understood the nation and its currents as well. Anne Newport Royall deserved more than she had received from her fellow countrymen. Mrs. Royall had to concur.

Nicholas Biddle paid his visitor the proper compliments. Mrs. Royall did understand the processes and directions of the bank and that knowledge was appreciated by the bank. Such ability to expound on finance could be very beneficial for those who used it wisely. It was a veiled suggestion, but Mrs. Royall knew exactly what Nicholas Biddle meant.

The old woman liked the man. Biddle was a charming rascal and a gentleman, but Biddle was less Mrs. Royall's concern than was Ely. Why did Biddle parade his friendship for that blackguard, that blackcoated magpie? For what reason did he lend his remarkable position and reference to such as Ely? The churchman was a scourge, a traitor who wanted to scuttle the whole fabric of the American government. For what reason did Biddle allow his name to be coupled with Ely's in any enterprise?

Nicholas Biddle could not charm himself out of Mrs. Royall's pointed questions concerning his relationship to Ely. He had to admit Ezra Stiles Ely had been his friend since his Princeton days and was his friend now. As for religion, churchmen often were carried away with thoughts better left unsaid, and he did not espouse everything Ely said. However, it could not be disputed that the man had been a galvanizing leader for the Presbyterian Church and was doing great works with its many societies. The very doctrine of thrift taught so well by its many publications had been most beneficial to the country, the people, and the bank, and those things had to be weighed in the balance. Mrs. Royall had to consider Ely and Biddle's friendship in that light, not as their enemies would picture it.

Their enemies! Mrs. Royall was Ely's enemy. Biddle was asking her to re-think everything she knew, discard it, and follow a line she knew to be untrue. If Ely was such a friend to Biddle and Biddle such a friend to Ely, both were the other's measure and neither was for her. Mrs. Royall thanked Nicholas Biddle for his kind expressions of appreciation for her work, but she had done quite well for herself so far and she would continue to be her own person. Mrs. Royall had one last query for the banker from Philadelphia. Was he really supporting Dr. Ely for a position with the U.S. Treasury? Nicholas Biddle knew when to be frank and honest with an equal opponent. He told Mrs. Royall no.

The president of the Bank of the United States had failed to woo Mrs. Royall to his side. He had not been able to do with her what lesser men had done with the likes of George Watterston and Tobias Watkins. Mrs. Royall could not be bought with charm, dollars, or the promise of instant success. In a way, Biddle, the literary dilettante, sympathized with the old woman. She was a remarkable piece of work. She had created herself and he respected that creation. Biddle's personal inclination was to let her be; others would not agree, but for the moment, Nicholas Biddle controlled the scene.

Mrs. Royall's visit with Biddle left her unshaken in her beliefs. Further, she had gained what she had sought. Dr. Ely was no contender in the treasury sweepstakes and she had established the definite connection between Biddle and Ely. Their collusion was in Ely's many acceptance and collecting societies and the monies they controlled. They were all in Biddle's bank, and he placed much reliance upon them. Neither Biddle nor Ely would be happy with where Mrs. Royall's discovery would lead in the weeks to come! The indomitable old woman had a new crusade to pursue. She had transformed her discovery of the alien control of the new American presses, the confusing blizzard of religious literature, and the obvious distribution of foreign ideas at the expense of American ones into a theory which the Jacksonians would accept and project.

Mrs. Royall's charges of conspiracy and treachery were no demented squeals to men of revolutionary tradition. They knew the effect of cabal and the basics of their history had taught them what excesses tyrannical religion could produce. When Mrs. Royall stated that men who preached the Kingdom of God were guilty of treason, men of reason believed her, for the Inquisition was still alive in their minds and no amount of Bible waving could dismiss it. The shadowy figures of prejudice and hatred which had defiled Andrew Jackson and his followers were real enemies with names and faces. Mrs. Royall did not hesitate to identify them: the Elys, the Biddles, the Beechers, the Blacks, the Waddells, the clerics of the Hartford Convention, and more importantly, their alien servants, the immigrants of the last decade, Britain's disbanded regiments in civilian clothes massing in the Washington offices of the American government. Nicholas Biddle had been correct in assuming Mrs. Royall's talent. The writer had not only discovered the dangerous game and its players, but she was at work to produce a counterforce to it. None of the collaborators were safe.

Chapter 14

God, Man, and Mammon in Washington

The grand jury convened on the first of May, 1829, in Washington. Its first task was untangling the affairs of Tobias Watkins and his office as fourth auditor, and hearing the charges the government would bring forth.

From the onset, it was acknowledged that the government would seek to widen the Watkins affair. There was enough evidence to indict Watkins, but Jackson's forces intended to extend the public investigation into who had so enlarged Watkins's prerogatives that the crime had been done, how it had been done, and why.[1] The new administration wanted to move to trial with a broad-based attack on the people and the system they had devised. It was an obvious move to effect the personnel and policy changes the Jacksonians sought, and it mustered spontaneous opposition to reduce the Watkins case to a simple charge against a simple criminal, thus ending all ramifications and insinuations. The case would not be in the hands of the government prosecutors alone but in the courts of judges who were holdovers from the old regime, most Federalist in theory and practice and following policies not welcome in the Jackson climate but unassailable in their legal refuges.[2] The Watkins case could be made a battle between judges and the people.

John Eaton was in charge of the Jacksonian attack. He had made the decision to keep Watkins out of the courts as long as it took to build a case not against the man, but against the system which corrupted him. He knew the courts would not be cooperative but that the new national press would, especially those editors who were masonic brethren. Biddle and Calhoun could have their Washington office holders, but John Eaton would enlist Jacksonian editors like Amos Kendall and Isaac Hill.

Amos Kendall signed on first. Watkins's desertion of his office in February left a position to be filled, and before Washington knew what was happening, Kendall had been proposed and confirmed.[3] With his help, John Eaton organized the Watkins case, building public opinion for a full-scale review of the financial shenanigans in the Navy auditor's office and his connection to the Biddle bank and its foreign operations. To that end, a remarkable series of letters were directed from Watkins, in custody, to his former superior, Samuel Southard, Adams's intimate.[4] Seeking to establish his defense, Watkins requested that Samuel Southard confirm certain of his instructions to Watkins regarding Navy vouchers, their distribution, and their use. Samuel Southard, an active politician in New Jersey, kept his distance from Washington and denied any role in the affair, but the disclosure of his strange sequence of position in the Adams administration raised questions.

112

Samuel Southard, a senator from New Jersey, had arrived in Washington in the Monroe administration.[5] His entrance had been prepared by his friend, Nicholas Biddle, and his first cabinet position had been as secretary of the Navy. In that capacity, he had established the system which had brought Tobias Watkins into the Navy Department and given him extraordinary authority over funds and expenditures. Southard had maintained his Navy position in the Adams administration and, in a sudden switch, had been appointed secretary of the treasury, a position he held for only two months in 1825. During those months, however, he effected the complete separation of the fourth auditor to the Navy. Southard then returned to the Navy secretary position and continued to administer that department until once again, in 1828, he was appointed secretary of war for a few weeks. He promptly appointed Colonel Nathan Towson as paymaster of the Army, with authority over Army funds to match that of Watkins' over Navy funds. In this capacity, Southard had served out the last few months of John Quincy Adams' regime.[6] The whole sequence was a most peculiar circumstance, and John Eaton and Amos Kendall intended to draw public attention to it by giving the review to Isaac Hill, the Jacksonian editor from New Hampshire.

Isaac Hill was asked to join the Jackson administration as second officer of the treasury. He had impressive credentials for the post. What the Jacksonians were trying in the Watkins affair, Hill already had done in a similar matter involving the Portsmouth Navy Office and the Portsmouth branch of the Second Bank of the United States.[7]

The selection of Amos Kendall as fourth auditor had bypassed John Branch, secretary of the Navy, and not one question had been raised. Without consultation with Samuel Ingham, secretary of the treasury, Isaac Hill was appointed as his second in command, replacing Auditor Lee.

Isaac Hill accepted the Jackson post; his newspapers gleefully trumpeted the relationship of his appointment to the Watkins affair. His name was presented to the Senate for confirmation. With Amos Kendall in Watkins' old office in the Navy Department, combing the books, and Isaac Hill to sit in the Treasury surveying that department's records, John Eaton had created an attack which left no further room for speculation. A full-scale assault was readied on the private manipulation of power that the last of the Federalists had hoped would carry them through these difficult days, an assault upon the links of the Treasury of the United States with the Second Bank of the United States.

The anti-Jacksonians regrouped on the Senate floor, led by the Vice-President. They determined that Isaac Hill would not sit as second controller of the United States. John Calhoun mobilized not only those who hated Jackson but those who detested Hill himself. Isaac Hill, publisher, a homely man twisted in frame who wielded a taunting pen, had twisted many a senator's nose. As his name was intoned before the Senate, Calhoun and his cohorts opposed Hill.[8]

Isaac Hill was a self-made man. He had taught himself to read and write, and by apprenticing to a printer he had acquired his further skills. A tough man, he had been saddled with physical difficulties from birth which would have submerged a lesser spirit. From his hard experience, Hill had evolved his own philosophy: Words meant little to a man accustomed to placing them in any context needed; actions were the things to be recorded. Early in his newspaper career, Hill had formed an aversion to the likes of John Quincy Adams, Daniel Webster, and John Calhoun.[9] The man who had come up the hard way disliked the self-assumed and self-confirmed aristocrat.

His solid alignment with the people had enabled Hill to build a small newspaper into a large publishing group which spilled over the borders of New Hampshire into the neighboring states of Maine, Massachusetts, and Vermont. Hill's empire was born in the areas most contaminated by the blackcoat press.

Isaac Hill had gained national fame with an *exposé* his papers had promoted in 1827.[10] He had uncovered a raid on the U.S. Navy Department's funds accomplished by the collaboration of local naval officials with the manager of the Portsmouth branch of Nicholas Biddle's bank. This money drain had been revealed because work at the Portsmouth Navy Yard, the main support of small businesses in the area, had come to a virtual halt in 1826, causing severe economic stress to the region. Investigating the situation, Isaac Hill had discovered that the money allotted to the Portsmouth naval facility had not decreased but was flowing in different directions. While ships rotted, pension payments had increased, and although the total expended by the facility appeared to be the same, the end result was not. Hill and his men had stumbled upon a clever cash flow diversion which effected the transfer of naval funds from government accounts to the Portsmouth Bank of the United States for pensions for deceased or fictitious persons. All was certified by naval officials. This cash flow had been carefully kept from view by a strange alliance between the bank and certain Washington officials, with a large assist from the Portsmouth naval offices. The trail of this skullduggery and the skill with which it was effected led directly to the manager of the Portsmouth branch bank, Richard Cutts, brother-in-law of James Madison, and to his subsequent indictment and dismissal.[11] This curious parallel to the Watkins case had produced the issue with which the Jacksonians had campaigned in New England against Adams and his coterie.

Isaac Hill, with the creation of a political issue, had taken the Portsmouth Navy Yard scandal and accomplished an invasion of the New Hampshire Legislature, stampeding that body into demanding that Congress force changes in the bank management in New Hampshire. These were changes which Nicholas Biddle did not want. To offset Hill's attack, Biddle had resorted to open dealings with his minions in New Hampshire and in Washington. He had blunted Hill's attack by getting Richard Cutts transferred to Washington. The man who had denigrated his connection to James Madison, former president of the United States, and was under indictment for criminal conspiracy, had been rewarded with the post of second comptroller in the treasury; he had milked out of millions. Richard Cutts sat in the post as Isaac Hill's name was proposed for the same post.[12] Hill's appointment was a cut with a double-edged sword.

Nicholas Biddle had entered into other curious arrangements in the Portsmouth affair. He had tried to destroy Isaac Hill and the Portsmouth businessmen associated with him. The Biddle bank had called loans and denied capital to those who supported Hill.[13] That issue was still smoldering and the sudden alliance between Kendall and Hill, under John Eaton's direction, raised the flames again.

Nicholas Biddle thought himself clever enough to direct the counterattack on Hill personally. His whole life was the result of his ability to affront and intrude where lesser men would not, and his very entrance into banking proved it. A man of letters with no training in finance, he had traded writing for banking in the Pennsylvania Legislature by trading ideas and votes.[14] The young man who knew how to use a pen had learned to figure with it in sums so staggering that no one was his equal in 1829. That power was Biddle's corrupter; he had come to fear no one, and he did exactly what he wanted when he wanted. This time was no exception.

Nicholas Biddle decided to gain control of the greatest voice in the United States Senate, to cement Daniel Webster to his enterprise. He had begun this by offering the management of the Portsmouth branch of the bank to Daniel Webster to confer upon whomever he pleased. Senator Webster had accepted this gift and assigned the lucrative post to his law partner, Jeremiah Mason.[15] The

Senator, known as the conscience of New England, had trumpeted to the world that God had rewarded him with yet another sign of his approval by harnessing Biddle's gold to his political wagon.[16]

Great men have great price, and Nicholas Biddle did not try to humble Webster; he offered him an open draft for any sum the Senator from Massachusetts might require. The bargain was struck as the debate on Isaac Hill's nomination began. The banker wanted assurance that the great voice would not indulge in any "expedient" change of heart, no matter the heat in the Senate chamber.

Daniel Webster did not think twice about accepting Biddle's new offer; he thought it was due him. He had a monumental ego, and God had confirmed him for this world and the next once again. Not even Nicholas Biddle's snide limitation deterred the man from Massachusetts. The banker placed no limit upon the amount of money Webster could draw from the bank save that of his, Biddle's, personal approval.[17] Daniel Webster became what Anne Newport Royall would not: vassal to Nicholas Biddle.

Biddle, having assured himself the control of the best voice in the Senate, moved on to the Treasury. Samuel Ingham was his next mark.

The capital had a very poor opinion of the secretary of the Treasury, even though his past association with John Calhoun had given him immediate confirmation. Biddle's offhand suggestion of a successor, Dr. Ely, and the selection of Isaac Hill without his approval had relegated the man to the status of nonentity. Samuel Ingham publicly acknowledged that he wished he had never come to Washington.[18]

Ingham had received his appointment to Jackson's cabinet for services rendered to the 1828 Jackson cause in Pennsylvania. A former supporter of Calhoun in the presidential sweepstakes, he had supported Jackson as Calhoun's fortunes waned, using his small printing operation to bolster Jackson's campaign.[19] As a result, the Jacksonians had raised no objections to his elevation to cabinet rank, for they acknowledged that he had contributed to Jackson's victory in Pennsylvania. It was not until the capital's preoccupation with the development of the Eaton attack that any questions arose about Ingham's loyalty. His unwillingness to take sides in the growing controversy caused Jackson and Eaton to leave Ingham in his post but take into their own hands full control of the patronage in the Treasury Department. Isaac Hill's selection without consultation with Ingham had resulted.

The Secretary of the Treasury needed a friend, and suddenly Nicholas Biddle appeared at his side. Isaac Hill became the wedge Biddle drove deep between Ingham and Jackson. Biddle had a bonus in hand. Samuel Ingham need have no future worries, for no matter the outcome of the battle being mounted on the Senate floor, his previous business background was infinitely valuable. The implication was not lost upon the businessman who found himself disenchanted with Washington political life. Samuel Ingham was enlisted to the bank's side, right under the noses of Andrew Jackson and John Eaton.[20]

The Senate of the United States met to consider the appointment of Isaac Hill as the second comptroller of the United States following the ouster of Richard Cutts. Daniel Webster led the attack. His great voice filling the chamber was met by the greater voice of Thomas Hart Benton of Missouri but Isaac Hill was not confirmed. John Calhoun seized the moment to adjourn the Senate, leaving Jackson with his appointees unconfirmed, including John Eaton.[21]

Nicholas Biddle had triumphed. The President of the United States had been handed a catastrophic setback. He had the government, but it was a rump one. With reckless abandon, Jackson's enemies gleefully quoted the words of Hill himself as they served up this unprecedented political insult to the new president:

You may say to all our anxious Adamsite friends that the barnacles will be scraped clean off the Ship of State. Most of them have grown so large and stick so tight that the scraping process will doubtless be fatal to them; but it can't be helped. Just add them to Zeke Webster's and Jerry Mason's list of "Jackson's Murders." 22

Jackson had the ship of state, but he had no crew to scrape those barnacles, and Daniel Webster, John Calhoun, and Nicholas Biddle had seen to it. With Hill's and other appointments unconfirmed, Samuel Ingham was safe to come out in open rebellion to Andrew Jackson and his long-time friend, John Calhoun, celebrated it.

A new Ingham paraded on the Washington scene. The old Federalists rallied around, praising him. Calhoun promised him complete command, and nothing would diminish his authority, not Watkins, not Portsmouth, not John Eaton, not even the President of the United States. Ingham alone would determine matters concerning his department and the Bank of the United States.

Ingham issued an open challenge to Andrew Jackson, stated in terms to please Nicholas Biddle. He complimented the bank and insisted that the anomalies under review were done by individuals removed. Ingham asserted he would take direction from no one but would consult with Andrew Jackson. Even as he said that, he questioned Jackson's ability to give logical directions in financial matters. He was in open correspondence with Nicholas Biddle and made the most of it. 23

Washington watched the change in Ingham with fascination. Not only had Samuel Ingham acquired new stature in his post, but his wife also emerged from obscurity. The capital's salons gained the stage once more.

Samuel Ingham had arrived in Washington alone to accept Andrew Jackson's summons to serve the new administration. Mrs. Ingham had remained at home in Pennsylvania to care for their young daughters until the time was more propitious for their debut. As a result, Samuel Ingham had chosen to take no part in the Eaton affair, and his wife had kept her silence also. The refusal of the secretary of the Treasury and his wife to be drawn into the cliques had occasioned much comment. The ladies of Washington had been particularly intrigued.

Those who boasted of "friendship" with the Inghams fell back on the excuse that the Inghams were practicing Quakers, known for keeping to themselves and reserving comment on other people's affairs. Even the Calhouns accepted this while the Jacksonians never thought otherwise, and Dr. Ely never considered the Inghams at all. To him they were heretics, and the fact that Mrs. Ingham had been actively associated with her husband in their business affairs did not sit well with him or his blackcoats. Dr. Ely's religious beliefs relegated all women to church and home, and Mrs. Ingham's business activity was not considered proper for women attached to his New Life Presbyterianism. Consequently, Samuel Ingham had been left to his own devices in his affairs and his wife had been allowed hers, conditions it was thought both appreciated. 24

Washington's view of the Inghams was in error. Even as Biddle learned that Ingham was a man who yearned to be recognized, so Floride Calhoun soon knew that Mrs. Ingham, the Quakeress who placed no store in the sophisticated amenities of capital life, was in reality a woman who wanted friends among the capital ladies. Further, Mrs. Ingham had lovely daughters whom she wished to present to a society in which she had a place thanks to her husband's rising position. Mrs. Ingham was no recluse wedded to seventeenth-century Quaker beliefs and joyfully joined the ladies of Washington in their morning and afternoon meetings. 25

The transformation in the Inghams came about quickly as they walked at last with their former friends, forgiven of their former political alliances. The Inghams were the new breeze which fanned the fire of the many capital hearths, and the dying embers of the Peg Eaton affair became a blaze again as Samuel Ingham and his wife were welcomed not only into the Calhoun circles but into the outstretched arms of Dr. Ezra Stiles Ely himself. Mrs. Ingham joined the New Life Presbyterians and sat with Floride Calhoun and Emily Donelson against Mrs. John Eaton.26

The Eaton affair once again was the main dish at every capital function. Mrs. Ingham's enlistment in the crusade and her gratitude for her redemption were apparent as she appeared everywhere, in feathers and lace, with the Calhouns and Dr. Ely. Washington was quick to make its latest assessment of the situation.

With Branch and Berrien, and now Ingham, the Vice President held the legal and money powers. The President held the War Department and the Postal Department; Martin Van Buren in the State Department was still an unknown quantity. How long could Jackson and his Eaton prevail against such odds?

Floride Calhoun did not take personal charge of this latest assault upon Mrs. Eaton; she let Mrs. Ingham, guided by Dr. Ely, carry the standard. That wily churchman, mindful of his own needs, boasted his influence with the Inghams as one more expression of good over evil. To celebrate himself and his oneness with moral power, he issued a pamphlet incorporating his charges from his letters to Andrew Jackson about the Eatons.27

The Calhouns were pleased to let him run with the attack. Ely's published assault was a more acceptable explanation for the Inghams' emergence and their change than was Nicholas Biddle's use of Mammon for men. Biddle knew it too; he let his friend take credit for this latest miracle—it was God's wrath at work, not a man's money.

These new machinations bore instant fruit. The old Federalists took heart and even the defeated John Quincy Adams found his voice again. General Jackson would not have his way with John Calhoun, Daniel Webster, and Samuel Ingham lined up against him, aided and abetted by Nicholas Biddle and his bank, with Ely and his blackcoats behind them all.

Ely was no stranger to the Adams family. John Adams, the second president, had been an early follower and appreciated the clergyman's philosophy. He had recommended Ely and his ideas to Thomas Jefferson in the exchange of letters between two ex-presidents in their old age.28

John Quincy Adams had responded to his father's beliefs in 1823 by joining Dr. Ely's new Presbyterians. He and his wife Louisa had purchased a pew in the Second Presbyterian Church in Washington. There they had continued to worship through his presidency.29 They had put from them their commitment to Unitarianism and they were not alone in this change. Even Edward Everett had flirted with the new concepts that Man, in his success in this life, mirrored his acceptance in God's order. This doctrine appealed to men who had been selected above other men and believed they performed better than their brethren. The scions of the old America could never redesignate themselves "aristocrats," but they could embrace a belief which celebrated their difference from other men as godly grace. In accepting a kingly God, they could not be accused of accepting a king, but the basic order was the same. In religion, the Federalists had found the political compact that had eluded them since the Revolution, and John Quincy Adams embodied their joy at this discovery. At last those Americans who feared democracy, the rule of the rabble, had a rationale to follow. Divine Providence had gifted some men more than others, and it was an excellent substitute for the lost nobility of the English crown.

John Quincy Adams, to effect the direction approved by his father, came out of retirement to support this concept and veneer it with historical Americanism.[30] Jackson's opponents believed they had a viable tenet to use in the political arena. John Calhoun and Dr. Ely had forged it in Washington, and Biddle could promote it nationally with his purse. Men would have to bow down before this new grace in order to rule. It would be employed against all opponents, against Jackson and his revolutionaries, and God would rule as He decreed through His representatives. The Adams forces regrouped behind their old leader to assist in one more assault on the Jacksonians. Once again those who believed in divine right would frustrate those who had revolted against it. Men of God, wedded to wealth, allied with traditional power, formed a partnership for another assault on the Ship of State. God and Mammon would continue to rule men in the United States of America. There would be a king for the nation, a kingly God with his appointed representative, not a mob-elected president. It was what Mrs. Royall had warned about for three years. Washington was being prepared for a new coronation, but the crown was still to be conferred.

Chapter 15

The Price of Being Right

The government investigators scrutinized the former office of Tobias Watkins as they prepared for his prosecution. John Coyle, Jr., the fourth auditor's clerk, feared this surveillance more than his fellows, for his father and the mission congregation still contended with Mrs. Royall. Every day he despaired of his position. His father and friends had been unable to devise any method to eliminate Mrs. Royall's threat to their well being, and his own was more precarious with every review. While they discussed this or that action against her, Mrs. Royall went on visiting Congress and had produced another book, *Travels in Pennsylvania*, the story of her successful action against their blackcoat brethren in Harrisburg. She promised more in Washington.[1]

Impatient with his elders, young John Coyle proposed his own plan. Sitting as he did in an office beset by investigation and its former executive under arrest had taught the clerk that legal apprehension removed one from active life. The arrest of Watkins had left his chair open for Amos Kendall, and even the man's friends had disappeared! It was obvious that the mere act of charging anyone with a crime cast the accused into the pit of self-defense, a condition which could be all consuming. It had stopped Tobias Watkins, a powerful man and personal friend of John Quincy Adams; why wouldn't it stop this dangerous woman?[2] It was a bold suggestion and young Coyle's elders listened carefully to the young clerk's argument.

They all had a chance if they could remove the old woman from the scene. Any legal attack could keep her at bay, and a successful one could destroy her. They could charge her with anything criminal, anything that could effect her arrest. They could say she was a disturber of their peace, she tippled too much. Any crime would do; they needed something to charge her before the local magistrate. Her arrest would provide the respite they all needed, for this threatening Jackson tide could pass over, leaving them intact if the old woman was not able to point them out.

Young Coyle had a capital idea; Mrs. Royall *was* a criminal to them. She was a heretic, and in their minds that was the worst crime of all. In Scotland and Northern Ireland they had known how to deal with the likes of her: She was a witch, and they had burnt her kind.[3] She was the blaspheming voice of Satan, a devil of darkness, and with her attacks on their God she was pulling the shades down on their glorious attempts to shine their God's light upon the American government. Indeed, Mrs. Royall was a disturber of their peace, and they had friends in the Washington constabulary to whom they could appeal for help against the old woman.

119

They exulted among themselves at the simple solution suggested by their young follower in Christ. John Coyle, Sr., had produced in his son the voice of God in answer to their prayers.

The Engine House Congregation leaders took their charge against Mrs. Royall to the local constable, the Honorable Beck. He heard his friends out, but he was not impressed. When and how had Mrs. Royall disturbed their peace?

The Coyles became angry. Beck knew that Mrs. Royall had caused trouble; she had accused religious people of disturbing her, had tried to get both Beck and Magistrate Young to act against them. The old woman had complained about Beck himself to his superiors that he had not done as she wished. The writer was a menace to them all.

Constable Beck did not dispute his friends' arguments. He would like nothing more than to comply with their wishes and arrest the old woman, but they would have to make their charges against Mrs. Royall to Magistrate Young, and he doubted that the magistrate could allow them. Had they forgotten that it was Mrs. Royall who had charged them with disturbing the peace and produced proof for that charge? Since neither Magistrate Young nor he had acted on that charge, they could not act against Mrs. Royall without endangering themselves and the Coyles too.

The fact of the matter was that the lady had very important friends, more than she had before. Constable Beck had no intention of focusing Mrs. Royall's attention upon himself, and he would not invite any glance from her friends either. He enjoyed his sinecure, and so did Magistrate Young. He advised his friends to go home and forget about the woman. He did not like to refuse to help them, but he was in jeopardy too. Mrs. Royall had a greater influence than all of them.

The action of the Coyles and their congregation friends was not kept secret. Mrs. Royall heard about this attempt for it was treated as a joke by her friends. The blackcoats on Bank Street were making inquiries as to how much she drank.[4] The writer was not amused. These people were not just trying to tab her a drunkard. They were after much more. She knew the capability of these blackcoats to make trouble, and she had seen her laughing friends lose their smiles when faced with other actions from these fanatics. Holy Willy and his precious son had shouted they would get her yet. "Your time will come!" they had said.

Lewis Machen, the Senate clerk, had kept apart from the Coyles for weeks. Mrs. Royall's blast at him in Black Book Volume III, had forced him to keep a low profile. He was with them but not openly. Young Coyle had made a good suggestion, but Constable Beck's refusal to cooperate placed the matter back in Machen's hands, whether he liked it or not. His friends on Bank Street had been joined by his congressional confreres and Lewis Machen had to help.

Young Coyle's thoughts appealed to the Senate clerk. The woman could be silenced with an action against her before the law. There were many brains in the Senate who had no love for Mrs. Royall; someone like John Calhoun, Henry Clay, or Daniel Webster could assist with legal procedure.

Lewis Machen took his problem to the known Jackson opposition in the Senate. From John Calhoun through William Wirt, Adams's former attorney general, he sought advice, but no one was willing to lend his prestige to the project. The woman was free to write what she pleased, and there was no legal way her congressional opponents could stop her. Congress had attempted to muzzle such as her during old John Adams' administration when Congress had passed the Alien and Sedition Acts against voices which sought to influence the Congress and the nation against the President, and those acts had been declared illegal.[5] The resulting outcry had destroyed the Federalists and brought Thomas Jefferson to power. Andrew Jackson had enough power, and his opponents were unwilling to attempt another muzzling to give him more! Lewis Machen would have to find other allies to help him with Mrs. Royall.

It was a disheartening search for the Senate office clerk. With Mrs. Royall's books in hand, he could quote her worst passages against the very people from whom he sought help, but still they would not act. Mrs. Royall was an unpleasant fact of life, but she was an old woman and Lewis Machen could pray that she would just die or go away. The Senate clerk did not feel he had the time to rely upon such a kindly fate. He was not elected to office and had no term of office or constituency to support him. Each day, the Jackson attack came closer.

The continuing investigation into Tobias Watkins' tangled affairs took a new turn. The curious actions of Samuel Southard, Monroe's and Adams' secretary of the Navy, began to surface in the public consciousness. Isaac Hill had not been confirmed, but his fine hand was behind this new development. The emergence of Southard from obscurity worried many in the Senate, especially William Wirt and Daniel Webster. Both men had been associated with Southard for years.[6] The publication of Southard's list of assignments under two former presidents, his extraordinary reassignments, and his return to the Navy Department was the stuff from which scandal could be made. Southard's movements were made suspect with the disclosure that he had installed the disbursement routes so abused by Watkins. A link had been established among the disparate elements of the anti-Jackson leadership in Washington for the first time. The umbrella which had shielded Jackson's many foes was the bank, and the handle was held by Nicholas Biddle. The strange alliance was not so strange anymore.

Somehow the news of Lewis Machen's quest reached Ezra Stiles Ely. Here was a group of little people, his people, in danger in the government. They wanted to silence Mrs. Royall, have her arrested and jailed, and remove her like a thorn picked from a finger.

Dr. Ely lost no time in contacting Lewis Machen, and the Senate clerk brought together the Bank Street fanatics with congressional officeholders fearful of losing their jobs. The search for action against Mrs. Royall was over. A prominent churchman, a man who had access to the highest circles, would solve their problem. All Presbyterians, they would be united in a great work, and they could exorcise the Royall devil. Dr. Ezra Stiles Ely, the leader of their church had wisdom beyond theirs. Here was a project well tested to use against Mrs. Royall.[7]

The meeting was a great outpouring of Christian grace. The man who commanded the Old Pine pulpit and with it had usurped command of a hundred such podiums had great experience with she-witches. He held his listeners spellbound as he intoned his action against the Mrs. Royalls of the world. In stentorian tones, he preached to them as he had those women he had chastised in Philadelphia:

> Common fame accused you of being a notorious scold, of ungovernable temper . . . . peculiarly abusive . . . .[8]

His words were punctuated by amens and hallelujahs. The laws of the church held that a woman scold was a criminal and her punishment was to be humiliation, even death. Dr. Ely told his listeners that he had taken the ancient charge and made it a crime in Philadelphia, and he would do so again in Washington. He would give them words with which they could bring the devil woman before the courts of the capital, and she would not escape God's wrath. Dr. Ely added his personal note. She had attacked them, but Mrs. Royall had attacked him, too, by her words:

Ely convert the heathen! He might cut Christian throats, or devour them, but make them, never!

He had no need to convert her; he would do as she had prophesied: he would cut her throat and devour her and his God would help him do it. Mrs. Royall thought she was right, and the Jacksonians thought she was right; Dr. Ely would make them pay a high price for their error.

Chapter 16

Who Is the President?

The second week of May, 1829, saw Andrew Jackson, the seventh President of the United States, take to his bed with a virulent respiratory infection.[1] This news pushed aside all discussion of Tobias Watkins.

Andrew Jackson had not been in good health for months. He was, at 62, the oldest man to ascend to the nation's leadership and like so many in his time had been through a lifetime of battles, illness, and injury. He had been wounded severely five times and carried pain through every waking moment. His wracked body proved to be unequal to Washington City's infamous swamp fever. For eight weeks, the President had been fighting that pestilence, but it had become more critical because he had treated it disdainfully, standing on his feet. He had been appearing briefly for official duties, but now the affairs of the nation had to be conducted wholly from his bedside. Andrew Jackson, President, was reduced to complete reliance upon his close associates to carry forth his presidential directives.

John Eaton again found himself designated Andrew Jackson's surrogate, this time in the implementation of all executive powers.[2]

It was impossible to keep the news of this development from Jackson's enemies, not with Jack and Emily Donelson so close at hand. John Calhoun and his friends were told of the situation as it developed. The illness of Jackson was the moment they had sought to move to assert control. Jackson on his back and John Eaton covertly conducting the nation's business was not to be tolerated. The Constitution did not provide for the removal of an ill President, only an incompetent one, and Jackson's enemies decided to move in that direction. It would be a difficult chore, for "incompetence" was hard to define, but they would have to accomplish it. It was impolitic to assert that the President was dying, because Jackson did occasionally arise from his bed and he could give the lie to such rumors even with a momentary appearance. The way would have to be prepared for the public to accept Andrew Jackson's disabilities. Accordingly, the first intimations that Jackson ruled from his silken bed like a Roman Caesar began to slip into the opposition press with all the luridness practiced so well in the last campaign.[3] The President was to be ruled an "incompetent" in more ways than one.

Jackson's illness forced Ezra Stiles Ely to put aside his project for Mrs. Royall to aid in this new and more important attack. The same mind which authored the scandal heaped upon the Eatons was now to assist in reducing Jackson to a manageable quantity for John Calhoun. The concept of the hard-drinking, poker-playing Jackson, a man reduced to his bed through his own excesses, was Ely's new theme. He reinforced this by portraying the men guiding Jackson as those who enjoyed the dissolute life with their chief. Ely was concocting another clever ploy, one directed at the Presbyterian, Methodist and Baptist sanctions against gambling and drinking. In lurid illustration and prose, Andrew Jackson, the seducer John Eaton, and their friends were depicted as God-defying men, immoral in their personal conduct, illegal in their assumption of the nation's affairs, working in secret against the good people. They constituted a hidden government and committed a "crime" against the constitution. The patent homily with which the picture was presented played on the "kitchen" cabinet and the country rudeness of the Jacksonians. It was created by artful minds who served the religious press and Dr. Ely. The tract societies, their publishers, and writers were at work on their favorite subject again: manufacturing "sin" to serve their own interests.[4]

John Calhoun took his first hesitant steps to assume control of the government. His friends counseled him to move fast, for as president of the Senate he had support against Jackson; but he hesitated. Six men constituted the official cabinet designated to hold the reins of the nation. The Vice President knew he had three with him, but he wanted a fourth. The Secretary of State was necessary to his plans, and John Calhoun believed he could be enticed to his side with the offer of the vice presidency to his, Calhoun's, presidency.

It was in the nature of the South Carolinian to think in his own interest. In service to his constituents, he followed his personal dictates even against their interests and had been rewarded for this independence by being re-elected again and again to Congress. His stand for tariffs and western expansion cost his followers much, but he was returned anyway, thanks to that ever-growing stream of new immigrants from Scotland and Ireland, many of them entering through the port of Charleston.[5] His agent in attracting and directing this power pack was his brother-in-law, Moses Waddell, and Calhoun opened his office to the newcomers. These immigrants had also flooded the War Department and West Point while he was secretary of war under James Monroe.[6] As a result, Waddell had provided Calhoun with his own troops, trained and ready to follow him. Thus, in 1829, two armies were in the field: Andrew Jackson's citizen militia and John Calhoun's Army professionals and their blackcoat allies.[7]

The best trained army in the world can do nothing if its leader will not send it forth. John Calhoun had all this on his side, but he wanted more. He wanted the approval of other governments for his assumption of the presidency and he felt he needed the secretary of state to accomplish that. He wanted Martin Van Buren to join him on his march to destiny.

Martin Van Buren had kept his distance from the Vice President and his wife. The man who was the designated secretary of state was a widower and had no wife to be enlisted in the salon controversies stirring the capital. He spent his time with four people. Bachelors Charles Vaughn, British minister to the United States, and Baron von Kudner, the Russian minister, provided company, but a singular woman and her husband provided the social life expected from one of Van Buren's rank. The Chevalier and Madame Huygens, he the Dutch minister, ordered the small parties at which Van Buren entertained[8] and it was to them that the Calhouns turned for support in this project.

The advent of the Jackson administration had been a difficult time for the diplomatic community. To those accustomed to pomp and gala, the inauguration of the new president had been a disenchanting affair. Jackson's extended mourning and his decision not to be a receiving president had been most confusing. The White House was closed to visitors except for the most necessary functions, and, despite protestations of friendship, the estrangement of the President of the United States from all diplomatic social ceremony made normal contact difficult. The Eaton affair, intriguing as it was, forced the diplomatic discreet to keep a distance. However, despite official silence concerning the volatile domestic situation, the astute foreign circle knew the Vice President and his lady were engaged in a peculiar conflict with President Jackson and his friends.

There were two accepted leaders in the Washington diplomatic community in 1829. The official "chef" was Sir Charles Vaughn, the British minister, a gentleman of liberal tendencies whose representation of the mother country, despite its enmity, was recognized as necessary to give the nation concourse to the world at large. The unofficial "chef" was the Dutch minister, the Chevalier A. de Bangeman Huygens, from the Netherlands, the senior diplomat in the capital and accredited to three presidents. His continuity gave him a potent voice in capital affairs. The Washington diplomatic salons, bowing to the British minister, looked to the Chevalier Huygens for the action to be pursued in any difficult situation, and 1829 was no exception.[9]

The Chevalier Huygens was the scion of a remarkable family with roots deep in ecclesiastical Protestantism, science and business. The Huygens family was the epitome of the kind of aristocracy liberal nations can and do produce. The Netherlands, like Britain, cherished a king and queen but governed with a parliament and, although not espousing democracy in either the French or American context, did proclaim republican tendencies. The aristocracy believed that men of excellence should govern lesser men, and the prime consideration in their assessment was not politics, but a new quantity: economics. The Netherlands had accepted that it was the balance sheet of commerce, not the divine right of rulers nor the votes of the masses, which bestowed favor upon men. In practice, the Dutch Royal House, a relic of divine right, conferred the privilege and rank upon those successful. It was difficult to determine which came first, divine right or business.[10] The Chevalier Huygens and his position were perfect examples of this dichotomy.

The Huygens family had been prominent in Netherlands affairs for over 200 years. Christian Huygens, a clergyman, product of the Reformation, had broken from the church into science and from science into business, with his creation of a theory of optics.[11] His nation had developed a new industry, lens and jewel cutting, as a result. Christian Huygens had not only invented a new system, but he developed the means to control the technical aspects of his new inventions, and this gifted his family with not only money but a continuing position in Dutch affairs at home and abroad. Christian Huygens had not produced any children, but his brothers' progeny had inherited his mantle and continued to exercise his power in business and government as the decades and centuries passed. Two hundred years of continuity in the exchanges of Amsterdam, Paris, and London had created for the name Huygens what a thousand years of blood and genealogy had for other famous names in Europe. This fact was not lost on the aristocrats, the republicans, or the democrats, in the new United States of America.

The Chevalier and Madame Huygens were long-time favorites in Washington. The combination they represented, the marriage of church and science to government and to business, was the ambition many, particularly the blackcoats, sought for themselves. Madame Huygens, a charming woman with a pedigree equal to her husband's, led the diplomatic salons since Sir Charles Vaughn was a bachelor. Madame Huygens was a good friend to Floride Calhoun; both shared a Huguenot background.[12] In ten years of association, these two women had organized the capital's society to their mutual liking, and Floride Calhoun presumed to capitalize upon that achievement.

It had been rumored for some time that Secretary of State Martin Van Buren enjoyed a surprisingly close relationship with the Chevalier Huygens and his wife. It was a circumstance not easily understood, given the different backgrounds of the participants in this friendship, and it had excited much comment. Martin Van Buren had been a personal friend to the Huygens since 1821[13] and a quiet affection had grown between the Dutch aristocrats and the American farm boy turned leader. It was based on a simple fact: Martin Van Buren was a Dutch-American who loved to celebrate his background and preferred to practice the customs of his origins with others who could appreciate and understand them. The Huygens interested Van Buren, and it was to them that he turned during his Washington service to keep alive his original language and customs. The American and the Huygens had talked, celebrated, and eaten together, secluded from the misunderstanding gaze of others in the nation's capital. It had been a profitable liaison for all three from the beginning.

Martin Van Buren had become acquainted with the Huygens during his freshman stint in the capital as New York's senator. His entry into their home had been accomplished by his deliberately seeking the Huygens out. A child of the Netherlands' New York, Van Buren's first language had been Dutch; he had not learned to speak English until he was eight years of age, and he thought in Dutch as well as he did in English.[14] Although he had assimilated himself into the English-oriented political life of New York, then that of the United States itself, he had employed common sense to exploit his "difference" in politics.

The Dutch were a sizeable constituency not only in New York but in the nation's business community, and his championing of different customs also earned other aliens' appreciation for the little man bound for Washington. Martin Van Buren had built his national career on this fortunate representation among Americans out of the mainstream of English attitudes. It was a circumstance the Huygens understood and with which they identified.

As a senator in Washington, Martin Van Buren had been a solitary figure. His two sons were away in schools, and he was free to seek out the camaraderie which pleased him. Van Buren had found it easy to ripen acquaintance into friendship as he joined the Huygens and, trading tales of his outlander Dutch background in New York, he gained their firm affection. The Huygens benefited from that friendship too. Not only was their American friend a man who understood their ways in this foreign capital, but he was a United States senator and then secretary of state. Huygens's government was pleased with such an association. Van Buren was well aware of the mutual benefits each gained from such an ethnic friendship.

The extraordinary success of Martin Van Buren was the product of his dual identity as a Dutch-American. He was the first national leader to capitalize on the capacity of the American melting pot to produce Americans. At a time when the nation was passing from its revolutionary fervor to the establishment of its own peculiar democratic character, an American who paraded "foreign ways" had a great advantage. The Anglophile homogeneity of the once-English colonies was under frontal attack from many sources. Two decades of immigration from other European countries had begun to create a multicultural community in the large Eastern cities, and those elements sought voices on the national level. Jackson had capitalized on the rising Catholic Irish elements, and Martin Van Buren based his ascendancy on the other non-English groups seeking recognition. He had woven his political magic by opening the doors to first this foreign group and then that, as these "alien" people had reached for power from those who sought to withhold it from them. His mastery of this intricate and fluid situation had produced his title "The Little Magician," a tribute not only to his political prowess, but to his clever promotion of his short stature, a physical property he used well against taller, more aristocratic men.[15] It also helped bring him close to the Chevalier Huygens, a man as short as Van Buren.

Martin Van Buren could be brought to John Calhoun's side if Madame Huygens would help her friend. Floride Calhoun had two things going for her as she moved to effect her purpose. As the wife of the Vice President, she was a leader of Washington society, each position sustained by the other. She decided to put both advantages into play and with them insure her good friend's cooperation.

Floride Calhoun's move on the diplomatic community was done openly. The Eaton affair invaded the foreign salons, and John Eaton knew immediately what was happening. The Vice President was moving to supplant the elected President of the United States, using Jackson's illness to assert openly that he was the legal successor. He sought full diplomatic recognition of his move. John Eaton did not panic; he knew that John Calhoun's political assertions were far from being realized.

The President of the United States still functioned, albeit through John Eaton and friends, and the Constitution of the United States did not allow succession easily or well without death. The President could be removed only by death or impeachment, not because of illness. Andrew Jackson was on his back but he had a tenacity to live. John Calhoun could trumpet to his small world that he was gathering to himself all the elements of victory, but he did not hold the presidency. Andrew Jackson did.

John Eaton moved to counterattack for Jackson immediately. If John Calhoun thought he had the cabinet, the President simply would not convene the cabinet. If Branch, Berrien, and Ingham wished to side with the Vice President and his cohorts to play against the President, let them. John Eaton knew how to undercut them all. Jackson's illness could be used by the Jacksonians too. It was an excellent excuse to set aside the bickering of a divided cabinet and protect the President's peace of mind. The President's policies could be carried out by friends close to his bedside as well as enemies praying for his death. John Eaton moved his group of friends immediately to assert Jackson's prerogatives. The general, accustomed to staff tactics, gave them the latitude needed to get their jobs done. The men about his bedside would be the "cabinet." John Calhoun could march up and down the corridors of the Congress, through the departments he thought he controlled, but Andrew Jackson was the commander; he held the presidency and would administer it. The designated cabinet be damned; it would be replaced by Jackson's own staff.[16]

The "kitchen cabinet" went into full and open operation, and John Calhoun and his friends ran steaming to their law books. This rump cabinet ought to be illegal, but was it? The cabinet was not an elected body, it was a selected group appointed by the President. If the President did not meet with it but instead preferred his friends, there was no constitutional admonition involved. The cabinet appointees, after selection, were expected to serve with the President for a full four years but it was not mandatory. John Calhoun thought to make it so; to enunciate the dictum that men so appointed could not be removed even by the man who appointed them. But even as this was said, the error became apparent. Wiser men remembered if no appointee could be removed, neither could John Eaton; that comment cooled even Calhoun's hot tongue. John Eaton was the man he wanted out of the government, but he could not afford to lose John Branch, John Berrien, and Samuel Ingham too. Martin Van Buren, the secretary of state, became more important than ever.

Martin Van Buren had kept a neutral stance for the first 60 days of the administration. Busy with "foreign affairs," he had kept aloof from all political and social intrigue. So carefully had he sidestepped the Eaton issue that no one in Washington knew where he stood, not even the Calhouns.

Martin Van Buren made his debut in the controversy just as Andrew Jackson's illness began to excite the capital to action. The Johnny-come-lately to

Jacksonian ranks appeared in public with Mrs. John Eaton on his arm! Not only did he walk in the streets with the hussy, but he escorted her to calls on his bachelor friends, Sir Charles Vaughn and Baron von Kudner. The Secretary of State accompanied Mrs. Eaton to the British minister's home and then to the house of the Russian minister.[17] So unexpected was this simple move by the ranking member of the cabinet, that no one was ready for it.

Washington had been prepared for a Calhoun *coup d'état*. The months of harassment directed at the Eatons, Jackson's illness, Eaton's administration of the government, and Peg Eaton's apparent lack of support in pressing her right to position had signaled the weakness of the new administration. Washington society had been prepared for the final act. The prospect of Mrs. John Eaton walking into the dens of lionesses, ready and able to devour her, had been the pleasant anticipation of those who had suffered two months of the Jacksonian reign. Fangs and tongues had been sharpened for the occasion, spirits had been roused from the depression of the attacks on Watterston and Watkins, and appetites had soared at the chance to savor a full feast at the expense of the Jacksonians. Martin Van Buren's temerity in volunteering as an escort to Peg Eaton was not what anyone had expected, but it was a moment which Martin Van Buren had long awaited.

The man from New York knew exactly what he was doing. Andrew Jackson was a sick man indeed, but his sickness had exposed the selflessness of his aides. John Eaton was a man devoid of ambition; he served only Jackson. He was a valuable ally to him who would be the next president. Andrew Jackson had selected no heir apparent, but it was obvious he could not accept John Calhoun. Despite Jackson's repeated assertion that the cabinet would not produce the next president, Martin Van Buren knew otherwise. The Jackson-Eaton partnership controlled the government by right of position. Jackson held the franchise, Eaton managed it, and any heir had to accept that fact. Martin Van Buren alone had the opportunity to achieve what every ambitious politician sought: He decided he would become Jackson's successor, the next president of the United States.

Van Buren was a master of political timing. He stepped onto the Washington stage at precisely the moment John Calhoun had planned to make his final move on Jackson.

Martin Van Buren had escaped the notice of the capital in the growing conflicts at hand because he was neither friend or foe to any of the contenders in Washington; he was an amorphous shadow, a product of the constant shifting of loyalties with which New York propelled men into public life. The Empire State's representatives responded to national questions like brokers, taking commissions on the sales of ideas to Congress, for influence and capital came from selling to the highest bidder. There were just too many ideas to be fielded to keep to a hard and fast position. Like the Dutch burghers who became British agents, New Yorkers were content with a momentary profit, but their questionable loyalty made them poor allies in any long-range activity. It was a historical circumstance which forced the state's leadership to keep its market situation liquid at all times. In effect, New York could not afford a national statesman since other states' politics, policies, and men were its main business.

Martin Van Buren was the epitome of the New York broker-politician. His entire life had been spent in political trade, the largest deal of all having landed him the State Department in the Jackson cabinet. He had exchanged a well-organized Jackson opposition left over from 1824 for the captaincy of the revitalized New York Jackson campaign in 1828, and with victory he claimed his spoils. Elected governor of New York in the Jackson landslide, he had deserted that post to take his new national position. Jackson and Eaton had planned to relegate the State Department to obscurity, a circumstance which had not bothered Martin Van Buren one whit.[18] He knew history well, and such an entry into the Jacksonian councils, even by a lackluster State Department, was an excellent vantage point for a clever man.

John Calhoun's assumption that Martin Van Buren would join him against Jackson was plain stupidity. The New Yorker had little regard for the South Carolinian. Van Buren had been the leader of William Crawford's drive for the presidency in 1824 and had been his running mate as vice president. It had been John Calhoun's devious maneuvering in that campaign which had aborted Martin Van Buren's entry into national affairs. Calhoun had taken for himself the vice presidency under John Quincy Adams, and Van Buren had been retired to New York.

Martin Van Buren had kept his dislike of his competitor to himself and cooperated with Calhoun in the Jackson campaign in 1828. In consequence, he had made many of Calhoun's cohorts his friends, including some who stewarded the Bank of the United States. Martin Van Buren also had a strong attachment to the new religion absorbing American Protestantism. As a matter of record, Van Buren had drawn upon the same forces in New York that Calhoun had used nationally. The New Yorker had plans for those influences, and they did not include Calhoun.

Martin Van Buren was well acquainted with the old Federalists, their policies, their men, and those who financed them. As Federalist politics had been assaulted, then submerged, he had assisted them to retain a modicum of control. Rufus King was living testimony to that cooperation. That old New Yorker, that Federalist of all Federalists, was yet a force in national affairs due to Martin Van Buren.[19] A most astute manipulator, utterly without scruples, Van Buren had the talent to satisfy his own desires and still convince others that he really represented theirs. Martin Van Buren knew how to turn his liabilities into assets.

It did not take long for Washington to know what the Secretary of State had done. The simple act of Van Buren extending his arm to Mrs. Eaton had revealed his side to the public. The man from New York had joined Andrew Jackson and John Eaton. It was a potent omen.

Peg Eaton was no longer a joke. In one afternoon's foray, she had broken from the ranks of the "fallen women" and invaded the diplomatic community, with the attendant boldness of the Secretary of State behind her. Peg Eaton had added her name to the list of those women who achieve international renown for the key to politics they provide. Overnight she gained a new title, *La Bellona.*[20] It was a salute to both the beauty and battle she signified, and not what Floride Calhoun had expected. The Vice President's lady had been eclipsed; just as she moved to call the favors owed her from the diplomatic community, the White House in her grasp, Martin Van Buren had pre-empted the action. It was a challenge Floride Calhoun could not ignore, one she decided to take up in her own fashion.

Floride decided to gamble that Jackson was so ill that he would keep to his bed, leaving the field to those who could gain it. Mrs. Calhoun proposed to assume, as the wife of the Vice President, full direction of Washington's diplomatic salons, moving to take precedence over the Secretary of State and Peg Eaton.

Floride Calhoun had hoped to enlist Madame Huygens to entice the Secretary of State to her husband's side, but Martin Van Buren had not waited for such gentle persuasion. He had bypassed his old friends and turned to his two bachelor companions to entertain Mrs. Eaton, men whom Mrs. Calhoun found it difficult to approach. The British minister, Sir Charles Vaughn, and his Russian friend, Von Kudner, were ranking diplomats, but the Huygens still commanded the capital salons. Madame Huygens was still available. Floride Calhoun decided to proceed with her original plan to counter Van Buren. She knew that what she had in mind was feasible but entailed great risk. Andrew Jackson favored Peg Eaton, and for any diplomat to render assistance to even the Vice President's wife in an attempt to ostracize her could be interpreted as political intervention and undue interference in American domestic matters. Neither the American government nor the foreign one could officially condone such an action. Mrs. Calhoun knew she was about to strain the best of friendships, but she had hidden allies in this difficult situation.

The Chevalier Huygens was not just a diplomat; he was a representative to Dutch-oriented trade and to certain religious circles in the United States. As the representative of the Dutch Crown, he enjoyed an official liaison to the Dutch Reformed Church, the American offshoot of the state church of the Netherlands, one wedded to the dignity of the Royal Dutch family.[21] This position was not an honorary association, it was a working cooperation. The Chevalier combined religion, trade, and finance with powerful influence which reached into most of the seaboard cities of the United States. The Dutch community held a heavy position in finance and trade in the existing money centers, and, through their holdings in the United States and abroad, they had become heavy investors in the Bank of the United States. This and the gradual alliance of the Dutch Reformed Church in America with the new brand of Presbyterianism brought together the Huygens, the Biddles, the Elys, and now, Mrs. Calhoun hoped, Martin Van Buren. If Van Buren did not know who his friends were at the moment, the Huygens had the capacity to change his mind. Floride Calhoun banked upon her connections and her friendships to accomplish this maneuver.

Madame Huygens was enlisted. She did exactly what Floride Calhoun desired. She cut *La Bellona* from her guest lists, but before Washington could react to that fact, another event eclipsed the Dutch minister's wife's action.[22]

On the sixteenth of May, John Eaton, secretary of war-designate, acting for Andrew Jackson, President of the United States, sent to Congress a list of specified charges against George Watterston, Librarian of Congress. The charges enumerated all the complaints Mrs. Anne Newport Royall had exposed in her three-month campaign against the Librarian.[23] The effect was immediate. Edward Everett's apology, the retraction of privilege extended to the tract society, and the reclamation of religious literature from government shelves, were facts accomplished. The Librarian stood alone, without a shred of defense.

To the long list of George Watterston's ill-considered actions, Mrs. Royall had added a new charge. The Librarian had misused his franking privileges to aid and abet inimicable interests to distribute false and misleading propaganda sheets throughout the United States, not the least among them those broadsides, campaign leaflets against Andrew Jackson and his wife, Rachel. George Watterston had been using his position in this unseemly manner for over a year; he had cost the Treasury of the United States an enormous amount of money and was continuing this illegal practice.

The proof was overwhelming. Not one voice was raised in George Watterston's defense, but several were raised in apology. Henry Clay and Daniel Webster did their best to excuse the poorly-paid and dedicated government servant but to no avail. George Watterston, unlike Tobias Watkins, had lived very well in the nation's capital. His fine house, his fancy carriage, and his parties gave no evidence of poverty, no possible excuse for his wrongdoing. George Watterston attempted to resign but Andrew Jackson fired him first.[24]

The removal of George Watterston took precedence over all other actions in

Washington City. The man so many had hoped to save was not saved. John Calhoun, the Vice President, kept a silence heavily weighted. His friends and supporters were stupefied and Dr. Ely in particular felt the loss. He had made it his business to save Watterston, and he had failed. Henry Clay joined in by writing to George Watterston what all his friends felt:

> Your removal from the office of Librarian . . . was a step in keeping with the despotism that now rules Washington . . . . I hope you and I live to see the nation rid of its present misrule, and the Jacksons . . . and the Eatons and the host of kindred spirits driven back to their original stations and insignificance.[25]

George Watterston's failure to keep his office despite the thunder from his influential friends caused many in the capital to ponder again Van Buren's actions. As the salons sought to evaluate this latest event, the answer came quietly from their own ranks. The Chevalier Huygens and his wife left on an extended trip to visit the Dutch-American communities in the cities north of the capital.[26] The salon gossip held that Madame Huygens had come under undue influence from Floride Calhoun, and the Chevalier did not approve. He had removed his wife from the councils of all those who did not wish to receive Mrs. Eaton. The Chevalier was not about to indulge in any confrontation involving his friend Martin Van Buren.

With the departures of the Huygens went the last hopes and pretensions of John Calhoun, his wife, and their many supporters. The Vice President would not succeed to the presidency after all. John Eaton and now Martin Van Buren had seen to that. John Eaton would move heaven and hell to keep his mentor alive, and Martin Van Buren would help him. Andrew Jackson, ill almost to death, was yet the President of the United States. The only question that remained was who would be his real heir-apparent.

Chapter 17

The Scapegoat

The sacking of George Watterston from the Library of Congress tore apart the alliance building on the hopes of John C. Calhoun. Suddenly, everything his supporters had prayed for was no longer there. The old regime would go. The Jacksonians, having found good cause for the removal of Watterston, now pressed for the wholesale removal of the holdovers. Andrew Jackson did not have to lift a finger. John Eaton had control of the maneuver, with an able assist from Martin Van Buren. The Jackson supporters stampeded the government offices, and they no longer hinted for position, they took what had been assigned months before.[1] The Vice President sat powerless as the deluge stripped away his supporters.

Mrs. Royall exulted in the changes. Jackson had the right to install his own men, and she argued that right as fervently as she had carried her crusade against George Watterston. She marched through the government halls lending assistance to the Jacksonians as they sought office to serve the President.

Jackson's opponents were decimated; Ezra Stiles Ely was particularly distraught. He had put aside his plans for Mrs. Royall for this effort against the Jacksonians, and the defeat of Calhoun's bid to replace the ailing Andrew Jackson had cost him dearly. The Presbyterian moderator had risked his national position in coming to Washington to save George Watterston; he had become enmeshed in the growing and expanding conspiracy concerning Jackson, and he had lost.

Mrs. Royall haunted him. That she-devil who walked the halls of Congress in victory, meeting with Eaton and his minions, exulted. He should never have put his original project to punish her aside to follow these other interests. Mrs. Royall should have been silenced. None of this would have happened if he had followed common sense. He had turned aside from his proper pursuits, had been distracted by vanity and power in Washington, and his God had swiftly punished him.

It was easy for the Reverend Ely to rationalize his position. As he did so, the light dawned. Mrs. Royall still remained, and so did he. The small band of men who wanted the woman removed and had approached him just weeks ago were in the capital still. He had promised to help them, had boasted that he could, and now he would. With their help, he would destroy this woman who had made a mockery of his friends, had blasphemed his God. It was time to gain God's favor once again.

John Coyle had prayed daily for the eminent churchman to come to the rescue of his people. The senior Coyle had accepted Dunn's and Machen's thesis

132

that it would take a leader of the Presbyterian Church to cope with Mrs. Royall, that it was necessary to mount a concerted effort with the highest echelons to meet her with equal influence. There was no doubt that although they, as little people, had suffered from Mrs. Royall's actions in Washington, Dr. Ely and his friends had suffered more. Sooner or later, Ely and his cohorts would have to move against Mrs. Royall, and they would be ready to aid in that effort.

It took Ezra Stiles Ely just three days to contact his Bank Street friends. The clergyman sent word to John Coyle, John Dunn, and Lewis Machen that he was ready to proceed against the woman and would require their help. He had a simple plan in mind, and they would be doing God's work to assist him with it. The Coyles, senior and junior, John Dunn, and Lewis Machen lost no time in promising their cooperation.[2]

The Coyles had had their own idea of the action to be initiated against Mrs. Royall. To them, the woman was a crazy old hag, mad with her new-found influence in the Jackson camp. They wanted to confine her in any way possible. Was she a drunk? Then off to the workhouse with her! Was she mad? Then off to the asylum! With the help of such a man as Dr. Ely, it would be so simple.

John Dunn and Lewis Machen did not agree. These men, close to the political spectrum changing before their eyes, knew that Mrs. Royall was not mad. The events of the past year had borne fruit for her and too many followers of Andrew Jackson in the new administration. There was no way that such a simple attack could be successful. A far more sophisticated assault would have to be launched, one that would eschew personalities, one that would make the old woman stand alone, severed from the "influences" she proudly claimed.

Dr. Ely listened to his new allies. Machen and Dunn were right, but they could be useful in the action if they would hear him out. Dr. Ely had a clever scheme in mind with which to hobble Mrs. Royall. The old woman was a witch, a heretic who blasphemed their God, but their God had given them a course of action against her.

Mrs. Royall had not just charged the men with treason, calling upon Congress to investigate them and act against them; she had attacked all New Presbyterians. So be it. It would be the New Presbyterians that would answer her. Even as she stalked the halls of Congress in pursuit of her large objectives, Ely thought to have her find it in men greater than herself and suffer the consequences. Government clerks were not adequate to handle this, but a government institution was.

Lewis Machen was ecstatic. The church would attack Mrs. Royall. Dr. Ely did not agree. The church was powerful and it did control many great men in the Congress, but Mrs. Royall had taken up her most punishing cudgels not against the church but against men associated with it. Dr. Ely had in mind to assist those who had the most to lose, his listeners. What he planned would hasten her downfall more than any outright church attack upon her. The action against Mrs. Royall would come from those who had suffered so openly from her attack, and Dr. Ely assured them they would keep their jobs doing it. His listeners were enthusiastic.

Dr. Ely suggested that Coyle, Dunn, Machen, and even Watterston could initiate certain charges, and they could enlist all their friends to make her guilty. They could do it themselves, without any public assistance from Dr. Ely, and yet show the world that Dr. Ely and all of his powerful friends stood behind them. They could convict her with all the arguments she had used against them, and God's will would be done.

Dr. Ely reviewed Mrs. Royall for his listeners. The old woman was preaching that the United States had passed through three crucial years. The country was under attack from blackcoats and missionaries. Mrs. Royall had accused men like Coyle, Machen, and Dunn with representing their religion first, the government second, and of attacking the Age of Reason. It was her argument that they had exploited the Sunday mail and Sunday business issues as they sought to take over state legislatures; it was her thesis that they had crept into employment with the national government to produce victory for their church and kind, to do with the federal government what they had been unable to do in the several states. Mrs. Royall had satirized them, their Bibles, their tracts, and their widening religious constituency. Let her speak it in an open court.

The Coyles were aghast. Mrs. Royall had written this, and she had said it, too, but why should they let her speak it in open court?

The wily churchman played his trump card. Was not Mrs. Royall scolding the world with these words, scolding the politicians with her diatribes and complaints? Well, their church had experience with such as she. It was a crime to the Presbyterians to do what this woman had done, and it was that crime Dr. Ely proposed that the men before him now charge her with. He, their leader, would work behind the scenes to insure the crime was recognized in the federal courts. They had only to do his bidding, and they would all be revenged upon the old woman and their God would be vindicated in all his glory.[3]

The clerks sat stupefied. It was a concept beyond them. The good doctor had an idea, but they could not grasp it. How could they do what the church would not? Dr. Ely had to reassure them it could be done because the church was all-powerful and would shield them as they sought justice against the woman. Mrs. Royall would not be attacked by religion, through religion, or for religion, but by the power of God's precedence. It would be done in such a way that no man could come to Mrs. Royall's defense for her persecution. The woman, by her own words, would be condemned. She had made herself vulnerable. Her words had sown the seeds of her defeat, and Dr. Ely knew how to make them sprout. The small clique listened rapturously. The clergyman asked them to consider his direction carefully.

Mrs. Royall was not just a woman, she had become a inimicable force. This woman with her pen had concocted a simple exposition most dangerous to everyone. From the loose ends of her loose life, she had fashioned a very personal account, and although she had cut a wide swath with it among certain men in politics, many more people did not accept her thoughts. It was Mrs. Royall who had proclaimed that religion and government did not mix, that they were not natural handmaidens but sworn enemies. She had promoted this hatred of religion by tying the church to a popular dislike of those who had money. It was that old woman who had declared that men in finance had joined the church in an assault upon the American civil government. It was obvious what she wanted; she had demanded that both religion and finance be chastised to save the nation. However, men, like themselves, knew the truth. Mrs. Royall was an anti-Christ and was using politics to serve her dreadful master. It was that truth which would save them all.

In pressing her attack on the church and on rich men, Mrs. Royall had gone too far. Many were ready to construe her words as irresponsible, disruptive. Dr. Ely was not at liberty to divulge those men, but they were powerful. These men would join in any effort to make Mrs. Royall ludicrous. Dr. Ely asked his new friends to trust him, to cooperate; it would be worth their while. The churchman would punish the woman with her own kind of argument but in an entirely new context. Revenge would be sweet for them all; with this he gained their complete support.

Dr. Ely knew what he was doing. More than the blackcoats were threatened now, and the opposition was growing. Mrs. Royall had discovered the strange alliance of religion with finance, but she was touching some hidden nerves even among friends. The Tobias Watkins affair was adding to her public following, but behind that facade, fear was increasing among those who smiled when she passed. Mrs. Royall was becoming a political figure. She was no longer an un-biased commentator, and her crusades were leading her onto dangerous grounds. To insure against more Watkins and Watterstons, public office was to be denied to all "blackcoats," but who defined the blackcoats? It gave pause to many old friends, and Mrs. Royall's assertions that blackcoat ties to the Bank of the United States were just as dangerous opened her definition of enemy to a broader interpretation than many liked.

Ely intimated to his new friends that Nicholas Biddle was not pleased with this new development. The situation in Washington was proving to be one crisis after another and with the split in the Jackson government, the bank was in greater jeopardy than ever. As other issues divided, the bank issues kept surfac-ing to bring the Jacksonians together. The charter which had established the Second Bank of the United States had years yet to run, but the situation devel-oping could submerge that legal fact. What Congress had granted, it could take back, and with criminal activity charged to the bank in the Watkins case and the trial being readied for the public, such discussion was harrowing indeed.

In all these considerations, Mrs. Royall's name played a part. The writer had produced the weave of events and incidents troubling the nation's religious and political waters since 1826, the cloth which bound Ezra Stiles Ely to Nicholas Biddle. This had influenced Congress against the bank. Thomas Hart Benton had been wooed completely to the Jackson side with its enmeshing of Henry Clay in the compact.[4] The Missourian was becoming an effective spearhead of the Jackson attack on the bank. As first one assault then another was launched against Biddle's empire, Mrs. Royall's own power increased. Her discovery of the "alien" influences massed within the government, of the working alliance between the charitable, religious, and mendicant groups serving the new religion, and those capital and money organizations stewarded by Nicholas Biddle now cast her as an expert in the matter. Dr. Ely was weaving his net carefully to catch Machen, Dunn, and the Coyles.

She who had revealed the collaborators now could define them, and the defi-nition she presented sealed her fate. The old woman had widened her influence too fast, and she had to be cut back as soon as possible. Nicholas Biddle had underestimated Mrs. Royall and her pen. No longer could he receive her as an-other writer, for she had become a menace to his bank. Mrs. Royall had broad-ened her power base, but Biddle was determined to narrow her support.

Ezra Stiles Ely was attending to Mrs. Royall in his own way, and he laid his trap very carefully. It was all very well that the woman spoke her mind and warned others about impending danger, but most of her listeners would not take kindly to her alarm. It had been his experience that without the religious pulpit, most people did not heed prophets and certainly not female ones. He knew how to deal with women who misunderstood their place and spoke out on issues. He had dealt with forceful female parishioners who had solicited public support from other women only to discover that other women were too willing to join against them. People, particularly women, did not want reform or change, and if they were aroused they would back those who represented authority, not those who tilted with it. Mrs. Royall would not be able to build a constituency of women, she had only men. The churchman knew that men would not back a woman under attack for acting like a man; their women would not let them.

Dr. Ely would not lodge a single attack on Mrs. Royall but a double or triple one if it could be accepted. The woman was to be charged with multiple crimes. She was to be indicted as a "common scold" in a remake of his actions in Phila-delphia, but he would play no open part in this action. He would let the Coyles,

Dunn, Machen, and their fellows carry his banner. Their complaints about Mrs. Royall would reduce her to a vulgar neighborhood pest who carried that vulgarity into the Congress to threaten the operation of the government itself. The Coyles would represent the Engine House Congregation, the Dunns, Machens, and more important people with much to lose. In this manner the churchman would put together two disparate groups as surrogates for the real elements in this fight. The Coyles would represent the church, the congressional clerks, and important men riding with the church. By localizing the attack, Mrs. Royall would be shorn of her important friends. Those who revered her for her perspicacity in national affairs could not defend her on the charge of neighborhood vulgarity, because they did not know her well personally. The little people who hated so well would eliminate the people who respected so much. If any of the well-known Jacksonians attempted to come to Mrs. Royall's defense, they would be tarred with the same brush applied to Mrs. Royall. Dr. Ely was sure that Andrew Jackson, John Eaton, or their allies would not come to the aid of a common scold.

Ezra Stiles Ely was as brilliant a manipulator as any in 1829. He had built his reputation in Philadelphia by employing ecclesiastical attack; resurrecting it from its ancient dust bins and giving it new life in the civil courts of Philadelphia. That success had produced fame and given him national prominence as the protector of the ancient faith. It had codified his religious philosophy. Dr. Ely had introduced into an American court a "crime" which by constitutional definition was unacceptable since the Revolution, and he had gotten a decision with it. That action in the City of Brotherly Love had been a great personal triumph, one he had enjoyed until the higher courts of Pennsylvania had ruled against his creation.[5] Now he had a chance to overrule those higher courts in Pennsylvania and in so doing mark American law with his will forever. His colleagues would produce a lasting monument to Dr. Ely and his fervent beliefs in Knoxonian and Cartwrightian doctrines. American law would be restructured by his God in a novel way indeed.

Mrs. Royall had been sent to Dr. Ely for this exquisite test of God's will. The writer would accomplish with her court appearance what would have taken countless fights in the many state legislatures to bring it about. The civil code of the United States was to be invaded by the ecclesiastical codes enunciated by John Knox, James the First of England, and Thomas Cartwright.[6] The Age of Divine Right would be codified forever in the courts of America and what had been denied Dr. Ely and his cohorts in Pennsylvania and New York would be imprinted upon the entire nation. Mrs. Royall would be charged with a crime against men which was defined only by God, Dr. Ely's God. Mrs. Royall would be sacrificed and the ceremony attended by many men. Unlike the sacrificed in the ancient ritual, Mrs. Royall would not be allowed to escape with only the sins of her words fastened to her; she would be met with a far more exquisite punishment. The spokeswoman for the Age of Reason was to reintroduce the Age of Divine Right to her country, to carry its mark with her wherever she went. Mrs. Royall was to become Ezra Stiles Ely's perfect scapegoat.[7]

Chapter 18

Indictment!

In just eight days, Dr. Ely had his plan in motion. The eminent clergyman gathered together the right people to manufacture this new crime for the consideration of American jurisprudence. There were some surprising people involved.

The most immediate of Dr. Ely's allies was Thomas Swann, prosecutor for the District of Columbia, a last-minute appointee of John Quincy Adams.[1] Mr. Swann continued to enjoy the prerogatives of his office because the Jackson replacement, William Jones, sat unconfirmed thanks to the adjournment of the U.S. Senate in the conflict proceeding between Andrew Jackson and John Calhoun.

Swann, like the Coyles, Machen, and Dunn, was scheduled for removal from office when the Jacksonians could manage it. He had much in common with the men Dr. Ely brought to him to make complaint against Mrs. Royall, and he heard them out. Although Ely's proposition had a strange sound to a man grounded in American law, Swann accepted it for presentation to the grand jury. Dr. Ely had crossed his first barrier.

The second was no more difficult. The sitting grand jury was foremanned by Colonel McKenney, Commissioner in the Indian Bureau, the patronage department created by Congress to oversee the nation's first welfare problem, the American Indian.[2] This gentleman was the general overseer of personnel and materials with which to accomplish the forced migration of America's original natives from land coveted by the growing nation. Congress had established this agency to satisfy the demands of General Andrew Jackson after his experiences with the Indians in 1812.[3] This department had become the Washington bastion of Jackson's enemies, thanks to the Federalist control of Congress, and Colonel McKenney sat in command of its behind-the-scene strategy to hobble Andrew Jackson's ambition. He had been hand-picked as the foreman of the grand jury to examine Tobias Watkins, a master stroke from Jackson's enemies, and he had a personal score to settle with Mrs. Royall.[4] Dr. Ely had arranged matters well for Mrs. Royall's presentation to this jury group.

It was all cut and dried. The Coyles, John Dunn, Lewis Machen, and George Watterston went in secret before McKenney and his panel to tell their curious tales about Mrs. Royall's scolding, her attacks on their peace of mind. More officeholders joined them: J.F. Frost, James Whitwell, Joseph Elgar, W.J. McCormick, and their wives asserted that the writer had disturbed them too.[5] Pressed hard by this litany without one word of rebuttal, with constant manipulation by Prosecutor Swann and exhortation from foreman McKenney, the grand jury was directed to produce Indictment 118,[6] in words written by Ezra Stiles Ely in 1825 for his Philadelphia assault upon the outspoken women in his Pine Street congregation.

The presentment handed up by the grand jury called Mrs. Royall "an evil disposed person," "a common slanderer," "a disturber of the peace, of the happiness of her honest and quiet neighbors." She was accused of "falsely and maliciously" slandering and abusing "divers good and quiet citizens of the said *county* to the common nuisance of the good citizens of the United States to the evil example of all others in like cases of offending." To this blanket condemnation of the woman and the commendation of Dr. Ely's past concoction, the phrase "against the peace and government of the United States" was added. In one day, Ezra Stiles Ely had done in Washington exactly what he had done in Philadelphia four years before. Mrs. Royall was indicted as a common scold, charged as a "common brawler" and a "sower of discord," all on the complaints of men removed and facing removal from office, and their women. The action of the higher courts of Pennsylvania had not been referred to once.

Mrs. Royall's indictment was presented for immediate execution by Thomas Swann but haste produced a legal error. William Brent, Mrs. Royall's old friend, found it when Prosecutor Swann handed the peculiar document to him for service. Thomas Swann had neglected to check the date of his manufactured indictment with the dates of the alleged offenses presented in evidence. The indictment, signed on May 29, 1829, cited an offense alleged to have occurred on June 1, 1829. William Brent did not inform Thomas Swann of his mistake. He rushed the document to Mrs. Royall and told her. He did not arrest her as an officer of the court but advised her as a friend.[7] She needed counsel at once, but she held her freedom in her hand.

Mrs. Royall lost no time in following William Brent's direction. Knowing Thomas Swann's part in the action, she hurried to the man slated to replace him for help. William Jones, a former secretary of the Navy, was a renowned reformer and an ardent Jacksonian. Mrs. Royall saluted the Pennsylvanian as "one of the first lawyers in the United States," and the appearance of the writer seeking his help produced it without fee.[8] With one glance at the document she held, the name of Thomas Swann, and the list of witnesses, Jones went to work.

The indictment was a patently illegal concoction; William Brent was correct. Considerations of constitutionality did not have to be discussed, for the date of the alleged offenses was enough. The date of the crime, obviously hastily inserted after the paper had been drawn, made the indictment invalid. There was no way that Mrs. Royall, or any other citizen, could be indicted for a crime, offense, or action said to have occurred after an indictment had been handed up. Thomas Swann could do nothing but concur, and Indictment 118 was shelved with the bold notation added by Court Clerk William Brent, "quashed by order of Attorney."[9]

It had been a comedy of errors, and Mrs. Royall's friends laughed with her. Ely had done his worst and had failed; his God had provided a slip and perhaps he would take heed from this heavenly intercession. Mrs. Royall could relax; her days of anxiety were over. What the churchman had hoped to accomplish in secret was out in the open, and he could do it no more. Mrs. Royall was relieved but not so sure. Ely had produced such indictments before in Philadelphia, and they had been knocked down by higher state courts. Yet he had produced this one in Washington. The record was not reassuring. She had to lessen her tension and she took her pen and with it put the capital's laughter to paper, Mrs. Royall outlined the events she had endured and the actions of her "good, quiet and honest neighbors" in dialect and sarcasm, just as she told the story to her friends and they told it to others:

About this time a council was held to which the good pious men of Capital Hill repaired.

Amongst these were some mighty good pious souls who were turned out of office, and others who expected to be turned out. This revived good holy pious feelings in their bosoms, and glorious was the outpouring of the divine grace.

"Oh, that we had our Holy Religion established," said Mucklewrath, "we would bring this heretic to a speedy repentance."

"Yes," said Hallelujah holding forth, "the inquisition is the thing: it would open her eyes to the light of our holy and precious religion."

Simon Sulphur, who had been closely engaged with the Lord, breathing pious ejaculations, begged leave to be heard. My friend, Coldkail, who had been chosen moderator, said, "Speak on brother, for Lord be thankit, I hae nae ill will against the leddy, gude thought she hae call's us names, and has set the world in a roar o'laughing at us!"

"I think for my part," said Simon Sulphur, "this woman is beyond grace, and if we can fall on some plan to remove her, that we might serve the Lord in peace, it would be best and never mind her soul, a civil prosecution is our only hope."

"I second the motion," said Holy Willy, "a little coertion is sometimes attended with salutary effects. Our holy meetings yield no refreshment to my soul as long as this heretic eats, drinks and sleeps, in peace."

Mucklewrath spoke next; not being a gifted man, he said but little. One of the Raws spoke next: "if we let this woman alone, I mean if we suffer her, gentlemen, to write more books, Black Books, she will Black Book us all out of office, I can swear to that. I suppose you've heard of being turned out today, and I'm of the opinion she ought to be had up, that is, I think, she ought not to be let alone for writing these Black Books. They say she is writing one now that is as bold as Beezlebub, and all them members of Congress bleevs every word that's in them books."

"Well, well," said Holy Willy, "we'll see about that very good idea, Mr. Raw."

. . . .

Counsellor Raw took the floor. He began by saying "I am clearly of the opinion that she might be prosecuted on various grounds. She is a disturber of the peace. Even cats would not mew for her. She wished to stop good pious boys from throwing stones on the Sabbath, and objects to mobs parading the streets at night, or pulling down houses, carrying off carts and steps, and other pious things. She even refused to let Justice Young and Judge Throwstones' sons play ball against her room door. Why it is only the other day she had the assurance to go to our corporation for a warrant to turn out some mighty good pious ladies of Capital Hill out of her own house. This you'll admit, is not to be suffered amongst us good pious people of Capital Hill. This, gentlemen will support an action of itself; only put the law on her, and she'll soon leave our good pious neighborhood."

Counsellor Raw's speech was received with great applause. Some praised his wisdom, while all applauded his piety.

Holy Willy seemed rather doubtful, "Statutes" said he, "some old laws for slight crimes, and our business is to find evidence. For instance, drunkeness—let us take up that—you know—all the ladies—you understand; that will put her in the workhouse."

Had I been a drunkard, a street walker, or a missionary, I should have been safe enough; for it is well ascertained I was the only woman on the Hill who was clear of those virtues.

It appears my godly friends had been at great trouble enquiring over the whole country wherever I had travelled, and corresponding with pious good men to pick some hole in my reputation for the good of my soul. Which of them could sustain such a trail?

"Well, well," said Coldkail, "we'll mack nae hustle about it too. Let's us meet this day eight days, and I'll hae a few cannie books. I'll con them owre wi muckle care at hame. She's as douce a hereteck as e're was stretched on ceron spile, prying into a' fock's business. For, by myself, then, honest Toby and holy Nourse man be turned not o' house and hame by her glibe pen; and she'll ne're stop, I ken her weel freends, till she clears us a' oot o' office; and gin ye find eveedence I'll find law; so gude enn' freends; a' must meet here as we first decreed."[10]

The Coyles, Machen, and Dunn had been joined by Thomas Swann and the capital roared with laughter. These were Mrs. Royall's "good and honest neighbors"!

Thomas Swann was not a respected man in the capital. The sophistry and then the stupidity with which he had manufactured Indictment 118 for Dr. Ely characterized the man to many people. Thomas Swann was known for his facility in skirting facts; it was a talent he had honed years before. The phrase he had written "citizens of the *county*" to cover for "citizens of the *country*," to create citizens when in fact they were not, was a dark shadow of his efforts from the past.

Thomas Swann had begun his public career in 1806 by leaving his native Virginia for Tennessee and better fortune. He was a personable man from good family, and he worked his way into frontier elite circles, those most opposed to Andrew Jackson. He made a name for himself among these people by masterminding the first barrage of innuendo directed against Jackson in order to stem the frontier lawyer's rising star. Young Thomas Swann first raised the issue of Jackson's matrimonial status using a new-found friend, Charles Dickinson, to feed the ultimate insult to the fiery Irishman after a horse race. Dickinson, angry at the loss of the race to Jackson, had snapped up Swann's whispered remark "a man so courageous as to steal another man's wife"[11] and shouted it aloud. For this slander, Charles Dickinson paid with his life, for Andrew Jackson had defended his and Rachel's honor with pistols at dawn. Thomas Swann, not content with the blood of Charles Dickinson, promoted the incident with letters to newspapers. Jackson had driven him from Tennessee by seeking him out and caning him, whipping him like a dog. Swann had sworn revenge, but Jackson already bore his mark. Jackson's pistol had killed Charles Dickinson, but Dickinson's bullet lodged itself so close to Jackson's heart that it could not be removed. The President of the United States suffered from the pain of it always.[12] That pain was worn in the name of Thomas Swann.

The Dickinson tragedy had sent Thomas Swann running from Tennessee, despised by friend and foe. He had gone directly to Washington City, where he had found immediate employment with the Bank of the United States, risen to the presidency of its Washington City branch,[13] and from that post, with the arrival of Jackson in the capital, had stepped into the last-minute Adams appointment as United States attorney and prosecutor for the District of Columbia. This parting gift from the retiring president, John Quincy Adams, was managed in time to handle the tangled affairs of Tobias Watkins for the bank against the Jackson thrust. Thomas Swann had been selected for removal from his post for his bank connections, and only the Senate adjournment, called by Calhoun, kept him in his office.

Thomas Swann had more in common with Dr. Ely than his fellow government workers and appointees. Both men served the same master: Nicholas Biddle. Thomas Swann had no personal reason to dislike Mrs. Royall. He had met her but once, just before Dr. Ely had approached him. He had heard about the woman and knew of her work, but his only meeting with her had been while visiting with his successor, Harrison Smith, in his old office at the bank.[14] There he had come upon Smith and Mrs. Royall engaged in argument about the merits of William Wirt and his hopes for higher office. That argument had cleared the bank offices and Thomas Swann, intrigued by the verbal abilities of the woman, had invited her to call upon his wife and himself. Mrs. Royall had never taken up his invitation, and Thomas Swann's involvement in her affairs was at the insistence of Dr. Ely, not his own brief encounter with her "scolding." The whole matter was in the nature of a legal lark, and Thomas Swann wanted to keep it that way, especially since it had failed. He had not expected to draw to himself the attention he had received, and he was anxious to see the business erased. The Jacksonians were breathing down his neck, and he had no other place to go. When Dr. Ely asked for further assistance, Thomas Swann said "no."

Mrs. Royall enjoyed her deliverance from Ely's concoction. The good churchman's hope that he could remain anonymous was not realized, not with Mrs. Royall marching the corridors of the government offices. If no one knew about Ely's connection to such obscenities as the "common scold," Mrs. Royall erased their ignorance immediately. Coyles, Machen and Dunn were not brilliant men, they were pawns and as for Watterson and his clique, they were proven crooks, out of government or on their way out. Mrs. Royall took no notice of them; she had a more interesting new "raid on the Treasury" to discuss and a very peculiar circumstance to go along with it.

In early 1828, Mrs. Royall had come upon Joseph Nourse, register of the Treasury, who was engaged in questionable activity. Visiting the Treasury, she had witnessed Mr. Nourse busily engaged in signing Treasury certificates in the company of Bank of the United States officials who were keeping count to pay him for his labors. Mrs. Royall was shocked that the register of the United States, the man paid to authenticate government notes, should accept extra payments from Biddle's bank for doing his duty.[15] This strange affair led Mrs. Royall to dig deeper into the matter.

The Treasury was a sacrosanct arm of the government and treated as such by Congress; it was the first department to isolate itself from "politics" by employing career people. Presidents came and went, but the Treasury clerks stayed on forever. As a result, those men within the security of the nation's finance department operated like lords of their domain. This situation had not offended Mrs. Royall before, but after noticing Joseph Nourse she began to question this continuity, this ubiquitous clique in control of the nation's money.

Joseph Nourse was not the only Treasury official involved in accepting fees. William Lee, the national auditor, was there beside Nourse with his hand out too. Mrs. Royall took after both men in *Black Book, Volume I* with a view to ending their practice of accepting extra money from the bank officials. Her comments had not excited anyone in the Adams regime, but Auditor Lee had done his best to retaliate. He had transferred David Henshaw, Mrs. Royall's friend in the Treasury Department, to the War Department where he had to serve under Colonel Towson. Henshaw, an ardent Jacksonian, had not accepted his demotion and had taken to drink to assuage his discomfort. Mrs. Royall had been upset by the action and more upset about Henshaw's drinking and set about to rectify the situation.[16] David Henshaw was meant for better things, and Mrs. Royall went to work to find them for him.

Mrs. Royall's enemies were alert to any attack they could launch in her direction. The news that Mrs. Royall was interested in David Henshaw gave rise immediately to all kinds of rumor and innuendo to warn others friendly with Mrs. Royall that they were in the same awful position. John Quincy Adams joined in this effort. The former president of the United States wrote in his diary on April 25, 1829:

A clerk in the War office, namely Henshaw, who was a strong partisan for Jackson's election, three days since cut his throat from ear to ear, from the mere terror of being dismissed.[17]

Ex-president Adams did not have his facts straight. Mrs. Royall had rescued her friend from the clutches of Colonel Towson. David Henshaw was no longer in danger of being dismissed, and he had not cut his throat. Even as John Quincy Adams wrote, David Henshaw had been put forward by John Eaton for the lucrative post of the Collector of the Port of Boston.[18] As David Henshaw and his family packed up for their move to Boston, Joseph Nourse disappeared from Washington. His flight sent the capital and the Treasury offices into frenzy and shock.[19] Mrs. Royall had done it again. Nourse, attacked in all three of her *Black Books*, had followed Watkins; the old writer had stripped him bare:

N***** is a little old man, crooked in body and mind; his face is round, dark, small and wrinkled, with two little pinking eyes; his countenance is contracted, and his manner clownish; he is the meanest man in the government, except Auditor L.[20]

Mrs. Royall knew well of what she wrote. Nourse had bolted from the capital because of another of her visits to his office, and this time John Quincy Adams was not president; Andrew Jackson was. She had followed a whim of the moment to check on the status of her pension payments, remembering Isaac Hill's experience in New Hampshire, since he had been so rudely set aside by the Senate rejection of his appointment. She had a personal interest in Nourse's office, for his pension group had some say in her claims for government reimbursement due her for her husband's expenditures in the Revolution. Since so many who were unentitled had received pensions from the Navy through the bank in New Hampshire, the woman writer wanted to know what was happening for those who were entitled.

Congress early had accepted the concept that those who had served the birth of the nation should receive restitution for what they had expended to give the nation life. In theory this was commendable, but in practice it was quite another thing. The nation had little cash with which to reward its heroes, and so the Congress, accepting the premise, had hedged its action by creating a group within the Treasury to review claims until such time as more cash was available to satisfy them.[21] Thus, the Pension Bureau had been established, not so much to do as not to do, and those who gained control of this new department used this power for many purposes, not always Congress's own. Claims against the government were closeted for review and the money apportioned and appropriated went to "friends" while the bureaucracy grew. These temporary sinecures became, in time, a power in themselves, stewarding funds which drew financial power to the clerks who passed upon them. Those who agreed with these new servants of the public had their claims paid, and those who did not never heard another word.

Mrs. Royall was in the latter group, and she learned to retaliate in her own fashion. Joseph Nourse had been revealed to be doing something he was not supposed to do and doing nothing he was expected to do, and Mrs. Royall told him so in no uncertain terms. The register of the Treasury sat as head of the Pension Bureau, holding the records in close secrecy; the man not only validated Treasury notes and certificates, the stuff which made the nation's money, but he validated the pensions too.

Open the door, N. I want to see what you are about. How dare you shut the door . . . I am one of the sovereign people, I merely wish to see how you perform your duties, we pay you a round sum. Maybe you are hatching Treason: I don't know that you English, if you are patronized, have a right to shut the door on us. No public office by law is allowed to be shut in business hours.[22]

Mrs. Royall had discovered Joseph Nourse and his employees not only signing Nourse's name to Treasury certificates under the direction of an employee of the Bank of the United States, but she found the same combination validating pension claims for people not entitled to them. Mrs. Royall found the register not only in collusion with an "Henglish" officer of the Second Bank of the United States standing by, counting each certificate and rewarding Nourse with a penny for each bill so authorized but an identical operation was in progress in pension claims. Joseph Nourse had been guilty of contravening regulations before but now Joseph Nourse was guilty of a crime in authorizing payments to people who should not receive them.[23]

Mrs. Royall had one more Nourse expose to bring to the public: The register of the United States of America was not an American citizen. The old man had been appointed to the Treasury by Alexander Hamilton, and no one had thought to ask about his allegiance.[24] As a member of the old Federalist establishment, he had sat through six presidents. It was an omission which shocked Washington.

Mrs. Royall had a method in her attack. Joseph Nourse enjoyed the direct commission to validate certificates not only for distribution in the United States but from foreign sources for dollar conversions. Most of those certificates came from England, increasing implications in context with the Watkins case. Mrs. Royall saved her best salvo for last. The British officer who had suggested the burning of Washington City in 1813 was Captain Joseph Nourse of the British Royal Navy, the register's own son.[25]

Mrs. Royall's extraordinary revelations concerning Joseph Nourse threw the old Federalists and their latter-day supporters into confusion. Andrew Jackson was expected to take a hard line with the Bank of the United States, but Mrs. Royall's new expose made it certain now.

Mrs. Royall's attack on Nourse was her third on the Treasury. In early 1827, the writer had singled out National Auditor William Lee for sarcastic remarks, and those had led to Lee taking a leave of absence rather than encourage Mrs. Royall and her friends to look closer at his office. With the presidential campaign about to break, that ploy had worked. When Tobias Watkins flew his coop, the bank, and its manager in Washington, Thomas Swann, had prevailed upon Lee to surrender his post to give the Jacksonians their first position to fill, one that went to Amos Kendall.[26] The bank expected no more trouble for this cooperation and this new tempest about Nourse was unsettling, particularly to Harrison Smith, Swann's successor at the bank's capital office.

Bank manager Smith decided to retaliate against Mrs. Royall in his own way. His wife Margaret had recently joined the ranks of the literary and was writing for the blackcoat press about Washington society, using words and events to heighten the attack on Peg Eaton. Now Mrs. Smith took after Mrs. Royall, demanding the "old harridan" be silenced.[27] With this step, Mrs. Smith sacrificed her disinterest in politics to reveal her connection with Ezra Stiles Ely. Mrs. Smith called for support against Mrs. Royall from all the good people of the capital, and the Engine House Congregation found itself with more important allies in its endeavor, as Dr. Ely had predicted

Dr. Ely was in a quandary with his legal assault upon Mrs. Royall. To place his religious stamp on American law, he had intended to sneak his legal concoction into the federal law books with the local charges brought by the Engine House Congregation in the district courts of the capital, but it had not worked.

Washington City was not like Philadelphia; it was a separate unit created by Congress to house the national government. Washington with its own laws and no precedents, was governed only by the Constitution. The founding fathers had been cognizant that the city which housed the nation's government had to be a model even to the courts which were to produce the new American jurisprudence undefiled by colonial precedents. Therefore, it would not be admissible in the district courts to use a device drawn from the magistracy courts of Philadelphia. The judges who sat upon the federal bench were not seedy local magistrates easily pressured, but precursors of larger legal values for the nation. These men would have to be approached with an entirely different consideration for review.

The experience with Indictment 118 gave Dr. Ely a new dimension with which to tailor his brainchild for admission to the federal law books. If he could get "common scold" by any strategem into the Washington court, the old ecclesiastical crime could enter the federal statute books by creating its own precedent and he could accomplish with one action what it would take hundreds of actions in the courts and legislatures of the many states to do. The fact that such an action would supersede the very Pennsylvania courts which had declared his legal brainchild null and void in 1826 only gave him greater impetus to continue.

Ely hurried to Thomas Swann with his new project, but the Prosecutor was not as receptive as Ely wished. The aborted Indictment 118 had not been a pleasant experience for the U.S. attorney. The affair had left a bad impression with those for and against Mrs. Royall. William Jones's exploitation of Swann's legal error and his success in quashing the strange legal abomination had caused adverse public comment. The churchman might have good reason to continue his quest, but Thomas Swann did not. It had been a gamble which had produced one loss, and Mr. Swann did not think he could afford another. He had no love for Mrs. Anne Royall, but one experience working with Ely had been enough. Thomas Swann was not refusing for himself alone.

Colonel Thomas McKenney had paid heavily for his compliance in Indictment 118; the Indian commissioner was no longer foreman of the grand jury. That body was in session yet, deliberating the Watkins matter, but Colonel McKenney had been removed summarily for cause from his post at the Bureau of Indian Affairs. That had eliminated him from the jury panel too.[28] Dr. Ely had cost the establishment a key man in a key position.

John Eaton had done the dirty work. McKenney had visited Jackson's war chief to plead for his job, only to hear John Eaton say, "Why sir, everybody knows your qualifications for the post; but General Jackson has long been satisfied that you are not in harmony with him in his views in regards to Indians."[29]

Colonel McKenney's expulsion from the grand jury had hurt Thomas Swann and his control of the Watkins affair for the bank and for himself. Dr. Ely had to bear the responsibility for that tragedy. No, Thomas Swann would assist him no further.

It was a trading session between Dr. Ely and the prosecutor. Dr. Ely demanded that Swann reconsider his decision and reminded him that he had the influence to make him do what he wanted, and that he could force the issue. There was William Wirt, Swann's good friend. It was no secret that John Quincy Adams' former attorney general harbored strong presidential ambitions and even as Ely talked with Swann, Wirt was known to be negotiating with the new anti-Masonic movement to form a national party to promote him as its candidate.[30] Certainly Swann's cooperation in this matter against Mrs. Royall could only hasten the successful outcome of such negotiations for Swann's former protege, now his benefactor. Was it not true that Swann sat as U.S. attorney because William Wirt had prepared Swann's commission as one of his last acts as attorney general?[31] Had not that good man spoken for him even as his own fortunes were declining?

Thomas Swann had no illusions about what the churchman was saying, but there was nothing he could say in rebuttal without making the situation worse. The prosecutor thought back briefly to the one chance meeting he had with Mrs. Royall. All his chickens were coming to roost in her henhouse, and he was sick of it all. He told Dr. Ely exactly how he felt. William Wirt or no William Wirt, Indictment 118 was done and so was Thomas Swann.

Ezra Stiles Ely tried a new tack. What about the interim appointment Mr. Swann enjoyed? Dr. Ely had friends who could make it permanent, with or without Jackson. Thomas Swann suffered Ely's long discussion of his relationship to John Calhoun, Daniel Webster, and Henry Clay. His comment was terse. If Mrs. Royall was so important to the good clergyman why didn't he take himself to these all-powerful folks, and get them to help him? Thomas Swann had his hands full with the Watkins affair, and they were little help there.

The churchman had reached an impasse, and he knew it. He had one last argument, a real bludgeon. The U.S. Attorney's differences with Andrew Jackson were not well known in Washington, but Dr. Ely knew all about that feud. It had something to do with Swann's disgrace a few years back, not the sort of thing to publicize. The clergyman had played an ace, and Thomas Swann knew it.

The Prosecutor had one last defense. He would be happy to assist the clergyman again against Mrs. Royall, but the fact of the matter was that he had no power to do so. Dr. Ely had proposed continuing an action now out of the U.S. attorney's hands, and if Dr. Ely was to ever have his common scold, he would have to locate a federal judge to give it to him. Thomas Swann could not pursue the matter unless a jurist could be found to accept Ely's concoction.

He suggested that Dr. Ely find someone to contact Judge William Cranch about it, since Cranch had been a bank lawyer back when it was the First Bank of the United States and was a cousin to John Quincy Adams, a fact that should count for something in this instance.[32]

It was no idle suggestion from the Prosecutor and Dr. Ely knew it. Thomas Swann was well aware that Indictment 118 was recirculating the capital requesting advice, and he had given it. The Prosecutor went about his business of saving Tobias Watkins and his bank, and Dr. Ely went about his.

Dr. Ely did go to William Cranch. On June 30, 1829, the churchman's strange concoction of common scold, contained in Indictment 118 and declared invalid the first day of June, became valid as Indictment 129 on the last day of June. The curious document had been redesigned by many legal minds. What no one would admit to association publicly had been perused in private, and savored, flavored, and improved. Thomas Swann did not put his name to it this second time.

Indictment 129 was an assault on the new American jurisprudence. The old religious crime forbidden recognition by the Constitution of the United States crept into federal law by Ely's back door. No mention was made of the Pennsylvania court's rejection of it; Judge Cranch allowed the charge as proposed by Dr. Ely. No polite consideration can be attributed to the jurist, for Indictment 129 differed from Indictment 118 in one aspect only. William Cranch accepted "common scold," by citing its horrendous history.[33]

The term common scold had a long, dark history in Scotland and Northern Ireland. It had been invented by John Knox and promoted by his cohorts to fasten tight control on their constituency by reducing it. Having used both men and women to overturn a nation, they sought to decrease the numbers of those they had to satisfy to keep power over their new holdings. Not being able to tell other men that they were unfit to share dominion over Scotland and later Northern Ireland, they moved against women and enlisted their men to gain their ends. Unable to employ arguments against women where an English queen ruled, nevertheless that queen gave them permission to use such in her rebellious territories where her enemies had to be punished.

John Knox and his followers had traded Catholic Mary, Queen of Scotland, for civil and religious dominion over the land that had been hers. Thus, from its very beginning, the term "common scold" was used by Protestant extremists against Catholic and Presbyterian women, by men who claimed vanquished lands as spoils for their assistance to a Protestant queen in her battle with a Catholic one.[34] The term had a special significance to the men who proposed to use it in 1829 against Mrs. Royall.

Andrew Jackson had ridden to power on two horses: the Masons and the Irish Catholics expelled from Ireland. Mrs. Royall boasted support from both too, her Catholic friends being Charles Carroll and Father Mathews, Catholic prelate of Washington.[35] Judge William Cranch's acceptance of "common scold" was not just an affront to Masons and Catholics, it was an open admission, the final proof of Mrs. Royall's thesis against Ely's religion and its intent and against Biddle's bank and its control.

Indictment 129, like its predecessor 118, was produced in secret, hidden in a week of much activity. The nation was readying itself for its annual Fourth of July celebration, this time with Andrew Jackson as President. Congress had left the capital to take advantage of holiday platforms for speeches and electioneering in bright, bunting-laden stages to present them in favorable light. Only the government bureaucrats and the President stayed to enjoy the expected quiet. John Eaton continued to work on the Watkins affair. John Branch was delegated by John Calhoun to keep an eye on both men. It was the perfect time for Cranch to sign the new indictment, since no one was minding his part of the store.

The last of June, 1829, saw an extraordinary calm descend upon Washington, D.C. All animosities appeared to disappear as the hot weather blanked the capital city. No one disturbed the languid humid days and nights; Floride Calhoun had left the city for South Carolina, heavy with yet another Calhoun soon to be born.[36] All seemed peaceful at last with the new administration.

Andrew Jackson kept to his White House and John Eaton to his office, both men busy with their affairs; Andrew Jackson particularly so. Dr. Ely's continuing letters rankled the man, and he was readying another reply. Taking advantage of the June quiet and his detractors' preoccupation with other deviltry, the President had produced his own version of the Eaton story. Weaks of investigation had sought and obtained affidavits to prove the accusations mounted by Ely and his friends to be false, and the President had in hand documented evidence with which to disprove Ely's written complaints. Knowing the good reverend was in Washington, Andrew Jackson directed a most courteous note to Ezra Stiles Ely telling him about his findings.[37] It was not the kind of White House measage the good churchman had expected to receive, and Dr. Ely decided to take his leave of the capital immediately rather than reply.

Thomas Swann had Indictment 129 on his desk, ready to go. Judge Cranch had cleared it for introduction to his court, and all it awaited was the moment for execution. Dr. Ely was given the privilege, and suddenly the churchman wanted it put aside. Even as everyone had left Washington, so must he. The Fourth of July was coming, and the General Assembly had called an annual meeting for that week. He, as elected moderator, had to attend. The prestigious leader of the New Life Presbyterians would be grateful if the Prosecutor did not serve the warrant upon Mrs. Royall until his return. Thomas Swann concurred. If Dr. Ely did not want to take advantage of Mrs. Royall during this week of inactivity in the capital or have her arrested to celebrate the Fourth, the Prosecutor didn't care. He was sick of the whole mess, and Indictment 129 was placed in his desk until such time as the clergyman could make up his mind to have it delivered. No one else knew the papers existed, not even William Brent, clerk of the court.

Mrs. Royall sat writing her version of Indictment 118 and its failure in her rooms on Bank Street, unaware of what was happening. William Jones had saved her from Ely's legal obscenity, and she was putting it to paper. The whole business was unconstitutional, and the federal courts were her protection. She let her pen carry her emotion to celebrate her own Fourth of July.

Indictment 129 sat in the prosecutor's drawer, a new document produced by a new collaboration. Colonel McKenney's name was not on this paper. The new indictment had been signed by Andrew Way of Gideon and Way, printers to the U.S. Senate, a plush appointment arranged by John Calhoun. Andrew Way had nothing to lose and everything to gain from this new association with Dr. Ely against Mrs. Royall. Gideon and Way had begun the printing of a popular new book for national distribution by the tract societies: Gideon's *Bible*.[38]

Dr. Ely left for Philadelphia. The President of the United States could wait for his reply. Dr. Ely had a different kind of answer for him, and he would choose his moment to deliver it. "Common scold" was about to become American law right under Jackson's nose. Dr. Ely gave thanks to his peculiar God!

Chapter 19

Arrest

July descended upon the Jacksonian America with an unexpected coolness. Storms gathered all along the coast, and torrential rains lashed Maryland and Washington. The weather enforced the isolation of the government.

Andrew Jackson had elected to remain in the capital, requiring his cabinet to do likewise.[1] There was much unfinished business in establishing his government, and he was still a sick man. Keeping to his bed, he was not in the public eye, but others were: his friends who surrounded him and those who still hoped to replace him.

The mail packet boats carrying news from the capital were kept busy during this period, distributing along the coast the latest developments from Washington. One newspaper, the *Baltimore American*, a small sheet maintaining a remarkably nonpartisan approach in this most partisan time, was busy with this information activity. Published every morning in time for the mail packet boats sailing from its small office at #2 South Gay Street, it was carried to Boston in 28 to 30 hours, to Niagara Falls via canal in 72 hours, and south to Charleston in 55 hours.

The *American*'s editors and publishers, Dobbin, Murphy, and Bose, did their best to capsulize events from the capital and review all available coastal journals for other tidbits with which to inform their public.[2] Their runners not only delivered papers for the coastal runs but solicited from captains and passengers in transit whatever other papers, journals, or information they had for use in their news coverage. Thus, this one small port newspaper presented an excellent coverage of the events of the times.

A new national issue was being made the first of July, 1829: transportation. The *American* covered it in depth. The nation was growing so fast in all directions that new lines of transport for people and goods had to be devised. Even as roads had been pushed through the wilderness, water, the age-old access to far parts of the world, had been made a domestic alternative for land routes throughout the United States. From 1818, canals had carried an ever-increasing share of the nation's traffic. Suddenly these water routes were in dispute.

The canal companies had grown up in the big states of New York and Pennsylvania. The brainchild of a popular governor of New York, DeWitt Clinton, the Erie Canal had given birth to so many imitations that canal building became a mania, providing safe routes to the furthermost reaches of every coastal state and expanding to towns of the Midwest too. Using river paths a most beneficent Nature had created, more comfortable and much cheaper water routes for commerce and transport were supplanting the primitive toll roads in almost every

148

state's interior. As a result, an argument had begun in the many state legislatures over this new development. It supposedly concerned the cost of the canals to the public, but actually concerned the loss of revenue to the owners and operators of the toll roads threatened with this new competition.

Early in this growing battle, DeWitt Clinton had enlisted Masonry, both operative and speculative, and the Masons, those who built and those who felt a kinship to those who did, had responded. Clinton was a Grand Master of the fraternity, but he had attracted masonic support because, committed to revolutionary change as they were, the new canal concept was in keeping with masonic purposes. Accordingly, the Masons found themselves the target of abuse from more than those who espoused divine right. The old Federalists, stewarding the existent money pools of the nation and holding the stock and bonds of the toll road and bridge companies, did not want their cash flow diminished by progress. This transport controversy cut through old friendships and alliances like a hot knife through butter.

As the canal companies had gained the future from the state legislatures, thanks to masonic support, the established financial groups fought back in their own way, resigning from masonic commitments, assisting anti-Masonic movements, and doing all in their power to stem the influence of the canals and the Masons who supported their development.[3] By June, 1829, this transportation war had reached its zenith. The Pennsylvania legislature, like that of New York, had committed more public funds for canals than roads.

The 1829 campaign, Jackson *versus* Adams, had seen an injection of this issue. Henry Clay, Kentuckian, using his congressional position, had sought to commit the federal government to roads by the simple device of appropriating federal funds to construct a turnpike connecting Kentucky to the East. This seemingly innocuous request was the opening gun for the old Federalist money pools to secure to themselves and their toll road operators access to capital funds denied them in the many state treasuries. The implication was clear. Federal assistance, superceding funding by the states, would commit the capital of the nation to roads over canals. Clay's action was, in effect, an attempt to override the popular opinion of his times.

Andrew Jackson had refused to take a public position on the matter. He had rejoined, when pressed, that the nation had far more problems than a road to Mr. Clay's Kentucky, and this simple put-off had put the road protagonists and Henry Clay in their place.[4] The road crowd had not dared to press it as an anti-Jackson issue, although many near John Quincy Adams had beseeched them to do so. As a result, the opening months of the new administration had not been faced with the matter at all. Henry Clay, and his many adherents, kept quiet but very busy, forming land companies with which to enrich themselves from what they expected to be a forced decision in their favor.[5]

Mrs. Royall had become embroiled in this transport battle early in 1826. As a constant traveler and fervent admirer of Clinton, she had enlisted on the side of the canal builders. For herself, the prospect of fast, quiet, easy water transport was far more acceptable than jolting trips in coaches over rutted and decaying roads. Further, the sight of so many skilled workmen harnessing Nature's great gift to America, its waterways and feeder streams, to provide wide area transport, stirred her. It was the most efficient solution to the growth of the nation. Water had carried men and goods to found the country, and now it would carry generations and goods to build it. It was the cheapest and the best answer to serve the distribution needs of the United States, since the wharves and docks already existed along the rivers and ocean fronts of the land. The canals would not only route products and people to the entire country but all America could compete with the world for the markets that existed in foreign climes. The benefits of such a growing business activity were not lost on the woman commentator of the American scene.

These facts were important to the nation in 1829. All that was lacking was an expression of interest from anyone highly placed in government, business, or finance, to loose the flood gates for either side. Accordingly, the *Baltimore American*, in its July 2nd edition, announced that on July 4 the President of the United States had accepted an invitation to dedicate the cornerstone of the last lock on the new canal linking Washington to an extensive network. Charles Carroll, the last living signer of the Declaration of Independence would attend the ceremony for the dedication of the new stone viaduct for the new proposed Baltimore and Ohio Railroad, a project of the Frederick Road group. Both ceremonies were masonic dedications, and suddenly a new element, railroads, had been introduced into the transport battle.

In the same edition, the *Baltimore American* dropped another surprise. Even as the anti-Masons were occupying an important position in the General Assembly meeting of the Presbyterian Church in Philadelphia, chaired by Dr. Ezra Stiles Ely, Dobbin, Murphy and Bose printed a letter *apropos* of this new movement within that church. Its heading told the tale:

MORGAN ACTUALLY FOUND

In April last, I being at Mt. Desert Island, a small craft appeared off the harbor and shortly—she had on board in all, nine men, who came ashore. The third man I saw was Capt. Morgan. He approached me—He went by the name of Herrington on board the schooner. He told me he had been at Newfoundland, that he was then a British subject; that he was conveyed down the St. Lawrence from Ft. Erie, that he should return to the United States, and Miller had in his hands money of his to the amount of $20,000, that he had been in the bay fishery. By his request, I have promised to publish this on my arrival in this town; let this put all further speculation at rest, as I have had ocular demonstration of the foregoing facts.

This letter was signed by Captain Ezra Sturges Anderson, a well-known leader in the mail packet business. Its effect on the growing movement against Masonry was immediate, for anti-Masonry had begun with the exploitation of the Morgan affair and the appearance of William Morgan found could mean only one thing: Those who had denounced the Masons had been part of a well-financed scheme with other aims to serve. Mrs. Royall's assertion that it all had been a publishing plot to push the sales of anti-Masonry propaganda written by William Morgan with David Miller was no longer only her opinion. The $20,000 alleged to be waiting for Morgan was a vast sum in 1829, one which could come from only one source: Biddle's bank! Mrs. Royall had revealed the strange relationship between the Elyite Presbyterians and Biddle's empire, and suddenly it came to a head. Ely's Presbyterians were meeting then in Philadelphia to propose the formation of a political wing, a new national party drawn from New Life ranks to be called the Anti-Masonry League. It was one more manifestation of the strange movement which had surfaced with Dr. Ely on July 4, 1827.

On Independence Day of 1829, a great storm blanketed the nation. The celebration was washed out; Andrew Jackson did not leave the White House to dedicate the canal lock, and Charles Carroll did not open the new viaduct. The President of the United States and the Great Relic of the Independence were not the only men to change their plans. William Wirt, John Quincy Adams's Attorney General, did not go to Philadelphia to begin his national drive for the presidency with the Anti-Masons and Dr. Ely's General Assembly, for the first time in four years, did not make the news outside of Philadelphia. The news of Morgan had knocked both out of the box.

So the Fourth of July, 1829, passed uneventfully, with only reports of rain-soaked masonic contingents marching to celebrate the nation's birth. On July 5th, the *American* reported the masonic ceremonies and then returned to the case of Tobias Watkins to titillate its readers. There was the prosecutor and his interests, along with the judge and his, and together they had occasioned constant delays. The *American* made the most of these facts. The public wanted to know why Watkins had bolted and run from the capital; the man was hiding something. The constant grand jury meeting and the list of those appearing before it could not be kept secret. Samuel Southard, the former secretary of the Navy, then the Treasury, then the Army became the star of the proceedings, despite his desire to remain anonymous. His connections to Swann, Judge Cranch, and the bank inflamed the public's suspicions, and the *American* kept them afire with another report.

While sequestered aboard a ship in Philadelphia awaiting his prosecution, Tobias Watkins had written two letters to Samuel Southard. Judge Cranch had refused the public a look at either of these pertinent writings. One letter had reached the former secretary via the post office, but the other had been removed by a Southard friend before it could be delivered. This strange interference in such important communication fueled the growing rumors of the contents of the papers in question.

More news broke on July 7th. John Eaton, secretary of war, announced another presidential interim appointment: Francis Scott Key, the renowned poet-lawyer, was appointed as U.S. attorney for the District of Columbia to assist the government with its case. With appointment in hand but no confirmation, Francis Scott Key produced for the grand jury copies of the forbidden correspondence between Watkins and Southard. At the same time, the letters were revealed to the nation by the *American*, reprinting from the *Alexandria Gazette* (Virginia), its report of the correspondence drawn from the *Baltimore Republican*. Samuel Southard, refusing comment, rushed to Washington.[6]

Watkins's letters to Samuel Southard were blockbusters. The first was a simple plea for help to a former superior, setting forth in explicit terms the directives Watkins alleged he had received from that superior. Samuel Southard was asked to come forward and speak for his former assistant. This letter had been forwarded through the post office, following the route that all letters took. The second letter from Watkins to Southard did not. This second appeal was a plea to corroborate the directions enumerated in the first letter to save a man who had served Southard so well, with promise from Watkins that for the secretary's witness in Watkins's behalf, Samuel Southard would not be implicated in any criminal activity, that Watkins would insist that the secretary had been guilty only of an excusable oversight. This letter had been extracted from the Philadelphia post office before it had been recorded as received. Tobias Watkins claimed that he had sent it, but no one would admit to having handled it. The appearance of both these letters set the stage for what was to follow.

Judge William Cranch could not deny these documents to the grand jury. The question of interference with the mails was a criminal problem and one that the grand jury had to consider in the Watkins affair. All Judge Cranch had left was his power to cite for contempt the newspaper responsible for the national dissemination of the letters and their contents. The *Baltimore Republican* was cited by Judge Cranch[7] while Francis Scott Key, seizing upon this emotion-laden moment, joined William Jones to demand that Tobias Watkins be moved to trial immediately. The court had no right to refuse public examination of the man and his words.

In just ten days, John Eaton had pried the Watkins case from the clever manipulations of Swann and Cranch. Watkins had been sitting in prison long weeks, stripped of all his colleagues and his confidence in their ability to help him. Eaton had taken advantage of the situation. Guessing that Watkins's former associates had left him to the mercy of William Cranch, with Thomas Swann to oversee their legal interests, Eaton had prevailed upon William Jones, Mrs. Royall's friend, to take over Watkins's defense.[8] Tobias Watkins, alone and without funds, had accepted William Jones, a former secretary of the Navy. It was obvious that if Southard would not come forth, another with access to Navy files and personnel knew how to force him to do so. Associated with William Jones was Richard Coxe, and he, together with John Eaton and Tobias Watkins, was a practicing Mason. The fraternity had joined hands again to protect its own, and for the first time since Watkins had been brought to Washington, before its Federalist courts, the Jackson administration would have a fair go in the controlled court of William Cranch.

Francis Scott Key had been enlisted by John Eaton on July 1, the same day William Jones had raised his voice for Tobias Watkins. William Cranch and Thomas Swann had been caught unprepared and had chosen the Fourth of July holiday to delay all the proceedings. Key's ploy with Southard's letters on July 3 frustrated that plan. On July 7, William Cranch denied Francis Scott Key and William Jones their joint petition for immediate trial and ordered the whole matter back to the grand jury only to find that Key and Jones had taken their petition to another judge for consideration. William Cranch, trying to bottle up Watkins with yet another grand jury examination, discovered that a fellow judge, Buckner Thurston, had successfully overruled him. The ensuing attempt by William Cranch to annul that action did nothing to enhance the district court's repute. The details of these stormy court maneuverings were carried by the *American* as its answer to Cranch's contempt order against another newspaper.

Judge Thurston's upset of Cranch's control threw Samuel Southard a curve. He went to John Branch, Jackson's secretary of Navy, for support. Before Branch could aid him, Andrew Jackson took a hand in the affair. With only a few hours' notice, he invited John and Peg Eaton, William Barry and his wife, and Jack and Emily Donelson to accompany him to Norfolk, Virginia, and, by order of the President, John Branch, secretary of the Navy, and his wife if she desired. It was announced that the President and Secretary Branch would inspect the Norfolk Navy Yard and installations. Rumor was that Jackson was very ill and wanted a brief respite, a cruise on the sea to restore his energy, but others guessed that Branch had been taken from the capital to frustrate Samuel Southard's needs. It was no secret that Jackson loathed Southard, who, as secretary of the Navy to Monroe, had claimed that the credit for the victory at New Orleans belonged not to the general who had won it but to James Monroe, the acting secretary of war at the time.[9] This sophistry which lauded a man who, with James Madison, had mismanaged the nation's defenses at Bladensburg, effecting the defeat of American forces that allowed the burning of Washington, had been too much for Andrew Jackson. Samuel Southard had backed down when faced with it, and he was to back down again.

As the *Potomac* steamed southward with its disparate passenger list, Ezra Stiles Ely returned to Washington. The prominent clergyman was a dejected man; the Fourth of July meeting of the General Assembly had not been a glorious affair. The planned political movement had not materialized, and the convention of blackcoats had filled its hours with nothing more rousing than the reports of seminary problems in Princeton and progress reviews of mission activities elsewhere, all of which entailed more demands for money from the growing press empire. The entire New Life movement had been downplayed, and Ely felt the frost creeping over him from the results of his manifesto of July 4, 1827. The news of Morgan had cast its pall.

Ezra Stiles Ely had suffered a personal blow during his church enclave in Philadelphia: He had been subjected to open criticism for his activities in Washington.[10] The general feeling was that the churchman had spent too much time in Washington, and his activities there had been costly. The loss of Colonel McKenney as chief of the Bureau of Indian Affairs had been a catastrophe for the blackcoats and their efforts among the Indians. Dr. Ely, by pursuing the common scold indictments, had cost his movement another important proponent in a national post, and his preoccupation with his strange legal matters was not worth such sacrifice.

The Bureau of Indian Affairs had been a paying preserve for "Christian" Army retirees and ministers for more than a decade. Andrew Jackson's experiences with British Bible wielders leading Indian movements and uprisings against the new American nation occasioned his demand that Indians be forced to migrate to western sites to render them incapable of any further deployment against the nation. This call had led Senator John Eaton to propose legislation to establish the bureau to facilitate Jackson's policies. That agency had been taken over even as it was voted into being and turned over to James Monroe's special favorites, among them Colonel McKenney, the Georgetown dry-goods dealer turned soldier at Bladensburg.

McKenney was infamous in the capital. Anticipating the British attack, he had sold his business and compounded his clairvoyance by running about the Bladensburg battlefield broadcasting to the American line that the British had breeched this position and that, an action many believed had contributed to the American rout in that battle.[11] Since James Monroe and his chief, Madison, had done no better, Colonel McKenney was a delicious affront to Andrew Jackson. Thus he had received stewardship of Jackson's brainchild.

Under McKenney, the Indians found themselves assisted by three disparate groups: the military and religious commanders allied to the anti-Jacksonians and the dry-goods merchants who were granted a trading monopoly with each tribe. These agents were supposed to preclude British intervention with Indians but instead formed their own political power pacts for other troublesome interventions. Retired officers, mostly political hacks with nothing more than honorary commands, joined missionaries to exercise command and control of public funds appropriated by the Congress to accommodate the Indian move west. Those public funds were supposedly spent in buying "goods" for Indians, but in truth the cash was diverted to business ventures, among them Bible and tract publishing houses. Far from the gaze of Washington City, the Indian agents had established personal political and financial fiefdoms with which to serve not only their own interests but those who bankrolled them. The Bureau of Indian Affairs in the capital operated exactly like the Pension Board of the Treasury, using its growing money control to reward friends and punish enemies and to stir up the Indians as needed to heighten the effect.[12] Mrs. Royall had been as acid in her criticism of the bureau as she had been with the Pension Board and her comments had been credited with McKenney's removal.

Suffering the loss of Colonel McKenney, Dr. Ely's friends did not subject themselves to criticism for the loss of the money power they had enjoyed and abused; they blamed him. The cessation of sales thanks to the removal of Watterston from the government and the end to free distribution of Bible tracts and now the loss of McKenney and the monopoly trading business was a financial blow to the General Assembly. These matters disturbed the churchman as he prepared to resume operations in Washington.

Dr. Ely had not been the only one to suffer loss over the Fourth of July weekend. It had been a costly holiday for the Engine House Congregation and its friends too. Calling upon John Coyle to proceed at last against Mrs. Royall as planned, Dr. Ely found the government clerk in a terrible state. That very morning the word had come that William Barry, Jackson's postmaster general, had signed the removal from office of Andrew Coyle, first clerk of the Post Office Department.[13] Barry had done this as the coach stood at his door ready to carry him and his wife to the good ship *Potomac* for that cruise to Norfolk with Jackson. The Coyle family was reeling from this blow.

Andrew Coyle had been the benefactor of the entire Coyle clan. The first Coyle to find employment with the government, he had sent for the others, and every member of the family had received his position from the recommendation of this more successful kin. Not only had the post office chief clerk made it possible for his relatives to gain their sinecures, but he had opened many other offices to Scots-Irish immigrants, particularly members of the Engine House Congregation. Andrew Coyle's precipitous fall from grace signaled trouble for the entire clan and their fellow exalters in Christ.

Ezra Stiles Ely's shock was as great as John Coyle's. It was bad enough to hear about Andrew Coyle's removal, but the news that Obadiah Brown, a Baptist minister, had been appointed to replace him was worse.[14] The new replacement for Andrew Coyle was a good friend to Mrs. Royall, and this new reminder of the power of that woman infuriated both men.

Brown had been encouraging the old woman for years. He was her informant and had joined her in her constant attacks on the blackcoats and aided her financially. This man, "the only honest priest" by Mrs. Royall's own pen, "that jolly, sensible man" rewarded with Andrew Coyle's position[15] was more than a godly man could stand. Parson Brown had taken possession of Andrew Coyle's office that very morning.

Ezra Stiles Ely could not contain himself. It had been a disastrous week, but the eminent minister could not drop his guard. He eased John Coyle's grief as best he could and then added the promise that Mrs. Royall would pay dearly for all the mischief she had done, including this last calamity. John Coyle would have his revenge; Dr. Ely had it in hand even as they spoke. They had only to straighten up and walk directly to Thomas Swann, and the old woman would be finished. It was the kind of action both blackcoats needed to quiet themselves.

Thomas Swann was not in a good mood. Everything was going wrong. It had been the worst week yet in the Watkins affair. Eaton's surprise appointment of Francis Scott Key had caught the Prosecutor in a bind. The man was celebrated for his poem, *The Star-Spangled Banner*, and he was an attorney in excellent standing. John Eaton had pulled a fast one, for with Key on the case and the Prosecutor's own prerogatives now invaded, Watkins would go to trial. Buckner Thurston had seen to that. Monday, July 13, Tobias Watkins would face the world, and there was nothing that could be done to stop it.

The sudden appearance of Ezra Stiles Ely and John Coyle in Thomas Swann's office the morning of July 9 was not what the Prosecutor wanted. He was sick of the Anne Royall mess, and there was no doubt the clergyman and his friend had come to see him about it. Thomas Swann resigned himself to their visit. Indictment 129 was ready and they could have it.

The churchman and his partner, John Coyle, were agitated. Andrew Coyle had been sacked from the post office and Obadiah Brown had been appointed in his stead. Swann commiserated with Ely and Coyle, but he did not know how important Andrew Coyle was to both men. Dr. Ely did not elaborate, but with Andrew Coyle out of the mail business, Dr. Ely's tract societies had lost their last hold on free distribution. Parson Brown was a known enemy to the Bible and tract groups, a Jacksonian through and through. Worse, he shared Mrs. Royall's adverse opinions of the blackcoats and their products. It was an end to another scheme. Dr. Ely could not talk about the matter with Thomas

Swann; he let John Coyle prattle on about his brother's loss. Ely allowed himself one comment. There was no doubt that Parson Brown would lend his voice to those upholding the Sunday mails against the anti-Sabbaticals, and that would be another blow to the hopes of Thomas Swann's friend, William Wirt, in his quest for the presidency.

Thomas Swann was not interested in conversing about the matter. When did Dr. Ely want the indictment processed? Dr. Ely's answer was short and to the point. He wanted Mrs. Royall arrested immediately.

The churchman and his friends had picked the right time for their assault. With the writer's mainstays out of Washington on the *Potomac*, no one could help her and her counsel, William Jones, was not available either. Mrs. Royall's lawyer was in Annapolis and would return to Washington the 10th, just in time to represent Watkins against further legal delay.[16] If they could execute the warrant for Mrs. Royall's arrest, take her that very afternoon, she could sit in jail over the entire weekend. Mrs. Royall should be taken late the next day.

Thomas Swann agreed. He placed Indictment 129 again in his drawer. He would give it to William Brent to execute at the last possible minute to insure that Mrs. Royall be taken too late for Jones to help. Ely and Coyle left Thomas Swann's office with a much lighter step.

Friday, July 10, dawned hot and heavy. Mrs. Royall had risen at six in the morning to write before the summer heat made her occupation impossible. She had enjoyed the quiet of the capital these past few weeks. The Engine House Congregation had been silent, the heat having cooled religious ardor, and open-air meetings in the park having taken their congregation. It had been a very good week since the Fourth, and she had much to write about.

The post office developments were the most interesting. William Barry had rid himself of Andrew Coyle and her old friend, Obadiah Brown, was in his place. She had been the first visitor to Parson Brown's new office and everything was working well. At last the Jackson administration was cleaning house. John Calhoun had adjourned the Senate without confirming Jackson's personnel, but Jackson's followers were taking the offices anyhow. They were dedicated men, and although they could not be paid until the Senate confirmed them, they had assumed their places. Jackson's name still carried more clout than Calhoun's cash! She was filled with pleasure as she wrote. She was writing her commentary about William Lee, Joseph Nourse, George Watterston, Colonel McKenney, and now Andrew Coyle. The very name Coyle set her pen to scratching as it had not before:

We want no hereditary offices, or officers . . . These fellows have been in office so long, that they consider it their inalienable right, and have raised a fair hue and cry, within a few weeks, that their employers thought proper to dismiss them, and employ others. "They have been in since Jefferson and Washington—they are faithful servants." What is that to the purpose? Have we not the right to employ whom we please to do our work? And why one set of men should be suffered to monopolize emolument or all, to the exclusion of another, I should like to know.[17]

Oblivious to everything but her pen, she continued to celebrate the Jackson removals:

Even our Presidents, members of Congress, etc. are elected, at short periods, from the mass of the people, and upon the same principle, all the subordinate officers ought to be changed. The best of men, we find from history, never have been proof against corruption; and to guard against this evil, the framers of our constitution wisely provided frequent rotation in office. It is essential to the existence of republics, and the only security to the liberties of the people.[18]

Mrs. Royall was waxing warmly to her recurrent theme. A breath of fresh air was blowing through Washington for the first time in over a decade, and it would clear the stale odor of privilege and favoritism which was throttling democracy. She laughed aloud as she thought about the arguments of those who did not want to go, and those who did not want to see them go. Their arguments had been trotted forth in great profusion and such wailing had not been heard since the Fall of Jerusalem. It was the fall of their city all right, and their cries to Jehovah would not save them this time. They had defiled their temples and been caught, and they would have to make a new start to gain the city back. Andrew Jackson had come and was taking Washington. Let the fools cry out; the nation would benefit despite the claims set forth for those in office. Government business held no risk for the initiate, only for those who, having had it, had abused it. As clerk after clerk fell before the Jackson axe, the cries would grow louder, but Mrs. Royall knew they would fall on deaf ears. The old had to give way to the new:

> I know it will be said that it requires practice to do the business of a clerk. No such thing: enough can always be found who understand bookkeeping, which is sufficient, and the measure itself will act as a stimulus to qualifications, where office and place are alike open to all. What incentive has the youth of our country, if offices and emoluments are to be perpetual.[19]

Old Jackson's fresh sweep had a youthful feel to it, and Mrs. Royall made the most of it. She thought of the blackcoat appeals to sympathy, their only remaining excuse, and then wrote:

> I had no idea that we had so much corruption in the government till I saw these abominable impudent remarks. I have heard a hundred times latterly. "What is to become of his poor wife and children," as though they had met with some awful loss by fire. What becomes of every man's wife and children who have never received one cent from government? Is government bound to take care of every man's wife and children?[20]

Here Mrs. Royall paused. She thought of Nicholas Biddle and his hired hands in the treasury:

> Preposterous impudence—a great pity indeed, that Mr. B. can no longer put his hand in the treasury, and squander it to his kindred.[21]

Biddle's kindred, those blackcoats, those clerks, those British bankers. Mrs. Royall loved her Jacksonians more. They had delivered on what they had promised:

> What would the people say if these men were not turned out? The cabinet are not to blame; they were placed in office for this very purpose. It would be as much as their places are worth, were they not to do so. I know a little more about this matter than any other editor in Washington, as it may be supposed, though I do not meddle with politics. I am not deaf, and am perfectly aware that it is expected of the present administration to make a general turn-out, and they were elected upon no other understanding; and why not? Is it not right? It is the voice of the people, let it be right or wrong.[22]

"I know a little bit more," she wrote, and so she did. All the muling and complaints of those removed had been covered, but yet, one did remain: that business about non-gentlemen removing gentlemen from office, the parting shot of those who thought themselves the chosen of God. Mrs. Royall saved the best sarcasm for them.

If these men had possessed the delicacy and independence of gentlemen, they would not have waited to be turned out . . . had they the proper spirit, they would not serve under a man whose politics they did not like.[23]

Mrs. Royall felt free and at peace as she sat penning these words. Her delight spilled over into her final rejoicing to her readers:

. . . this reform has taught the people a lesson, which I trust they will improve substantially for their good. They have discovered that the want of rotation in office has created a host of nobility in fact, who consider their fellow citizens born their vassals, and bound to maintain them, and that because Lord John has succeeded to the place and title of his father—his son, the young Count, ought to succeed him, and so on . . . though they are not called by their titles, they assume the pomp, receive the revenue, and exercise uncontrolled insolence over their fellow citizens—the very source from whence they received their power![24]

All the Coyles were in mind with that! Lord John and his son; they would be next. The assumed aristocracy of those who followed the new God was too much for the republic, and it was on its way out. The new American government looked at the nobility its predecessors had created. It was time to clear out not only the top clerks but the bottom ones too. The Hensons, the Bakers, the McCormacks, the St. Clarks, the Sprigs, the Dunns, the Machens, the Elgars and the Lowries should be removed, and as she enumerated their names she heard the first pounding at her door.

Constable Beck stood there on the doorstep. At first there was a wide smile on his face, but as people stopped to stare, it became a quick frown. Mrs. Royall stood quietly saying nothing, her presence speaking for her. With a loud voice tuned for the crowd forming, he announced that he had come to take Mrs. Anne Newport Royall to answer charges witnessed before William Cranch, chief judge of the Circuit Court of the District of Columbia. Mrs. Royall stared at her neighbor, redfaced from his exertions, in disbelief. What was he talking about?

Constable Beck drew himself up into the best symbol of authority he could muster. The crowd was swelling with young ruffians from the Engine House. The officer of the law waved a paper for all to see. Mrs. Royall took it from him and reviewed the words. There it was, in black ink on parchment, and very official indeed:

DISTRICT OF COLUMBIA, to wit:

THE UNITED STATES OF AMERICA,

To the Marshal of the District of Columbia — Greetings:

WE command you that you take Anne Royall, late of Washington County if she be found within the county of Washington, in your said district, and her safely keep, so that you have her body before the Circuit Court of the District of Columbia, to be held for the county aforesaid, at the City of Washington immediately to answer unto the United States of America concerning a certain misdemeaner by her committed as it is presented to

Whereof fail not, at your peril, and have you then and there this writ.

Witness W. Cranch, Esquire, chief judge of our said court at the City of Washington, the 10th day of July, Anno Domini one thousand eight hundred and 29.

Issued the 11 July 1829

W. Brent, Ck.

Mrs. Royall read the document again. Her voice found itself: "I must tell Counselor Jones." Constable Beck was very stern. There was no time for that; Mrs. Royall was bid to come immediately. She would have to surrender herself to him there and then, to be taken to the keep immediately. She could see her counselor on Monday. The crowd was jeering and laughing.

Mrs. Royall asked more information of the constable. Beck shook his head. He did not know the charges and it was no concern of his. The judge's name was there and that was all he needed to arrest Mrs. Royall. Mrs. Royall studied the document in her hand. Did Constable Beck know why the phrase "on the Monday" had been inked out and "immediately" had been substituted? Constable Beck knew nothing about the alteration, but "immediately" was there and he would do it now. Mrs. Royall looked again at William Brent's signature on the document. This man was an old friend of hers; why had he not warned her about this? He had written "immediately" over "on the Monday of." The crowd grew larger, wondering about the delay, and then began to call to Beck to do his duty.

Constable Beck was not happy with the mob at his back and insisted that Mrs. Royall come then and there, or he would force her. Suddenly Mrs. Royall understood. Ely and his Engine House friends were at it again. They had thought of something new. For a moment she felt fear, but she held her ground. She looked at the document again. "The 11th of July, issued the 11th of July, 1829." She handed the paper back to Constable Beck. He could not serve her this day with this paper. This was July 10, and the paper was not valid until July 11. There it was, over William Brent's signature! Constable Beck looked at it carefully, and Mrs. Royall was right. The writer was relieved. William Brent had sent her warning again; she loved that man.

The crowd was menacing, not understanding the action at the top of the steps. Mrs. Royall could feel the danger. She spoke to Constable Beck. She would spare him a second trip tomorrow and go to the court with him now if he would allow her to get a few things. Using her best smile, she pressed her luck and his, leaving him to handle the mob in the street below. Could she have a moment to gather her things, her small necessaries, for no doubt she would need them for the keep over the weekend? Constable Beck had no choice. He turned to the crowd and announced that Mrs. Royall needed something and she would be quick about it, for Judge Cranch was waiting. It was 1:00 p.m.

Mrs. Royall stepped into her rooms. Summoning her maidservant, she sent her for Sally Stackpool. There was a nasty crowd forming, and Counselor Jones had to be summoned. Only Sally could do it. Gathering up her things, she returned to Constable Beck.

Mrs. Royall walked proud and erect beside the constable. The crowd pursued them, pressing in on their sides. It was a disorderly parade, and Mrs. Royall knew that Beck and she were all alone. Not one friend was among the host engulfing her. If the girl did not do as she was told, no one would know what was happening. Even as this thought came to mind, good, dear Sally was there, returning from her errands. Sally saw her and ran to her, pushing away the crowd.

Mrs. Royall offered no explanation, and Sally asked for none. The writer asked her friend to fetch William Jones and then run to whatever friends were still in the city. Mrs. Royall had no intention of remaining in Constable Beck's keep for the weekend. Sally understood her assignment; Mrs. Royall proceeded with her growing retinue.

The parade reached the court and William Brent came out, surprised at Mrs. Royall's appearance. The Prosecutor had surprised the court clerk with the writ signed by Cranch that morning, a *fait accompli* which Brent had to execute. William Brent, knowing the thoroughness of his friend, Mrs. Royall, had deliberately dated the writ July 11 to give her a day to prepare, yet here she was! One look at the crowd, and William Brent knew why Mrs. Royall had come. The old woman had exercised common sense to walk safely with the constable rather than remain at home to be molested by that mob. Brent sent word to Mrs. Royall's friends with his clerks. It would be well to have a welcoming committee to oppose that mob, and Brent himself went to the newspapermen to tell them what was happening. When Mrs. Royall reached the top of the court house portico she found a welcoming group ready to receive her, this time her friends, and together they faced her enemies behind her. The Engine House ruffians were left standing on the court steps, Mrs. Royall was in jeopardy no longer. She was on a stage and she had an audience to prove it. She entered the halls of justice in no fear and it was not what Ely, Coyle, Swann, or Cranch had wanted at all. Mrs. Royall had not been arrested and could not be arrested until July 11, but one more of her crusades had been set in motion.

Chapter 20

The Washington Merry-Go-Round

Mrs. Royall did not spend the weekend in the Washington City keep. Dr. Ely and his cohorts were deprived of their hope to place the woman writer among the fallen women of the capital for two days of humble pie. William Brent had seized upon the extraordinary crowd forming before the court to interrupt the Watkins case and bring forth William Jones to assist his client.

Counselor Jones was angry. Thomas Swann was a bigger fool than ever, and with or without William Cranch this invalid summons would not stand. The prosecutor would have to spell out the charges immediately. William Jones entered an objection to Constable Beck's writ.[1]

Thomas Swann had not prepared for such quick counteraction for Mrs. Royall. Both he and Cranch had been too busy deliberating about their next move in the Watkins affair to bother about Ely's common scold. Accordingly, William Jones's immediate action for Mrs. Royall forced the prosecutor to assent to counsel's demand that Mrs. Royall be returned home and allowed her freedom. She would report on Monday, July 13, with William Jones.

Thomas Swann was beside himself with anxiety and then the thought occurred to him that Mrs. Royall's maneuver was a stroke of luck. William Jones's demand that Mrs. Royall have until Monday, July 13, to answer the writ was what they needed for Watkins. Here was the perfect chance to delay Watkins's trial, an opportunity they had not found in the law books. If Judge Cranch would arrange to bring Mrs. Royall to immediate trial on Monday or any day of the next week, Tobias Watkins's trial could be postponed. The papers and the public could criticize all it wanted, but Mrs. Royall could be given precedence. The old woman could go free over the weekend, but the judge could declare that it was adequate preparation for her trial and she could appear before him on Monday or Tuesday. Tobias Watkins would not! William Cranch took Thomas Swann's unexpected gift.

Mrs. Royall returned to her home in a state of suspense. She did not know the particulars of the charges upon which she had been arrested. She suspected it was Ely again, but Thomas Swann had not provided any details. William Jones had told her not to worry; there would be no trial until everything had been clarified. It was all she had, and she had to accept it despite her misgivings. She knew something terrible was afoot and suspected that Ely had new allies.

Back in court, Thomas Swann and William Cranch had become active collaborators in a new scheme. Mrs. Royall's affair could preempt Tobias Watkins and his matters. The old woman was manna from heaven, Ely's gift, and both men enjoyed the long weekend, relishing their deliverance from Watkins on Monday. Neither guessed that Jones and his associates knew what they were up to.

William Jones, former secretary of the Navy, had been working with John Eaton, secretary of War, and Amos Kendall, the new fourth auditor, preparing his own bombshell for Swann and Cranch. Even as Mrs. Royall had surrendered herself to Cranch's court, a barrage of criticism had been planted in the *Baltimore American* to fuel public dissatisfaction with William Cranch and Thomas Swann. It began "It is now nearly two months that this matter has been, in one form or other, before the court," and the statement applied to both Watkins and Mrs. Royall. It was a prelude of what was to come.

William Jones had in hand information that Tobias Watkins was not the only culprit in the scheme to defraud the government both at home and abroad. Jones had appealed to loyal clerks in his old department, men tied to him but not to Jackson, for pertinent information and had received it. Navy agents in New York and Boston had done with their more subordinate positions what Watkins had done. William Jones, working with Jackson's appointees as U.S. attorneys in both New York and Boston, moved to have these men indicted. By Monday, July 13, the word was out that Watkins had been joined by new defendants and their crimes were the same.[2] Francis Scott Key joined with William Jones in demanding that the government be allowed to consider evidence presented against Purser Hambleton in New York as well as the Navy agent in Boston to examine the extensive network with which Watkins was associated. This bombshell was tossed into Cranch's court hopper on the very last moment of trial on Friday, July 10. William Cranch never had a chance to rule against it. Once again Buckner Thurston had given his approval and the die was cast. William Jones gave William Cranch one more headache. He entered a motion to take the whole Watkins matter out of the District of Columbia court and transfer it to New York, where the pertinent facts were already available.[3] This shock to the bank crowd, this affront to Judge Cranch, was too much. The Philadelphia money colossus now knew it was not fighting just Andrew Jackson but a competing financial monolith in New York. William Cranch found he was not destined to have a quiet weekend after all, and he was not alone in his discomfort.

The weekend of July 12 was not a pleasant one for Mrs. Royall. William Jones had reassured her that she had nothing to fear, that everything was under control. Dr. Ely and his cohorts would not be allowed to abuse the law, and Mrs. Royall had much better legal minds on her side than her enemies did. It was little comfort to the woman who knew she had to appear before William Cranch on Monday morning, even though she had confidence in her counselor. There was nothing to be done about the situation, however, so Mrs. Royall went about her affairs, writing what she thought. She gave vent to her spleen about this latest assault, and she had a good idea of why it was still happening. The word was out that the General Assembly of Ely's Presbyterians had been disturbed by the Morgan revelations, and Mrs. Royall was being credited again with it all. Also, the Pennsylvania Legislature had criticized the administration of Dickinson College under "Pope" Duffield, an earnest follower of Ely, and had denied them further state funds.[4] Mrs. Royall was sure the new attack upon her came from three of her latest victims:

> It may as well be explained here, that the good pious people of Capital Hill were only the catspaws of Dr. Ely and Pope Duffield . . . the agents of the General Assembly.[5]

Duffield, the sanctimonious fool she had put to rout in Carlisle, Pennsylvania had been in Washington trying to drum up congressional help to stop the world on Sunday and had been scuttled during his absence from home by his own state legislature while meeting with Ely and the Engine House fanatics to do her in. She could not help wondering what they had planned for her in revenge:

> But these would never have dared to make the attempt but for the items in the first volume of my Pennsylvanian. These items raised the wind; and all the discarded officers, and those who expected to be turned out, offered their services. I had long thwarted the godly people. Now was their time to measure their strength, if ever. Many weighty state matters were at stake—the new Congress was soon to meet (Oct. 1829) I had influence there—I would be in favor of turn-out—I would unite with my friends in the Congress to oppose the Sunday Mail Bill—I was a bar to their outpourings—I even foretold the swindling of Nourse and Watkins—I told too many truths—I must be put down—but how was it to be done? "She must have powerful friends or she would never dare to attack the first people in the government. She must have some secret friend. She has thrown off the mask and come out a Jackson man. It must be some of these. A prosecution is the thing to draw them from their hiding places. We will then attack them separately, and may finally overcome." Of all this I was apprized; and to save trouble, if Dr. Ely, Duffield, and their tools of Capital Hill wish to know my friends, their names are at their service, viz: Truth and Independence. It is needless to name my enemies. Had they not been fools as well as knaves, they might have known my friends. Those who vindicate the truth have the whole world for their friends.6

Mrs. Royall indulged in this bravado to rebuild her flagging spirit, but she knew that the court was with her enemies, and Ely would use it as he had in Philadelphia if he got the chance:

> "Law, law is the thing. (The Gospel was taking a nap). Put her in jeopardy, you will soon find her friends. This will show if the administration is with us. It will prove whether the President is of the true evangelical faith or not." The party prayed again and had a precious outpouring. All who opposed reform flocked to the holy standard. These were backed by the good sound Presbyterians throughout the Union, with oaths and money at their service. So that my conversion might be called a law-full convention and full of law. Thus armed the crusade began against an old woman. It was David and Goliath.7

Mrs. Royall spent her whole weekend writing to assuage her feelings. It was well that she did. William Jones was convinced that the new attack on Mrs. Royall was as illegal as the first and that Mrs. Royall was a pawn used by Swann and Cranch to delay the Watkins case. He spent all his time on that affair, not Mrs. Royall's.

Counselor Jones was determined to show Swann and Cranch that they did not have command of the Watkins situation. Tobias Watkins had admitted to using vouchers from other Navy agents to accomplish his transfers. This was a criminal act of misappropriation. Monday he would raise this in court and demand an immediate trial on this simple fact. Hambleton, the New York Navy agent, had pled guilty and his admitted disgrace would be the best defense Watkins could put forth. The whole matter could be pried from the restraint that Cranch had placed upon it.

Having decided on a course of action for Watkins, William Jones considered Mrs. Royall's problem too. He was disturbed by Judge Cranch's order that Mrs. Royall report for trial Monday morning, two days after writ for arrest. Such an action did not serve the ends of justice, and Cranch knew it. For a federal judge to take such a precipitate action, there had to be a reason, but what could it be?

Cranch had been a willing agent in the many delays in the Watkins matter and this could be just one more excuse for more procrastination. If it was, Watkins' plea for immediate examination in the light of recorded evidence could force Cranch to change his plans. William Jones set himself to the task.

Watkins alone would not be enough to effect what the counselor had in mind. Mrs. Royall had to enter the picture. There was no way that the writer could be brought to trial without knowing what her crime was. Swann had produced an indictment which meant nothing; the prosecutor would have to give up the details before a trial could proceed. The defendant was entitled to know what she had been accused of having done, and no judge, federal or otherwise, could amend the legal code and American legal practice to eliminate that basic right. Watkins's plea for his trial to proceed for a simple and documented act of criminal intent could not be put aside to proceed in an action against a woman whose crime was undefined. The prosecutor's neglect in producing the particulars with which he intended to charge Mrs. Royall would preclude Mrs. Royall from facing trial on Monday.

William Jones savored his moment of triumph; he was about to prove that another member of the old regime was not up to new considerations. There was a new legal game yet to be played in the nation and it was called justice over privilege.

Monday morning, July 13, 1829, dawned bright and hot. Mrs. Royall had risen early and prepared carefully: As she was about to depart, she was surprised to discover a delegation at her door. It was not from the Engine House Congregation but from the local newspapers. The word had gone out that something remarkable was about to occur in William Cranch's court, and the best way to see the action was from beside Mrs. Royall. All of Washington's young newsmen were at Mrs. Royall's door to escort her to the court.[8] It was a gesture which touched the woman writer deeply.

William Jones awaited his clients. Mrs. Royall arrived on time, with her coterie of newspapermen. Tobias Watkins, in custody, would appear when needed. Mrs. Royall came first, for Judge Cranch had so ordered. William Jones produced his argument, and the *Baltimore American* reported it on July 14:

> Mrs. Royall—The National Intelligencer of yesterday states that this lady appeared before the Circuit Court of the U.S. on Monday, to answer to indictment found against her during the term by the Grand Jury, for certain alleged improprieties of conduct, denominated in legal phrase "common scold," "common slanderer," "brawler," "common nuisance," etc. The defendant's counsel entered a demeurer to two out of three counts of the indictment, which the counsel for the prosecution agreed to submit to the court without argument. The defendant also asked a continuance of the trial to Friday next, on the ground of absence of two witnesses material to her defense. The indulgence was granted, on the understanding that if she was convicted, the expense (growing out of the repeated attendance of many witnesses) would be paid by her. The trial was accordingly postponed until Friday.

William Jones had been successful. Judge Cranch, faced with Watkins's simple plea and the matter of the Navy agent in New York pleading guilty to the same misdirection of funds, was forced to reconsider his plan. Further, Mrs. Royall could not be brought to immediate trial. The prosecutor's failure to provide Mrs. Royall and her counsel with the full statement of the charges against her was an error. Without any legal brief, Counselor Jones had forced the issue and asked for dismissal of charges so poorly drawn as to constitute no charges at all. Judge Cranch could not deny William Jones his request without careful judicial review. Mrs. Royall would not be used to interfere with the trial of Tobias Watkins after all.

Mrs. Royall was not aware of her pawn position in the matters before William Cranch's court. She knew her head was on the legal block, and she was confused about William Cranch's actions in regard to her. She knew and respected the man and thought him an eminent jurist and a friendly Unitarian. After one morning in his court, she knew something was not quite right about William Cranch and his treatment of her.

Mrs. Royall was dismissed for the week. The judge had not reacted kindly to William Jones's legal argument. Seeking to place some sort of onus upon Mrs. Royall in the light of his having to grant her request for delay, he had resorted to the use of innuendo to cast some blame upon her to relieve his own frustration. His order that she could have her continuance, but bear the expense of the delay, supposedly for witnesses who would have to come again, shocked the court listeners. William Cranch had displayed bias against Mrs. Royall in a blatant fashion.

William Jones was not upset. He had taken the measure of this court, and nothing could surprise him. At least Mrs. Royall had a delay, and there would be no rump trial. Mrs. Royall would have her day in court. The two witnesses not available for Monday would be available for Friday next, and there was no single attendee in Cranch's court who did not know who those witnesses would be. Andrew Jackson and John Eaton were in Norfolk, Virginia, but they would be back in Washington in time for the next appearance in Cranch's court. It was an anticipation which filled Mrs. Royall's friends with glee and her enemies with mixed emotions.

Mrs. Royall returned home in exactly the state of mind with which she had left that morning. She was grateful for her astute counsel, but she could not help but marvel at her enemies' machinations. They had known the President and the Secretary of War were out of town, as were most of Mrs. Royall's other friends, and they had effected her arrest to take advantage of the situation. They had lost the immediate trial, but they would try again to railroad her. There was no doubt that the court would help them. Why William Cranch was with them was a question she would investigate in her own way.

Mrs. Royall stayed close to her home for the week, writing notes to friends in the capital and without. They had to hear the facts from her, for she had no doubt that her enemies were circulating their own version of Monday's events. Her disappearance from her daily rounds of the capital's offices inspired her foes to spread the "news" that she had fled the city to escape prosecution. This sensational report found its way to New York through the religious press, and even such a good friend as Mordecai Noah, the New York editor, printed the story. Mrs. Royall heard about it with disbelief. When she read the story Noah had published, her disbelief gave way to dismay. The tale was of Constable Beck's fearful arrest of her embroidered with the usual blackcoat canards. Describing Beck as having quaked in his boots, "this veteran of the Battle of Bladensburg," Noah reported that Beck would have preferred to face "a rhinocerus rather than come within the pale of Mrs. R's tongue." The tale continued, "The marshal has so contrived matters as to afford her a hint of her intended arrest, and she has taken advantage . . . and decamped."[9] This story was the cruelest cut of all, and from one who had been Mrs. Royall's ardent supporter. The man who had invented flamboyant reporting and to whom Mrs. Royall had recommended James Gordon Bennett as a Washington correspondent should have known her better. Mrs. Royall wrote Noah what she thought of his sensational nonsense, and Noah rectified his mistake in large print in his next *New York Morning Courier and Enquirer's* edition:

Be it known, Anne Royall continues to reside on Capital Hill, receiving the daily homage of her friends, and dispensing terror and dismay among her enemies!"[10]

The daily homage of her friends included James Bennett, Richard Wallach, and James and Thomas Brooks, young men she was grooming to follow her in informing her editors and friends of developments in Washington. Mrs. Royall had created a new form of newswriting based on observation, facts, and constant notations in a personal diary. Working from her journal led her to call her work "journalism."

Mrs. Royall was the first practicing journalist in the American sense of that word. Addison and Steele with the *Spectator*, and *Paul Pry* were individual efforts.[11] Mrs. Royall expanded her efforts by opening her discoveries to the editors of newspapers throughout the land, writing letters and comments in her own diary and her own publications. In effect, she established the first national news service providing background information to men too far removed from the capital to have access to her sources and proved so successful with this innovation that young men gathered for tutelage in what they knew was the course of the future. Mrs. Royall, involved in government and politics, had enlarged the personal journal's concept to include who, what, when, where, and then why to give journalism the format it has enjoyed ever since.

Mrs. Royall was attended daily by her young proteges after her arrest because she had not only developed a new profession but was about to test her right to continue it. They were there to help her fight for that freedom in a court of law. Her young men knew why she was under attack, and the fact that men, not government, set out to silence her made it a unique case. If men succeeded now, no newspaper could survive attack in the future. If speaking the truth and forcing action with it was disturbing the peace, they would have no future. The Washington newspaper fraternity in 1829 sided with Mrs. Royall to protect themselves. The old woman had opened the path to power and influence, and none of them were about to let other men take it from them! This dedication to her protection by newspapermen wrought immediate changes in the reporting of events in Judge Cranch's court.

The Watkins and Royall cases were entwined in the nation's press. A legal dance was in progress before a federal judge and it had far-reaching consequences. Both Watkins and Mrs. Royall were actors in a larger drama, and the writers wanted the public to join them in examination of the real issues. The presentations of both cases were made into tandem *cause celebre*, and even the opposition press was drawn into it.

In New York, the Royall battle was joined between Major Noah and his competitor William Leet Stone. Colonel Stone had not liked Mrs. Royall since their first confrontation in Saratoga Springs. A holdover from the Hartford Convention and a follower of Ely, Stone and his *New York Commercial Advertiser* went to great lengths to heap praise upon the grand jury and its indictment of Mrs. Royall in words most curious:

> It required no ordinary share of courage, in any three and twenty men, to make so daring an attack upon the right of this belligerent woman.[12]

This strange statement was followed by a lengthy letter from a practitioner of a newly promoted "science," phrenology, that attempts to analyze a person's character by charting the bumps on his head. This communication, signed "Phren and Logos," revealed that the author claimed to have "seen, conversed with and observed Phrenological indications in Mrs. Royall. Gentlemen, she is beyond a doubt *partially* insane." This was intended to explain the necessity for the attack upon Mrs. Royall's rights.[13]

The *"partially* insane" Mrs. Royall kept her wits about her, leaving her case in the hands of William Jones. Tobias Watkins had the priority, for as long as he was to stand trial, Mrs. Royall could not. The addition of Francis Scott Key to the case gave impetus to the collaboration between her counsel, serving Watkins too, and the government prosecutor. Thomas Swann was forced to sit on the sidelines. The *National Intelligencer* congratulated the change:

> Our readers will perceive that at last there is some prospect of this fatigu-
> ing case coming to issue and conclusion . . . The Counsel for the prosecu-
> tion deserve credit, for their perseverance as well as their authority, the
> commendation may also be bestowed upon the Counsel for the defense for
> their untiring zeal—dis-interested as it must be—and the eminent ability
> which they have displayed in defense.

The game in Cranch's court was playing to a close, and the newspapers of Washington were glad. Mindful of Cranch's contempt citation against the *Baltimore American*, the *National Intelligencer* skirted the problem of judicial criticism well:

> . . . and all voices award the Court unqualified praise for the patience it has
> evinced throughout this case, unprecedented here for its duration . . . its
> elaborate opinions . . . and all this apart from and in addition to the mass
> of other business, civil and criminal, which it has dispatched during the
> protracted term![14]

This comment, following an editorial complaint about the glut of court cases waiting upon Watkins and Royall, said it all. The court business was at a standstill and all Washington knew it.

Mrs. Royall did not go to trial on her scheduled date of the Friday next. This time she was not responsible for the postponement; the court was. Tobias Watkins's affairs had to be resumed. Once again William Jones was correct in his assumptions. Thomas Swann, seizing upon the defense argument that Watkins, admitting complicity, demanded trial, tried to keep the action to one against a man who had defrauded the government. William Jones counterattacked, citing the complicity of others, among them Samuel Southard, former secretary of the Navy, the Treasury and, the Army! Judge Cranch, trying to keep the case in line for Swann, impounded all papers presented, and ordered the court closed to the public.[15] A near riot ensued. The *National Intelligencer* reported:

> The great anxiety which this trial has produced upon the public mind may
> be estimated by the numbers which assembled in the court room yester-
> day, to witness the proceedings.[16]

With the gallery in an angry mood, Judge Cranch promptly modified his hasty ruling.

Tobias Watkins sat through trial Thursday and Friday. Thomas Swann moved to move the case to the jury without argument, but Key and Jones would have none of that ignomithat of y. The counsels demanded the right to sum up for both the government and the defendant, and Judge Cranch could not deny that right. Mr. Swann, being unprepared, asked for delay. Judge Cranch gave him relief by adjourning court until the next morning. This was at 2:30 p.m. Friday, July 17, 1829.[17]

Saturday came and Watkins still held Cranch's courtroom. Thomas Swann did not appear to deliver the summation for the prosecution, but Francis Scott Key presented for the government. At 11:00 a.m., Key concluded the government case, and the matter went to the jury. In exactly 35 minutes, the jury returned with a curious verdict:

> Dr. Watkins is guilty of having received $750 in his official capacity and applying same to his own use.[18]

This decision, recording an admitted fact but placing no positive blame, was seized upon by Jones immediately. Counsel for Watkins's defense asked clarification of the verdict. How could Tobias Watkins be guilty of receiving funds in his official capacity? Key, for the government, concurred with William Jones. This issue was forced upon the court, and Judge Cranch had to send the jury back for further consideration of its verdict. This time the jury returned with a greater sophistry: "Dr. Watkins was guilty of having, in his official capacity, obtained and applied to his own use, $750, money of the United States."[19] This insistence on semantic confusion forced the judge to dismiss the jury and adjourn the case until Monday, when presumably the verdict would be reconsidered.

It was a strange situation. Tobias Watkins had a verdict and yet he did not. He was in jeopardy still, and on Monday it could begin all over. Another trial was a possibility and the government would get another chance at the man and the men behind him. The *National Intelligencer* believed it was the only solution, for the other matters before the court had not been reported on by the jury: "It is presumed that the trial of the individual for the fraudulent obtainment of $300 will come on." A new jury would have to address itself to the individual counts of the indictment.[20]

William Jones sympathized with the government, and especially with young Key. The Jacksonians wanted another shot at their enemies, and Key was expected to produce it. But time was running out. Cranch was not instructing the jury properly; he was also aiding and abetting the suppression of the other counts before the court. Jones expected that the verdict Monday could be just as inconclusive as the one on Saturday. The vouchers included in the government's evidence were many, and each implicated Watkins and the other fiduciary agents involved in the case. The jury could not avoid decision about them all and single out one voucher, making no comment about the others. Tobias Watkins could spend his life in court answering each and every voucher. Yet William Jones had no doubt that John Eaton and Amos Kendall would continue with this to get at the bank crowd and their illegal manipulation of government accounts.

William Jones did not look forward to Monday. He gathered up his papers with only one bright thought: At least he did not have to worry about Mrs. Royall and her affairs over the weekend. The shenanigans in Cranch's court meant a few more days to iron the peculiarities in the indictments against the woman writer. Thomas Swann had produced three distinct counts against Mrs. Royall: one, that she was a "common slanderer"; two, "a common scold"; the third, "a common brawler." William Jones had moved for dismissal of the "common scold" count, since it was not a listed statute. He had entered objection to the language of the other two counts as not being specific enough to sustain in the action. "Common scold" was an insult to American law, and Jones had questioned the inference involved in a court allowing it. The court could not make laws but only interpret them, and the common scold charge was not written into American statutes and should not be before a federal court. William Cranch was attempting to force the issue and, as with Watkins, William Jones knew there was more to the affair than was apparent on its surface. Another weekend to study the matter was welcome indeed.

Mrs. Royall had attended the previous day's court session, and William Jones had requested permission to excuse her from sitting through the Watkins trial. With the prosecutor, Francis Scott Key, concurring, she had been allowed to return home. The *National Intelligencer* reported it:

> Mrs. Royall was yesterday in court, prepared for her trial, but owing to the occupancy of the attention of the Court by the case of Dr. Watkins, she was most ungallantly compelled to return home, without passing through the ordeal, for which, we have no doubt, she was fully prepared. [21]

Mrs. Royall may have been fully prepared, but her counsel was not. The writer's witnesses were back in town; John Eaton and President Andrew Jackson had returned to Washington on late Wednesday afternoon, but there had been little time to contact them. Unbeknown to both Mrs. Royall and William Jones, Andrew Jackson had taken to his bed, the rigors of the trip having proved to be too much for his delicate condition, a fact that was made known by Friday afternoon to Mrs. Royall's enemies by the young Donelsons.

The rumors of Jackson's confinement had reached Mrs. Royall and on Saturday morning, while William Jones continued with the Watkins defense, Mrs. Royall went to the White House to pay her respects to the President. She was admitted to his sickroom, and there she saw her friend in his abject misery. [22] Andrew Jackson knew of her difficulty. He would be happy to appear for her if only he could. A few more days rest, and perhaps he would have the strength. The prosecution of his friend, this fine woman, was a dastardly thing, but not unexpected from the kind of people they both had to confront. Mrs. Royall eased her friend but feared for his life. If anything should happen to him the nation would have John Calhoun and his blackcoat hordes to deal with, and for herself that would be a fate worse than she contemplated now. The President was not to think about her problem. The weekend was upon them, and Dr. Watkins's trial would continue on Monday and Tuesday. By Wednesday perhaps the President could appear. It was an optimistic note on which they parted. The President smiled. At least Mrs. Royall would have John Eaton at her side.

The delay in Mrs. Royall's court appearance had been Heaven sent, and she could not help but remark upon it to Sally Stackpool when she returned home. The President might recover in time to appear after all, if Watkins kept Cranch busy. What a scene it would be to confront Cranch, Ely's followers, and their friends with President Andrew Jackson himself. Mrs. Royall may have been compelled to return home ungallantly as reported by the *National Intelligencer*, but the delay could produce marvelous results.

Back in Cranch's court, the Watkins case adjourned after 2:00 p.m. until Monday. Gathering his papers and talking to Francis Key, William Jones prepared to depart. It had been a long and extraordinary Saturday session; the court usually closed at noon. Even as he turned to leave, Judge Cranch stopped him. The trial of Mrs. Royall would proceed immediately, Cranch said. Counsel was to produce the defendant in court, there and then. William Jones was astounded and then angry. Mrs. Royall was not in court, the judge knew it; she was at home where she had been sent by the court itself yesterday, as the terms of her liberty required. William Cranch did not dispute William Jones. He turned to the marshal and ordered him to bring Mrs. Royall before his bench. William Jones, astonished by the impetuosity of the judge's action, objected. Mrs. Royall did not require the marshal to bring her to court; William Jones would send word, and his client would respond as required. Judge Cranch, taken aback by Jones's strong objections, softened his stand and allowed Jones to send for Mrs. Royall. Calling an hour's recess, he ordered Jones to be ready for trial at 3 p.m.

William Jones sent his associate, Richard Coxe, to bring in Mrs. Royall and her witnesses. Runners were sent in all directions, the young newsmen doing their duty for a fellow writer. Meanwhile, the Coyles, the Dunns, the Machens, Watterston, McCormick, Frost, and Elgar miraculously appeared in the courtroom. William Jones knew they had been standing by, waiting for the trial they had been expecting. It made him more angry than ever.

Mrs. Royall appeared in answer to the hectic summons. She came into the courtroom quietly, noting her friends among the visitors filling in. Her "newsboys" had done their duty well, and the room had as many for her as against her. The court bench was another matter. The judge and prosecutor were on one side and her counsel on the other. She looked them over very carefully. Mrs. Royall had described Judge Cranch once before in print, but this time she took a closer look and decided she would have to amend her description:

> Judge C. was described formerly as resembling Judge Marshall (the Chief Justice). This is incorrect, owing to my having seen him but once in the dusk of evening. He is younger than the Chief Justice; has a longer face, with a good deal of the pumpkin in it (though my friend said the pumpkin was in his head). Let this be as it may, I was always partial to Judge C because he is a Yankee—a Unitarian, and a near relation of my friend the ex-president Adams.[23]

Judge Cranch was no longer a Unitarian. Like John Quincy Adams and Louisa he attended Ely's Presbyterian Church.

The jury was presented and Mrs. Royall transferred her attention to the members as they filed in. The panel from which her deliberators were to be chosen sat to the right of the bench, but before she had time to draw any conclusions, two more judges appeared. Buckner Thurston and James S. Morsell joined William Cranch on the bench. If anyone doubted the importance of Mrs. Royall's trial before, they did not now! If John Eaton and Andrew Jackson were to appear in this courtroom, William Cranch had prepared himself well. Mrs. Royall made her notes quickly:

> Judge Thurston is about the same age as Judge Cranch, and harder featured. He is laughing proof. He looks as though he sat upon the rack all his life, and lived upon crab apples. They are both about 50 years of age. The sweet Morsell, who seems to sit for his picture, is the same age, his face round and wrinkled, and resembles the road on Giandott, after the passage of a group of hogs. He is thick and short. They all have a worn look, and never was three judges better matched in faces. This was the court called the Long Parliament by whom I was to be tried. I did not know for what.[25]

Mrs. Royall still did not know and neither did most of those in the courtroom. "Common scold" was undefined, and the bar of Washington had descended upon the courtroom, curious as to what this new legal innovation entailed. Congress had visited upon the District of Columbia the laws of Maryland, but common sense had precluded that entire old code from inundating the courts before. The lawyers had turned out to see how heretofore archaic legalisms could be justified in the present instance. Mrs. Royall watched the crowd grow; she knew the importance of the move against her:

The court house was crowded, as the trial was the first of its sort ever tried in the United States, and excited much interest.[26]

Mrs. Royall was surrounded by lawyers who, with Clerk William Brent, paid her all possible attention and respect. Her young newsmen were led by James Gordon Bennett, Erastus Brooks, and Richard Wallach, each convinced that the attack on Mrs. Royall represented an assault upon freedom of the press. The courtroom buzzed with great anticipation.

William Jones offered Mrs. Royall the right to challenge the jurors as they were called, but Mrs. Royall declined. She had taken her measurement of the court, and one Marylander was like another among the panel before her. She concurred with the young newsmen in dubbing it the Long Parliament, so dour were its members and so representative of Irish Presbyterianism. Mrs. Royall wondered aloud where in all Catholic Maryland they could have found so many Roundheads![27] Mostly country bumpkins with but few representatives from Washington, they would entertain no favor for a woman who could write. Mrs. Royall surveyed them well:

> There was George Upper Leather, Will Chisset, Overdone Carr, Jack Pill Box, John Stirrup Leather, Phill Yardstick, Tom Lapstone, Dick Tape, Bob Bouncer, Hall Saucepan, and the others I did not know: but it would puzzle Hogarth to paint them—[28]

Since there was not one among them she would have picked, she saw no reason to reject them. It was a stacked jury, and together with the witnesses grouping against her, she knew what the outcome would be before the trial began. She turned to William Jones and told him so in her characteristic way:

> I shall make a proposition to my friends in Congress to have the whole painted and put in the Rotunda with our national paintings, reserving a conspicuous place for myself.[29]

Mrs. Royall referred to the controversy about the mural "Justice," then about to be painted in the Capitol.

The trial began with a recitation of opinion from the bench. William Jones had requested a clarification of the charges upon which Mrs. Royall was to be tried. What was "common scold" and what application could such an ancient charge have in an American court? Further, the other counts in the indictment were so general as to be lacking in qualifications for "crime," and the inclusion of the phrase "common nuisance" cast doubt upon the use of the indictment since it referred to a peace issue handled by magistracy courts and presented no original issue for consideration by a federal panel. Just how did the charges of "common slanderer" and "common brawler" apply to Mrs. Royall, and on what evidence could such claims against her be sustained? Mrs. Royall was not a "common" person; her accusers were more "common" than she, and their claims, even under the ancient statutes, had to be judged in that light. William Jones had handed Judge Cranch a difficult problem.

Judge Cranch spoke for the court. William Jones had scored with his attack upon the first and third counts of Thomas Swann's indictment against the writer. Mrs. Royall was not a common slanderer nor a common brawler. However, since "common scold" was a historical indictable and had been applied in areas covered by English Common Law, "common scold" was acceptable under the congressional mandate which made the laws of Maryland pertinent to the District of Columbia. Mention had been found concerning the ancient statute in the archaic records of England, and therefore the charge would stay. Judge Cranch would entertain no further argument on the issue and trial would commence forthwith.

William Jones and his partner Richard Coxe sat with Mrs. Royall. Coxe, the younger man, would handle the questioning. Thomas Swann, his case to be proved by a single incident of "scolding," had John Coyle lead his parade. Mrs. Royall recorded his testimony herself:

> "Hear, O Israel," the testimony of Captain Coyle. He began to place his feet as though he had set in for a four-hour sermon. It was quite an out-pouring of christian love; but I only have room for a short extract. He said I called him a damned old bald headed son of a bitch, not only once but three times![30]

And Mrs. Royall had; she admitted it. "He is the only person in the world that ever heard me swear."[31]

Coyle, Sr., was followed by both his son and son-in-law, who presented no specifics, only tales of "labored nonsense of no weight." They were followed by George Watterston. The former Librarian of Congress paid Mrs. Royall many compliments, "alike honorable to himself" and with the same quiet intonation delivered his *coup d'etat*. Mrs. Royall indeed had called all Presbyterians cut-throats, and the witnesses against her were all Presbyterians. The courtroom burst into laughter. Mrs. Royall had written it far more often than she had said it.

Watterston was replaced by Lewis Machen. Mrs. Royall really had fun with him. She wrote:

> He looked like Satan's walking staff. His long face, roached hair, and af-fected gaity had complete stage effect. His testimony amounted to noth-ing but a history of our acquaintance, of no consequence.[32]

The spectators did not like Machen, and his friends became restive too. The hour was late and everyone wanted to get on with it.

It was one of the McCormacks who set the Court in a roar. This congressional clerk was immediate sport for the lawyers and livened up the proceedings. Mrs. Royall reported his witness *verbatim*:

> He said I sat in my window, one Sunday, with a book in my hand, which he supposed was my *Black Book*. Mr. Swann, the prosecutor, asked if that was all. McCormack replied that he could say more but he didn't want to in court. Mr. Swann pressed him to do so and McCormack did.
> "I was walking with some ladies, one day, and she asked me if I wasn't ashamed to walk with them old maids."
> Swann, amused, commented, "Well, maybe they were old maids."
> McCormack drew back. "No they wasn't for one of them was my sis-ter."[33]

This exchange brought the courtroom alive with laughter. Spurred on by this attention, McCormack continued. He accused Mrs. Royall of having described his friend in her book. Thomas Swann asked how he knew it was his friend, since Mrs. Royall had not used any name. McCormack brought down the house again.

"Why, by the description I knew it must be him, it was so exact!"[34]

The merriment in the court grew, and Thomas Swann was forced to a new tack. The prosecutor asked McCormack why he thought Mrs. Royall sat in her window. McCormack supposed it was to see what was going on in the Engine House prayer meetings.

"She could see in, then?"

"Oh, yes, she could see everything that passed." By this time the spectators were hooting and howling, and Judge Cranch demanded order in the court. Judges Thurston and Morsell said nothing, their stern faces relieved only by a flicker of discontent. A comedy routine had been heard which would play the riverboats and the palladiums for years to come, with many variations. Mrs. Royall's pen immortalized the "that was no lady, that was my sister" routine forever more!

After the McCormacks, John Dunn made his witness. Mrs. Royall went to work on him as he sat in the witness chair.

> Dunn is another walking staff—his hair mackarony—his arms over six feet extended—his face pale—his nose hooked, with a grey goggle eye, Shakespeare's smile. His testimony was about my encounter with the snapdragon.[35]

John Dunn complained that Mrs. Royall had scolded his wife, but he neglected to say Mrs. Dunn had scolded Mrs. Royall first.[36]

Thomas Swann did not call all his witnesses. As required, John Dunn had provided the instance of scolding, but the two succeeding witnesses had provided such ludicrous recitation from the stand that Mrs. Royall was advised by the lawyers about her to take out an immediate writ *de lunatico inquirendo* against them. Mrs. Royall's loud rejoinder that she had the notion to take out such a writ against all of her accusers set the court in another uproar.[37] Thomas Swann rested his case while he was ahead. He had presented his proofs and to allow the oafs to take over would not be wise. Mrs. Royall was a "common scold" because she had written the *Black Book*. Several persons therein portrayed were recognizable to their friends, and he had one solid incident of her swearing and scolding. The prosecution retired.

Richard Coxe rebutted for Mrs. Royall. He cited the fact that the writer had the right to write her books, that if someone portrayed in print was recognizable to his friends it was no slander or scolding, but the truth. Anyone had the right to speak sharply when impeded by someone like Coyle or Dunn; no crime had been proven and no crime was present. The courtroom roared its approval but Cranch overruled Richard Coxe. An incident of scolding had been cited, and one instance of that act was enough.

Suddenly, John Eaton appeared. He had slipped in to the courtroom during Richard Coxe's statement and now came forward, begging the indulgence of the bench and requesting to be heard immediately. The court granted his petition. John Eaton took the stand and testified that Mrs. Royall was not common in any way, did not scold, and was, in his judgment, a fine lady.[38] John Eaton averred he spoke not only for himself, but he was nevertheless not allowed to continue.

The courtroom stirred. Andrew Jackson would not be there. Mrs. Royall had one official witness, but not the one everyone had come to hear. Secretary Eaton was followed by a number of women who testified to the writer's fine manners, her abilities, her lack of "common" description:

I had but a few witnesses, knowing how it would end. Secretary Eaton
and a few ladies. Their testimony was clear and unequivocal, and directly
opposed to the testimony of the prosecution. But, as I understood, several
of the officers of Congress were summoned on the part of the District, I
summoned a few too, particularly General Bailey, to rebut the testimony
of Machen. The General took sick upon the strength of it and did not appear. Mr. Hickey did attend, but unfortunately he was deaf in one ear (I
hope Congress will find a clerk who can hear out of both ears) and the
good ear was always turned to my house and the deaf one to the Blueskins.[39]

However, Mrs. Royall did produce a witness who gave the court the best
laugh of the day. Henry Tims, the Senate doorkeeper, gladly testified for his old
friend.

Mr. Tims was pure gold, he never flinched. I hope the Senate may keep
him in office as a reward for his honesty. He ought to have a statue to perpetuate the fact that one honest man was found in the government. He
said, "he never knew me to slander but two people in his life, and that was
himself and Mr. Watterston, and that was when she said we were the clev-
erest men in the city!" This we may say put an end to the business for the
day, as the whole were convulsed with laughter, except Judge T. In fact,
the whole of the examination kept the house in an uproar. Such another
ludicrous farce was never played before a judicial tribunal.[40]

Henry Tims's performance characterized the entire proceeding against Mrs.
Royall for the nation. His act was satirized not only by himself, but by all who
were interested in the affair. It was a comedy routine which found its way into
every small weekly and town daily. It was a Royall gambit which was to live on
for many years.

Mrs. Royall's trial was at an end. Prosecutor Swann suggested that the case
go to the jury without summation. Richard Coxe agreed to forego his counsel's
argument with the provision that Mrs. Royall be allowed to speak on her own
behalf. He had promised her this privilege on this, her day in court. The defendant could not be denied. Mrs. Royall wasted no time in availing herself of her
moment. She addressed herself to the court and especially to the jurors.

Mrs. Royall cited her role as a citizen-guardian of the rights of others. She
asked the court and the jury "to defend her against oppression, to prove themselves the protectors of personal rights and liberty, warning them against sanc-
tioning a system of clerical domination, and persecution, which if not checked
by the freedom of speech and of the press, and these defended by independent
juries, would produce a state of things which would endanger the judge on the
bench, and even the President himself,—declaring that this system and the prosecution, were part of a general scheme, of which the attempt to stop the mails
on the Sabbath was another feature."[41]   In seven minutes, Mrs. Royall covered
her cause and sat down to watch the results of her appeal. She had no illusions
about the jury but she knew her impression upon her friends and the newsmen
behind her.

Mrs. Royall was found guilty. The jury had not cared one whit about the
larger issues, but only the muzzle to be placed upon her by the court in carrying
out the sentence. The writer's reaction was a characteristic one. She turned to
Marshal Beck and requested that the next time she was tried, he summon twelve
tom cats instead of twelve Bladensburg men.[42]   Her voice carried to the crowd
her comic allusion to the "bravery" of those who had "defended" Washington
City at the Battle of Bladensburg in 1814. It appeared that the convicted "com-

mon scold" was going to speak her mind still, and not even the court would stop her. Her supporters rushed to her side, and foremost among them was Marshal Beck. Andrew Jackson had not appeared, but the implication of John Eaton's testimony was enough for any fence-straddlers.

Mrs. Royall did not stand in William Cranch's court like a convicted felon. Surrounded by lawyers and newsmen, she was protected from the disapproval of Cranch. Thurston was angry at the verdict, sitting on the bench in a black mood, and what Mrs. Royall had taken to be his lack of sympathy to her was her best defense. The writer noted it later in her journal:

> Judge Thrust-on looked as fiery as Mount Aetna, so displeased was he with the verdict.[43]

Mrs. Royall had taken his measure well. Thurston was not with her, but he was against the travesty played before him. He could have stopped the legal farce himself, but certain forces were at work upon him too. The blackcoats had intimated that his dark moods and his drinking were reason enough to remove him from the bench, and Buckner Thurston still entertained hopes for the Supreme Court.[44] Mrs. Royall was glad that Judge Thurston had displayed his unhappiness, for it did make things more pleasant for her at the moment.

William Jones had expected the verdict. The sudden summons to trial on Saturday afternoon at the insistence of Cranch and the proceedings had been unmistakable signs. He had turned the case over to Richard Coxe, while he himself monitored the proceedings carefully. He had all he needed for an appeal, and he told Mrs. Royall there would be no sentencing of her that day, nor the next week, and, if Jones read his law well, there would never be one. The long-feared trial was over, and it had been nothing to fear after all. Mrs. Royall was triumphant in her defeat.

Young Richard Coxe had absented himself from the post-trial gathering in the courthouse. Noting Thurston's displeasure, he had hurried to him to ask the judge to suspend judgment, and Thurston had granted his request. Mrs. Royall was to be permitted her freedom. Thomas Swann objected. The trial had been enough of a farce, but for Mrs. Royall to be allowed freedom without security, never. At the mention of "security," the legal name for money, most of the lawyers thronging the writer scattered, but the newsmen held their place. Two young men whom Mrs. Royall had never seen before, Thomas Dowling and Thomas Donohoo, both newcomers with the National Intelligencer, came to her immediate aid and posted bond for her.[45] Mrs. Royall was appreciative to them for this quick action, but she was bitter that the National Intelligencer had not recognized the principle of her prosecution before the trial. She told them so in unmistakable terms:

> Though you have done yourselves and the noble fraternity to which we belong, immortal honor by this generous act, yet all the water of the Potomac will not wash out the foul stain of this infamous prosecution.[46]

And so it happened that an American citizen was tried in a United States Court on a charge which the framers of the Constitution had thought to be prohibited in American jurisprudence by the reason embodied in that founding paper. Official Washington was stunned. Mrs. Royall had been found guilty of a charge no one believed and was free only because of this strange disbelief. The Baltimore American, copying the National Journal, told the country at large about it on July 21, 1829:

The trial of Mrs. Anne Royall, indicted on a charge of being a common scold, took place Saturday last. There was some difficulty at the commencement, in determining what constitutes a common scold. The opinion of one of the authorities quoted is, that the person so designated must be always scolding. If so, we need look no further for the perpetual motion, after a single conviction grounded on that authority. More rational lawyers, however, seem to think that where the scolding is so loud and frequent as to be a common nuisance, it is sufficient to constitute a common scold. But according to some of the witnesses, Mrs. Royall although frequent in her vocal exhilarations, was not always loud, but, on the contrary, had inflicted some of her linguadental severities in a very soft tone, and with a very smiling countenance, coming up, in fact. to the poet's description, and showing that she can smile, and smile, and murder while she smiles. The punishment also is a perplexing subject, for the lawyers seem to have ransacked the Maryland code in vain to find some precedent, and among the negligences of the Congress may be enumerated the omission to enact some befitting penalty for a common scold. It is true, that the ducking stool in England had been the stool of repentance to many a scold, but there seems to be an awful consequence resulting from that punishment, since some authorities had laid it down that it confers upon the criminal the privilege of being a common scold forever afterwards, with impunity.—To Mrs. Royall, one ducking would be a cheap consideration for this inestimable privilege.

Many of the respectable citizens who live on Capitol Hill appear to have been prodigiously annoyed by this gifted dame, whom Petruchio would have found harder to tame than Kate the Curst, and such a universal terror of her, except among the boys, infects that whole region, that man and woman, priest and layman, would rather make a circuit of a mile than venture beneath her eastern window which overlooks Jersey Avenue, and from which she edifies herself, probably with a view to the future edification of the world, by studying the weakness, and practicing upon the fears of the neighborhood. No wonder than that the inhabitants of Capitol Hill should rise en mass and flock to the Court to give testimony against this animated apple of discord which the fates had thrown into the midst of them. They testified sundry wicked sayings of their tormentor—which although they relaxed the features of bench and bar, will perhaps be found insufficient to relax the sterner countenance of justice—and various outrages upon the peace and harmony of society. Mrs. Royall was also heard, first by her counsel, secondly by her witnesses, and lastly by her eloquent self. Nevertheless the jury ungallantly found her guilty and the Bench, still more ungallantly ordered her to be locked up until she found bail for her appearance to receive judgment, which was arrested by her Counsel. "This is a pretty country to live in" said the indignant persecuted, as she heard the mandate for her incarceration.[47]

This embellished tale captured the incident for the public and the story of Mrs. Royall's jailing gained currency despite the fact it did not happen. Her "newsboys" were at it again. The mother of journalism became the victim of it.

Richard Coxe filed a brief with the court challenging the charge absent from specific statute in the federal codes or the Maryland code since the Revolution. The brief was an obvious device to bring the "common scold" under constitutional review, a test Dr. Ely and his friends did not want. Excited by this development, Washington City was divided into camps for and against Mrs. Royall, and the catch-all legal position Congress had forged for the District of Columbia. Mrs. Royall's friends mounted a movement in the Congress to re-examine the statutes under which that body had placed the capital and an attack on the non-specific codes of Maryland.[48]   Her foes marshaled their forces against both movements and added an innovation of their own.

The Navy yard, Washington's largest government employer, had been the first of the government offices to feel the lash of Mrs. Royall's tongue and pen. Her attack on that costly facility had begun the Jackson assault on the capital office holdovers. Naturally, this group of "public" servants could be enticed into action against the "common scold." The Navy yard shipwrights lent their talents to the construction of a singular device, at government expense, and then offered it for public inspection. At the direction of Commodore Tingley, a ducking stool was created, in model, to illustrate the kind of engine of destruction on which the ancient punishment for the "scold" was carried out. Its appearance titillated the capital, enlarging the audience for the drama yet to come. Mrs. Royall noted its effect herself:

> A rash effort was made to induce the court to condemn me to the punishment of ducking . . . .
> To be prepared for this event, they had a machine made at the Navy Yard, so constructed, that I could not have survived the operation. The model was at City Hall, and consisted of a shaft, which was to be eleven to fifteen feet in length, and at the extremity of this, I was to be fastened—this shaft was to be worked by a windlass, by a great number of people, and was to go round like a windmill, with such rapidity, that, from the circumference of the sweep . . . first in the river and then in the air—it was said I could not have survived one sweep of the machine! The model was made at the Navy Yard and brought to the holy people for their approbation, and being approved, everything was to be in readiness at a moment's warning; when I was to be instantly seized and carried off before my friends could come to my aid—all the boys and negroes, and holy people were to be there, and shout and make a great noise, and my death, which would have been inevitable, would have been ascribed to the coldness of the water![49]

It was a most peculiar device but no comic matter for the Holy Willies. From the beginning, they had been led to believe that the ancient and archaic punishment was to be inflicted, and they had been sorely disappointed that she was not jailed immediately in preparation for what the ancient statute had set forth. Dr. Ely had inflamed their desire for the customary punishment prevalent in Northern Ireland for such as Mrs. Royall, and the latter-day Scots-Irish in Washington were ready to mete out this action on this outspoken woman. The matter of the suspended judgment and the possibility that Mrs. Royall might escape this retribution led many of them to suggest that they take Mrs. Royall and duck her themselves. The shipwrights, most of them members of the Engine House Congregation, had not only lent their ingenuity to the construction but had improved upon the old design. Mrs. Royall was not to be lowered into the water vertically, but swept through it horizontally in a great circle sweep, insuring that she would remain under water longer. Commodore Tingly had sanctioned the building of the new ducking engine because he had a score to settle with Mrs. Royall. She had questioned his right to be decorated for bravery in the War of 1812 since he had fought no battle and produced no heroic action, but had burned the Washington Navy Yard before the British burned the city.[50] Her well-publicized attack on his administration of the yard had only added to his difficulties, and there was a continuing congressional investigation of his entire command as a result. Commodore Tingly would have loved to have turned the wheel of the new ducking engine himself. The Navy yard worked as one man to turn out this new assault on Mrs. Royall.

The display of the Navy yard's ingenious invention at the City Hall did not have the desired effect. The crowds came, but the crudeness of the device and

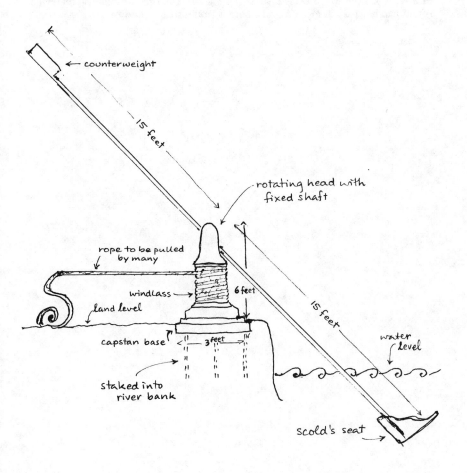

← counterweight

15 feet

·rotating head with
fixed shaft

rope to be pulled
by many

windlass

land level

6 feet

15 feet

capstan base

3 feet

water
level

staked into
river bank

scold's seat

**Washington Navy Yard's ingenious ducking machine,
the first Washington merry-go-round**

its obvious intent, its historical reminder of the hated inquisition, made Mrs. Royall a more sympathetic figure. Mrs. Royall found herself being cheered by the mob whenever she appeared, and Judge William Cranch and his blackcoat friends found themselves objects of ridicule. The whipping post and the old stocks were on their way out, thanks to the United States Constitution, and yet this eminent American jurist had opened the door to the possible introduction of a relic of even worse ecclesiastical repression. The first Washington merry-go-round had been set in motion and where it would stop nobody knew.

Chapter 21

Will the Punishment Fit the Crime?

The crowds thronged City Hall to see the first merry-go-round in the American capital. The exhibitors spun it again and again for the curious. Many hands could increase the speed with which the bench circled first over land and then into water with a great splash and a wide wake. It was an engine of destruction, and although the crowd laughed as they watched it, the laughter subsided as they turned towards home.

Mrs. Royall could not stay away. The reports of the new invention intrigued her, and she went to the city hall for a personal demonstration. The crowd followed her, and the aged writer took this new notoriety and the idiocy it represented in stride and walked with her head held high. She insisted upon a complete examination of the device. Indeed it was clever, and who would have expected that the Navy yard, which built so few ships, would have the talent to build this new "iron maiden"? It was a pity that the shipwrights could not do the job they were paid to do, repairing rotting ships and building new ones.[1] Mrs. Royall's remarks were a telling rebuttal to the nonsense at hand.

The thinking citizens of Washington City were distressed about the machine. Tingly and Cranch had opened a Pandora's box! If the federal courts could be lent to such indignity, perhaps it was time to reform them. It was not what Judge Cranch and his colleagues wanted at all.

In 1829, the federal judiciary was almost sanctified. The brotherhood of the bench and the lawyers associated with the courts had insulated this group from criticism. It was a refuge which the old regime enjoyed even as it was assailed in the other branches of the government. Andrew Jackson's opponents took full advantage of it, counting upon the control of the courts to soften any mandate this unwanted president might think he had. Jackson had the White House and might take Congress, but those who held the courts could overrule both.

The federalist remnants had full control of the bench; judges were drawn from men who had achieved education, fame, and renown in law. Who were these, but the scions of privilege? Men who made the best living from the law, from its business and its politics wedded to finance, were elevated to the judiciary; their opponents were not. The courts of the United States in 1829 were bastions of privilege in a nation created to reduce such privilege. Not even an Andrew Jackson, victorious in election and standing valiantly for democracy, could change the courts or the judges who held them. So long as the bench maintained its dignity, its authority could not be impugned. William Cranch had visited upon his federal bench an indignity which placed it in jeopardy.

The federalist benchwarmers should have been warned by the Tobias Watkins affair. Papers kept from the public and trial dates postponed had raised the

179

wind but not yet the storm. Judge Cranch had tinkered with judicial involvement, but as yet he had not been accused publicly of misusing his bench to thwart justice. Now he faced that accusation. The new Washington merry-go-round propelled the federal courts into the limelight, and it was an illumination they simply could not stand.

The Jacksonians asked the first question. Who was Judge Cranch, and how did he come to sit upon his bench? William Cranch owed his appointment to his family connection with John Adams. He was nephew to former president John Adams and cousin to former president John Quincy Adams, and, although an appointee of Thomas Jefferson, he owed all his prominence to that Adams link.[2] Suddenly the questions produced an answer for the men who had taken Mrs. Royall's side. Judge Cranch was Adams's instrument of revenge.

Judge Cranch had not expected to attract inquiry to himself, and his misadventure would be responsible for blowing a hole in the dike the proponents of privilege had erected through the terms of six presidents as a bulwark against runaway American democracy. Cranch, evading the intent of American law in order to keep faith with his secret constituency, gave the Jacksonians a surprising entry for court reform. Once again Mrs. Royall had led them to it.

Andrew Jackson had not considered the possibility of court reform. In fact, he was in such disregard of the matter that, wanting to rid himself of the head of the post office, he had appointed that office holder to the Supreme Court, knowing full well that Joseph McLean was his enemy.[3] Cranch's conduct of the case of Mrs. Royall forced the new administration to regard the federal courts in a new light.

The proceedings against Tobias Watkins had alerted the President and his aides to a lack of sympathy on the part of William Cranch as the government sought to dig deep into the strange financial manipulations besetting the U.S. Treasury. The government sought to investigate corruption, but Judge Cranch blocked any action, bottling up facts and preventing examination of necessary documents. This had been done under the guise of protecting Watkins's rights, but the sudden about-face of Cranch in the Anne Royall matter cast a new cloud. Cranch was no conservator of constitutional tradition.

William Jones was the first to note this. Handling defense for both defendants, he had watched Cranch take opposite positions on both. It made no sense that one rule applied in one matter and was reversed in the other. Counselor Jones was an eminent lawyer who knew he was dealing with a judge less interested in justice than in maintaining a political position. As a result, two men faced one another, skirting open disrespect, but their contempt for each other became obvious as the days passed. Judge Cranch held the upper hand, but William Jones, with his political position, held a key which even Judge Cranch did not want turned. Each knew that behind the scenes was a large group of men controlling a great financial empire who were bent on using the courts for their own purposes. If Counselor Jones tipped the action to the right people, all hell could break loose. Something untoward was occurring, and the growing carnival atmosphere was destroying the repute of the district's federal court.

Tobias Watkins appeared for his second trial on the Wednesday following Mrs. Royall's *tour de force*. The former auditor faced explanation for yet another set of vouchers, but this time Judge Cranch did not have sole direction of the affair. The same three judges who had sat for Mrs. Royall now sat for Tobias Watkins. All of Cranch's actions in regard to impounding certain documents were overturned, and the public heard in the court what it had read in the newspapers.[4]

Samuel Southard and Tobias Watkins had indulged in an extraordinary correspondence. The public drew the only conclusions it could from what was presented. Secretary Southard must have made the arrangements whereby Tobias

Watkins had been able to direct cash to certain Navy agents for extraneous accounts. He delivered some of that cash to himself and to personal agents of Southard's, all with the connivance of the Second Bank of the United States. The letters cited details of how the money was channeled, how a voucher written for the Washington Navy Yard could be converted into a bank draft in New York and the cash transported to the bank in Philadelphia, lodged there in a private account bearing Watkins's name, and then delivered to others. The jury, aghast at the implications in this routing of the nation's money, refused again to render a simple verdict; it would not declare Watkins to be guilty alone. Judge Cranch instructed the panel to find against the defendant, but the jury held out against him. Cranch discharged the jury. On Saturday morning, July 25, one week after Mrs. Royall's trial, Tobias Watkins was awarded a new trial.

The convicted Common Scold was back at her customary haunts. Cranch's court had not destroyed her but made her famous. People went out of their way to approach her and wonder with her about the terrible legal attack she suffered. It was an opportunity to expound upon her theses. Did they know that the charge "common scold" was the brainchild of that blackcoat Dr. Ely, concocted from Presbyterian precedents declared illegal in English courts but admitted to an American one by the Presbyterian Cranch? Her lawyer had a new brief before that jurist challenging him to cite the existing American statute which would admit this ancient and archaic ecclesiastical law as precedent for "crime" in America. No matter how Cranch ruled, court reform was in the making, and Mrs. Royall intended to pursue it:

> Now, I wish to know, if instead of hunting up old obsolete statutes, it be not the duty of every Judge to support the constitution and the bill of rights which are in force in this District? I wish to know if every act of a Judge is not upon Oath, and if it not be their duty to tell the jury what is law and what is not law? This they are sworn to do! This the Court did not do on this trial. Why did the Court not sum up the evidence, and tell the jury what it was? I trust the Senate of the United States will seek into this matter, and if the Judges have violated the constitution, put it out of their power to do it a second time. Since our judiciary united with the good sound Presbyterians, it is time for honest men to unite too, if there be any. No man's life is safe now, as I shall show more clearly than I have done.[5]

Those who had massed against the woman writer were not inactive. The bank crowd had become part of the action against her. The president of the Washington branch of the Second Bank of the United States, Harrison Smith, had applauded the new Ely concept and his wife, Margaret Bayard Smith, the social chronicler of the capital, had popularized the matter in the right circles, the Adams-Calhoun clique. Anne Royall "ducked" was a sight they would have paid any amount of money to see. Every tale they could trot out to prove the crassness of their enemy, they told. It was during this time that the story about Mrs. Royall forcing John Quincy Adams to interview by catching him bathing in the nude in the Potomac and sitting on his clothes until she got what she wanted became current.[6] This example of the woman's impropriety with the president of the United States was accepted by the Smiths and their friends as an appalling example of a most uncouth woman, but the rest of the world loved the determination of the writer who had displayed such ingenuity.

The Elyites applauded their mentor. The good clergyman received congratulations high and low for his ingenious method of humbling that awful Mrs. Royall. Fun was poked at a woman who cared little for clothes, spent her time writing and dared invade the life of her betters. Dr. Ely had taken her measure. In-

deed she was "common," and she was a "scold." Not one of the Washington
bank crowd thought for a moment that Mrs. Royall would win. They had the
cards stacked against her, a pot of gold with which to up their ante, and they
could not conceive that such an impecunious scribbler would ever match them.
It was a case of self-congratulation, not self-examination! Ezra Stiles Ely was
their leader; Nicholas Biddle was nowhere in sight.

Richard Coxe's attack upon William Cranch was not read by Ely and his followers as the beginning of an assault upon court procedures. The suggestion that
Judge Cranch was finding it difficult to phrase an answer did not upset Dr. Ely
or his friends. If Cranch was having trouble, Ely had access to all the material he
would need to frame a masterful presentation of the legality of "common
scold." The clergyman sent word via Thomas Swann that he was prepared to
assist the court.

An irate Thomas Swann received the latest Ely suggestion with contempt.
The "common scold" was proving to be a problem in American courts. Judge
Cranch had gone out on a limb to get what Ely wanted, but the appeal Coxe had
mounted was another matter. There would be no trial for this, just argument
between learned men, and it would be recorded for others to read. Ely's help
was welcome, but it was no insurance that the action against Mrs. Royall would
be sustained. Cranch was not alone in this matter any longer; there was Judge
Thurston.

Swann's implication that Ely's "common scold" would not be sustained was
frightening to the clergyman. If Judge Thurston was a problem, Dr. Ely would
find a way to handle him. Swann had inferred that someone with great influence would have to take Judge Thurston in hand, and Dr. Ely knew someone
to do it.

Ezra Stiles Ely thought it was time to ask John Calhoun to take an active part
in the proceeding against Mrs. Royall. The clergyman had asked little of his former classmate from Yale but had done Calhoun's bidding with the Eatons. He
had the right to ask a favor. John Calhoun and he had grown from the same
stalk, guided by the same hands: the one a Yalie about whom his classmates had
said that "he made a profession of religion before he was 14",[7] the other one
who had a profession of both religion and politics before he was 20. Certainly
the man from South Carolina could lend a hand with Judges Thurston, Morsell
and the higher courts, perhaps with Justice Marshall too. Judge Cranch had to
receive a free hand.

Buckner Thurston was a brilliant judge, but he had a drinking problem which
produced rages bordering on insanity. A full bottle sent in his direction could
remove him from the bench for days. Judge Morsell had debts galore, and Harrison Smith and Thomas Swann, members of the bank, would know what to do
about that. Justice Marshall, the Chief Justice of the United States, had feet
deep in the clay of land he had taken in "reward" for his sedentary service to
the Revolution, land denied other more worthy men.[8] The situation was tailor -
made for scandal. It would be no hard task for the Vice President to remind
Justice Marshall that Mrs. Royall was a potential threat and should never achieve
review of the "common scold" matter.

Dr. Ely envisioned the court in his control, but there was William Jones, that
clever lawyer; he had reason to work for Mrs. Royall, for he expected to take
Thomas Swann's place when and if the Senate met to confirm Andrew Jackson's
new U.S. attorney appointments. If Jones could be enticed out of town with a
fat fee from the canal company, Mrs. Royall would be left completely to the
inexperienced Richard Coxe. Dr. Ely knew the man who could take Jones out
of town. William Wirt was representing the canal company in Alexandria, and
an appeal to him could solve the problem; he would use William Jones in his case

if Dr. Ely requested it. The clergyman from Philadelphia decided to try all his plans at once. He could foresee no problems: Judge Cranch would be delivering an opinion, not presiding at a trial, and there would be no move for John Eaton to make in that she-Satan's behalf.

All these possibilities became realities. Judge Thurston went on a drunk and held his head for days, unable to fathom any court proceeding. Morsell kept his own counsel, counting his notes and wondering how else to pay them. William Jones was called to Annapolis by William Wirt, and together they argued for the canal companies being sued.[9] Richard Coxe did inherit the Royall case, all of it, with the promise of receiving the Watkins case too, for that was the only account which would provide remuneration for his services. Richard Coxe found himself with a new young associate, Stephen Smith, Harrison Smith's younger brother.[10] The stage was set for the final play against Mrs. Royall.

Judge Cranch took immediate advantage of his power. On Tuesday, July 27, he had the editor of the *Baltimore Republican* jailed for "contempt" for having published the forbidden testimony in the Watkins case. Then Cranch threatened all other publications following the *Republican's* lead.[11] In the same hour, he ordered Richard Coxe to submit a more comprehensive brief concerning his objections to the judgment of Mrs. Royall, and Richard Coxe was given two days to do it. Cranch announced that Mrs. Royall would be sentenced July 29.

Dr. Ely went to work on his supporters. Mrs. Royall was an infidel and his God knew how to take care of such as she. Ely's contacts responded to his call. The battle was on in the courts, and what better place to begin the Kingdom of God in the United States of America?

The blackcoat press had advance notice of Cranch's moves. The jailing of the Baltimore Republican editor was held over the heads of the other papers, including the *Baltimore American*. To prepare the public for what was coming, sudden reprints of trial accounts unfavorable to Mrs. Royall appeared in papers which had carried better notices of her ordeal. On July 30, the *American* reprinted a verbatim account from Colonel Stone's blackcoat paper:

MRS. ROYALL'S TRIAL

From the correspondent of the *New York Commercial Advertiser*

Washington, July 23

For want of something more worthy of your sprightly and various columns, I send you some account of a trial which has excited some interest, and occasioned some gratification among the lovers of the ludicrous. I refer to the trial of the redoubtable Mrs. Anne Royall. As you have been in the presence, and possibly admitted to kiss hands, I need not describe to you that truly royal personage. Her brazen front, twinkling eyes and Billingsgate voice, are all present, I dare say to your fancy. She has long been putting to trial the public forbearance in Washington, which has been to her a city of refuge. Driven from Alexandria by the threat of being carted and "dumped down beyond the city bounds, and from Richmond" by the first steps of a process for imprisonment, she favoured us with her august presence in the metropolis, where by dint of brass, begging and scribbling, she has contrived to get her bread and cheese, together with a great name. With unabashed face and an indomitable assurance, she has pushed herself into the audience rooms of all the Heads of Departments, and, as is said, into that of the President himself, (of whose friendship she makes a loud boast). Good, easy Mr. Carroll, who has more houses than tenants, and more tenants than rents, permitted her to inhabit a large deso-

late three story house of his on Capital Hill, in the neighborhood of a
building frequently used for holding religious meetings, and on Sunday
mornings, for the assemblage of a Sunday school. At the window opposite
this building, the old bellwether was in the habit of establishing herself and
gratifying her malignity, by loudly ridiculing, and grossly insulting the
teachers (of both sexes) who are in the benevolent work of gratuitously instructing the poor. Nay, the poor children themselves could not escape,
but were berated as blackguards, beggars, impudent varlets, etc; while the
teachers were tauntingly asked why they did not convert them? Why they
did not teach them manners? Whether these were their Christians? with
other questions in the same strain. So far this was carried, that some of
the young ladies were actually afraid to pass. Nor could they come within
hearing, without having themselves outraged by language, to which no delicate female could listen. The Mayor was appealed to, but in vain; and at
length, an information was lodged with the Grand Jury, accompanied by
a list of the most reputable witnesses. Mr. Swann produced an indictment,
two counts of which were quashed by the Court. On one of them, however, after a delay of more than a week, the lady was at length brought to
trial, being escorted in a carriage from her lodgings, by a Toison d'Or in
the shape of a constable—She had engaged the services of Mr. Coxe, a lawyer of great acuteness, who was much amused at being retained by a client
of so novel a character.

The appearance of the prisoner (loudly greeted by the boys around the
door) and the reading of the indictment, excited much mirth throughout
the Courtroom. But these smiles all vanished on the examination of the
first witness for the prosecution, who testified to outrages on the female
part of his family, so gross and abominable, that a general feeling of indignation put everything of the ludicrous to flight. The only provocation for
this usage was the fact that the gentleman himself was an elder in the
church, his son a prominent and active promoter of every object of a pious
and benevolent character, and his daughter (a very timid, diffident, retiring girl) one of the Sabbath School teachers. None of the family done
aught to provoke the virago, yet she had not ceased to pour out on every
one of them torrents of the most coarse, vulgar and obscene language,
until they could not appear even at the windows of their houses. Other
witnesses testified to the abuse of sisters and mothers, (for had she confined her attacks to men alone, the prosecution would never have been
undertaken) and that both in the public street and in their own houses.

The testimony on the part of the prosecution being closed, that on behalf of the prisoner followed—and here the farcical part of the scene com-
menced. She had sent a summons for her alleged friend the President, but
he did not wish to figure in such a field and he was very properly excused.
Not so his Secretary—a summons proving ineffectual, she issued a sub-
poena, when lo, Mr. Eaton, nolens contens, had to make his appearance.
Being pressed for time, he was permitted to give his evidence out of turn.
It was delivered in short metre, with no great appearance of delight. It
amounted in fact to nothing, being merely that when Mrs. R. was in his
room, she was not guilty of any misconduct. An Irishman by the name of
Holohan was next called. The man is engaged in digging a bank of earth
opposite Mrs. R.'s above, and lives next door to her. Being asked if he ever
knew Mrs. R. to be engaged in scolding or slandering, his replies, delivered
in the broadest accent of the turf, occasioned great merriment. They were
flat against her. "Sure enough, I have heard her often shouting at people
from her window—but I was too busy with my carts to give any great
attenshun. It's true, your Honors, what Mr. C. says—she did shout at him,
and call him Ould Holy Willy, that's a sure, and he was in the coach all the
while, riding in a funeral." Deflated in her hopes of Holohan, she next
called little Tims, the door keeper of the Senate. (of "more porter Tims
memory") This worthy perhaps you have seen—if so you remember his
maniken shape, his red picked snuffy nose, and ludicrously pompous man-

ner. Coxe began by asking him if he knew Mrs. Royall to be a common scold. Now it so happens that this witness (more suo) had been somewhat familiar with that out of which the devil often comes without the aid of a conjuror: his eyes winked,—or snapped, I believe the term is,—his frame see-sawed over the centre of gravity, and, with his right hand protruded, he answered the lawyer's question by another. "Pray, sir," said Tims, "what is the proper and legal definition of a common scold? When can a scold said to be common; for as being a scold you know all women are that." Now what gave point to this query, was the fact that it was the very question which Coxe himself had put to the court on a previous motion to quash the indictment. The wary counsel gave it the go-by, and changing the shape of his question, said, "Well then, Mr. Tims, did you ever know of Mrs. Royall's slandering anybody?" Tims promptly answered, "Yes, sir,— she has slandered me." This was rather a stumper—coming from her own witness. "You, Mr. Tims, how so?" "Why sir, she has said, aye and printed it too, in her book, that I am very clever—and to that I make no objections; in fact, I believe on the whole, it is true. Take me altogether I certainly am a very clever man; but she adds—and a very exemplary man. Now that is a slander!"

This was too much. The court roared: bench, bar and jury, all lost their balance, and while even the sedate Judge Cranch sunk his head between his hands and shook in his chair, Tims himself was the only person left unmoved. He looked round grave as an owl. Just opposite him stood Mr. **** laughing immoderately. Tims catching sight of him, again opened his oracular jaws. "Yes sir, and I know of her slandering one other person besides me." Indeed; who is that? "Why, there's Mr. ****, she says in the same book, that he and **** are two of the handsomest men in Washington; now I leave it to the whole world if that is not a slander!"

The effect of this you may imagine. In vain, the constables roared out "silence!" The Courtroom shook to its foundations, and it was some time before the trial could proceed. Her witnesses having been examined, and all proved alike treacherous, the accused proceeded, in propis persona, to address the jury. Advancing her wrinkled visage and swaying their souls with the majestry of her outstretched hand, she proceeded to obtest and objure them, as they love liberty and their country, not to sacrifice both in her person. They stood not only for the present age, but the guardians of posterity. This prosecution was but one branch of the general conspiracy of the blue-and-black-hearted Presbyterians, the Priests and Missionaries, against the freedom of speech and of the press. If they were permitted to succeed, who could answer for his home or fireside? Nothing would be safe—bigotry and all the horrors of the inquisition would overwhelm the land, and nothing would be left of all for which her husband and the other worthies of the Revolution had shed their blood on the tented field, etc., etc. But I blush to add, that the force of even such eloquence was in vain. The Jury, neither melted by suffering beauty, nor fired by the remembrance of posterity in danger, returned a verdict of Guilty—and, to crown the evidence of our barbarism, the Judge informed her that unless she found bail for her appearance until the sentence should be pronounced, she must be remanded to prison. On hearing this, she exclaimed, "This is a pretty country to live in!" and left the courtroom in company with the constable. Sentence is not yet pronounced—and this paragon has already forfeited her bail by attacking a gentleman in the street. He disclaimed, however, to enter a complaint—so the matter lies over. The general opinion is, that she will be sentenced to a fine and short imprisonment, and that her punishment will be remitted by a pardon from the Executive, but this I think must be a party slander. Yours, etc.

Having concluded, she turned round to the lawyers and said, "Well, was not that fine!"[12]

Mrs. Royall entered into the spirit of this press war, even though her own head was the quarry. Having had the worst, the rest had to be better. It was obvious that Cranch had taken on more than his friends had planned, and reports such as Ely's did more to hurt than help the judge. Dr. Ely had done her a favor, with his story appearing after all the others. As Christ had been prepared for the sacrifice before the judges and Pontius Pilate, so Mrs. Royall was being prepared too. Her supporters made the most of this simile.

William Jones had removed himself from Mrs. Royall's affairs, but he had assured the writer that her prosecution would come to naught. What Cranch was doing was simply not constitutional. There were no more stocks allowed in the District, despite precedence in the Code of Maryland and there would be no ducking stools either. Cranch and his blackcoat friends could do their damndest, but there would be no return to the Dark Ages. Mrs. Royall was to keep her good sense of humor and let Richard Coxe handle the situation.

A sense of humor had been Mrs. Royall's best weapon since the beginning. It had honed her satire to the point where her pen could cut with a quip better than a saber. The Navy yard's ducking contraption was no liability for her; it was her best asset during this difficult wait. With the concurrence of her lawyer, she publicly promoted the punishment designed expressly for her and with that promotion continued to discomfort and harass the judge who had brought it all to pass. It became the symbol of her entire prosecution and editors who wrote against her found themselves saddled with the ducking stool whenever her case was discussed. Judge Cranch, in accepting the ancient charge, had placed himself in an awkward position. Could he order the ducking stool reinstituted in America? The Washington bar said no. Judge Cranch is in the unenviable situation of having accepted an ancient charge which prescribed a punishment invalid in the United States, and that was proof of the invalidity of the prosecution in the first place. The judge was caught in a legal crossfire.

The brief that Richard Coxe submitted and argued was a classic joke in legal terminology. The *National Journal* told the story:

July 30, 1829

The motion made by the Counsel for Mrs. Royall, in arrest of judgment, was argued yesterday by Mr. Coxe. He suggested to the Court that, according to the authorities, there was no discretion in the Court to adjudge any other punishment to a common scold than the ducking-stool, and a learned English judge respited the judgment in a case of this description, because he was of the opinion that a ducking would only have the effect of hardening the offender. There was another consequence of this punishment, to which he called the attention of the Court, which was the privilege, which according to legal writers, it conferred on the delinquent of ever afterwards scolding with impunity. He begged that the Court would weigh this matter, and not be the first to introduce a ducking-stool, which had been obsolete in England since the reign of Queen Anne, reminding them that the very introduction of such an engine of punishment might have the effect of increasing the criminals of this class. If the Greek legislators would not enact a punishment for a crime not unknown to them lest it should induce persons to commit that offence, the Court might now suffer themselves to be influenced against the introduction of the ducking-stool, lest it might lead to an increase of common scolds.

Mrs. Royall, who seemed to be as much entertained by the argument as any other person, occupied herself in taking notes of the proceedings, and smiled very graciously when Mr. Swann expressed his desire that she should enjoy the benefit of a cold bath with as much privacy as possible. She was informed that notice would be given her when the Court should have made up its opinion upon the motion on arrest of judgment.

Indeed Ezra Stiles Ely and his collaborators had created a monster, but it was not entirely their own. Richard Coxe and Anne Royall had taken it from them, using their own cues, relying on the Constitution and its *dicta* against cruel and unusual punishment, and constructed their own version of the "ducking stool." If "common scolds" there would be, let the prestigious federal judge be forewarned that he would have to lay his reputation on the line to keep them in the body of American Law. Richard Coxe and Anne Royall were having great sport with Ely's brainchild. If Mrs. Royall's enemies feared her now, let them beware of her after the court had conferred the title upon her! The English precedent had been raised by those seeking to please an English Queen who had been displeased by her Scots-Irish subjects and their treatment of women. Queen Anne's determination to erase the right of religious fanatics to abuse women, and by inference abuse her, had reformed the English law. Men who sat as judges would have seen their heads roll if they had not, and another Anne in another time had decided to win the same point in the United States of America.

The challenge was before Judge Cranch; the other judges had been removed. With the Washington bar sitting in the court, Richard Coxe threw his argument at Cranch while Thomas Swann sat through it, disinterested. He had warned Ely and his many friends of the consequences. He no longer cared, for that morning he had learned that his days as U.S. attorney were over; the very men who had promised to work for his retention had agreed to replace him after all. It was a blow softened by one fact only: William Jones would not replace him; Francis Scott Key would. The Jacksonians and their enemies had agreed to accept the man who had written *The Star-Spangled Banner* in a compromise constructed from a threatened court reform.

Thomas Swann sat in Judge Cranch's courtroom in his official capacity for the last time. Although he could not abide Mrs. Royall's opinions, Swann decided he would have no part in the insane attempt to introduce the ducking stool to America. No one would tarnish him with this legal obscenity. The prosecutor sat in his chair and looked at Cranch, Ely and his minions, the lawyers on the benches, Francis Scott Key, and Mrs. Royall and Richard Coxe. He was glad he was relinquishing his job. This was one case where the punishment would never fit the crime, for any of those involved.

Chapter 22

The Last Laugh

Richard Coxe had planned a bold strategy for Mrs. Royall. William Jones and he had been convinced from the beginning that the whole "common scold" proceeding could not stand the scrutiny of American law. The legal problem was to force the judge to recognize that fact and, failing that, to force the other judges on the federal bench to take notice of the seriousness of the situation. Judge Cranch had made enough errors to mount an appeal but Jones and Coxe knew their opponents would try to keep the matter from higher consideration.

Richard Coxe had decided on a two-fold attack: the matter was to be kept as ludicrous as possible, and Judge Cranch was to be the butt of his own involvement in the legal abomination. Coxe had two advantages: the Navy yard's "merry-go-round," authorized by Commodore Tingley, lent credence to Mrs. Royall's justified "scolding" of men in government misusing public funds, and Cranch's obvious lack of judicious sense in threatening Mrs. Royall with corporal punishment for writing truth while Tobias Watkins, an admitted thief, was placed in no such jeopardy in the same court by the same judge. It was the stuff with which Mrs. Royall's many editors and friends could create a climate for the more important work Richard Coxe had to do.

Public opinion was rallied to Mrs. Royall's side. Judge Cranch was in error and had shown his bias. The judge had failed to instruct the jury to put aside considerations of slander and brawling as invalid to her prosecution. The jury had been allowed to consider those counts in the verdict and had expressed its "guilty" finding based on all three counts of the original indictment. Judge Cranch had compounded his error by asserting, when reminded, that one instance concerning any of the three counts was enough for a jury to find Mrs. Royall guilty of all. He had refused to correct his error.

Richard Coxe went to work with a full assault upon Judge Cranch, but Cranch could not accept it as such. He had to accept Coxe's brief while he wrestled with a way to keep it from the review of the higher courts.

All Washington was watching, and Cranch could not afford a slip. He had to handle his opinion very carefully to promote what Americans would not accept lightly, to wed English common law to American constitutional law to facilitate its reinstitution in the United States. The old Federalist believed that the new nation had to be wedded to the old for the union of both. Ezra Stiles Ely believed in an English-American theocracy; Cranch believed in an English-American legal system. He could not stop the mirth of his colleagues nor the public's feelings about the ducking stool, but he could tie the ends of justice to his decision and have his own laugh on his detractors. He intended to redefine American law to include English law, giving legal precedent for the "common scold" charge.

188

Richard Coxe had produced a voluminous brief. He had searched the statutes for William Jones in the original hunt for the meaning of the charge when it was first presented. Coxe contended that the English common law stated that the only acceptable punishment of a common scold was to duck, and the English courts had removed the charge "common scold" from active use. Further, ducking was precluded from use in the new United States of America because it defied the constitutional prohibition against such punishments. "Common scold" also abrogated Maryland's Bill of Rights, thus infringing on American precepts. Richard Coxe sprinkled his brief with quotes from the ancient legal sources, as Judge Cranch had his initial opinion. From Jacob's dictionary, an antiquated definer of legal terms from the Dark Ages of English law, he took "a woman indicted for being a common scold, if convicted, shall be sentenced to be placed in a certain engine of correction called the *trebucket, tumbrel, Tymborella, castigatory,* or *cucking stool,* which, in Saxon, signifies the scolding stool, though it is now frequently corrupted into ducking stool, because the residue of the judgment is, that when she is so placed therein, she shall be plunged into the water for her punishment."

Not content with this archaic recitation, Richard Coxe found more old English cases to cite. One hundred years before, in Queen Anne's time, the whole matter had been settled. In *Queen vs. Foxby,* 6 Mod 11, Coxe cited "note, the punishment of a scold is ducking"; and Holt said: "She was convicted by the justices of the peace, at their quarter sessions at Maidstone, upon an indictment for being a common scold, and judgment that she should be ducked; whereupon she brought a writ of error, and hereupon the sheriff let her go at large, there being no fine or imprisonment in the judgment." Richard Coxe had slammed his legal gauntlet in Judge Cranch's face. No precedents existed for further use of ducking for common scolds, and there were no fines or imprisonments inherent in the charge in even ancient judgment. An American court, a federal one at that, had claimed jurisdiction over a crime which did not exist in either American or English common law, and now Cranch had to explain why Mrs. Royall had been charged and tried on the matter in the first place.

Judge Cranch did not have a pleasant week constructing his reply to Richard Coxe. An enterprising tinker, Irish by birth and Roman Catholic in religion, had come to the capital at the height of the "ducking stool" fever, and viewing the Navy Yard model, had improved upon it by setting up a working model on which people could ride as an amusement. People were paying to ride this ducking stool wheel, not into the water, but round and round on the ground. The merriment and amusement attending the device only heightened the tension in the court and in the bar, which watched the matter getting out of hand.[1]

At length, Dr. Ely and associates realized that the new memorial to their "common scold" prosecution was running against them. The blackcoats marched to the Washington constabulary and demanded that the Irishman and his merry-go-round be stopped. The tinker, alerted, moved his contraption out of Washington City and into a friendly field owned by Daniel Carroll. The Presbyterians in the capitol, watching the crowds stream out to join in the fun, preached mightily against such delights of the flesh but to no avail. Ely's pulpits and their hellfire and damnation were no match for the ingenious invention of an Irish gypsy. Mrs. Royall became a household word even to those people who could not read, and the common scold was becoming a new national celebrity. It was not happening the way Dr. Ely had envisioned it all; the woman was not being ostracized; the public was not about to stone her; she was not being treated like a convicted criminal. Instead, she was being hailed as some sort of new national heroine. Judging by the crowds who waited for a ride on the tinker's merry-go-round in Carroll's field, there were more people who wanted to join Mrs. Royall on her ducking stool than there were those who wanted to duck her.

The entire Royall prosecution had been Ely's brainchild. Remembering his successes in Philadelphia with members of his own congregation, he had expected to achieve the same effect with Mrs. Royall. Ely had hoped to make Mrs. Royall such a joke that women ever after would stay in their domestic roles, leaving the affairs of state and religion in the hands of men. Dr. Ely counted on his pursuance of the "common scold" charge to provide a national vehicle to laugh independent women out of existence. Women on the streets meant only one thing to him: they were whores, not national commentators.

As Ely had envisioned, a national joke was in the making but it was his own blackcoats. Andrew Jackson's lusty followers had discovered what Mrs. Royall was all about. Men and women who never read suddenly knew what the old lady had written and, taking to the "merry-go-rounds," they danced about them as they had reveled about the hickory poles for Jackson. The spectre of the French Revolution danced through Washington's streets but this time, the guillotine had been replaced by the Navy Yard's wheeled ducking stool.

As quickly as the Royall affair had begun, it had to be ended. Judge Cranch was handed the quandary. His friends wanted *finis* to the matter, but he had an opportunity to alter the future of national jurisprudence. That was more enticing. His friends had sought for years to soften the effects of the Revolution, and now he had the means in his hands. Judge Cranch, Federalist to the core, could provide a semantic fort for the forces of privilege. He would write his opinion; Mrs. Royall would be ensnared in the law. She wrote about her dangerous position herself:

Finding appearances against them, old Mr. Coyle, generally skulking round my house, made affidavit that I met him in the street and abused him, and called him perjured.

"Oh, dear sir," to Mr. Swann, " 'wrap' the mantle of the law around me and save me from this woman." A great beast like him. How could so small a woman as I, hurt him? If he was afraid, why did he not keep away from my house? What brought him there? Now the fact was this: running down my steps in a great hurry, one evening, I ran plump upon Mr. Coyle. I laughed as usual, and said, "We would have the pleasure of walking together." "Ah, old woman," said he, "your time is short." What do you threaten sir? "Take care, don't go too far." He either wrote or went to Judge Cranch (can't tell which, though I heard the Judge tell it) to complain and the Judge told him the substance must be in the form of an affidavit, and he produced the affidavit in Court, which I immediately contradicted by another. Now I should like to know, whether Judges, consistent with their oaths, can give advice in matters pending before them?"[2]

John Coyle, Sr., charged Mrs. Royall with violating the terms of her release, disturbing his peace again. She reacted characteristically. She wrote immediately to the prosecutor, Thomas Swann.

Dear Sir:

I think it very unkind in you to believe my enemies whom you see are so bitter against me, the face of things contrasted. This old Mr. C. is always around my house, annoying me with all sorts of noise, so far did he go evening before last that he came to my own door — not in the street — threatened my life. I am about to have measures taken to bind him to his

good behavior. I therefore appeal to you what steps to take, I have no
peace in my life from the whole gang.

Yours,

Anne Royall[3]

This unexpected letter from Mrs. Royall shook Swann loose from his leth-
argy. The old woman could charge John Coyle, Sr., with "a threat to her life,"
and that could blow Cranch's latest ploy sky high. He went immediately to
Cranch.

Judge Cranch and Thomas Swann knew what to do to head off Mrs. Royall.
John Coyle had to charge Mrs. Royall at once with threatening him. They
would accept his complaint and not hers; she was a convicted common scold. At
last, Mrs. Royall could be fined and held to the peace, and there could be no
complaint about that sentence. John Coyle was happy to comply with this
expert suggestion.

On the morning of July 31, eighteen hours after the promised data for judgment on Mrs. Royall, Thomas Swann produced John Coyle's latest charge
against Mrs. Royall instead. The woman had violated her terms of release, and
Mrs. Royall's letter to Swann was produced as corroborative proof of Coyle's
allegations. Judge Cranch declared it evidence of the fact that Mrs. Royall knew
she had breached the peace and was trying to cover for her mistake; therefore,
Mrs. Royall now had to take the consequences.[4] Richard Coxe and his client
could do nothing but listen.

None of the Adams family was ever renowned for a sense of humor, and
Judge Cranch, their connection, was in keeping with their dour condition. This
jurist, still memorialized for his stern countenance and the fact that he liked to
inflict extreme punishment, wrote his opinion. Answering Richard Coxe, he
worked to cement English law to American law, including its obsolete antiqui-
ties. William Cranch tossed his own gauntlet to the Washington bar and to the
federal courts. Like it or not, lawyers made their living not by upholding Reason but explaining the irrationalities of ancient precedence, and Cranch gave
them an objective lesson in how their knowledge of archaic and obtuse items
forced other people to come to them in order to find "justice." William Cranch,
lawyer, knew exactly how most of his legal brethren would react. They would
laugh, but they would laugh among themselves as they sheared their clients for
sacrificial slaughter.

It was an artful opinion which Judge Cranch delivered. Mrs. Royall stood
before him not only as "common scold" but also as a disturber of the peace she
had been warned to keep as the terms of her release. Judge Cranch wove together both charges and drew his punishment precedents from them. "Common
scold" might be an obsolete term but "common nuisance" was not. Judge
Cranch dwelt lovingly on the old English semantics to hammer home that Mrs.
Royall, the common scold, would have been treated far more harshly in ancient
times:

Lord Coke says — 'Trebucket, or castigatory, named in the statute, signifieth a cucking stool; and trebucket is properly a pitfall, or downfall, and, in
law, signifieth a stool that falleth down into a pit of water, for the punishment of the party in it, and "chuck" or "Guck," in the Saxon tongue signifieth to scold or brawl (taken from cuckhaw, or guckhaw, a bird, qui
odiose jurgat et rixatur) and ing, in that language, (water); because she
was, for her punishment, soused in the water; and others fetch it from
cuck-quean i rellex.[5]

With such nonsense, Judge Cranch forced Mrs. Royall to stand before the court, sporting with argument that not only were scolds so treated but bakers and brewers also for failure to pay taxes. Although only a woman could be a scold, the same punishment was no longer the criterion; only crime was the consideration. Any constitutional argument raised because only women were involved was no longer germain to the issue since men had enjoyed the "baths" too! Judge Cranch warmed to his legal lecture:

> It is therefore clear, that the punishment . . . was not confined to scolds; and that this citation from Lord Coke does not justify an inference that ducking was the only punishment which could be inflicted upon them. It should be said that such an inference may be drawn from the etymology of the word "cucking stool" which he derives from a Saxon word signifying to scold, that inference is rebutted by the more probable etymology given by Burn (3 Burns's Justice, p 225) who says — "The common people in the northern parts of England, amongst whom the greatest remains of the ancient Saxon are to be found, pronounce it ducking stool, which perhaps, may have sprung from the Belgic or Teutonic 'ducken,' to dive under water; from whence also, we probably denominate our duck, the water fowl; or rather, it is more agreeable to the analogy and progression of languages to assert, that the substantive, duck, is the original and the verb made from thence; as much to say, to duck is to do as the fowl does." So that the name of the instrument, and not because it was used for the punishment of scolds only. The words tumbrel, terbucket, castigatory, cucking stool and ducking stool, are used synonymously by the old writers, as well as the old statutes.[6]

Richard Coxe and Mrs. Royall sat and listened to this legal nonsense. Judge Cranch had taken the challenge and returned it with the full use of his judge's prerogatives. Mrs. Royall noted wryly that it could have been written by Ezra Stiles Ely as Judge Cranch continued:

> Now, for that the judgment to the pillory or tumbrel (as hath appeared before) doth make the delinquent infamous, and that rule of law is, that the justices of the assize, oyer and terminer, jail delivery, and justices of the peace would be well advised, before they give judgment of any person to the pillory or tumbrel, unless they give good warrent for their judgment therein. Fine and imprisonment, for offense finable by the justices aforesaid, is a fair and sure way.[7]

Judgment at last had arrived, but Judge Cranch was not going to finish so easily. He let his listeners hang on his every word, and drawing out his argument, reminded all present that such precedents were binding only on justices of the lower courts, not on judges of the higher courts such as he. Lord Coke was giving advice to underlings, not to peers such as Judge Cranch. Any punishment was within his discretion, and he cited another curious precedent to nail his right:

> Thus in the case of The King vs. Thomas and wife, convicted of keeping a disorderly house, the wife was in prison, but the husband had run away from his bail; affidavits were made that the prisoner was in so weak a condition that a bodily punishment might kill her. The ordinary judgment in this case is pillory; but for misdemeaner, the court is not tied down to any particular punishment; and being a married woman has nothing to pay a fine withal, the punishment must be imprisonment. The judgment was, that she be imprisoned for a year, and then to find security for her good behavior for seven years.[8]

Richard Coxe was aghast. What was the old man talking about? Mrs. Royall sat stunned. "Imprisoned for a year" The Court erupted. Judge Cranch demanded that the court restore order; he was not done:

> It is said — 'All common nuisances to the public are regularly punishable by fine and imprisonment at the discretion of the judges; but in some cases corporal punishment may be inflicted, as in the case of a common scold, who is said to be properly punishable by being put in a ducking stool.
> Also the offence of keeping a disorderly house is punishable, not only with fine and imprisonment, but also with such infamous punishment as to the court, in its discretion, may seem proper.[9]

The courtroom erupted again and in vain did Cranch try to quiet his domain. William Brent, the clerk of the court, and Marshal Beck did nothing to quell the outburst. Mrs. Royall sat white with anger; it was obvious the game this judge was playing and his reference to "disorderly house" was indefensible. Mrs. Royall sat wondering how long Cranch would speak. He could have his sport with her now, but she would have hers with him. The pandemonium continued.

Judge Cranch demanded order again, and this time he ordered the defendant to stand. Mrs. Royall complied, and the courtroom quieted. The lady was no felon facing a judge but a woman standing on right facing a man speaking wrong. The spectators were with her, crushing her opponents with their emotion. Judge Cranch, with utter disdain, went on with his opinion; he was weaving archaic law and obsolete rulings into federal law:

> If a part of the common-law punishment of the offence has become obsolete, the only effect is, that the discretion of the Court is so far limited. The offence is not obsolete, and cannot become obsolete so long as a common scold is a common nuisance. All the elementary writers upon criminal law admit, that being a common scold, to the common nuisance of the neighborhood, is an indictable offence at common law.[10]

Judge Cranch had equated the archaic "common scold" with "common nuisance," redefining it as an indictable offense. Richard Coxe reached over and took Mrs. Royall's hand. At last they had the case for a higher court. Even as the lawyer considered this, Cranch finished his opinion and his last words were almost lost:

> This Court is therefore of the opinion, that although punishment by ducking may have become obsolete, yet that offence still remains a common nuisance, and, as such, is punishable by fine and imprisonment, like any other misdemeaner at common law; and that, therefore, the motion in arrest of judgment must be overruled.[11]

The court erupted again. Richard Coxe was on his feet. Judge Buckner Thurston had granted that arrest of judgment. Judge Cranch called the court to order again amid the lawyers' and newspapermen's jeers. The district court had not witnessed such a scene in years.

Judge Cranch went on to deny the motion for a new trial. No argument presented by Mrs. Royall's counsel was acceptable. Mrs. Royall had been cited as a common scold, accused of scolding in one instance, and the jury had judged her to be guilty. That was enough. Further, the other indictments, despite the ruling against them, were just considerations of the court and the fact that the jury had not been instructed to disregard them or the evidence admitted for them had no bearing on the matter. Cranch said "the counts were not a matter of evidence; nor could they have been so understood by the jury; and they could not be separated from the good count, upon which the issue had been joined."12 The lawyers stood stunned. Cranch continued with his judicial semantics:

So here, although the jury might have supposed they were trying an issue on all the counts, and may have given their verdict, because they thought one of the bad counts supported, if the Court is satisfied that the evidence was sufficient to support the good count, the court ought not, in its discretion, to grant a new trial.13

The district court was crowded; almost every lawyer in the city was present. For the first time, the Washington bar knew it had a judicial problem on its hands. Court reform had begun as a whisper, a mist rising in the last month, but this decision could make it a Jackson whirlwind. The courtroom was hushed as lawyers and newspapermen strained to hear Judge Cranch.

Mrs. Royall was ordered to come forward before the bench. As she walked, her defiance was apparent to all. She was prepared for the worst from this American judge who did not represent America but the forces against it. "Imprisonment for a year; fines, seven years good conduct" was in her mind. It would not stop her from writing what she thought. Prison or not, fine or not, she would keep her pen going against such as this black-garbed judge and his black-coated allies. Even as she stood where she was placed, straight and tall with pride, she steeled the others in the room for what was to come.

Judge Cranch asked Mrs. Royall if she was ready for judgment. She replied loud and clear that she was. He sat back, looked about the courtroom and then spoke his decision.

"Mrs. Royall, you are fined ten dollars and you are to give security for your good behavior for one year and to stand committed until the fine and costs should be paid, and the security given."14

The courtroom was silent, stunned. Ten dollars and a peace bond. Judge Cranch had been playing a game. All those semantics, all those ancient words and threats, meant nothing. Laughter began and then rose in intensity, breaking like a tidal wave. Richard Coxe stood up, grabbed Mrs. Royall and hugged her. Ten dollars; it had all been a joke!

Mrs. Royall did not laugh. She watched as the men about her, and her few women friends, found release in their mirth. Ten dollars and a peace bond! For this a federal court and the American law had been abused. It was like Philadelphia in 1824. That city had laughed at "common scold" too, at Ely and his pretensions, but the laughter had been short lived. Mrs. Royall was the seeming butt of it all; but was it a joke? Mrs. Royall did not think so.

The courtroom laughter relieved everyone. It appeared that all those present thought they had won. Those against Mrs. Royall had a guilty decision against her and a judgment to cite; those for her could laugh it off as another strange legal exercise in semantics resulting in a minor fine. Confusion attended it all. No one was really sure what the judge had said when they thought about it, not even the newspapermen present. The *National Intelligencer* reported on the decision on August 1, 1829:

MRS. ROYALL: The Court, after it had delivered its opinion in the case of Mrs. Royall, gave judgment against the Defendent: that she be fined $10 and costs, give security in the·sum of $250 for her good behavior for one year and stand committed to prison until the sentence be complied with.15

Who paid the fine, who went the security so reported? The record does not tell, and the defendant wrote a different tale. The trial over, an appeal denied, Mrs. Royall noted:

> This was late on Saturday evening. The next day, on the blessed Sabbath, those wretches circulated a report through the city that I was in prison. This report was carefully forwarded to Secretary Eaton's. From the testimony he gave in Court he was expected to be one of those secret friends. General Eaton, not knowing them as well then as he does now, immediately signed a bond together with the Postmaster General and others who were at his house, and sent a messenger off with it to the Marshal to release me — and any man who would not have done so, must have the heart of a beast. But Secretary Eaton had not the honor of being my security, though doubtless he would have considered it so.
>
> The judgment was a fine of ten dollars — the cost fifty — but who paid it, whether it was ever paid or not, I never heard.[16]

And she never did. The controversy attended the verdict in such volume that no one could sort it out. What had Judge Cranch ruled upon? Was it "common scold" or the written affidavit of John Coyle alleging Mrs. Royall's scolding of him after the trial? Whatever it was, the Washington bar did not care to know, and Judge Cranch did not elaborate. Mrs. Royall did not pay the penalty, and Richard Coxe thought it best to let the matter lay. Perhaps that was what William Cranch had wanted after all: his opinion filed and no challenge mounted. It was the solution to the mess which had engulfed them all. True to her fashion, Mrs. Royall had the last word upon the matter:

> And it was a case of much importance, the Court took several days to make up their opinion. It was surmized that this interval was to ascertain the public voice — "whether the punishment of ducking would be suffered to be carried into execution." What the object was I know not. It would have been a serious business, to say the least and the Court had a hint of this . . .
>
> Much to the honor of Mr. Cox, his defence was able, clear and pointed. He adverted to the Bill of Rights, to the constitution — and proved this savage statute had never been in force in this country; and deprecated the disgrace of introducing such an inhuman law into our country — too shocking for men much more than an aged and respectable female, whose husband had fought for our independence. He appealed to the justice and humanity of the Court, in a style of feeling, energy and pathos, that would have touched the heart of the most untamable savage, and urged the illegibility of the law in toto. Being thrown so many ages back, Mr. Coxe was compelled to use the phrases of those barbarous ages, which was a mixture of Saxon, Roman and Norman. While he was pleading, I was amused with my sweet Morsell. He kept his eyes shut, and looked as though he was peeping into rat holes. — There was not much amusement in the looks of the other two — Whether it was Coke upon Littleton or Littleton upon Coke, I am at a loss to say. Their faces grew as black as the hour they were appointed, and seemed to be taking different shapes. It was complete stage effect — nothing wanting but the rack.[17]

And so it happened that "common scold" passed quietly into the statute books of American jurisprudence on July 31, 1829. The legal question of how common nuisance could become an indictable offense, subject to federal court treatment, was never raised by the learned counsels. It was an oversight noticed by no one but the woman involved. Mrs. Royall wrote: "Every legal man will be astonished, that the grand jury of our metropolis, should be so ignorant as not to know these charges could not be brought before them. A drunkard, or an abandoned woman infesting the streets can be committed to the workhouse as a common nuisance; but no such thing is recognizable by a grand jury."[18] Why no action was promoted against "common scold" on this basis by a member of the Washington bar will never be known, but obviously Judge Cranch knew his lawyer brethren better than they knew themselves. Without legislative enactment "common scold" became law, in the presence of many of the nation's first lawyers, and not one of them said a word.

Ezra Stiles Ely did achieve the impossible on July 31, 1829. He abrogated the Constitution of the United States with this "crime" and his friends did assure that this invasion of American law would not be reviewed. The blackcoats had a free hand to try their will in all the member states of the union. Mrs. Royall knew what Dr. Ely and his cohorts intended. She had not forgotten Philadelphia in 1824-25 and was free to work against them. Let the fools enjoy the new Bladensburg Races: With Andrew Jackson and John Eaton, Anne Royall would have the last laugh.

Chapter 23

Consequences

August heat cleared the streets of the capital and stilled the government offices. The great courtroom drama was over, and Mrs. Royall was back in her home, at her desk. It was a time for reflection.

Anne Newport Royall had been made the "Common Scold." Richard Coxe had been right. The writer had a new title, and she would have to assess its effect. She had to write to her friends and her editors and judge their reactions. She went back to work with a zeal that belied the steamy weather.

The answers came fast. Mrs. Royall's case was a *cause celebre* for her editors, and the Jacksonians were making her a heroine. The court case had not been misunderstood by her friends, and people who had not known of her, who had never read a word she had written, responded with encouragement. The Washington merry-go-round had made her a symbol of resistance to court tyranny and injustice, and Mrs. Royall discovered she had a new kind of fame.

The capital support for the writer had become a national affection. Ely's well-laid plan had not prevailed. Mrs. Royall had departed the federal courtroom not to laughter against her but to titters against the men who had worked so hard to abuse her.

The weeks of isolation before and during trial had not been a loss for the writer. She had used her time to complete another book and in response to the Bladensburg Jury, its verdict of "guilty," and Judge Cranch's penalty "joke," her book rolled off the press with her version of the trial. *Black Book, Volume III* had sold 3,500 copies, but *Travels in Pennsylvania* sold 7,000 within a week after her travail.

Mrs. Royall's caustic delineation of her difficulties and her enumerated enemies received a wider publication than the accounts put forth by her opponents. The American public was invited to express its own opinion, and it did. None of Mrs. Royall's oppressors escaped. Ex-president Adams, his connection to Judge "Crunch" exposed, once again was an Adams against freedom of the press.[1] The Jacksonian press made the most of this new abuse, recalling old John Adams and his Alien and Sedition Acts.

Mrs. Royall was inundated with invitations from her masonic friends and from men and women who now opposed the Elyites, asking her to visit their small communities and tell all. With these requests came many donations and with orders for her book still arriving, she discovered she had enough money to tide her over until autumn and decided to enjoy a well-earned rest.

It had been a difficult five months. The Jackson victory at the polls had not yet become government in Washington. The army of recruits General Jackson had led into the capital had generally not found offices, and the few that had sat unapproved by the adjourned Congress. Jackson's enemies had planned well, and Mrs. Royall was more aware than ever after her experience with Judge Cranch and the district court. The whole government had to be reviewed, and she took the time to do so.

There were annoying interruptions. The blackcoats had not disappeared. Ely had gone back to the City of Brotherly Love, but his brethren in the capital were after John and Peg Eaton again. The Reverend J.N. Campbell of the Second Presbyterian Church, true to his mentor, was manufacturing new crime. The Eatons were said to be guilty of murder: He said Peg had aborted a child, Eaton's child, while still the wife of Purser Timberlake. Pastor Campbell asserted he could prove it and was moving for review of his charges. Mrs. Royall heard the rumors as they began, and the writer went to the defense of her friends:

> These men, discovering Secretary Eaton was not a brute like themselves, immediately attacked Mrs. E. with charges as foul as they are false and malicious. The dastardly cowards! Thus to make war upon women! One Whiteside, now in the pay of the government (to its disgrace) said "He was glad Mrs. J———— was dead, as she was not fit to keep company with the ladies of Washington." The members of Congress may judge of that. But Mrs. E. being very popular from the elegance of her manner and her superior understanding, stands in their way.[2]

And she let her friends know why she was involved:

> Thus people can see these Sunday-Mailmen are for moving every obstacle that opposes them. Another falsehood — "I am in possession of some secrets of Secretary Eaton and lest I might disclose them, he is compelled to do everything I ask him." I ask no favors of Secretary E! — I want none! nor have I but one fault to find with him, and that is not secret, which is keeping such knaves as they are in office.[3]

Mrs. Royall's defense of Secretary Eaton carried the Eaton affair far afield from the capital. For the first time, the blackcoat renditions were countered by someone friendly to the Eatons with as wide a base as theirs.

The blackcoats counterattacked: Noah Webster and his new dictionary were enlisted against her. The man who claimed he was the world's greatest lexographer set out to define scold in blackcoat terms, using Mrs. Royall's trial as his basis. Mrs. Royall acted characteristically to this information:

> Even Webster's dictionary was appealed to. By the way, I have a crow to pick with my friend, the North American, for lending his paper to some idiot to puff off this twenty years of labored nonsense. Does the North American think his paper can change dross into pure metal? The North American well knows that Webster and his Dictionary too, are nothing but a laughing stock to the whole country.[4]

Noah Webster was not a great contributor to the English language to Mrs. Royall. He was a son of the Hartford Convention who had been rewarded for his treason by being given years of aid and subsistence in London by the English, years which produced his dictionary.[5] Mrs. Royall knew Noah Webster; she had met him in 1826, and writing about that encounter to Jared Sparks, the biographer of George Washington, she had penned: "Webster is just the pompous blockhead I have described him . . . . he is the most dangerous because the most deep." She was disturbed by "the deep designing puritanical conscience" of the man who had "taken upon himself the responsibility of the mighty dictionary." Mrs. Royall knew that Noah Webster was in service to the blackcoat publishers, for he who had only known failure before was now their hope.[6] She believed he was out to purge the American tongue of its character, reducing it to a pale copy of English and reserving unto himself and his clergy friends the right to determine what words should or should not be used. She had argued with him about American expressions, and she felt that he was just one more manifestation of divine right, this time with the purpose to censure popular speech. Mrs. Royall enjoyed picking on Noah Webster and never more than now. These diversions did not keep the common scold from her purpose.

For five years, Mrs. Royall had been preaching the need for facts in the United States. She corresponded with editors in a dozen cities and eighty small communities encouraging commercial journals to include information to enable people to judge national directions. She had been successful not only with friends but with enemies, as her experience with Ely and his blackcoats proved. She was ready to launch a full-scale crusade to get her kind of writing in every journal and advertiser in the land.

Mrs. Royall had picked an ally for her project. John Eaton knew about newspapers and their influence. He had bought the *Washington Gazette* in 1825 and converted it into *The Telegraph* with Duff Green as editor. With it Eaton had prepared Andrew Jackson's campaign for the presidency, giving Jackson a voice in the capital.[7] She knew the part her pen had played in that affair, and she knew the opposition press·response. John Calhoun had taken leadership from Henry Clay, Daniel Webster, and William Wirt because the religious and the Biddle papers had backed him. The Jacksonians still had the capital, but they did not have Philadelphia and they needed new voices in New York, Hartford, Boston, and Pittsburgh. It was time to send her newsboys, her "Jimmies," abroad to print facts, real news for the people to know. Andrew Jackson had to speak to the entire country! Mrs. Royall decided to take her plan to John Eaton.

The Common Scold had a suggestion for a counteroffensive to the growing blackcoat press. If Eaton agreed, Mrs. Royall would like to recommend her young men, James Bennett, James Brooks and his brother, and young Richard Wallack as editors for friendly publications. Her boys knew Washington, the full facts of government, and directions that should be before the public. She had it in mind to suggest to her good friend Mordecai Noah and Mr. Webb in New York to do what John Eaton himself had done with the *Telegraph* , and she would personally recommend her Jimmies to them as their editors. Mrs. Royall had one other suggestion. Wasn't it time for two small New York papers to become one larger and increase their voice?

It was a wide-ranging subject before Secretary Eaton and Mrs. Royall finished their discussion. Both were conscious of the part the printed word played in giving support to the President, but both approached the problem from different views. Eaton knew how to finance a paper but not how to present it, and Mrs. Royall did. Mrs. Royall's plan to employ both their talents for the Jackson cause on a national scale was not dismissed by John Eaton. They discussed possible plans and the difficulties in depth.

In 1829, political payoffs were usual for avid supporters. Printing contracts for government notices and legislation were distributed by legislatures. Further, Mrs. Royall's own revelations as to how the blackcoats used the post office and Watterston's franking privilege to distribute religious literature alerted lay publishers to the possibilities. The U.S. mail was the only means of disseminating information on a nationwide basis and another avenue for political exploitation, one the Jacksonians should utilize.

Mrs. Royall was frank with her friend. She had discussed her ideas with her good friend, Obadiah Brown, the man appointed to replace Andrew Coyle as the chief post office clerk. Parson Brown, a Baptist and sworn enemy of the Elyites, knew about the religious and opposition press and its tactics. Like Mrs. Royall, he was alert to what must be done to counter their influence. With the post office now to be a cabinet department, it was time to put that agency to rights. Parson Brown hoped to reorganize the postal services and remove old regime holdovers, particularly those who had served the blackcoat menace. However, there was a problem. In moving to rid the post offices of those guilty of using the department for religious interest, he found himself assailed with petition against change inaugurated by the prevalent religious press in the South.9 There had to be more Jackson papers if this government was to prevail, and action had to be taken in print, not just at the ballot box.

John Eaton was impressed. Brown was not just another supporter, he was a brother Mason and a philosopher as well as a well-spoken minister and self-made man who was as much involved with the needs of Man as he was with the Word of God. The new post office chief clerk did not respect those who let others do their thinking for them. He had published his own paper, and he believed that information had to be available to people. As a Baptist Christian, he preached knowledge of the Bible and what it said, not what others said it meant. For this reason he had been opposed to the tract societies from the beginning, recognizing them as attempts to lead men and women astray. As a Jacksonian, he had traveled to enlist supporters for Jackson as the answer to the iniquities promoted by the black-suited missionaries in the back country. While Mrs. Royall had traveled the North rallying Masons and reasonable men to the defense of freedom, Obadiah Brown had traveled the South. Now as operations officer for the post office, he was tied to Washington and had suggested that Mrs. Royall take over his territory in the South, that she should do what she planned with her young friends in New York in the cities of the South.10 Mrs. Royall should take her new fame, her renowned pen, and her insight into South Carolina and find more young men to edit papers for Jackson. Obadiah Brown thought it was time to mount an offensive against the Vice President in his own home territory.

Mrs. Calhoun had left the capital heavy with child, but she was not just giving birth to another Calhoun; she had begun to organize all of South Carolina behind her husband, reaching over into North Carolina and Georgia too. Calhoun's home, Clergy Hill, had a great attraction for the rising blackcoat interests in the South, and even some Baptists were being enticed. Obadiah Brown had heard from Joel Poinsett that Charleston itself was falling for the Calhoun ruse.11 The Minister to Mexico was back in his home territory, having helped deliver Tobias Watkins to Philadelphia.

John Eaton knew that Charleston, once the most bustling port in the South, was in great malaise. John Calhoun's tariffs had wharved the ships, but since the loss of shipping had been felt most in these first months of Jackson's new administration, Jackson was being blamed. The action against the Jacksonians had been carried into the streets of the city even as Floride Calhoun had come home to Charleston.12 Joel Poinsett had elected to go to his city and counter this situation.

Charleston was not just another American port; it was the capital of the South, for from its docks moved all the commerce of that region. Organized as a trading entity, it maintained itself apart, regulating its commerce and pooling its capital. Its life was structured by breakfast clubs, morning meetings which set the exchange rates for all produce and commerce, making policies which made or broke traders.13 Joel Poinsett was important to the Jacksonians because he had organized Charleston for them, and it had been his stratagems which had kept the whole of South Carolina in Andrew Jackson's corner, and Eaton knew that control was threatened.

Floride Calhoun had arrived home with a large retinue of blackcoats and an unlimited purse. Clergy Hill, the plantation home she had brought to John Calhoun, had blossomed forth in new splendor. As it did, it became the center of a new movement. Throughout South Carolina, as Charleston waned, voices were heard suggesting it was time the Plantation South declare its independence from the Manufacturing North and go it alone in market and tariff negotiations with London. Shades of the Hartford Convention! These arguments that the northern states promoted tariffs, that the federal government enjoyed this funding, and that the South was thereby impoverished was a potent issue in old Charleston. The fact that John Calhoun had advocated, promoted, and voted for the hated tariffs was lost because there was no press to exploit those facts. Instead, with Floride Calhoun's return, talk of separatism was born anew in the salons of the best families.

Joel Poinsett had recognized this strategy and warned that unless Andrew Jackson did something to counteract this nullification movement, he could not maintain control. The fact that the movement became more emotional as the Charleston distress spilled over into the land was a situation only the President could handle. A secessionist campaign was growing, waved on by falling cargo shipments and declining bank balances and crop prices, and Joel Poinsett had few resources left with which to counter the problem. He was mobilizing what support he could, but the South had to be mobilized from Washington. The fact that the author of the hated tariffs was benefiting from this assault was certain. It was led by the same people who had led against Andrew Jackson in 1828. There was no doubt that John Calhoun was increasing his constituency for another assault on Andrew Jackson.

John Eaton knew that Obadiah Brown was right. Mrs. Royall's plan to place her newsboys in positions to influence opinion had to be done. There was only one problem. Mrs. Royall had young men for New York, but did she have any for the South? Mrs. Royall had her answer ready. Since she had developed talent in Washington for New York, she thought she could develop more talent elsewhere.[14] She thought she could find young men in Atlanta, Georgia, and even Mobile, Alabama, and perhaps young women too. She was willing to accept such an assignment, if John Eaton and Parson Brown would underwrite it with letters of recommendation and finances. The chief post office clerk would make the necessary arrangements for her travel and provide the list of people to contact; she could use her reputation and roust the Jacksonians out of their beds into the streets against Calhoun and his threat to the United States.

Mrs. Royall had her mission for the autumn, and it was her own. The blackcoats and Calhoun would not give up until they had destroyed the United States; Mrs. Royall would defeat them again. She began her new crusade by going North first.

Mrs. Royall's suggestion that Bennett and Brooks become editors[15] of the New York papers of Noah and Webb was approved, and John Eaton went to work to effect the merger of the *Courier* and the *Enquirer* to give New York a large publication to hawk the Jackson views. Mrs. Royall went north with her boys to start the project and to collect the money due her from Philadelphia and New York booksellers while Parson Brown arranged for her southern tour. She left Washington City the first week in September, 1829, just as Richard Wallach, her young man "with the affection of a son" moved from the ranks of lawyers and, with the concurrence of Duff Green, became editor of the Jackson *Telegraph.*[16] It was a move which startled the capital, for Duff Green had been thought to have enlisted in the anti-Eaton crusade. It was an auspicious beginning for Mrs. Royall's new venture.

The Common Scold walked in triumph through Baltimore, and then on to

Philadelphia, in Ely's own territory where the booksellers had scorned her. Here Mrs. Royall found herself lionized and courted and not just by the Ingersolls. She went on to New York, which like Charleston was in the throes of a shipping depression, and even as her old enemy Colonel Stone and his New York *Commercial Advertiser* inveighed against her,[17] she was celebrated for her courage and praised for her suggestions. Noah and Webb welcomed the young editors. Bennett received his editorship immediately, for he had been Noah's Washington correspondent for a year, and young Brooks was employed as a writer-editor to develop the news along Mrs. Royall's views.

Mrs. Royall completed her business in New York in less than 36 hours. She took leave of her young men with regret and a promise to collaborate with reports of her progress through the South. She was pleased with both her Jimmies and would live to see Bennett become the most famous editor-publisher of his times and James Brooks, a pioneer American journalist of her stamp, accepted by a new profession born because she had shared her talent with them.

Mrs. Royall returned from Philadelphia with William B. Lewis, Andrew Jackson's personal secretary, and Peg Eaton aboard a government packet boat. William Barry, postmaster general of the new department, and William Jones, Washington postmaster, joined them. Parson Brown had made exceptional arrangements for his very good friend.[18]

Postmaster General Barry and William Jones were surprises for Mrs. Royall. William Jones, counselor, had eschewed the promised appointment as United States attorney, leaving it to Francis Scott Key, for the more lucrative position as postmaster for the capital. They had come to Philadelphia to inaugurate the new Delaware canal mail service, and Mrs. Royall had been invited to join them on the first mail packet boat to traverse the canal. Starting in Philadelphia within sight of Ely's own church, the mail carriages carried not only sacks of mail for the Sunday trip, but Peg Eaton to cut the ribbon and trip down the canal with them. It did not matter to Mrs. Royall that the day was a rainy one, but one incident did give her pause:

> I happened to turn around when lo! Mr. Lewis, full of mischief, was conducting Mrs. Eaton with the umbrella carefully held over his head![19]

This prank did no harm to Mrs. Eaton, whose curly red hair just glistened more with the dampness, but Mrs. Royall could not help wondering about it. She had discovered that William Lewis had placed his daughter in school not in Tennessee from whence he came, nor Virginia where schools were many, but in Philadelphia, and she did not approve:

> In Philadelphia there is neither refinement, taste, nor science; nothing but tracts and Sunday School Union.[20]

Mrs. Royall did not know it, but Major Lewis had chosen a Presbyterian school for his daughter.

The canal trip was a great adventure. Peg Eaton kept the party alive all the way with her wit, and the august company of men was very attentive to both women. As it was, the writer could celebrate her luck in this encounter in more ways than one. She was in on the first and last counteraction Jackson would make against Ely, Towson, and Reverend Campbell, in the Eaton affair. Peg Eaton was returning from New York and Philadelphia with proof positive that the Presbyterians were liars.

There was no entry upon any hotel registry to show that Peg Timberlake had ever registered with John Eaton in the hotels where Ely and his friends had asserted they had. Major Lewis and Mrs. Eaton were returning with the evidence Andrew Jackson required to boot clergymen and friends from his office, calling them liars, and defamers of women. Soon the whole matter would pass into oblivion. Mrs. Royall put aside her misgivings about Major Lewis's daughter to join wholeheartedly in the extended celebration.

The Common Scold had in hand the first consequences of her prosecution. She had not been destroyed; she was a famous woman, and she had powerful friends. The Elys of the world had not obliterated her; they had created a New Mrs. Royall, and she was girded for battle with stronger armament than ever.

Chapter 24

Accomplishment

There was a special committee of one waiting for Mrs. Royall on the mail packet's arrival in Baltimore. Sally Stackpool waited impatiently for the boat to dock. Mrs. Royall was surprised to see her friend so far from Washington.

Sally was breathless as she gave the news. Mrs. Royall was not to return to Washington City but to proceed immediately to Norfolk on another mail packet boat now waiting for her. Parson Brown had sent Sally to tell Mrs. Royall that her presence was needed at a constitutional convention precipitously called for the State of Virginia and scheduled to begin in Richmond in two days.[1] It was news to Mrs. Royall, and she wasn't sure what to make of it.

What was this constitutional convention in Richmond? That, Sally informed Mrs. Royall, was what she was to go to Richmond to find out. The Virginians in the capital had decamped two days previously and were heading there too. The western counties of that state, by surprise petition, had demanded and were convening a convention to consider basic formulas for representation not only in Virginia's legislature but in the national Congress. It was rumored that a schism was about to engulf Virginia.[2]

William Jones, the last to leave Washington before the Delaware canal mail service inauguration, volunteered information. The political infighting which had begun in South Carolina, its Separatist movement, had found another expression in Virginia. From the little he knew, petitions had been circulating throughout Virginia's western counties and had been produced as a surprise for autumn consideration and convention. Mr. Jones did not have to say another thing; Mrs. Royall understood immediately. The blackcoats were up to their old shenanigans. Even as they were working to split South Carolina and the South, they were working on Virginia too, the mother of American presidents.

The western counties of Virginia. How well Mrs. Royall knew them and their people. Western Virginia, with hill sections like South Carolina, was the bulwark of the Scots-Irish and their peculiar religion. Ely and his ilk had made serious inroads there. A petition circulated clandestinely in that section meant only one thing. The blackcoats had taken the fight against Andrew Jackson out of Washington into the South, just as Parson Brown had said they would. Mrs. Royall needed no instructions; she knew what was expected of her. She would monitor this, bolster her friends, and report on all. Sally could return to Parson Brown with the message that Mrs. Royall was on her way, her journal in hand. Within four hours of her arrival in Baltimore, Mrs. Royall set sail for Norfolk, Virginia, franked through by Parson Brown with free passage by ship and stage to Richmond, the sudden Virginia Constitutional Convention her destination.[3]

The coastal voyage to Norfolk was a welcome respite from the hustle and

204

bustle of her New York trip. Alone Mrs. Royall walked the deck of the *Poca-hontas*, enjoying the ocean breezes on the most modern steamer of its day. It was a taste of luxury, and it accented her quandary. She was on her way to accomplish in Richmond what she had done so successfully in Pennsylvania the year before. However, there were differences in this assignment, and Mrs. Royall had to consider them carefully.

Richmond was not her favorite city. That capital of Virginia did not have many pleasant memories for the woman writer, for Richmond was the seat of the bureaucracy which had beggared her, stripped her of all she had, and then sent her forth penniless to face the world.

She felt uncomfortable about joining them in anything and wrestled with her problem by employing reason, trying to set her mind at rest. As she walked the decks, she thought back on William Royall and his love of western Virginia, the people he had led to settle there, and the mountain ridges she had called home. It was even more unsettling to her mind. The major's followers could have petitioned for this convention, for they were underrepresented in the Virginia Legislature. With this she balanced her bias against the blackcoats, those opposed to Andrew Jackson in this call to convention, her mind arguing both positions for control of her pen.

Soon she began the overland trip to Richmond. As Mrs. Royall boarded the stage, she could take little comfort in her mission. Always her heart and mind had been one, but this time it was not to be. It preoccupied her thoughts as the stage careened across the land for Virginia's capital and the convocation of a convention in which her friends had chosen to shore up the old Tidewater aristocracy as the lesser of two evils.

Mrs. Royall found Richmond a city in frenzied anticipation of momentous doings. The convention was acknowledged to be an offensive in a new conflict which could decide national destiny. Jackson's enemies had a new counteroffensive and they had laid all their hopes on its line for their future. Every group opposed to the President was in the city: the remnants of the old Federalists, the new religionists, and, behind both, the shadow of the bank. One man was on their mind: John Caldwell Calhoun, the Vice President. The South Carolinian was the only one left in the administration who could reverse Jackson and his policies, and he was in danger. The recent events in Washington had been a setback to his hopes, and his friends hoped to rebuild a foundation for him with this flanking move in Virginia's capital.

Mrs. Royall rode through the city aware of what was at stake. Calhoun! The name had become as offensive to her ears as that of Ezra Stiles Ely. She never thought of the tall man from South Carolina without seeing those gloomy clerics who were his secretaries and aides. Once she had admired the man. At least she had recognized the truth so many others rejected.

As the carriage made its way to the inn, Mrs. Royall noted there was a new Ely church larger than all the others, and right across from it another Biddle bank. The sight jolted her, and as she looked from one to the other, both looked like temples dressed with Greek columns, the only difference being that the church had a steeple and the bank did not.[4] She wondered if she had missed this in viewing Ely churches and banks in other places; in the next city or town, she would have to pay more attention to this proof of alliance. She enjoyed her thoughts.

Biddle was in trouble. He was not admitting it publicly, but the Bank of the United States was in difficulty. Although its charter ran to 1836, the revelations of the bank's involvement with the evolving cases of Watkins, Nourse, and the strange actions of Samuel Southard gave credence to the charges of the bank's tinkering with politics. Those complaints were beginning to stampede the opposition to the bank. Nicholas Biddle feared the consequences; his careful control did not dispel the reality. He had tried to buy her and then failing that, his minions had assisted those religious idiots from the Engine House Congregation. Mrs. Royall was well aware of the connections of the bank to Thomas Swann, and to Harrison Smith, whose wife served whatever Biddle wanted. The Smiths had set out to destroy her even before the trial. Margaret Smith had written some of the more slanderous allegations against Mrs. Royall. Mrs. Smith had paid for her husband's continued position with the bank and her easy route to publication fame. All these matters passed through Mrs. Royall's mind as she gazed upon Richmond's temple of finance; she was thinking less of Ely on this trip and more about the bank. To a woman whose greatest forte had been the utilization of intuition, this was a sign; she would look for overt signs of Biddle's influence in this new convention in Richmond. As the carriage moved on its way, she turned and looked back at the Ely church and the bank's temple. They were one and the same, but like Janus, the Roman god, they sought to delude the public understanding by presenting two faces to the world.

Mrs. Royall spent her first hours in Richmond contacting Thomas Ritchie, editor-publisher of the Richmond Enquirer, the young man who had befriended her on her first trip to that city after her release from debtor's prison in Alabama.[5] He was a Mason, and Mrs. Royall knew she would get the straight facts from him.

Thomas Ritchie was frank with Mrs. Royall. The Biddle bank did have a hand in this convention. John Randolph had proven to be an enemy to the bank in Congress and the convention would strip that imperious landholder of privilege.[6] Editor Ritchie did not hold back any facts, for he knew her bias against the Tidewater aristocracy and Ritchie himself had no love for the old order, for he could never join it. Mrs. Royall did not abhor John Randolph, for the old aristocrat had committed himself and everything he had to the United States. She did not know John Randolph as an imperious lord but as the great American thinker and an able supporter of Jackson and his policies in the Senate.[7]

The bank was involved in the convention for another reason: John Calhoun.[8] The Vice President was the only man who could stop anti-bank action, but the recent in-fighting in the administration had weakened him. With a new Congress to convene, Calhoun had to be restored to power, and Virginia offered a good chance for just that, and Thomas Ritchie was for it. The western counties could take over control in the state's legislature and the Congress if they won this convention, and John Randolph would be removed from the Senate. Thomas Ritchie hated Randolph, and for him the bank was serving the purpose of democracy.

Mrs. Royall saw the bank's purposes but not with Thomas Ritchie's eyes. John Calhoun was the reason for this convention and she was interested in how the summons to meet had been effected so quickly.

Thomas Ritchie explained. The movement had begun among Mrs. Royall's own people, the men William Royall had led to settle in mountainous western Virginia. The Blue Ridge farmers, Scots-Irish, had been summoned to do God's bidding, join Calhoun, and achieve their rights. Sunday after Sunday, their preachers had hammered at the inequities in representation in Virginia. The hill people, like the small landholders in the Carolinas, had nothing in common with the plantation lords of the Tidewater country. Scots-Irish, not English in origin, they cherished their rugged individualism, their fierce independence, and their pride.[9]

Standing in the pulpits of the hill churches, the preachers had exhorted against Andrew Jackson to no avail at first. Frustrated by loyalty, the churchmen had turned to their northern brethren for help, and that help was forthcoming. What would happen in western Virginia if free white men were told that the nation counted them as equal to slaves in apportioning representation in Virginia and in the Congress of the United States? How would these prideful people react to the news that they were counted with slaves? Many did not know about the Virginia method of apportionment because they could neither read nor write. What if the pulpit informed them of their ignominious status?

It was a ploy tried with great success in the North. There, workmen seeking places in the growing industries of the towns and cities had been frustrated in finding what they wanted. Capital had not been expanding rapidly enough to provide the jobs that the new immigrating clerical forces wanted, and as anxieties grew, the problem was blamed not on the lack of money for development but on southern "lords" who, with slave labor, had frustrated the hopes of free men. Southern slavery had been made the North's excuse for no jobs, for low wages, and for mismanaged local economies. The campaign against slavery was paying great dividends for the blackcoats.[10] The Virginia hill people were not interested in jobs and factories, but slavery could be used to incite them too. In 1829, the Bible society tracts using the hill people's pride as free men and their lack of knowledge about Virginia's political processes were read from the pulpit like the word of God. How could free men, white men, sitting in those churches, tolerate being counted as equal to black slaves in the apportioned representation to the Virginia House of Delegates and in the Virginia delegation to the Congress of the United States?[11] Week after week, this was hammered home until the free white men were roused to passion, a passion which was to have far-reaching political consequences.

Ritchie reminded Mrs. Royall that there was truth in the new movement. Virginia did apportion its representation on a two-thirds rule, a formula for equalizing the interests of the old Tidewater area with the interests of western Virginia development. From the beginning of the United States of America, Virginia had been in a state of change. The old plantation society, dependent upon slaves and large holdings of land, watched while the outer perimeter of its state was divided into small upland farms worked by families or individual owners. From the first call for revolution, this had been the main stumbling block to Virginia's political unity. As a result, a compromise had been worked out to give Virginia the unified voice she needed in the structuring of the nation. Plantation and family farm would have an equal share in the voice Virginia gave to the new world. The large plantation and its slaves would be counted in representation with a formula: two slaves plus one freeman in the Tidewater would equal three freemen in the uplands. This two-thirds rule had allowed Virginia to set aside its internal bickering and join the growth of American independence, a most successful collaboration since Virginia had provided four of the seven presidents of the United States to date.[12] This was the compromise rule which now was placed under a frontal attack led by the same forces which used southern slavery as an excuse for all problems in the North.

Thomas Ritchie showed Mrs. Royall some of the tract society publications which had blanketed the western hills. Mrs. Royal assessed them: The blackcoats were at it again, but this time it was in the name of justice for white men and hatred was being aroused against the black slave. There was no end to the corruption which these missionaries would do to attain their end. She spoke her mind: the South could not be taken by such as John Calhoun without dividing it, and the South could not be divided against itself as long as a John Randolph stood in the halls of Congress speaking with great power and reason what had been Jeffersonian ideals but now were Jacksonian policies. Calhoun and the blackcoats had hit upon another masterful plot and, tying it to their other movements, they posed a national danger in Richmond. Mrs. Royall no longer was in a dilemma: it was the union not of Virginia but of the United States of America that these followers of Ely and Biddle threatened.

Mrs. Royall was right. The movement in western Virginia had been a very studied call to action, too well executed to be spontaneous. Promoted by certain clerically garbed members of the northern intelligentsia, the whole action had been paraded as a movement against human indignity with slavery and its monstrous practices as the passion-rousing theme. The movement had entered the region as early as 1816, but coming from England first and then from northern sources, it had not gained much adherence in these southern hills. However, a new format had been created. The anti-slavery crusade was being pressed among these people with a call to prejudice as men and women were asked in their churches how they could continue to tolerate being equated to black slaves by the land-holding Tidewater aristocracy. The Scots-Irish pride was assailed continually, and gradually the hill people were pushed to action. No one knew it was political until the movement was overwhelming. Many an Elyite preacher in the western region established his niche with this new doctrine and honed his oratorical power to a fine edge, achieving a cutting blade so sharp that[13] it caught the rest of Virginia unprepared.

From the pulpit came the first demands for petition to reconvene to reform this terrible inequity. Free men only, free white men only, should be entitled to representation. Why should men like John Randolph present himself and two black slaves as equal to three other white men? The time had come for western Virginia to rise and take the state! The hill people were more in numbers than the white men of the Tidewater, and they were exhorted to join and win. It was potent argument, and in six months it had submerged Andrew Jackson in an issue which could only benefit John Calhoun.

The Virginia Constitutional Convention came to be in the fall of 1829. Called to action by petitions circulated and signed in the churches on the Virginia frontier, it was a hidden assault upon Southern tradition, particularly upon the tradition supporting Andrew Jackson. Hidden from the national eye, it was to be the vehicle hitched to the engines being constructed in Philadelphia by Ezra Stiles Ely, in New York by Gardner Spring, in Connecticut by Lyman Beecher, and in Boston by William Garrison. "Abolition" was to be its name, and it didn't mean the abolition of slavery but of the United States.[14] Nurtured within the walls of the New Presbyterian churches, it was maturing and infecting the Congregational Church, the Dutch Reformed, and other Protestant sects seeking dominion above the government. It was proposed to have its first public test in Richmond, take that state, and then march on the nation.

It was no secret in Richmond that the petitions which had produced the constitutional convention had been amassed at religious services. It was loudly proclaimed. The church was the perfect cover for this political assault, for John Calhoun could not sanction an open attack upon the South and its historical institutions, not if he wanted the South to support him against Andrew Jackson. The black man was to be a vehicle by which the blackcoats, having failed in their designs in the Northern legislatures, planned to take the South by convention, dividing it, confusing it, and changing its image to their long sought theocracy.

Mrs. Royall knew what she had to do. It was her task to rally all reasonable men behind John Randolph as he carried the debate against the change, and she had to be seen and heard as Andrew Jackson's personal monitor of the proceedings. Richmond had to know that, far from participating in a hidden action, its convention was being watched from Washington.

Andrew Jackson was no stranger to this kind of political manipulation; he was thoroughly acquainted with missionary efforts to divide and conquer the country. Andrew Jackson was not a general this time, but the President of the

United States and the blackcoats were not employing Indians but whites against blacks, using the same threat of insurrection. There was an army yet within the borders of the nation, and it wore its black coats in great numbers in Richmond!

Mrs. Royall had not given up on Thomas Ritchie. The man did not like Randolph, but he was titually with Jackson and he still held great affection for her. She decided to test his position to evaluate just how strong the bank really was. Thomas Ritchie was no blackcoat, but was he for Calhoun over Jackson?

Mrs. Royall went to Thomas Ritchie again and told him she was in Richmond by direction to remind those attending the convention that Andrew Jackson was watching them all, including James Madison, James Monroe, and Chief Justice John Marshall. John Randolph was to be supported to keep Virginia intact. No amount of public preaching about "reform" was to disrupt the tenuous union of the states while Andrew Jackson was President. The nation was not to be divided by this strategem, dismembered in the many state capitals. This was the crucial issue, not representation, and Thomas Ritchie, two former presidents and the Chief Justice of the United States Supreme Court had best not forget it.[15] It was potent argument from the Common Scold and the man and woman who opposed the Tidewater aristocracy put aside their personal feelings for Andrew Jackson and the nation.

Mrs. Royall attended the Virginia Constitutional Convention, her appearance unexpected, and the blackcoats were unhappy. Two ex-presidents had been guiled into participating as Virginia's first citizens. James Madison, 79 years of age, was to open the proceedings, and James Monroe was to be nominated to preside. Both men, chafing in their retirement, accepted, expecting great acclaim for their re-entry into the political lists.[16] Mrs. Royall's shadow blocked that spotlight, and the spectre of Andrew Jackson behind her submerged them.

The writer had arrived uninvited to this convention, but she attained the floor within a day. Sitting first in the gallery, among the women, annoyed at the enormous bonnets of the members of the Presbyterian ladies aid societies about her, foolish women lending their presence to politics, she could stand their tittering no longer. Standing, she made her presence known with loud voice sharp with annoyance:

"I am astonished the sergeant-at-arms would suffer these mantua makers and milliners to intrude upon the convention."[17]

Everyone knew Mrs. Royall was present and the Common Scold had made another mark. The next day not one convention bonnet was to be seen, and Mrs. Royall was invited to sit with the delegates on the floor of the convention before the rostrum. She was recognized as the personal representative of the most important man in the nation and accorded instant rank due her for her role. "Several of the members bowed to me, amongst them Mr. Monroe. I think he is the most diffident man in the world,"[18] she wrote. It was no compliment to the past President, but then it came from the woman who knew the message sent by Andrew Jackson to his predecessors. Madison and Monroe could preside in Virginia, but they no longer presided over the United States of America!

From the moment Mrs. Royall took her seat before the Richmond dais, the end of the Virginia Constitutional Convention could be predicted. John Randolph would carry his important burden to victory. The long exhortations of the Blue Ridge pulpits could not be turned into enough ballot strength on the floor, and their self-publicized popular will evaporated as Mrs. Royall tramped the halls and inns, buttonholing old friends and comrades of William Royall. The galleries, packed with Elyite Presbyterians, cheered on as Chapman Johnson, their champion and the bank's vassal, declaimed against John Randolph, but their cheers and their puffery did not move the delegates. One by one, they slid back to reason. One observer wrote:

It is difficult to explain the influence which John Randolph exerted. He was feared alike by East and West (Virginia). The arrows from his quiver, if not dipped in poison, were pointed and barbed, rarely missed the mark, and as sseldom failed to make a rankling wound. What made his attack more vexatious, every sarcasm took effect amid the plaudits of his audiences.[19]

Mrs. Royall led the cheering section for John Randolph from the convention floor. The Senate's great orator excoriated the same influences Mrs. Royall deplored in print, and he tagged them with not seeking to improve the Virginians' lot but with attempting to destroy Virginia to effect their purpose to destroy the nation. No son of Virginia, after Randolph spoke, would vote to give his state to the blackcoats, and Virginia remained intact. The ploy to schism Virginia and thence the South failed; Andrew Jackson could count on Virginia to back him as he moved to assert his policies.

Mrs. Royall didn't spend all of her time at the convention. She went looking for Chapman Johnson, the leader of the opposition. This man who inveighed so heavily against slavery had purchased several of the old Royall slaves after the Richmond courts had taken them from Mrs. Royall. It was a circumstance Mrs. Royall decided to use, and announcing that she was interested in the welfare of her old retainers and how they fared under this blackcoat disciple, she went to see them. She was denied admittance to the Johnson lodgings and refused a glimpse or a word with her old slaves. Chapman Johnson had not come to the door himself but sent his wife instead. Mrs. Royall made her point and several more: "I wonder at Mr. Johnson's choice of a wife." She used the words Chapman Johnson had used to comment upon Andrew Jackson's Rachel.[20]

Mrs. Royall, ever mindful of history, called upon famous Dolly Madison. Unable to engage a carriage in crowded Richmond, she walked the two miles to the house leased by the Madisons for this event. A hot dusty Indian summer day had given way to rain, and when Mrs. Royall arrived, Dolly Madison opened the door to a mess. Mrs. Madison administered to Mrs. Royall's needs in a way which took the writer's breath away, and overwhelmed, she wrote:

I expected to have seen a little dried-up old woman, instead a young, active, elegant woman stood before me — the self-same lady of whom I had heard more anecdotes than any family in Europe or America. No wonder she is the idol of Washington. Chiefly she captivates by her artless though warm affability. She and affectation are farther apart than the poles. She is a tall, straight woman, muscular, but not fat, and as active as a girl. Her face is large, full and oval, rather dark than fair; her eyes dark, large and expressive. She is not handsome, nor does she ever appear to have been so. She was dressed in a plain, black silk dress, and wore a silk checked turban. Her curls were black and glossy.[21]

Dolly Madison was everything Mrs. Royall could have expected, for the famous lady had not changed. This woman who had gone about the White House calmly removing from its wall the mementoes of the nation's strength while her husband as president deserted the field of battle at Bladensburg before the British, knew how to care for a revolutionary relic:

She would run out — bring a glass of water, wipe the mud off my shoes and tie them. She pressed me to wait with much earnestness to await dinner. She appears young enough to be Mr. Madison's daughter.[22]

Mrs. Royall did not accept Dolly's invitation to dinner. In good conscience she could not, for Mrs. Royall thought James Madison to be a fop who, having led the Bladensburg race from the British, even now would do strange bidding save for strong warning from Andrew Jackson. She was not kind to the former leader in her pen portrait: "a small aged man . . . dressed in plain Quaker colored coat and his hair is powdered."[23] James Madison was out of step, for men no longer powdered their hair in Andrew Jackson's era.

The Common Scold enjoyed her stay in Richmond and between the convention sessions she visited the booksellers and found them most cooperative; she increased her sales and her subscription lists and engaged in banter and argument. Everywhere she went she found greater approval than condemnation. Not once did she suffer from her recent trial experience. For every one who turned a back on her, there was another to praise her for courage and truth. She had a new opinion of Richmond to erase the old.

As Mrs. Royall left the city to return to Washington, she saw again the new Presbyterian Church and the Greek temple of the Bank of the United States emptily facing one another across the deserted street. She contrasted this scene with the taverns of the town, which were full of people and ablaze with light. Mrs. Royall knew that all was right with her world, and she could tell John Eaton and Obadiah Brown that Virginia was not in John Calhoun's pocket—all the money in Biddle's bank could not buy it, nor all the God in Ely's prose raise it.

As Mrs. Royall entered Washington City once more, Vice President Calhoun departed it.[24] The collapse of the Virginia convention forced him to decamp and hurry south to Charleston to seek the comfort of his wife and escape the wrath of Andrew Jackson. The disparate political groups that had supported Madison and Monroe disavowed association with John Calhoun and were filing into place behind Old Hickory. The hidden assault upon the South's political and social base was out in the open, and John Calhoun was not its beneficiary.

As the New Life Presbyterians had entered the waters of political action to gain supremacy, so now did the Baptists and other evangelical groups to oppose them. It was as Parson Brown had called it. The South could be summoned to crusade; it was fertile ground for Mrs. Royall, and John Calhoun's desertion of Washington amidst the falling debris of the Virginia convention proved it.

Mrs. Royall returned to Washington with the report the Jacksonians wanted. John Randolph carried the Virginia convention and did so with considerable help from the Blue Ridge people themselves. The blackcoat blitz had overreached itself and exposed its flanks. As in the skirmishes about the Sabbath, one day a week of exhortation by men who said they spoke for God was not enough to erase six days of working experience for men and women of reason. Mrs. Royall could add that most people preferred to stand on their feet, not sit on their knees.

The Common Scold returned to Washington in triumph, and any remaining stain from Cranch's court was erased by the President and his friends. Mrs. Royall was included in all the official guest lists and the parties were many. Obadiah Brown had suggested Mrs. Royall wait on her trip South until John Calhoun's moves could be assayed, and she enjoyed every one.

Andrew Jackson was on the mend and had taken the Eaton affair in hand again, demanding this time that Eaton's detractors produce evidence, not continuing innuendo against his friends. Peg O'Neal had traveled to New York with Major Lewis to find what hard evidence had been manufactured against John and her and found none. The doctor said to have witnessed her abortion was dead, and his wife was revealed to be in the throes of Ely's religious mania. Accordingly, the president had called his full cabinet to meeting on the night of September 10 and presented his proof in an extraordinary showdown with the Eaton's clergy accusers.[26] The Reverend Campbell and his mentor Dr. Ely had been given full liberty to say what they would, but they were short of facts and not one member of the cabinet backed them. The blackcoats were revealed. Dr. Ely weaseled by admitting he never had seen proof of his allegations but had been relying on the Reverend Campbell; he had been doing his duty to inform the President what others had said. Reverend Campbell came to the meeting with Francis Scott Key acting as his lawyer to protect him from charges of libel and slander. It was not a pleasant affair.

Reverend Campbell fall back on an original excuse. He averred he had erred in his dates concerning the Eatons' activities and was sure he could correct them and would do so if the President wished to take the matter to court. Andrew Jackson knew just what court of law the wily Presbyterian clerics had in mind and would have none of such an explanation. Judge Cranch had made his reputation with Mrs. Royall and the public had enough of such justice. The President issued his own warning to Ely and Campbell: If they persisted in their tales, he, the President of the United States, would tell the world what liars and blackguards they were. Their allegations that John Eaton had copulated with Peg Timberlake in 1821 and produced a child she had aborted were falsehoods, for John Timberlake had been present in Washington that year. The clergymen would not be allowed to manufacture new dates to continue this dastardly game. The President would make public the transcript he held in his hand, signed by the cabinet, a document which would refute any further allegations in the matter. It was the end of the Reverend Campbell, and he knew it. The Washington cleric was dismissed by Andrew Jackson as a liar; neither Dr. Ely nor Colonel Towson came to his defense. Reverend J.N. Campbell walked out of the White House with a debt owed him by his cohorts, but he had lost the President of the United States as a parishioner, and with him every other important Jacksonian in Washington. Henceforth the blackcoat dominie would minister to the spiritual needs of only those opposed to Jackson's administration.

This was the end of Ezra Stiles Ely's peculiar attack upon John and Peg Eaton. Andrew Jackson had seen the sordid business through to its end like the lawyer he was. He had listened with courtesy, received the Philadelphia cleric, heard all charges, and then demanded proof. Dr. Ely and his friends could provide no evidence, and now the matter was closed. Henceforth it would not be allowed any official notice, but Andrew Jackson knew that the innuendo would linger, even as it had with his beloved Rachel. The President had done the best he could, and now it was up to his associates to either support or deny him. Andrew Jackson had forced his cabinet to assent and proclaim that John Eaton was morally fit. The charges against him were false, and now it was left to men of good will to put this nonsense from them and get to work.

Mrs. Royall settled in to enjoy this new climate in the capital. Andrew Jackson was leading at last, and Richmond had dispelled the notion that he could be dislodged. There was no way that the blackcoats could win; everyone knew who they were and what their strange connections meant. What was to be done about them was yet to be seen, but Ely, Beecher, Duffield, Black, and Spring had been chased back into their churches, their alliance with Biddle a rising question. The strange attack on the government, the President, and his friends had been turned back, and the woman who had alerted them was famous. The Common Scold had become Andrew Jackson's public conscience. The President of the United States had conferred the rank upon his old friend and now was about to confirm it.

District of Columbia, TO WIT:

THE UNITED STATES OF AMERICA,

TO THE MARSHAL OF THE DISTRICT OF COLUMBIA—Greeting:

We command you that you take *Ann Royall late of Washington County*

if *she* shall be found within the county of Washington, in your said district, and *her* safely keep, so that you have *her* bod*y* before the Circuit Court of the District of Columbia, to be held for the county aforesaid, at the City of Washington, ~~on the~~ ~~Monday of~~ *immediately* ~~next~~; to answer

unto *The United States of America concerning a certain misdemeanor by her committed as it is presented to*

Hereof fail not, at your peril, and have you then and there this writ.

Witness *W Cranch* Esquire, chief

Judge of our said Court at the City of Washington, the *10* day of

July Anno Domini one thousand eight hundred and *2 9.*

Issued the *10 July 18 2 5*

W Brent Ch

118

United States
ags. } *2d.*
Ann Royall

Quashed by order of attorney

Common nuisance.

True Bill
F. A. McKinney Foreman
John Coyle
Witness – *J. Coyle Senr.*
Geo. Waterston
Jos. Elgar
Jno. O. Dunn
Raul. Dunn

*124 cu Appl.
May 1829*

The United States
ags. } *2nd.*
Ann Royall

*Recorded in Crim Record
Nov fol. 465, 66, 67, 68*

Common nuisance.

And W. Way Foreman

Mr. Dawson

Witness – *Jno. Coyle.
Jno. Coyle Junr.
Geo. Waterston
Jos. Elgar.*

Bottom: covers showing two indictments of Ann [sic] Royall, as well as those in league against her. Top and next three pages: court documents.

Saturday July 11. 1829. The Court met pursuant
adjournment. —

Present

The Honble   William Cranch Chief Judge
50.   Buckner Thruston &
              James S. Morsell } Ass.^t Judges

United States } Recognizance in the sum of $100
               } for her app: on Monday next and attending
               } this Court from day to day until
in Royal   } discharged. & in the mean time to be of
               } good behaviour. } —

        Court Adjourns until Monday Morning
next 10 Oclock.

        Monday July 13.th The Court Met
pursuant to Adjournment
                Present.

The Hon'   William Cranch Chief Judge.
51.   Buckner Thruston &
              James S Morsell } Assistant Judges

Court Adjourns until to morrow Morning 10. Oclock

Tuesday July 14.th The Court Met pursuant
Adjournment
                Present
              Wm. Cranch. Chief Judge
Hon   { Buckner Thruston &
52.   { James S Morsell } Assistant Judges

United States   } 1829 Cri Appearances –
             Jury Sworn (on 2d Count in 8th Decr)
     vs   } Verdict Guilty
             Mo. in Arrest of Judgt.

Mrs. Ann Royal }

Alfred H Boutcher – Sworn for U.S.   for Traverser

George Cover	John Coyle	Hon. Jns. H. Eaton
Overton Carr	John Coyle Jr.	Mrs. Black
Philip J Berry	Geo. Watterston	Mrs. Greer
John H Clark	Wn. O Dunn	Henry Tims
William Archer	Christopher H Dunn	John Hollohon
Henry Ault	J. J. Whitwell	Fredk. May
Peter Casanave	Wm. S McCormick	Capt. Hickey
John Myers	Dr. T Frost	John Underwood
Robert White	Lewis H Machen	Mr. Polk
Thomas B Griffin	Charles McCormick	
Richard C Washington	Geo. W Dawson	

First adjourned the Monday next 10 OClock

Monday July 20. 1829 The Court met
pursuant to adjournment –

          Present
          William Cranch Chr. Judge
The Honble   Buckner Thruston &
       James S. Morsell } Assr. Judge
   57

Court adjourned til 10 OClock to morrow morning

Dis. of Columbia } May Term. 1829.
County of Washington }

The Jurors of the United States for the body of the county aforesaid on their oath and affirmation present that Ann Royal ~~~~ has been in the habit of late, to wit, on or about the 1st day of June instant, and at sundry times since and before. That period of using opprobrious and indecent language to respectable females and gentlemen in the public street, while going to public worship, such as charging them with going to commit dirdy of ~~darkness~~ ~~catawauling~~ and other false and offensive charges, and has at the time aforesaid and at sundry times before, and of late threatened John Coyle and his family and many other good citizens with saying and writing scandalous things of and against their character. Such as saying she supposed the children found dead in the canal, was the fruits of their catawauling, which is her term for prayermeetings, and other malicious and false sayings and writings, such as thief, villain, hypocrite, &c to the great annoyance of females; and citizens of the capitol hill and to the disturbance of said good people in the discharge of their religious duties, to the disturbance of the peace and good order of ~~society~~ and to the common nuisance of society. On the evidence of said Coyle and Oswald Dunn.

and the

foreman

Witness
J. Coyle Jr.
Geo. Watterston
Jos. Elgar
John O. Dunn
Christ. H. Dunn
Mrs. Rachel Dunn
J. G. Whitwell
W. G. McCormick
J. T. Frost
L. H. Machen.

Top: The United States Bank, Philadelphia. Bottom: Jackson kills the bank: Biddle (with horns) and newspaper hirelings scurry for their lives; Jack Downing, symbolizing the people, hurrahs.

Andrew Jackson (painting by Ralph Earl). The General turned citizen-president had two regrets: "I did not hang John C. Calhoun and shoot Henry Clay."

Top: Henry Clay, the "statesman" created by Biddle to stem the Jackson tide against the United States Bank. Bottom: John C. Calhoun, who fled the capital when Blackcoats struck coins for him as president of the Southern States of America.

Top: Daniel Webster, Blackcoat sympathizer bought by Biddle. Bottom: left, Mrs. Emily Donelson, Jackson's niece and hostess; right, Mrs. John C. Calhoun, who led the social boycott against Peggy Eaton and helped ruin her husband's chances for the presidency.

Chapter 25

Vindication

On December 7, 1829, President Andrew Jackson sent to the Congress of the United States his first annual message. It was a report eagerly awaited by friend and foe.

Mrs. Royall sat in the congressional gallery to hear what Andrew Jackson would say about his first ten months in office. The words about to begin would mark the Jackson Era for the presidency. The writer had a great stake in what Jackson said, for she had made certain predictions to her editor friends and the message this day would make her or break her. If her opinions found echoes in Andrew Jackson's words, the Common Scold knew she could bear her title proudly for the rest of her days. She could scarcely contain herself as the full Congress readied itself to hear the first statement of Jacksonian policy.

The great hall was hushed as the message began. This was no polite audience listening only with courtesy. Andrew Jackson was about to tell his Congress what he wanted from them, and desperation gripped Jackson's enemies while the President's men sat in pleasant contemplation. All eyes were on John Eaton.[1]

Andrew Jackson began his report with the customary reference to foreign affairs. All was peaceful on the frontiers of the nation, a condition the country had never known before. The hero of New Orleans had deterred the rest of the world from indulging in their usual acts of harassment against the young nation, and Andrew Jackson expected to keep it that way. It was a quiet but effective slap to the Cassandras sitting on the opposition benches. The President had accomplished with his hard line what his more "peaceful" predecessors had not. Ten months had passed without a single depredation against an American flag, an American ship, or an American border post. Mrs. Royall joined the huzzahs as they flooded the chamber.

Andrew Jackson then turned to his real concern: the reform of the national election process. The gallery gasped. The President called for Congress to deal itself out of the procedure, leaving it to the will of the people to insure that never again would the desires of the people be thwarted by the temptation of a single man to name his own reward"[2] All eyes turned to Henry Clay. Andrew Jackson had speared his enemy without even mentioning his name.

The President was not finished with Congress. The national legislature should limit the presidency to one term, four or six years, no more. The Congress sat stunned. For the first time, Jackson's opponents received his words with approval. A single term! Jackson was recommending something they could use. Mrs. Royall was not surprised; she had made the suggestion.

The President wanted a single term because the people had a right to change. The nation's problems lay in the fact that too many men held public position

213

too long and as a result did not serve the interests of democracy or the right of the people to expect change. The nation needed new blood constantly, not mingled and lost with the old but fresh and strong, to meet the exigencies of tomorrow. A single-term president would be free to boot out the old, take on the new, and not worry about political machinations to make himself one of the holdovers too. American democracy could thrive only on change, not on the corruption of office with privilege. Mrs. Royall cheered. Andrew Jackson had used her own words. Watterston, Watkins, Nourse and Lee—what they had wrought!

Money was next on the President's mind. The general waded into the problems of finance like an old swamp campaigner hot in the pursuit of an enemy. Tariffs had been raised as an issue by his opposition, but those tariffs were not of Jackson's making. The very men who now raised the wind against them had introduced them.[3] Those tariffs had been visited upon the nation not as an isolated sin from the North but by the collusion of many men, one of them a famous leader of the South. John Calhoun had been jabbed. Those hated tariffs had been imposed to produce the revenue with which the federal government financed itself and every other thing the Congress wanted. North, South, East and West shared equally in that pot. The federal government had to have revenue, and until other money was available, the tariffs would have to stand. Of course the tariffs could be reduced, but Congress would have to lower its items to be budgeted. The President did have a suggestion for increasing revenues, but Congress would have to vote it. The public lands could be sold more rapidly, and with the resultant income to the U.S. Treasury the hated tariffs could be phased out. The President was more than willing to do his part and had done so; he had ordered the national debt to be repaid, reducing useless outlays for interest, payments which bought nothing for the present, and paid only for past excesses. It was up to Congress to cut proposed expenditures for certain representatives and their political interests, for roads and improvements for those states wanting what other states had provided for themselves. It was a savage cut at Henry Clay, and the hall hummed.

Mrs. Royall listened eagerly. Andrew Jackson had begun the assault she had predicted on the present fiscal policies of the nation. How clever the old man was, and how perceptive John Eaton could be! The anti-Jacksonians had resorted to sectionalism to battle the new President, but Andrew Jackson had countered them with the union of the states and the wisdom it represented. If the West wanted special treatment, Andrew Jackson had warned he would remind the South and the North about it. Here was a man for all the nation, and Mrs. Royall was with him more than ever.

The President of the United States had told the nation that he would not tolerate one state taking advantage of another. His simple declaration against national funding of projects successfully built by states themselves was a warning which penetrated deeply into his audience. Already the political bargaining had begun among the many powerful congressmen of the few powerful states, and Jackson intended to stop it. Henry Clay had led this new movement, fielding legislation which on the surface was exemplary but was a raid on the federal treasury. His proposal to build a national road to link Kentucky with the rest of the country might benefit the citizens of Kentucky, but the greatest advantage would be to the Second Bank of the United States. Andrew Jackson knew it.

Clay had proposed that the federal government fund the national road by having the federal treasury back the bonds to be sold by the bank to build it. These bonds, once marketed, would be sold in competition with the private bonds already on the saturated market, paper issued by small groups backed only by the revenues received from the canals and roads already built. The intent of the Clay proposal was obvious. The Kentuckian was engineering, with Nicholas Biddle and his bank, a run on existing paper aided and abetted by the federal government's superior guaranty. There was no doubt that the bank, with loan paper backed by the U.S. government, could ruin the market for loan paper backed only by tolls. It was a move to take control of the entire market and at a price which the bank itself would set, with the use of the federal treasury. Andrew Jackson would have no part of it.

The Congress sat silent. Mrs. Royall could hardly contain herself. It had begun; the attack on the bank had begun! She was ecstatic. Jackson's announcement that the Maysville project was unacceptable to him, plus his intent to pay off the national debt meant only one thing: both would reduce the bank's ability to meddle in national affairs and muddy the country's political waters. Jackson was out to decrease the bank's share of the nation's cash flow and increase the public's share. His suggestion that the public lands be sold more quickly to anyone who wished to purchase them was a sword which cut in two directions at once. It would increase the money in the government purse, and its effect on existing capital was a raid in reverse. Henry Clay wanted roads in Kentucky for greater access to commerce for his constituents and more money for the West, and Jackson would give it to him. Money would flow fast from Philadelphia to the West with the sale and development of the public lands, and Nicholas Biddle and Henry Clay would have no control of it. Mrs. Royall chortled aloud.

The Congress knew history was in the making, history over which it had less control than the man whose message was setting it. The President had served notice that he was going to veto Clay's carefully devised legislation, and he had done it in a way which no one could counter. No one state was to receive help from the public treasury at the expense of the others. It was potent politics and everyone in Congress knew it. If anyone was going to use the treasury it was Andrew Jackson, not Henry Clay, John Calhoun, Daniel Webster or Nicholas Biddle.

The rest of the message had to be anticlimactic; at least that is what the listeners thought. They were to be surprised again.

Andrew Jackson called for the formation of a new Home Department to equal the position of the State Department. The nation was large, and attention should be given to the relations between the states and their many inhabitants. This suggestion caught the audience unprepared. A Home Department? Mrs. Royall was enthralled. It was what she had proposed last year when the first revelations concerning the extraordinary expenditures for foreign affairs and accounts had assailed the national mind. If foreign states got so much, why shouldn't American states get it too; after all, the government was set up to benefit Americans, not aliens. Mrs. Royall knew that every government department meant more money and although it was satire at first, misuse of funds for resettlement of the Indians had made the idea even more potent. Mrs. Royall did not intend to miss a word of this proposal.

Andrew Jackson was true to the woman writer. He explained the need for his Home Department. The constant pressure of the needs of the states and the Indian question dictated the need for a government group to deal with these entities properly. For example, had not the government been entreated to negotiate with the Indians as though they were a foreign power, an independent sovereignty within the borders of the nation? Andrew Jackson did not approve. Savages were not in that class, and no one knew it better than he. The truth was that the Indians were part of America, not a foreign nation, and like the states themselves, were an internal and interior domestic concern.

The time had come to stop the intercession of strange groups pretending to represent the Indians as ambassadors from a foreign nation, men who were not

Indians but self-appointed leaders who served foreign interests, not American ones. The Indian Bureau had taken the wrong tack but was continuing it. So long as large federal sums were involved, it was a pressing concern of Andrew Jackson and his administration. It was a bombshell, and it exploded over the Congress with white heat. Andrew Jackson had not made a proposal, he had thrown a challenge.

Jackson's proposal for the new Home Department was an open attack on the Indian Bureau, and his listeners knew it. The President had assaulted the sacred cows of the United States Senate, of John Calhoun, Henry Clay, William Wirt, and a host of others tied to the missionary grid. In calling for an end to the Indian Bureau, a finish for the great bureaucracy carefully constructed by John Calhoun to serve his interests, Andrew Jackson was going for Calhoun's jugular. Without the Indian Bureau, John Calhoun could control no government funds or cater to the political needs of the men he needed to assist him to power.

Mrs. Royall's presence in the gallery made the moment more exciting. This woman had called for the end to the Indian Bureau, and now Andrew Jackson had made it his public policy. Andrew Jackson was not dismantling the Indian Bureau, he was disarming the blackcoat army his enemies needed to march against him. The President was on the offensive, battling the hypocrites who served traitorous interests from American government offices and used American government funds to do so. Colonel McKenney! Andrew Jackson knew.

The audience understood an exceptional event was in the making. The President had sent his measure of the year to the Congress, couched in quiet language, but behind the words were weapons and arsenals of fact designed to strip his enemies one by one. Never before had a president used an annual message in this way and the hall was dizzy from the implications. How much further would Andrew Jackson go?

The President was not finished. Even as the galleries and the chamber settled, Jackson took a shot at a sacred entity, the United States Navy.

In time of peace, we have need of no more ships of war than are requisite to the protection of our commerce. Those not wanted for this object must lay in harbors where they decay rapidly . . . become useless.[4]

Tobias Watkins had come home to roost, ably assisted by Isaac Hill and Mrs. Royall. The President had taken a bead at the Navy's malfeasance and the expense of it, which did not benefit the nation but improved the Bank of the United States' foreign exchange operations and its concomitant foreign calls against American treasury funds. The general knew it was nonsense not to have an army on the frontier and yet build ships with no place to go and no war to pursue. Like the Indian Bureau, the Navy was a center for his foes, and Andrew Jackson would tolerate them no longer.

The Congress was caught up in the fever of anticipation now. The President was not finished. What would come next? Mrs. Royall listened more intently than ever, for she had predicted what his next issue would be.

It came quietly, so quietly that many missed it:

The charter of the Bank of the United States expires in 1836 and its stockholders will most probably apply for a renewal of their privileges.[5]

The crowd came alive. Jackson was on the bank!

In order to avoid the evils resulting in the precipitancy in a measure involving such important principle, and such deep pecuniary interests, I feel I can not in justice to the parties interested, too soon present it to the deliberate consideration of the legislature and the people.[6]

A gasp rode the hall like a storm wave hitting the beach. Andrew Jackson had begun his war on Biddle and his bank. The President would not fight it on the floor of the Congress where votes could be brought, but served notice he would take it to the people:

Both the constitutionality and the expediency of the law creating this Bank are well questioned by a large proportion of our fellow citizens, and it must be admitted by all, that it has failed in the great end of establishing a uniform and stable currency.[7]

Andrew Jackson had declared war in powerful language, signaling his first attack. Mrs. Royall literally jumped for joy. Rising, cheering, she led the applause. Andrew Jackson had confirmed her thesis and her prognostications. He had not left a single item behind. As she had wanted, the juggernaut had been attacked in all its elements. No longer could any Jacksonian claim he did not know the enemy; either he was with Andrew Jackson or he was not. The veneer had been stripped from every enemy and in just the same way Mrs. Royall had revealed them to view in the first place. All their guises, their political stances, their centers, their press empire, and their financial compacts had been taken on one by one, and Andrew Jackson had put his presidential stamp on each action. It was her truth, her printed truth, and let them call her a common scold now, indeed she was an uncommon prophet!

Andrew Jackson confirmed Mrs. Royall's personal influence in his message. He called Congress's attention to the laws governing the District of Columbia. There was no doubt that he had Mrs. Royall's famous case in mind as he expressed these words:

Placed by the Constitution under the exclusive jurisdiction and control of Congress, the District is certainly entitled to a much greater consideration than it has yet received. There is a want of uniformity in its laws, particularly those of a penal character, which increases the expense of their administration and subjects the people to all the inconveniences which result from the operation of different codes in that so small offense is punishable in unequal degrees, and the peculiarities of the early laws of Maryland and Virginia remain in force, notwithstanding their repugnance in some cases to the improvements which have superceded them in those states.[8]

Judge Cranch's joke would bring reform to the courts. It was a dividend he had not expected, and Mrs. Royall was jubilant. Even as all eyes turned to the aged writer in recognition of her travail, Andrew Jackson delivered his last blow. He called upon Congress to set aside the charter of the Bank of the United States and its private authority and create a bank within the treasury to serve the needs of the nation without the threat of being unconstitutional in its operations. The bank war had not only begun, but Andrew Jackson had taken the first battle.

Pandemonium took over. The young newsmen rushed to Mrs. Royall. She had done it again! Indeed she was the nation's seer, America's common scold, the American public conscience. Andrew Jackson had confirmed Mrs. Royall's opinions and her diatribes. In many of the words she had used herself, he had set the policy of his administration. If ever a blueprint had been drawn for a public message at any time in history, Mrs. Royall had drawn it. The old woman, who had summoned the courage to take pen in hand and survey her country, had been vindicated of all charges from her enemies by the President of the United States before a joint session of the Congress of the United States. But vindication had only just begun.

The next few weeks were a celebration for Mrs. Royall. The terrible days of July faded from memory as the import of Jackson's message carried through the nation. The war on the bank was in earnest, and for the important nuances in what was happening in the nation's capital, editors wrote more and more to their famous correspondent. It was important to know who and what stood with Jackson or the bank.

Both sides in the growing financial conflict mobilized forces. Andrew Jackson moved to weld his cabinet together, and the bank and its allies aimed their offensive at the West, particularly Jackson's home state of Tennessee. It was to be a showdown; the bank intended to survive. With Washington divided, the war was carried into the small towns as well as the cities of the nation. Every possible pressure had to be brought to bear on the White House, and the bank worked assiduously to protect itself.

Andrew Jackson's center of strength was the Mason brotherhood. Throughout the South, the masonic halls were the bastions on which the Jacksonians depended for their position. In the lodges, brothers sworn to aid one another were summoned to respond to Andrew Jackson. As in the Revolution, the Masons responded. Jackson's enemies returned the fire.9

The blackcoat press led the attack. Rekindling every innuendo from the Morgan affair, a quasi-religious assault was mounted against the Masons, this time in the South and West. The godly were called to arms against these ungodly. Money was poured openly into this new venture by the bank. Anti-Masonry was promoted as a political movement, God's own, well financed by Nicholas Biddle and his minions in his branch banks. The man from Philadelphis threw all caution to the winds. Andrew Jackson wanted war with the bank, and Biddle would give him war. If Jackson thought he had an army in the Masons and Democrats, Biddle had a large one in the missionaries and their followers, the Indians, too. The blackcoats and the frontier savages more than equaled the veterans who had marched with Old Hickory; the bank was more than the government itself. Nicholas Biddle believed he had one other advantage over Jackson: he had money.10

From the beginning, both sides were equal. Neither the North nor the South had been captured by the bank or Jackson. Nicholas Biddle relied upon Daniel Webster and John Calhoun for both these sections, but Andrew Jackson had sent his two lieutenants to counter them. Martin Van Buren operated from New York for the North, and Joel Poinsett in Charleston for the South. In only one area did the bank hold a clearcut advantage: the West. Henry Clay had it in his pocket, but he wanted a high price for it, even from his friend Biddle.

With the religious press carrying the bank's offensive, a virtual blizzard of political tracts descended upon the land. The theme was the same: Jackson was out to destroy the nation; the man had gone mad. The President was threatening not just the bank but the national resources, and this story was carried with lurid headlines into the West. The public lands were coupled with Jackson's rush on the bank, but the profligacy with which Biddle threw the bank's capital into his battle began to alarm the bank's trustees. As the money and paper flowed west from Philadelphia, Biddle's own supporters became frightened. Despite Nicholas Biddle's assurance that the West was the battering ram which could roust Andrew Jackson from the White House, others were mindful that the bank's heart was being revealed. With Ezra Stiles Ely and the various captains of the Elyite acceptance societies, Biddle held his base together. So much money spent would be returned via the tract society route. The bank and the New Presbyterians were linked nationally for the first time.11

The Elyite Presbyterian halls became the bank's centers in the very towns where the masonic halls were Jackson's. Using the pulpit to spread the message, the Presbyterian congregations were told that heaven was with them and would signal its approval by showering them with all kinds of good works: schools, roads, homes, and farms. The West responded as it had in the petition battle for Richmond. The bank advanced money for improvements Jackson said he would not. The access to such money was controlled: those who sided with the bank and the blackcoats, could have their share of it. The bank even mounted its own version of the public lands sale. If land was needed, the bank would buy the land and distribute it to its friends. Great land companies had been formed in Philadelphia to operate in the Transylvania region from Tennessee, through Kentucky to Indiana for speculation, and now these companies went after settlers, men and women carefully screened as to viewpoint. These land companies had charters which read curiously like manifestoes of independent nations, all directed from the bank's boardrooms and managed from Ely's Presbyterian headquarters in Philadelphia.12 Jackson had more than the Indian nations to deal with now.

The bank strategy was obvious. Two men were being promoted against Andrew Jackson: John Calhoun and Henry Clay. Daniel Webster had been bought publicly and was out of the presidential running. Nicholas Biddle believed that Andrew Jackson could do nothing about these men. The Vice President sat over the Senate, untouchable, and Henry Clay's hatred of Jackson made him unreachable by any administration strategem. The bank orchestrated all the actions against the Jacksonians with money. Thanks to the cooperation of the previous Congresses, Nicholas Biddle, president of the Second Bank of the United States, had loads of money at his disposal, while Andrew Jackson, President of the United States, had little.

The bank and its blackcoats were successful in the West, where money was short. Money promoted as the answer to all evils had a momentary effect. If the South chafed under the tariff, the North wanted more factories, if the West wanted roads, the bank could provide the relief. Biddle threw the bank's cash about with abandon. He had to woo more friends and punish his enemies. Loans were given or called as to the allegiance of those involved. Paper was redeemed at full value or discounted at loss wherever and whenever the bank wished to make its point.13 It seemed as though Andrew Jackson could not answer.

Mrs. Royall sat in Washington assessing the conflict. Her informants and correspondents kept her apprised of latest developments. As the bank gained the momentum, even her editor friends felt the press of the money issue as business and commerce controlled by the bank were applied against them. They wrote to her about it, and she replied in her customary fashion. She had her own ideas about money; men had need of it but not as much as they thought. In her own case, she lived from day to day, kept a roof over her head and bread on her table; she recommended that action to her friends. She never saw much of Mr. Biddle's paper; she used her own. She bartered her books for necessities and even small luxuries; surely her friends could do the same.14 Nicholas Biddle could keep his paper, hers was just as good; in fact, it was better, for it bought her freedom and independence. She made it herself, and then set its value, backed by her common sense. Mrs. Royall wrote her hard-pressed editors to stand firm and do likewise, for then their asset value would grow, for themselves and the nation. To allow Biddle to control was to be reduced to serfdom. It was a potent argument, and she found many to agree, particularly James Gordon Bennett. This correspondence kept her occupied while the issue over money and Biddle's use and misuse of it grew.

Money was the main issue in the small towns and cities, and it became the main issue in Washington too. Even as the rest of the country was being subjected to the buying power of the bank, so now was the Congress. Mrs. Royall kept on the prowl with daily visits to the Capitol to see who had fallen and who stood fast. There were many men who would sell their souls for a mess of potage, not the least among them Daniel Webster.[15] The tales of his indebtedness to Nicholas Biddle had reached awesome proportions; it was rumored that the great orator from Massachusetts didn't even own his own tongue, Nicholas Biddle did.

Andrew Jackson sat in his White House apparently doing nothing during this period. Many believed he could do nothing. When asked by friends about the money situation, Biddle's control of it, Jackson, like Mrs. Royall, would resort to small patent homilies about it, about his own experience. Biddle's paper was of no importance to the general; he liked gold and silver and a few good men who knew what they were doing.[16] Gold and silver and the labor of a free man were worth more than all the paper the bank could put into circulation. It was a curious answer to the uninitiate, those in Biddle's pocket, but to the men about Jackson, and at least one woman, it was a signal. Andrew Jackson, in his quiet way, had redefined money, and in so doing had unsheathed a double-edged sword. Like Mrs. Royall, he too watched the men about him, for many of them did not care what guise money wore so long as they had lots of it. Jackson's personal preference for gold and silver was in effect a silent promise to his supporters which meant much to men speculating in the confused paper market prevailing: gold and silver meant more than Biddle's paper.

The Richmond convention had warned the men near Jackson that their leader was on the offensive. Mrs. Royall's reports from that city and the defeat of the combined opposition made the anticipated bank war no longer an equal contest between Jackson and Biddle. The astute secretary of state, Martin Van Buren, pointed the way for others to follow. Suddenly Martin Van Buren was the new confidante of Andrew Jackson, and this new alignment signaled a new political stance.[17]

The bright days of winter brought Andrew Jackson to his feet with a new zest. With the final chastisement of Ely and his friends and the worst of the Washington swamp fever behind him, the President turned to his recuperation with vigor. Daily exercise was in order, and the President was a superb horseman. William Lewis, busy with Jackson's correspondence, John Eaton, preoccupied with strategy and staffing, were unable to ride with their chief on his leisurely excursions; so this task fell to Martin Van Buren. As secretary of state to a chief executive who believed the less foreign relations the better, Martin Van Buren had much time on his hands. He could canter forth at the general's pleasure, and with those rides the wily New Yorker had the link he had sought for so long to bind him to the next presidency.

Martin Van Buren wanted to be president of the United States. From the beginning he had waited for his chance to assert his candidacy. John Calhoun's bumbling, revealed by Mrs. Royall, had eliminated the Vice President, and Martin Van Buren did not need Nicholas Biddle.

The New Yorker had his own financial clique and had moved them into place as the bank controversy erupted. There could be many more rewards for men who worked with the President than for those who worked against him, and it did not take much Van Buren persuasion to convince other New Yorkers that they could reap the harvest from the seeds of dissent Biddle was busy sowing. Not even pulpit blandishments of the New York blackcoats could hold the New York money pool in check, not with Martin Van Buren to remind them just how big their reward could be. Nicholas Biddle was dispensable, and it was time that a New Yorker took his place as the financier of the nation. Martin Van Buren had that replacement in hand even as he began his move on the presidency. The leader of the New York financial pool was the son of its founder. Colonel James Hamilton was Alexander Hamilton's heir. Colonel Hamilton had no connection to Biddle or Philadelphia. After all, it had been a Biddle who had given the first asylum to Aaron Burr after the famous duel with Alexander Hamilton.[18] Philadelphia was a competitor to New York in most financial matters, and Nicholas Biddle's reconstruction of the Bank of the United States had put intense pressure on New York for over a decade. The New York pool would welcome an opportunity to even several scores, and Colonel Hamilton had personal reason to assist.

James Hamilton had been part of the Jackson camp for years, before the advent of Martin Van Buren. With Biddle close to Adams, young Hamilton had chosen to keep his position intact by joining the other side, and he had been rewarded for his strategy by becoming part of the Jackson inner circle. Like the son of many a great man, James Hamilton hoped to surpass his father; it was rumored that he had eyes on the presidency. He was part of the administration, having served as interim secretary of state while awaiting Martin Van Buren's resignation as governor of New York.[19] Now, late in 1829, her served as minister without portfolio to Andrew Jackson. There was no doubt in Martin Van Buren's mind that James Hamilton would assume any role he thought would serve his own interests, and Martin Van Buren had such a role in mind.

The end of the Virginia convention had brought ex-president James Monroe to Washington to explain his role in that meeting. Friends had prevailed upon the former president to make known his personal position to Andrew Jackson, for there were questions as to his loyalties. The forum for this exchange of information was a White House dinner honoring the former president, and on November 21, 1829, one old man was hosted by another. As they supped, a story was whispered among several guests.[20]

Was it not wonderful to see two men on such friendly terms after so much bitterness? Tench Ringgold, Monroe's grandson, marshal of the District of Columbia, was especially pleased. Ringgold, a friend to Mrs. Royall and Colonel Hamilton, warming to the occasion, remarked that it was about time. After all, James Monroe had been the only real friend Andrew Jackson had in Washington during that turbulent Florida period. If it had not been for the former president, Andrew Jackson certainly would have been court-martialed and would never have reached the White House. These remarks were heard by the men sitting near to him.

Major Lewis expressed surprise at such information. It was a Jackson understanding that John Quincy Adams and John Calhoun had stood by the general in that crisis, but Colonel Hamilton and Tench Ringgold held to their assessment. Adams wrote his famous letter in support of Jackson because James Monroe dictated it, and it had been John Calhoun, Monroe's Secretary of War, who had wanted to court-martial Jackson.

Major Lewis, Jackson's personal secretary, said nothing to the President at the dinner, but when the guest of honor had retired and the Jackson confidantes were sharing an intimate moment with their chief, Lewis turned quietly to his former brother-in-law, John Eaton, and asked if Eaton was not surprised by Hamilton's and Ringgold's version of the old Florida controversy. The mention of Florida brought Jackson's demand as to what they were talking about, and John Eaton was obliged to repeat for all what had been said at the dinner. It was a momentous revelation.

Andrew Jackson digested the new information in silence; perhaps it was another nasty story. Major Lewis opined that he did not think so, since he himself once had seen a letter in the possession of Colonel Hamilton from Governor Forsyth of Georgia, which told the same story as attributed to William Crawford, secretary of the treasury for James Monroe. Andrew Jackson turned to Major Lewis and ordered him to go to New York immediately and bring that letter back with him. As the President retired, those present knew that John Calhoun had been dispatched forever by a clever strategem, and it was not Colonel Hamilton who had done it; it was Martin Van Buren, the man who had not uttered a word! Tench Ringgold was an aide to Martin Van Buren, and the revelation of such a letter in Colonel Hamilton's possession had to have serious consequences.[21]

The letter which began this curious political maneuver did not come back from New York with Major Lewis. Colonel Hamilton refused to produce it and to excuse himself had fallen back on the compact between gentlemen which did not allow for the revelation of private correspondence without permission of both correspondents. Colonel Hamilton would contact former Governor Forsyth, now Senator Forsyth, upon his arrival in Washington, and the senator could discuss the facts with Major Lewis and Andrew Jackson. It was a masterful put-off, at least the way Major Lewis related it.

Senator Forsyth was contacted, and he referred the matter to William Crawford himself. There the story rested as December drew to a close. A tenuous chain, without proof, had been constructed linking John Calhoun to an action against Andrew Jackson. It was an operation which had the unmistakable Van Buren touch.

The White House was engulfed in new controversy, but John Eaton went about the Jacksonian business with his usual thoroughness. The bank war was on, and the West had become the major battlefront. With John Calhoun being temporized in Washington by events beyond his control, Nicholas Biddle had vested most of his hopes in Henry Clay. That Kentuckian was Eaton's major objective.

The President's call for the sale of public lands had triggered a new march on Washington City, a new Jackson army to remind the Congress of the popular support the President enjoyed. From north, south, and west came thousands of land speculators and farmers, potential settlers expecting Congress to take immediate action on the land sales and hoping that the first come would be the first served with the promised land. This inundation roused some of the northern representatives to fury—they were the voice of the industrial North and the blackcoats too, and they had little interest in opening the West. Among them was Samuel Foot of Connecticut, a Hartford Conventioneer. As the hordes of public land seekers filled the inns and halls of the capital, Senator Foot lost his temper and with it his discretion.

On December 29th, 1829, Samuel Foot introduced a series of resolutions in the Senate of the United States to limit land sales by several strategems. First, no land areas were to be opened for sale until all lands heretofore made available were sold; second, that federal funds be saved by closing the Surveyor General's office; and third, land sales be confined to those who had the proper assets to insure their development. From the moment the Foot resolutions appeared, their inspiration was obvious. The Bank of the United States had begun its counterattack to Jackson's message. Jackson could have his land sales, but the bank meant to maintain control. Land sales would be limited, and the bank and churches would be among the few entities to qualify for purchase. The center of the growing Jackson power in the government, the surveyor general's office and its frontier associates, would be dismantled. The battle joined, the debate began forthwith.

The Jacksonians selected Thomas Hart Benton to carry their voices to the

Senate floor. This Missouran would take on Henry Clay and Samuel Foot, and on the morning of January 21, 1830, the great argument started.[23]

The galleries were full, and among those who came to hear was Mrs. Royall. At last the Jacksonians would face, in open combat, their enemies. With John Calhoun presiding, the Senate was the arena. The audience knew something remarkable was to occur; both sides had lined up their strongest artillery. Mrs. Royall was interested in Daniel Webster, for he was Biddle's rear guard.

Thomas Hart Benton rose and fired the first volley. Rough hewn, this giant of a man spoke in a voice which gave a force to words which their content did not always confer, a force which could obliterate opponents. Senator Benton was not a polished orator like Daniel Webster, nor a preacher on classicism like Calhoun, nor a poetic lawyer like Henry Clay, but he was a bellower with a sonorous voice which the people loved. Like a bull to the attack, the sheer bulk of the man moved quickly as his voice thrust at his adversaries. Every word could be heard, and he kept the floor once he had gained it.

Senator Benton spoke to the gallery. Andrew Jackson should have his land sales without any resolutions to limit them because the cause of democracy dictated that the people's lands be made available to the people. The West was not a fiefdom, not owned by any one man or group of men, but land in common. It held the destiny of the nation, and common men wanted that land to give that destiny to the country. Mr. Foot represented men who would do anything to prevent other men from migrating to the better life, away from factory owners and managers, low wages, and bondage. Andrew Jackson had made a promise to these people that he would lead them forth to a full share in the nation, and the public land sales were the first movement to fulfilling that promise. Land, good cheap land, with people on it, meant growth for the nation, better growth than people working in dirty factories for cheap wages which served only the northern capitalists. The West wanted more people and would suffer no more meddling with its future. Public land sales would give people the use of dead land, and it was what the government intended from the beginning. Land should not be "banked" to lie fallow until future speculation gave a profit to the privileged. Thomas Hart Benton accused the North of trying to stop the growth of the West not to help the nation, but to maintain its control of it. It was a Jackson jolt delivered with a Benton bellow.

The Jackson position had been presented. Land sales would benefit the entire nation by pouring money into the U.S. Treasury, putting people on the land and increasing their desire for the world's goods; the growth of this great package would increase the asset value, the trade, and the market for all the American people, not just the few who sought to benefit from what the nation owned. The galleries went wild. Thomas Hart Benton had spoken as the leader of a new West, and he had extended an invitation to men in the North and South to join him in this new western progress.

Samuel Foot did not answer Senator Benton. Daniel Webster spoke in his place. Benton had to be stopped! Jackson's call, through Benton, threatened the old northern compact and the bank, and the great debator from Massachusetts turned his fire directly on Benton. How did the man from Missouri dare to imply that the North wished to inhibit the growth of the West for any purpose but Reason itself! The West had been opened and land was available still where settlements had already been established. It was the North's intentions that such land be sold first before the costly process of development was extended to areas which would create more problems for the nation as a whole. There were the Indians to deal with, and also the slaves. To open the West as Jackson wanted was to inflame men again, to destroy the Missouri Compromise. Surely Senator Benton did not want that.

Daniel Webster's game was apparent immediately. Slavery was to be made the issue, not land sales.[24] Robert Haynes of South Carolina rose to rebut. This fellow senator from John Calhoun's own state attacked Webster. The question was not how Benton dared to attack the North, but how Webster dared to raise the slavery issue. The North resorted too often to this kind of argument to stifle true debate.[25] Benton joined Haynes. Once again the senator from Massachusetts was up to his old tricks, trying to stop debate on an issue by raising another not pertinent to the effort at hand. The whole issue of slavery, an institution dying of its own volition, was made a burning, searing wound in the national fabric to serve the purposes of northern interests who used it to cover their own foul purposes. Benton bellowed forth that he, for one, was tired of so-called apostles of Christianity who promoted abolition, not to save the slaves, but for other purposes. Benton roared it would be wise for self-proclaimed voices of Christ to remember that when their Lord walked the earth, 99 men in 100 were slaves, white men, brown men, yellow men, black men, and yet Christ said not one word about slavery. It was recorded that Christ's greatest voice, St. Paul, went so far as to return a runaway slave to his master.

The challenge took Daniel Webster off his podium. Softly the senator from Massachusetts said he did not mean to impugn a section or a state; he was recording history. The southern states could keep their slavery problems, but the North did have an interest in how slaves were used to effect certain southern representation in the Congress.

Shades of the Richmond convention! Mrs. Royall noted it immediately. Webster was up to no good.

Benton bellowed like a wild ox, and Webster retreated. Webster agreed the North would abide by the original compact which had set representation in the Congress; however, he was reminding the Senate that the North was not alone to be impugned as to its motives in debating legislation. If the South could claim northern interference in its interests, the North could make similar complaint about the South. Mr. Webster affirmed that he would take the Union and the Constitution as it was.

Robert Haynes would not take this from Webster. He was happy that the senator accepted the Constitution, and he was glad that Daniel Webster had put from him his past experiments with the Hartford Convention's dissident philosophy, its less-than-exemplary support of the Constitution and the Union in 1814. It was good to have Mr. Webster affirm that his part of the country now accepted the U.S. Constitution and, perhaps having done so, it would stop interfering continually with the several other states, for in this manner, less pressure would be put on the great national union.

Haynes' reference to the Hartford Convention and the North's sponsorship of it drove Webster to fury. Who was the man from South Carolina to speak thus of Northern conduct in 1814 when in 1829, his own state was engaged in a peculiar exercise in state protest against the Union? This reference to the recent public meetings and legislative resolves promoted by the pro-Calhoun forces in South Carolina against the tariff and other Jackson policies opened a new line of attack.

Mrs. Royall watched intently as the public lands debate was submerged in this transformation of issues. Daniel Webster was playing his usual clever game. He had introduced a subject with which to force two new issues to keep one issue from being discussed. It was a signal that Nicholas Biddle did not have the strength on the floor of the Senate to pass the Foot resolutions; so the whole matter was to be mired deep in the mud of passions, not reason. The bank was answering Jackson's war call with another war call of its own. Daniel Webster was to open a new conflict, one to absorb Andrew Jackson's talents. Andrew

Jackson had begun his battle with Biddle on one front; Biddle would return his fire on many more.[26]

The runner to the White House carried the news. Webster was debating Haynes, but not on the public lands; Webster was using slavery, complaints against the South to raise the nullification issue. Daniel Webster was constructing a new public stage for John Calhoun. The states were to be embroiled in battle against the federal government. Webster's allusions to Union dictated it.

Andrew Jackson took the news calmly. "Good." The real battle was surfacing. Union! All the divisions would have to march openly now. Webster had made union the paramount issue. It was ironic; this spokesman for Northern regionalism, this apologist for the Hartford Convention, for the first action of separatism used against the Union, had invoked union. Andrew Jackson was not fooled. The bank was playing a desperate game. Using Calhoun, it was threatening the government that if Washington thwarted it, it would destroy Washington. Daniel Webster was playing Biddle's clever game for Union discussed was Union divided. Andrew Jackson, President of the United States, would teach the president of the Bank of the United States a lesson in tactics. The bank and Webster had raised the spectre of nullification; Andrew Jackson would haunt them out with it. The bank would be annulled, not the Union![27]

Mrs. Royall was sitting in the Senate gallery watching the drama unfold when the summons came. Robert Haynes had just finished with tweaking Webster's nose with references to her now-famous prosecution. Webster had made stentorious exposition of how the Constitution bound the states to the Union and how no legal authority could disrupt that constitutional lashing, not even an obscure legal authority. Robert Haynes had replied that South Carolina would not search for any obscure authority as a certain judge from Massachusetts had with "Coke upon Littleton," so recently to express its interpretation of the Constitution. Robert Haynes, looking up at Mrs. Royall as he expounded on his statement, assured Mr. Benton that "whenever any attempt shall be made from any quarter to enforce unconstitutional laws, clearly violating our essential rights, our leaders will not be found reading black letters from musty pages of old law books."[28] This clear reference to Webster's good friend, Judge Cranch, and his reading and decision in Mrs. Royall's famous case, brought down the hall and punctured Daniel Webster's semantic balloon. Mrs. Royall was caught up in the moment along with the rest of those present and at first did not hear the whispered call to her.

Mrs. Royall was needed immediately. Obadiah Brown had asked for her. Hastily she rose, tearing herself from her moment in the debate and as she did, Senator Benton chided Daniel Webster again for his part in the Hartford Convention when he reminded Webster, in Mrs. Royall's words, that he had not always marched under the Union flag but just a few short years ago had marched under the Hartford five-striped banner with the slogan "Peaceably if we can, Forcibly if we must!" It was a tale Mrs. Royall had made popular, and as she left the Senate, Daniel Webster was crying out against it.

Parson Brown was in exhilaration when Mrs. Royall arrived. The word had come from Jackson via Eaton that Mrs. Royall's southern tour should begin. Could Mrs. Royall leave Washington by January 30th? It was important. It was just three days' notice, but the postmasters could be alerted in hours as she went on her way.

Mrs. Royall had been packed for the road for weeks. Gladly she would leave Washington and the Congress to its wine and sin, and "to Mr. W. to be the conciliator of those conflicting interests which are now convulsing the Union."[29] Parson Brown and she had a good laugh on that one. Union, and Webster the defender of it! Old Hickory knew how to use that. John Calhoun's nullification, that was her business and she knew what to do with it. "Nullification talk is silly—the result of money, tract, baby cap and pin cushion religion. It is wholly without reason."[30] It was her new crusade, and there were eight state capitals before her. Mrs. Royall was embarked on a journey which would bring her absolute vindication.

Chapter 26

Retribution

When Mrs. Royall left Washington City on the morning of January 30, 1830, she was on the most important mission of her life. In her portmanteau were messages from Andrew Jackson to particular persons enroute, provided by John Eaton, to establish the framework for the new project the Jacksonians had decided upon. That new project was based upon certain writings Mrs. Royall had produced, and the author of those suggestions was being put to the test of her stated opinions. This time she would not only report, but she was to participate in the solutions to the problems she found. Mrs. Royall was to contact and then recommend certain people to Washington for assignments in the project to be completed. Momentous events were in the making and the woman who had spent so much time in predicting them was to have a hand in their happening.[1]

The tour had been planned with care. Mrs. Royall was not well the morning she left, and suffering from fever and cold she was carried aboard the stagecoach bound for Virginia and points south. Sally Stackpool feared for her old friend, but Mrs. Royall would hear no remonstrance. The stage was as comfortable as her rooms, and there was great work ahead. Mrs. Royall had been entrusted with Andrew Jackson's personal message to one prominent man as well as his presidential respects to many others, and nothing could stop her. As the stage left Washington, she was enroute not to report American history but to help write it.

The carriage proceeded along the route mapped by Obadiah Brown and as it did, crowds met it at its stops. Parson Brown had done his work well. The word that Mrs. Royall was moving again on the country brought out both friends and enemies. Mrs. Royall's celebrity went before her and with lodgings booked well in advance she was met by Jacksonians anxious to show their support and opponents desirous of knowing what they faced. Mrs. Royall was on tour again, selling her published work, but she had added a new element. She was a Washington ambassador with letters in hand. Mayors, state officials, county and town clerks, congressmen, even senators not in Washington would come forth to greet her. It was an extraordinary reception for a woman called the Common Scold.

Mrs. Royall was embarked on a new endeavor. Carrying letters to certain individuals, she was introduced as a woman who knew what was happening in Washington. She carried with her a careful exposition of certain information to be imparted to certain people to solidify Jackson's support and operations in the months to come. As Mrs. Royall progressed, she left behind a solid phalanx of enlightened citizenry who knew exactly what Andrew Jackson planned to do, men and women thoroughly indoctrinated as to who the enemy was, what garb it wore, and what the Jackson offensive would be. It did not take too many stops before the enemy knew the role she played. Mrs. Royall was Andrew Jackson's advance guard in his war against the bank and she was carrying his orders to his allies as she passed!

Mrs. Royall was a national figure. Her fame had gone before her, but the preparations for this trip trumpeted the fact further. Her mockery of her enemies' cherished beliefs was no longer just her opinion, it was a Jacksonian doctrine. As the woman rolled on across the Virginia countryside with the force of the government behind her, her enemies had to construct some action against her.

The blackcoats dared not mass themselves at her stops and oppose her openly, for to do so would prove her thesis. Instead, they sent against her the seemingly innocent, the irresponsible. As her carriage approached Charlottesville, Virginia, the first large-scale confrontation had been planned. Mrs. Royall had invaded blackcoat territory, and they would show her how dangerous that route could be.

Charlottesville, Virginia, was the home of the University of Virginia, child of Thomas Jefferson's hope for the enlightenment of the new world. By 1830, Jefferson's light had been extinguished by a cabal of Tory sympathizers and blackcoat clergy, a situation aided and abetted by Chapman Johnson. Missionaries had gained the classrooms of this greatest of new American institutions under the pretext of teaching Greek and Latin, and instead had introduced Bible tracts and the New Presbyterianism in all its doctrinal and financial splendor.[2] In five short years, the University of Virginia had been transformed from the heart of American Reason into a factory making youthful blackcoats who bore the name "blueskins" for the hours spent in church pursuits in cold halls rather than in intellectual pursuits about a fire and a convivial table. Young blueskins were the innocents the blackcoats would send against Mrs. Royall.

Mrs. Royall entered Charlottesville in the late afternoon, and as her carriage headed towards her inn, mobs of students raced after it, pelting it with whatever was at hand. The "witch" had come to town and as the people of Salem had once been sent out against women in that town, so the rowdy youths in black coats and breeches were propelled against her. As the chase became a riot, the townsfolk rallied about their messenger from Jackson, and the blueskin youths were sent packing. With the town to protect her, Mrs. Royall went about her business, the scandalous activity of the students in training for blackcoats having prepared Charlottesville for the message Mrs. Royall presented. It was an eye opener in more ways than one. Mrs. Royall, visiting Monticello, Jefferson's beautiful creation, found that the famous home had been invaded and vandalized, and the perpetrators were obvious. Mrs. Royall wrote about her shocking discovery:

> In the garret we found Mrs. Jefferson's spinet broken . . . It stood amidst heaps of coffee urns, chinaware, glasses, globes, chairs and bedsteads.[3]

Jefferson's Monticello had been ravaged. It was a Royall revelation which shook Charlottesville to its roots, forcing a re-examination of the black-coated presence at the University.[4]

The University of Virginia surprise sent Mrs. Royall on to Farmville, to look at a blackcoat institution there. Hampden-Sydney College, where she said they "manufacture blueskins by wholesale and retail,"[5] but this time the students did not chase Mrs. Royall down the streets; she chased them. Terrorizing the tract spouters with her presence and reason, she rallied the plantation owners against them. The lord of the plains, John Randolph, came out to greet her personally. This Tidewater aristocrat, the man who carried the Jackson day at Richmond and was destined to be the last of the great Virginians, rode to meet Mrs. Royall and take from her the message she bore.[6] As he saluted her and his white horse bore him away at a gallop, Mrs. Royall's reputation was made forever in William Royall's land.

On to North Carolina went the intrepid dame. On March 4, 1830, the *Raleigh Star and Gazette* gave the first official notice of Mrs. Royall's visit and purpose:

> On Friday last, our city was visitted by Mrs. Royall. Her fame had long since reached us; and her arrival threw our tranquil metropolis in commotion. Many visitted her, while others seemed desirous of avoiding her. All who saw her affirm that they never had seen the like of her before; and all who came within the range of her colloquial power were fully convinced that she wields a weapon equally as powerful as her pen.[7]

This was the signal which opened the rest of the South. Mrs. Royall rolled on in triumph, gathering friends and adding them to lists forwarded to John Eaton for Andrew Jackson's designs. One of the Carolinas was not John Calhoun's, and Mrs. Royall went on to the other.

Mrs. Royall headed for Charleston, South Carolina. It was a different reception along the way; Parson Brown's arrangements had gone awry. In the towns, no one came to meet or talk with her. The post office conduit had been short circuited by Calhoun supporters sitting in its South Carolina offices. Mrs. Royall did not dally where she was not wanted. Vermont was a long time ago, but its experiences had made a lasting impression. "If looks could kill I most certainly was dead!"[8] said the old dame and moved on to Charleston.

Joel Poinsett was Mrs. Royall's contact in Charleston, but he was not in the city when she arrived. Poinsett was in the back country, rounding up non-Elyites among the Huguenots, Baptists, Catholics, and the Masons. Open warfare had broken out in the South Carolinian towns, with blue-cockaded blackcoats marching in army phalanx in preparation for the nullification battle Calhoun was promoting.[9] Floride Calhoun had come home to Clergy Hill to have a baby, and what a baby it was! The Calhouns had split South Carolina, for John Calhoun was to be president if he had to structure a new nation to achieve it. Mrs. Royall could not be angry with Joel Poinsett.

Charleston was a city in depression. Mrs. Royall could not believe it. This once most beautiful of all Southern cities, where culture, theater, music had rivaled the best of Europe, was caught in the vise of blackcoat gloom and Bible censure. Man was down on his knees praying for forgiveness, and no one was working. Mrs. Royall could not stand it. Alone in a city of religious fanatics, she went forth to the city square and called upon any man or woman of reason to come forth and hear the truth as sent by Andrew Jackson. It was a good ploy, for it brought forth some supporters. Waving her gold-headed cane like a flag, she walked the streets of the once-lovely city demanding to know where its once-lovely people were. She called forth those who cherished the White House, not Clergy Hill. Few Christians answered her call, for they were gloomy New Life Presbyterians. Finding no response, Mrs. Royall turned to the Charleston Jewish community. Together they found mutual delight.

The "charming Israelite," Jacob Cardozo, owner-publisher of the *Southern Patriot*, took Joel Poinsett's place. To him she gave the Jackson message. He immortalized her in return:

> Mrs. Royall is certainly an exception to her sex in all particulars. The inordinate influence of the clergy and the Ladies, in American Society, were the burthens of her complaints, and she rated us, in our editorial capacity, in good set terms, for our submission to such influence.[10]

Jacob Cardozo was enlisted by Mrs. Royall and he, in turn, arranged for "levees" to spread her Jackson word. Two beautiful young women from the Jewish community attended to Mrs. Royall's every need. She commended the Mistresses Joseph in letter and print to Washington, and John Eaton listed the Cardozos and the Josephs for Jackson posterity. Joel Poinsett had not abandoned Mrs. Royall. He did contact her through a young aide, a surgeon from Massachusetts. John Holbrook, founder of the South Carolina Medical College[11] and a fervent admirer of her writings, had suffered from the blackcoat attempts to subvert his medical school as they had subverted the University of Pennsylvania Medical College. The Bible was no match for an anatomy book, and John Holbrook had been holding them off with that reason.

John Holbrook brought the news of Poinsett's search for support in the outlying countryside against the army Calhoun was building. Jackson had to have a citizen army to stop the destruction promised by this latest Clergy Hill effort. The word was out that John Calhoun would be the first president of the Confederacy, and that Clergy Hill would be his White House. It would only be over Joel Poinsett's body. ' The center of Poinsett's effort was the city of Camden, one hundred miles away. Camden! The name rang a distant bell in Mrs. Royall's mind. Could it be the same Camden where her husband had fought a battle in the Revolution? She had to see Poinsett and help raise the Jackson force.

Mrs. Royall followed her inclinations. She went to Camden, and her visit held more than one pleasant surprise. There was a young editor in that town whose name she had come to know well. Constan Freeman Daniels, a name on letters which had defended her brilliantly during her trial, was the editor of the *Camden Journal*, no longer an unknown citizen in defense of a woman's rights.[12] It was an extraordinary meeting for two minds so much alike that henceforth they would never be apart.

With Editor Daniels, Camden celebrated Mrs. Royall. William Royall? The town still remembered him, and there were men still alive who had served with him on the battlefield. Mrs. Royall toured that battleground with the city counsel and Mayor Thomas Salmond declared a holiday in her honor. The City Council paid her bills. Editor Daniels rhapsodized as he caught the town's reaction to his new friend:

> The annals of Camden will hereafter show 1830 as the year particularly glorified by the transit of Mrs. Anne Royall. Farewell dear Mrs. Royall . . . our citizens look upon her as the Queen of Flowers![13]

The Queen of Flowers! Joel Poinsett, botanist extraordinaire, was busy gathering his blossoms in the countryside, pinning his poinsettias on his followers, but Mrs. Royall had them wrapped up in a bouquet for him on his return. Daniels's praise did not go unrewarded, for Mrs. Royall commended the young man not only to Jackson and Eaton but to her editor friends in New York. It was the start of a long and fruitful relationship not only for Mrs. Royall but for the Jacksonians. Mrs. Royall established a dynasty for the Daniels family by passing through Camden in 1830; such was the power of the Common Scold. She did well by Jacob Cardozo and the Joseph family too; their names still illuminate American annals.

Mrs. Royall left South Carolina on March 25, bound for Augusta, Georgia. She had been 23 days in John Calhoun's bailiwick and set in motion a counteroffensive against Nicholas Biddle and his bank. Her beloved Jews were masters at finance and with Poinsett and his Huguenots, Masons, Catholics, Biddle and Calhoun's Presbyterians would not have everything their way. Mrs. Royall rolled on into Georgia with tales of her latest accomplishments preceding her.

Mrs. Royall had very important business ahead of her in Georgia. Here she was not only to evaluate the Jackson support, but she was to meet with certain political people who had been against Andrew Jackson before but were willing to discuss a change of heart. William Crawford, once a competitor in the presidential sweepstakes, was down on his luck and, due to the strange circumstances of the James Monroe dinner at the White House just months before, was again on Jackson's mind. Andrew Jackson wanted William Crawford's version of the 1818 move against him during the Florida campaign. If William Crawford would tell Andrew Jackson what was really said and done by John Calhoun and John Quincy Adams in that Monroe cabinet, Andrew Jackson would remember him well.[14] Mrs. Royall had been entrusted with the message to Mr. Crawford.

William Crawford might have been President of the United States, but fate dealt him an unkind blow. Just as he was nominated for president in 1824, he had been felled by a stroke which had paralyzed him, removing him from active campaigning. John Quincy Adams had taken the presidency because of Crawford's misfortune, but the Georgian's shadow muddied national politics. Martin Van Buren's post in the Jackson cabinet was a tribute to William Crawford, for Van Buren had been Crawford's running mate. Mrs. Royall also carried personal remarks from Martin Van Buren to the Georgian.

It was the first time the writer had participated in the political machinations of the White House. As her carriage rolled towards Augusta, the crowds grew larger as though the people had been tipped to her role. This time her receptions were crowded not only with Jacksonians but with Baptists, Catholics, and old-line Jeffersonians. As if to accentuate the fact that a new force was riding through Georgia, a Catholic priest joined Mrs. Royall, his black cassock an affront to the hated blackcoats.[15]

Mrs. Royall arrived in Augusta on March 30. It had been a triumphal procession across the state, and the *Augusta Chronicler and Advertiser* headlined her visit on March 31:

Nothing was talked of, or heard of, or thought of, but Mrs. Royall. On Thursday she received company, and everybody—that is anybody—not to mention some she had set down as nobody—paid their respects to her in person . . . . and her rooms were a squeeze.[16]

Men surrounded the writer. William Crawford came, a pale shadow of a man reduced to service in a lowly post for the state of Georgia. Mrs. Royall had good news for him. Andrew Jackson was interested in his plight. They had much in common, these two men who had fought all their lives for the nation's good. Andrew Jackson wanted to know the truth about the alignment of the cabinet during the threat to court martial him in James Monroe's cabinet. It was a moment of truth, and William Crawford knew it. The woman bringing the news from Washington about this matter also brought with her the first news about the Jackson banks. The blackcoats had chosen to initiate their southern anti-Mason effort in Georgia, but the brethren were to stand firm, William Crawford included, for the Jackson banks were to be soon a reality in the war against Biddle and his friends. Crawford approved a movement and a deal was struck.

Mrs. Royall rallied the old-line supporters of Old Hickory in Georgia, and, with William Crawford, she healed a breach of long standing. As the word went forth, she was inundated with visitors. The Georgia women might be in Ely's pocket, but Mrs. Royall made sure that many of their men were not. So complete was her victory in Augusta that Moses Waddell, Calhoun's mentor and brother-in-law, kept to his University of Georgia home and never came forth to confront her.

Mrs. Royall traveled to Savannah where a most pleasant surprise awaited her. Colonel William T. Williams, Savannah's mayor, responding to a note from Robert Berrien, Jackson's attorney general, was on hand to greet her.[17] Berrien's gesture was unexpected, for he was close to John Calhoun. Mrs. Royall surmised that the news of William Crawford's conversion to Jackson must have had its impact and with the Jackson banks no longer empty talk, Calhoun and Biddle had lost their monopoly on the future. Colonel Williams owned the local bookstore and confirmed his new allegiance by taking 50 copies of Mrs. Royall's work, subscribed for more to come, and paid her for all in advance. Indeed, this part of Georgia was having a change of heart. Colonel Williams wanted a good report back to Washington.

Mrs. Royall's southern tour had been a smashing success to date, but as the news about the Jackson banks gained currency, a new mood set in. Mrs. Royall's views that the President planned to aid and abet the establishment of new banks in opposition to the Bank of the United States signaled the new Jackson strategy. The President was interested in a new financial network, and he had the power to construct it by rerouting government funds. Mrs. Royall was contacting men who had the capacity to take part in these anticipated ventures[18] and suddenly Jackson's enemies reacted: her tour had to be delayed until some defense was mounted against this new blandishment. The word went out through the blackcoat lines that the woman from Washington was to be hampered until other measures could be taken to stop her progress.

The harassment began in earnest in Macon, Georgia.[19] Mrs. Royall had been booked for passage on a well-known river boat, and suddenly a group of missionaries appeared on board. Demanding that Mrs. Royall be put ashore, they threatened to take all the cargo from the boat. The captain, facing the loss of his payload, appealed to Mrs. Royall. No provision had been made for this, so Mrs. Royall discreetly withdrew and went by horse and carriage to Columbus, Georgia. It was a retreat she did not enjoy, but when word reached her that William Crawford had told all in his own hand to Andrew Jackson, she was mollified. She threw her energies into her task in Columbus with a new vigor.

Mirabeau Bonaparte Lamar, editor of the *Columbus Inquirer*, was Mrs. Royall's escort about town and country.[20] An ardent Jacksonian, he had played an active role in the expulsion of the Cherokees and Creeks, and he hated the blackcoats as much as Mrs. Royall did. With Lamar, she rode out to the ruins of the Indian villages and the wasteland appalled her. If only those innocents had not allowed the missionaries to lead them into actions against the United States. Young Lamar and she discussed the Indian agents and their close alliance to the black-coated missions. Mrs. Royall did not know it at the time, but her dissection of the Washington currents would so inspire a young man that he would take himself to Texas where Mirabeau Bonapart Lamar would become the first president of the Texas Republic, the man who would lead Texas into the United States.

On to Alabama went Jackson's emissary. This was the state Mrs. Royall called home. Here she had proved herself as the inheritor of her husband's estate, with a singular success in Huntsville still part of her repute. It was her investment in salt properties which had increased William Royall's wealth so much that his family and her own had sought to take it from her. That success had led her to her failure in the Richmond courts, but she had conquered all adversity and she could survey her "home" once again with delight.

Montgomery was a memorable visit for the writer. Here she came upon a young nephew to the hated blackcoat leader, Lyman Beecher, who turned out to be no follower of his noted relative, but a man of reason who found his way into her heart. Young Beecher was the recipient of countless tracts and Bible society publications from his illustrious relative, all intended to convert him to the ways of the new world, but young Beecher had used them in a singular fashion. Mrs. Royall wrote about it:

There are a great many goats in Montgomery, and Mr. Beecher stuck the tracts on their horns and sent them forth to spread the gospel!21

Young Beecher had found a lovely way to get his uncle's goat, and Mrs. Royall knew how to use it to get a few more blackcoat goats.

From Alabama, Mrs. Royall headed down river to New Orleans. This was to be the last leg of her trip through the South, and she prepared for a pleasant journey. She had been ticketed for the very same steamer on which she had sailed for Richmond and Washington just eight years ago.

Mrs. Royall eagerly looked to a nostalgic reunion with captain and crew, but it was not to be. The writer discovered the old steamer was strewn with Bible tracts, on tables and in shipping bales, to be distributed along the Mississippi. What bits and pieces she could lay her hands on went over the side. Macon had been enough. This captain could take his pick: mail contracts with the black-coats or with the U.S. government. By now Mrs. Royall was recognized as the personal agent of Andrew Jackson and John Eaton, and the captain made his choice. Mrs. Royall arrived safely in New Orleans.

Jackson's city awaited her. Mayor Denis Prieur and the Masons' Grand Mas-ter John H. Holland came to greet her. The city which owed its life to Old Hick-ory was pleased to receive the famous Mrs. Royall. A triumphal tour awaited America's favorite writer. It was to be the final moment of success on her tour. This port, which opened the heart of America to the world at large, was most important to the Jackson design. This bit of France in America did not have a single blackcoat in sight, and with French Catholics and Huguenots massed about her, Mrs. Royall had a very good time. New Orleans had no love for the dour Scots-Irish Elyites; in fact, they loathed them for their role in the War of 1812, but there was one Irishman the people of New Orleans loved, and he was Andrew Jackson.22 It was the perfect end to her long trip, and Mrs. Royall made the most of it.

New Orleans had no religious censure or hypocrisy, and the Jacksonians ruled. The battlefield where Jackson had saved the city, and with it the nation, was maintained as a memorial, and Mrs. Royall toured it and marveled at the victory Jackson had produced. As she discussed the great event with her new friends, she saw a city bustling with commerce which the Bank of the United States did not own. New Orleans had many banks with which Jackson could deal and many men willing to assist in his new endeavor. Mrs. Royall sent long lists of names to Washington for Jackson and posterity.

There was one name in New Orleans that Mrs. Royall did not report on favor-ably. The bookseller, Benjamin Levy, a friend to Edward Livingston and Martin Van Buren, proved to be a double-dealing merchant.23 Mrs. Royall had con-signed her final shipment of books to him for this end of her trip. Although she had requested that he send them to her on arrival, they did not come, nor did any accounting of them. She had to take herself to Benjamin Levy to request an explanation. He gave her a desultory one: The books had arrived but had been destroyed in the rain, and therefore he had not received them. Mrs. Royall was furious. Even as she talked with Mr. Levy, she noted the bales of Bible tracts ready for Mississippi shipment that stood about them. She knew instantly what had happened to her books.

Benjamin Levy was a agent of the Bible societies in New Orleans. It was he who consigned their shipments up-river, in collusion with the blackcoats and their missions to the Indians. Her new friends in the city confirmed her observations, and with it she wondered aloud at Benjamin Levy and his relationship to Edward Livingston, and Martin Van Buren.

Mrs. Royall had to stay longer in New Orleans than she had planned. Her books had to be replaced, so she waited for them, taking orders from other booksellers not affiliated with the Bible and tract cargo business along the Mississippi. It was a momentary respite, and she loved every minute of it. Madame Herries, with whom she stayed, was a woman who knew everything about the Delta country, and Mrs. Royall received an education in French language and customs.24 It would be with regret that she would leave this great town for Washington again.

News came with her books. Obadiah Brown had an important addition to Mrs. Royall's mission. Would the writer head north along the Mississippi to Tennessee? Things were not going well in Jackson's home state; Judge White and some of Jackson's close cohorts had turned against the President, and an instant survey had to be taken.25 It was a summons to action Mrs. Royall could not refuse. Her *southern tour* would have to be two volumes instead of one.

Preparations were hurried. Mrs. Royall packed for a hard journey, for this time there were no advance notices or lodgings. Once she left New Orleans, the writer would be on her own in hostile territory. Time did not allow for Parson Brown to make the necessary contacts, but he would do his best. Mrs. Royall would have to exercise the element of surprise and take her chances, for this time friends could be enemies. It was a fluid situation, for the blackcoats and the bank had been busy these past few weeks sapping Jackson's strength at its very roots in Tennessee.

Mrs. Royall's new itinerary would be the long trip up the Mississippi to the very center of the new nation. There would be few who would assist her as she went, and she would have to find her own quarters and introductions. She was booked on a friendly steamer, one which owed much to Parson Brown and the post office, and that would be her only advantage. On board she would be safe at all times, but not necessarily on land. The blackcoats owned the settlements along the river; they staffed the Indian agencies and Biddle and his banks owned what they did not. Mrs. Royall had an apt description for what she was about to invade. Noting the bales of tracts and goods consigned to the missions, she called the great Mississippi the "Bible Belt." It was a good title, for it was the territory into which the blackcoats had poured hundreds of thousands of tracts bought and paid for by George Watterston using government funds and his Library of Congress privilege to distribute them, with an able assist from another old foe, Colonel Thomas McKenney. Mrs. Royall was marching into the heartland of all her enemies. McKenney's missionary friends ran the Indian posts, and the cargo landings along the great waterroute were managed by Army groups controlled by Colonel Nathan Towson. As if that was not enough, it was really John Calhoun's country, manned by his appointees from his service with James Monroe and sustained by his vice presidency. Mrs. Royall was a courageous old woman, but even she must have trembled when she considered what was ahead of her.

The enormity of her problem was apparent as the steamer left New Orleans. Standing at the stern to bid a fond farewell to a city which had received her so well, Mrs. Royall noted that there were no fortifications about the city to be seen. John Holland26 had called that fact to her attention as he explained why and how the city of New Orleans kept the Jackson ramparts standing and in good condition. It was the only modicum of security the city had since Washington had seen fit to deny it any other fortification. It was a circumstance which John Holland asked Mrs. Royall to bring to Jackson's attention on her return to Washington. The frontiers of the nation had been left to men with strange alliances too long, and something should be done about it. Mrs. Royall knew she was about to make another discovery.

The answers began to come as the river was breeched by the river steamer. There were no fortifications in New Orleans, but 300 miles above the gateway to the United States the first army installation could be seen not on the west side of the river, but on the east. From that sighting, Mrs. Royall carefully noted each army outpost as the riverboat made its progress. Every day another was seen, and as the riverboat approached, blackcoats could be seen in great profusion on the landings. Much money had been spent for "defense" where defense was impossible. Andrew Jackson had taken after the Navy in his December message, but he should see what the Army had done with government money, constructing mission centers for the blackcoat army, not for the security of the nation.

Twelve hundred miles from New Orleans, Mrs. Royall came upon the greatest Army installation of all: Jackson Barracks. There it sat, named for Jackson in the euphoria that followed his victory at New Orleans. What an obscenity it was. John Calhoun had memorialized Andrew Jackson all right, but Mrs. Royall had her own comment for the former Secretary of War's production: "fortifications of so much style and cost. What enemy would come here? Not the Indians in the heart of the country. Why were these fortifications not built at New Orleans, where a foreign enemy might one day invade us?"[27] Mrs. Royall had her answer even as she wrote the question. John Calhoun had provided employment, contracts, shipping, and trade with which to build his political future with the blackcoat direction of the western territories, and they still held this frontier in their Bible grip. Mrs. Royall knew exactly what was being trekked to the Indians: Bibles and guns. They traveled in boxes that were interchangeable.[28]

St. Louis became Mrs. Royall's destination. Two weeks on the river had given her all the proof she needed of the blackcoat operations. Staying aboard the vessel past Memphis, she had surveyed the Indian agencies in particular. These posts were growing centers competing with recognized state governments and, as such, were in direct competition with the United States of America.[29] The Indian Bureau had constructed theocratic centers all along the frontier, centers which did not recognize Andrew Jackson as the President of the United States but were committed to his enemies instead. There was one last hope. The main western headquarters of the Indian Bureau were in St. Louis, headed by General William Clark, the brother to the great George Clark of the Lewis and Clark expedition. Mrs. Royall would go to General Clark with her findings and her complaints.

General William Clark, the superintendent of Indian affairs, was an old acquaintance from Mrs. Royall's Sweet Spring days. Arriving in St. Louis, she sent word that she was there to see him. General Clark never appeared but word went forth to deny her all accommodation, and the writer found herself confined to her riverboat and its decks. The Indian Bureau ruled St. Louis, controlling the bulk of the cargo shipping on both the river and its many tributaries as well as overland distribution and the stores within the towns enroute. The order against her placed Mrs. Royall in a very difficult position. She was not only denied a bed on land but social pursuits as well. No one was to speak to her or give her any assistance.

General Clark had made a great mistake; the lady from Washington knew exactly how to deal with such as he. She stood by her rights, and the riverboat captain stood with her. The steamer remained at the docks. If Mrs. Royall would not be welcomed ashore, she would haunt the docks of St. Louis until she was. But Mrs. Royall was a woman of action, and she knew who was responsible for her reception. She would see General Clark himself, and to do so, she obtained a floor plan of the Indian agency offices, plotted her moves, and then, on a sultry afternoon, invaded the agency and cornered the old general in his office. The old man was astounded. He pled sickness for his defense, but Mrs. Royall did not buy it. She accused him of lending his office to those who had no right to it and misusing his authority. She had written to Washington about it, and she would publish her comments for the world to read what General Clark did in St. Louis, how he used his post:

> I found the house (Headquarters) very large; part of it filled with trifles with which to allure the poor indians out of their annuities — another part of the house, under the appearance of hospitality to indians, the more readily to fleece them, is allotted to those unsuspecting visitors. This was a large room on the first floor, and was then full of indians. I pushed briskly through them and found Clark in a remote room, cooped up like an old rooster . . . He is only the shadow of a man, scarcely sane, reduced to a skeleton, feeble, superannuated and fit for no business in the world.[30]

General Clark had been reduced to a puppet managed by his blackcoat advisors. The Bank of the United States had ruined the Clark fortunes, stripping both him and his brother of the land they had received from a grateful nation, and this was his last sinecure with which to survive. Nicholas Biddle had a strong hand in this. Biddle's name was associated with Clark, Biddle having edited his journals and having promoted the land deals which had pauperized the great man, had procured this post for his brother.[31] Unlike Andrew Jackson, General William Clark had not had the heart and courage to put from him the past and take on the future. He had succumbed to his enemies and now fed from their hands, grateful to be alive. Mrs. Royall had no compassion for a hero with such clay feet.

The agency guards forced Mrs. Royall to retire, but her verbal confrontation with Clark set the whole town to talking. The blackcoats and the bank controlled St. Louis, but the tongues of its people were another matter. Mrs. Royall had spoken aloud what others knew to be true, and once out, it was fair topic for conversation. People began to appear at the boat, ostensibly to gawk at this strange woman, but many found a way to sneak aboard and talk with her. No one dared to offer food and lodging though, for the Indian agency controlled their right to do business and even their lives, for there were drunken Indians and the threat of instant death:

> It is very plain that the Presbyterians are in possession of the Indian Agency and the Army. Remote from the great mass of the people, their plot could ripen before the people are aware of it.[32]

Determined to see the matter through, she wrote Secretary Eaton about it. If he did not hear from her again within the next few days, he could call out his army for her! Such was the hostility the old woman knew. Mrs. Royall, cherishing her safety, told everyone what she had written. It had its desired effect. A young couple, Shepherd by name, running a school unconnected with the blackcoat enterprise, came at night and under cover of darkness, and took her in. With them she stayed until transport to Illinois could be arranged.[33] Day and night she was watched, and again she left by night to avoid trouble to her young hosts. She slipped over into Illinois, and there her reception was entirely different.

Obadiah Brown had been busy in her behalf. Illinois was Jackson territory, and Governor Ninian Edwards came to greet her. The tales of Mrs. Royall's confrontation with General Clark in St. Louis had reached Springfield, and Edwards, a former senator to Washington, came to assure Mrs. Royall that Illinois was not blackcoat territory.[34] The Jackson banks were no longer rumors now, and Mrs. Royall's role in Andrew Jackson's new plan was apparent. Ninian Edwards was pleased to enlist himself in Jackson's new offensive against the bank and against Mrs. Royall's hated blackcoats.

Illinois was a welcome respite for Mrs. Royall. The weeks along the Mississippi had been trying. The day-to-day confrontation with her enemies had exhausted the aged writer, and she took a four-day vacation in this hospitable state.

Rumor had it that her mother and her half-brother were somewhere in Illinois or Indiana, and she sent out queries about them. Friendly editors assisted. Mrs. Royall would be pleased to hear any information which could lead her to her family. With this done, she proceeded immediately over land by circuitous route to Nashville, Tennessee, her goal on this extended tour.

The blackcoats had invaded Jackson's home state like locusts bent on stripping the fields. From the moment of the defeat of the British at New Orleans in 1815, Jackson had been a target of these new religionists. Retribution would be visited yet upon the man who slew so many thousands of their brethren, and the promised offensive had produced one notable confrontation.

Even as Mrs. Royall rode through Jackson's land, she reminisced about Jackson and the early blackcoats. The general's arduous nine-hour support of Pastor Craighead, that old-line Presbyterian who had been accused of heresy by the new Elyite faction in 1820, came to mind. The President's tolerance of his wife's religious fervor and her capitulation to the very forces which were bent on destroying both of them, his building of their own church to shield her from the scandalmongering her "Christian" friends had visited upon her, enhanced the problem before her. Indeed, these Tennesseans were strange people.

The nation celebrated Andrew Jackson for his stand against these blackcoated enemies of America, but his own people had joined them. With Andrew Jackson and John Eaton in Washington the blackcoats had enjoyed a free hand, and Jackson's own friend had succumbed to their blandishments. Hugh White, Jackson's oldest friend, had been lured with a promise of the presidency for himself and had joined the latest blackcoat effort to accomplish his ambition. Using his well-publicized closeness to Andrew Jackson, White had preempted the leadership of the State of Tennessee and was moving heaven and earth, but especially heaven, against not only Andrew Jackson but John Eaton. Hugh White had not forgiven John Eaton for attaining the place he had assumed would be his when Jackson triumphed. These facts were on Mrs. Royall's mind as she rolled across Andrew Jackson's home state.

Town after town were visited and if Mrs. Royall had doubted any of the tales of duplicity about Hugh White she had heard in Illinois, she did not doubt them now. The President had been eclipsed by his friends turned enemies in his own heartland. The Elyite fanatics were everywhere, and the church which Andrew Jackson had striven so mightily to keep from their infestation had been taken too. Pastor Craighead was dead, and even his own son, lured by bank money, was on the verge of joining his father's enemies.[35] The blackcoats, luring the women of Tennessee, had strengthened their hold upon them with Rachel Jackson's death. Indeed the Lord had shown how to deal with sinners with that woman. The story was everywhere that Rachel Jackson died of grief because she had heard her sins told in public and had willingly given up her soul to the Lord to be cleansed. The women of Tennessee were praying that her husband would soon follow her for the same purpose. The rumors of Jackson's illness had excited mass prayer meetings to that end. Mrs. Royall was appalled

at the intellectual devastation about her. Not even her own experience with the
young Donelsons had prepared her for the Tennessee she found.

No one came to greet Mrs. Royall as she entered Nashville. Mindful of her
mission, Mrs. Royall took matters into her own hands and went to the editors
of the city herself, but none would publish notice that she was in town. Men
she had known to be friendly before were no longer, and Mrs. Royall had her
own explanation for that: "Considering the politeness of the editors before, I
can think no other than they are bought up by the U.S. Bank."[36] Mrs. Royall
set about unbuying them with the notion of Jackson banks and her own brand
of reason.

Mrs. Royall made one important discovery in Nashville: Not all the old-line
Presbyterians were lost. Several of the university leaders were holdouts from the
all encompassing theocracy of the Elyites. Dr. Philip Lindsley and Dr. Bertrand
Troost spent evenings with Mrs. Royall recalling their fights against the likes of
Ezra Stiles Ely and his minions.[37] How they wished Andrew Jackson were in
Tennessee to set his example before his people! How could people forget so
soon? The General had sat nine hours on the hard pew of his church, and the
presence of the extraordinary lawyer had turned back the onslaught on Craighead and the old-line church leaders. What a contrast to the women now sitting
on the velvet bench pads of the churches, giving themselves to this new hysteria.
Mrs. Royall left for posterity her own memento of her visit to Nashville, the
plight in which she found the city.

> Once flourishing Nashville is an example for those who wish to know the
> Bank and the Blackcoat. If it is wished to see the horrors of the banks and
> the tyranny of the priestcraft, visit the Tennessee city. Independence
> crushed, the citizens stripped of their all, not only in Nashville, but the
> state is swallowed up in monied monsters.[38]

The transformation of Tennessee had taken just thirteen months of concerted
activity. From a Jackson bailiwick, it had become Biddle-blackcoat territory, a
stronghold which stripped Mrs. Royall of the last vestiges of her usual optimism.
Reason had not been insurance against folly here; money had subverted the best
of minds. The bank and the blackcoat alliance were marching through the West,
no longer as the strange alliance she had found in Pennsylvania, but as an open
assault on American institutions.

Mrs. Royall had little good news to report to John Eaton and Andrew Jackson. Indeed, most of their old friends, including Judge Overton, Andrew Jackson's personal overseer of his affairs, were leaning in the wrong directions. It
would be well for John Eaton to look carefully at his own comrade in Washington, his former brother-in-law Major William Lewis. In Nashville it was said that
he was an active participant with White and Overton in a number of ventures
financed by the Bank of the United States.[39] Such information had to be a
blow to John Eaton, but perhaps it would explain how the constant assaults
upon Peg Eaton were used to distract Jackson's attention.

Mrs. Royall turned her footsteps north to where she could do something.
This time she was headed for Kentucky, Henry Clay's stronghold. The man who
had stolen Jackson's election to the presidency in 1824 and given it to John
Quincy Adams was himself preparing for a bid for the presidency. There was a
circumstance Mrs. Royall knew how to exploit: Clay against Calhoun, and Biddle torn between the two.[40]

The word had gone before her, and Louisville paid her no heed when she arrived. Then Samuel Penn, a descendant of William Penn, who published the
Daily Advertiser, announced that Mrs. Royall, the woman who had saved Penn-

sylvania, had come to Kentucky and the Jacksonians should come out to meet her.[41] The Jackson banks were on every tongue. When, what, where and who were the questions asked and her rooms were thronged with seekers after information. Mrs. Royall had it, thanks to John Eaton and Obadiah Brown. The Jacksonians were to put their houses in order, withdraw all public funds from the local branch of the Bank of the United States, and wait for further orders. Illinois was doing so already. In Kentucky, the Baptists were stronger than the Elyite Presbyterians, and Parson Brown had alerted his brethren for his famous friend. No spendthrifts, they had awakened from a long sleep as they watched the wagons arrive from the East, loaded with blackcoats claiming lands said to be owned by the bank, and the Kentucky hill people were ready for counterattack[42] The Kentucky press was still free and had long opposed the East, the bank, Biddle, and the blackcoats, indeed blackguards of every description, including Yankee peddlers.

Mrs. Royall heard about Francis Blair of Frankfort, Kentucky. This young man from Virginia had a pen which cut deeply into the same enemies she dissected, and had led a successful fight in the state against the Biddle bank, sponsoring the Kentucky movement to tax it. Such success merited Jackson's acclamation, and Mrs. Royall sent John Eaton a recommendation that he be sent for and brought to Washington.[43]

Mrs. Royall left Kentucky sure that Jackson's designs were in good hands and entered Indiana. She had been warned that if she thought Tennessee was infested with black locusts, she had seen nothing until Indiana. Mrs. Royall was not deterred by such reports. The lists of Indiana Masons were long, and the writer knew her brethren would not desert her.

As Mrs. Royall proceeded through Indiana, the Masons rallied behind her, even those who supported Henry Clay. Samuel Parker of Belleville placed his lodge above his politics, and he announced Mrs. Royall's visit in the most honest of appraisals, a call which set the tone of her visit thereafter:

> Though the undisguised independence of this lady has rendered her obnoxious to a few of the powerful classes of the country, yet her literary talent, and the deserved celebrity of her many literary productions, will elicit the attention of the public wherever she may go. We never spent an hour more agreeably than in her company. She is very communicative — all life and interest. Her minute observance of all the public evolutions of several of the recently passed years — the extensive range of her travels and intelligence . . . and the vigor of her imagination, together with a never flagging vivacity of countenance and conversation, conspire in giving her, and her writings, a peculiarity of zest and texture.[44]

Samuel Parker learned to know Mrs. Royall well. Through his efforts, Mrs. Royall found her long lost half-brother, Colonel James Butler, and with him spent a most agreeable week. The crowds who came to see this famous lady from Washington forced Mrs. Royall to abandon her brother's farm and move into a hotel in town. Samuel Parker would never forget Mrs. Royall; he would keep up a lifetime correspondence with her.

It was Colonel James Butler who told Mrs. Royall where their mother could be found.[45] From the last information he had, she was living with his sister, Mrs. Cowan, in Edenburg, halfway across Indiana. It meant backtracking 100 miles, but Mrs. Royall knew she would never pass this way again; so she undertook to do so. Newton Claypool, the wealthiest man in the Indiana country, sent her in his carriage to Rushville. Rushville proved to be such a den of blackcoat iniquity that Mrs. Royall hurried on her way in the only vehicle available to her, a farm cart so much like a tumbril that even she acknowledged her shock.

Tumbril or not, the cart did get her to the stage route on time, and on she went to Edenburg. Mrs. Royall was in the heart of the blackcoat effort for the Indiana plains, but that was not what disheartened her. Her mother had moved on, along with most of the populace. A bout of fever had settled over lowland Indiana like a plague, this time the cholera, and most of the settlers had gone west to escape it. Mrs. Royall noted that most of the people she met "hoosed," coughed and wheezed, and she wrote in her own characteristic way about it.[46] Indiana was too flat, too heavy with timber ("the air cannot circulate"), and surrounded with Indianans coughing, wheezing, and spitting, Mrs. Royall nicknamed them "hoosiers" for all the hoosing they did. Mrs. Royall's name for Indianans caught the public fancy and that state's everlasting title, the "Hoosier State" is a lasting memorial to Mrs. Royall's 1830 visit.

Mrs. Royall did not find her mother in Edenburg; the old lady had moved on to Springfield, 'Ohio, and her famous daughter decided to visit her for one last glimpse of her past. Mrs. Royall headed north to Indianapolis, and here she found what her Kentuckians had warned against. Indianapolis was worse than Nashville, Tennessee. "The Presbyterians have tract depositories, a press, and several societies in the place, and people hired at sixty dollars per month to carry tracts throughout the State."[47]

The lady from Washington stayed long enough to investigate the tract peddlers and their connections. Learning who she was, blackcoats invaded her rooms and tried to seize her luggage and papers and finally forced Mrs. Royall to call for help from Noah Noble, a brother Mason and brother to Senator James Noble.[48] Noble did not respond, but the senator's son-in-law did. He sent her on her way to Danville, where she was subjected to even worse abuse. There, the blackcoats serenaded America's public conscience with "obscene songs, and, the windows being up, they threw in dirty water and rioted until late in the night."[49] Despite this, Mrs. Royall concluded Indiana was not lost to Jackson, for only three cities were amiss: Rushville, Danville, and Indianapolis. They were all centrally located, and the rest of the state was uninfected. It made her trip to Springfield a pleasant one.

Mary Butler was 78 years of age when her 61-year-old daughter found her again. After ten years, the old writer faced an older woman who was still active in treating the afflicted with herbal skills she had learned from the Indians. Each took the other's measure and liked what she saw. It was a farewell, because the miles between them would never allow such a meeting again. Mrs. Royall enjoyed her brief moment with her mother and then left, never to look back again; she would have no time for regret. As she left Springfield, the Jacksonians had begun their first public assault on Biddle's banks and the panic had begun.[50]

Cincinnati, Ohio, was Mrs. Royall's next destination, but she had to cross Indiana again. The war on the bank was an open battle. Biddle had thought he could control the expected conflict until all his troops were in position. General Andrew Jackson had decided otherwise. He had the means to force his enemy into precipitous action, and he had set them in motion. Mrs. Royall could gloat, as she passed along her way, that the men she had contacted weeks before were well afloat in the deepening crisis. Jackson's supporters had prepared well, but the blackcoats and the bank men had not. Town after town had withdrawn its funds from Biddle's bank, and the blackcoats stood in line before the closed temples of their ally's empire. It was a sight which did not sadden the lady from Washington. God would deal out retribution, would he? Well, Jackson had dealt out his own, and she had a large hand in it.

It was a three-week trip to Cincinnati, and by the time Mrs. Royall had reached this Queen City on the apex of the Ohio, the panic had begun to reach epic proportions.[51] The Biddle bank had begun to counterattack, but as it did it cut its own ground out from under it. Having spent a year calling loans from enemies and refusing cash to them, the only business it had was with its friends. Andrew Jackson had waited just long enough for the bank to carry out its announced purpose of punishing foes and rewarding friends, and now he had all his enemies in one big blanket. He had only to pull the blanket and freeze them all out, and he did. Wherever the Jacksonians controlled the local governments, funds had been withdrawn from Biddle's empire and placed in the new Jackson banks springing up all over the countryside. Cincinnati, a blackcoat center like Indianapolis, was hit the hardest of all the Biddle centers. Mrs. Royall wrote about it in her own inimitable style. The bank was foreclosing its own friends' properties, punishing its own little people, visiting upon its allies the retribution it had promised Jackson and his friends. The tavern where she was lodged was a perfect example of what was happening. It was a blackcoat property taken over by the bank that very month. Further, the servants were in abject misery. Why? Again, the bank! Mrs. Royall had compassion for the establishment's cook for that poor woman was without shoes, and Mrs. Royall organized the visiting boarders to contribute to buying a pair for her:

> The poor thing burst into tears, called me an angel and said if I had not given her the money the constable would have taken her that night. 'This is just what I owe the tract society. So sure as I haven't the money to pay, the constable is sent for me. He took me away once.'
> 'But why do you subscribe?'
> 'You are obliged to subscribe, if you work for a living, or nobody would hire you. All the servants and waiters about the tavern have to subscribe $5 per year.' Several were standing by and said it was true.[52]

Mrs. Royall knew then and there the blackcoat menace was over. If this was happening to the little people who had been enticed to place their faith in Ely's God, Ely could hold them no longer in subjection to his power. Andrew Jackson was doing the right thing because the bank and its allies, the blackcoats, were exposed for what they really were: money grabbers peddling grace for every cent they could lay their hands upon. The panic was proving her thesis. The bank, by foreclosing its own friends' properties, had shown its collusion. She was proud to have assisted in this event, and she looked back over the past seven months with pride. She hoped the situation was the same in Nashville, Indianapolis, Danville, Rushville, and St. Louis. Oh, if only John Eaton had done something about that old fool William Clark! The blackcoats knew exactly what was happening to them. They knew the role Mrs. Royall had played in their crisis at hand. A frustrated Presbyterian cleric, full of Elyite bravado, challenged Mrs. Royall to debate in an unsigned letter to the Cincinnati papers. Mrs. Royall accepted with her own published rejoinder to him and his kind:

> I view all those schemes as vile speculations to amass money and power and the Sunday Mail plainly proves your object is to unite Church and State. I am opposed to those schemes because the money is taken from the poor and ignorant, as no man of sense would pay for the gospel which is to be had without price. I will be happy to see you Sir in my rooms or in public.[53]

The poor cleric never came forth. Perhaps he, too, lost everything in the days that followed; he could have been threatened with the constable had he still owed for tracts his followers had not paid for. Mrs. Royall spent her weeks in Cincinnati cataloging all the ramifications of the present and future Jacksonian actions. Late in October she began the final leg of her journey home to Washington.

Pittsburgh was a short stop on her homeward journey. By now the pressure on the Biddle empire had mounted so that Mr. Biddle's minions were beside themselves. One was G.W. Holdship, a bookseller with whom Mrs. Royall had been acquainted since her first trip to Pennsylvania in 1825. Mrs. Royall had met his brother, a paper manufacturer, on that very first tour, and through him G.W. Holdship himself. Both men had been Masons and of inestimable assistance to her. Naturally she would drop in on either of them in passing.

Entering Holdship's store to inquire about him and his brother, Mrs. Royall was confronted by a young blackcoat, Charles Plumb, clerk in the store. She announced her presence and asked that Mr. Holdship be so informed. Young Plumb refused her entrance. A fervent anti-Mason, the clerk knew who Mrs. Royall was, and he engaged in an argument with her. Mrs. Royall expressed her surprise that such as Plumb should be in Holdship's employ, a traitor as he was. Plumb took a cowskin belt, and with it the 20-year-old youth beat the 60-year-old woman. Mrs. Royall only escaped with her life because of her new bonnet, heavily laced with horsehair padding.

This attack became an instant Pittsburgh sensation, for it galvanized the competing passions engulfing the city. Assault charges were filed against Plumb, and Mrs. Royall became the focal point of all the latent fires being fanned as the panic marched from West to East. The same crunch which had toppled Cincinnati now gripped the Pennsylvania iron city, and tempers were very high. The Jacksonians controlled the city and county government, and Mrs. Royall was their darling. The prosecutor did his best, but young Plumb was let off with a minor fine, $20 and costs. Another judge was in the bank's pocket, another blackcoat in black robes. Mrs. Royall learned that not only had Andrew Jackson suffered the desertion of old friends, but she had too:

> Holdship was my firm friend until he found that I was opposed to the Bank. He manufactures paper for the Bank. He has all the presses indebted to him for paper . . . ships vast quantities to the Western and Southern states. If the Bank, which I suspect for this foul deal, would do such a thing now, what will it do if rechartered? Therefore, ye who value liberty, crush the monster before it be too late.[54]

With these words written in her journal, Mrs. Royall took her leave of Pittsburgh. Still afflicted with pain from the attack, she said goodbye to the city which had produced the first blackcoat, Preacher Black. It was a calculated farewell, for the intrepid woman writer carried with her a thousand blows with which to effect her own retribution against blackcoat and bank. In her hands were the lists of men and enterprises which would be the network of Jackson banks, the "pet banks" which would finish Biddle and Ely forever.

The court comedy in Washington had begun her tour, and the court farce in Pittsburgh had ended it. The Elyites had their tracts, but Mrs. Royall had her notes. Her enemies believed in an eye for an eye, and Mrs. Royall would give them a law for a law. There was no way they could stop her now.

Chapter 27

"Respects to Mrs. Royall"

Mrs. Royall returned to Washington on December 6, 1830. As she disembarked from her carriage, she clutched her notebooks tightly. She had lists of friends for John Eaton and Andrew Jackson, as well as a wealth of information about the new America awakening from the indulgences of the past half century. All of it was tailored to the needs of the new administration.

Washington City was ready for Mrs. Royall and her intelligence. The capital was in a state of frenzy. John Calhoun, the Vice President, had been deposed, and everyone knew it even as he sat presiding over the Senate. Andrew Jackson had begun a relentless attack upon his second officer, an attack which had begun with the receipt of William Crawford's letter.[1] The old regime was tottering, and its allies had been thwarted. It was what Mrs. Royall had hoped to find; all her enemies were publicly Andrew Jackson's and the President of the United States had the situation well in hand.

Even as Mrs. Royall prepared for her report to Obadiah Brown and John Eaton, she knew her work on the road had been completed. The blackcoats and the bank were finished. As the panic had begun in Illinois and rolled on through Indiana, Ohio and Pennsylvania, lashing New York and the North, her enemies had mobilized against Jackson with the same scurrilous and hysterical outpourings they had lavished upon the man and his wife in 1824 and 1828. In sonorous tones of the Elyite pulpit-pounders prayed mightily for relief from Jackson's "madness." In their extremity, they again attacked the well of Jackson's support, the Masons. This time they had no William Morgan with which to belabor the fraternity; they resorted instead to an open political movement drawn exactly from the propositions set forth by Ezra Stiles Ely in his infamous July 4, 1827, manifesto against the Constitution of the United States. The blackcoats were openly recruiting "for the Christian March" and so beset with adversity were they that they deigned to include the hated Catholics in their plans.[2] As the panic rolled on, they would even invite consortium with Jews, people they had begun their campaign against.

Mrs. Royall had forecast these developments. There was nothing these religious fanatics and their allies would not do. Money was their true god, and they used its power to buy what they could from the confused markets at hand. The blackcoats did attain some success; they took such good Jackson allies as Mordecai Noah and James Watson Webb with large loans and promises of support.[3] Neither of these men had the same fortitude as Mrs. Royall. She too had felt the effects of the growing financial squeeze, but she would not sell her policies for a loan. Noah and Webb deserted, but not Mrs. Royall's young men. James Gordon Bennett and James G. Brooks left their New York mentors to their new

243

apostasy and went forth and founded their own newspapers to support Jackson.[4] Rumor credited Mrs. Royall with a hand in this. Two sides were represented with full press; it was to be a war to the finish.

Andrew Jackson proved his mastery of the situation. The nation, alerted to the real effort by Mrs. Royall, was the President's strength. The financial communities, interested only in money, vacillated and wavered. Martin Van Buren, holding tightly to his future, worked valiantly to appease his friends and still please Andrew Jackson. The Little Magician resorted to some brilliant maneuvers to accomplish his aim. He set out to surround Jackson with new cronies whom he hoped would temper the old man's directions, and Edward Livingston, the man Mrs. Royall "reserved" in her mind thanks to Benjamin Levy and New Orleans, became the pivot of Van Buren's hopes.[5] It was a closet action which was to have far-reaching consequences.

Fate had brought Mrs. Royall into the controversy in the beginning when she had discovered the strange alliance between bank and church, and fate was to propel her into action again.

Martin Van Buren had achieved the impossible: He had replaced John Eaton as Andrew Jackson's daily confidant, but he had precipitated a personal crisis with this move. Van Buren's supporters were being unsettled by the growing financial crisis and Colonel James Hamilton, his own ambitions curtailed, was not happy that his New York financial community was involved in the counteractions resulting from the outland attacks on the Bank of the United States. Nicholas Biddle had chosen to reply to the President of the United States by calling upon his foreign connections to lend him support and that call involved Martin Van Buren's great friend, the Chevalier Huygens.

The New York money pool had believed itself to be well insulated from the movement directed at the Bank of the United States. It had prepared for the expected upheaval by setting its own operations in order and conducting its own raids on the bank's local supply. New York had no strange alliance to any church or theocracy to bring upon it Jackson's retribution. Hamilton and his friends were not allied to Ely's Presbyterians nor Beecher's Hartfordites. Lyman Beecher could fill a New York hall at one hundred dollars a head for his contrived causes, and the Bible societies were just as flourishing and the saving societies just as accumulative, but by and large, the Episcopalian Hamilton and his Dutch Reformed friends believed they were apart from the blackcoat element in New York. It came as quite a surprise to find they were not.

New York was enmeshed with the blackcoat offensive in America. New York City sat on land leased from the Episcopal Church and the Dutch Reformed Church, both entities having acquired the land as holdings during the upheavals that forced both English and Dutch to return home during the Revolution.[6] Further, that land, supposedly controlled by native boards, was actually in the hands of the headquarters of each church in London and Amsterdam, represented by English and Dutch officials stationed in the United States to steward these properties. The Chevalier Huygens was the titular agent for the Dutch Reformed properties in New York. He was also the bearer of Biddle's bad tidings to the New York financial fraternity.[7]

Martin Van Buren could not sit by and watch his friend, the Chevalier, threaten his ambition with his position in this matter. As secretary of state, Martin Van Buren was in a post to do something about it. The Chevalier Huygens had to be recalled and sacrificed to his friend's ambition.

The Chevalier's recall was demanded, and Martin Van Buren did not do one thing to aid his old friend.[8] He had the vice presidency in his grasp, and he was not about to relinquish it. The Chevalier Huygens and his wife, the couple who had hosted so many pleasant family evenings for Martin Van Buren, left Washington as requested. As they went, the fate of the Bank of the United States was sealed.

The crosscurrents in Washington following the recall of the Huygens kept Mrs. Royall busy assessing the situation for her followers in a series of letters. She had hoped to enjoy a well-earned rest, but it appeared that she would not get it. The battle against Biddle and his bank and the associated blackcoats had taken on some strange colorations.

Martin Van Buren had never been a favorite of Mrs. Royall. She had met him on her first trip in New York when he was busy undermining DeWitt Clinton and had watched him as he entered the Jackson lists. She would watch him as he gained the President's ear, sharing his confidence with John Eaton, William Lewis, and William Barry. The aged writer did not trust Little Van;[9] there was that association with the Huygens, and then there was Edward Livingston.

Martin Van Buren was worth watching. If he was to survive in the fluid financial situation assailing the nation, he had to remove all those not privy to his plans. Van Buren had no compunction about bartering away principle, but there was one man close to Jackson who would not. John Eaton sat beside Andrew Jackson, and while he was there, Martin Van Buren could not gain control. Ambition was no match for Eaton's selfless dedication to Jackson, and the departure of the Chevalier was a situation that Van Buren could turn to his advantage[10] in this difficult circumstance.

Floride Calhoun had enmeshed Madame Huygens in the anti-Eaton affair, and the Dutch diplomat's wife had gone so far as to refuse to greet Peg Eaton. Martin Van Buren decided to use this fact to absolve himself of his friend's removal and to erase any damage that might accrue from his desertion of a friend. The public would be told that Huygens had to leave because Mrs. Eaton was causing continuing friction within the administration. The Little Magician would do with John and Floride Calhoun's concoction what they had been unable to do with it themselves. He would ride to the presidency on the Eatons' removal from Jackson's counsel.

Martin Van Buren enlisted William Lewis in his machinations.[11] The major needed money for his Nashville involvement, and his daughter was involved with a foreign diplomat; foreign banking connections would be most welcome. John Eaton had been William Lewis's brother-in-law, but that was a long time ago. The major willingly joined against the man who had been his friend, even as he had joined in the Hamilton-Crawford affair so late in explanation to his mentor, Andrew Jackson.

It had an immediate reaction. Important Jacksonians were quoted as admitting that Peg Eaton was a continuing and disturbing factor in the government, and the rumor was allowed to run, assisted by comments from Andrew Jackson's closest "advisors." This sudden recurrence of a theme, propounded by Jackson's enemies and now espoused by his friends, sent the scandal to the tip of every tongue as though Andrew Jackson had never dispatched it.[12] Martin Van Buren, continuing to socialize with the Eatons, was the epitome of grace, but his friends were busy using the new Eaton assault to rekindle Van Buren's past ties to religious groups involved in the matters at hand.

It was the Little Magician's double dealing at its best. On the one hand, Martin Van Buren was the defender of Mrs. Eaton, and on the other, he was the concerned confidante of President Andrew Jackson, disturbed by the old man's habit of letting his heart run away with his head as the new slanderous attacks mounted against the Eatons. As the public defender of record of Mrs. Eaton, Martin Van Buren knew exactly what to do with this new circumstance: He would undermine husband and wife by resigning from the Jackson cabinet amid this latest flurry, leaving both to the tender mercies of those who were ready to ask why. The Eaton detractors could use Martin Van Buren, who had seemingly despaired of his original support of friends and was admitting his mistake in such a gentlemanly way. Martin Van Buren handled this very well. He went to John Eaton to tell of his despair with a cabinet so split as to be ineffective and requiring dissolution. All should resign to let the President have a free hand. It would solve all difficulties, including the constant scandal for the Eatons themselves. There was so much they could do in other positions for the President. John Eaton listened and agreed, and it was done.

Andrew Jackson could accept the resignation of Martin Van Buren but not John Eaton. Jackson knew Martin Van Buren wanted to be president but from a Jackson cabinet, never.

John Eaton fell back on his personal situation. The President did not understand; to him, Eaton's desire to leave was desertion under fire. Martin Van Buren made sure that Andrew Jackson continued to think it so. It was the end of John Eaton.[13]

Mrs. Royall sat amidst this latest intrigue, unable to believe this succession of events. John Eaton was letting Van Buren's future engulf him and his wife. Just as victory was in Andrew Jackson's grasp, Martin Van Buren effectively had sidetracked all action on the bank issue and the growing attack on the hold-overs in government and had taken unto himself the growing impetus of the administration. The old man in the White House was losing his grip! With the appointment of Edward Livingston as secretary of state, replacing Van Buren at Van Buren's own request, Mrs. Royall was sure that everything she had worked for was in danger. Livingston and Levy were coupled in her mind. The impending exile of John Eaton back to Tennessee was the last straw.[14] Mrs. Royall could sit with her letters no longer. The time had come for more positive action.

Mrs. Royall decided to galvanize her press contingents. She and Sally Stackpool took to the road together to travel the old northern routes to talk to friends and editors. Surveying opinion and gathering promises of support, the writer and her assistant returned to Washington with the necessary assurances that what she planned would be welcome indeed. She found General Duff Green, the mentor of the *Telegraph*, the Jackson paper in the capital, willing to underwrite her in a weekly exposition of comment aimed at the old Jacksonians, away from the direction that Martin Van Buren was leading.[15] Mrs. Royall was to rally the old-line supporters against the new line emanating from the White House, controlled by the New York Federalist clique now holding the old general in virtual confinement, due to the expulsion of his friends. Nicholas Biddle was bad, but this new compact was worse. Biddle held Philadelphia, but Van Buren and his friends had taken the White House and throttled all possible opposition. The old Jacksonians had to be shocked into action. Pressure had to be brought upon Major Lewis, Eaton's former brother-in-law, the man who had opened Jackson's bed chamber to Van Buren's control.

Mrs. Royall chose the title *Paul Pry* for her weekly national review from an 1825 comedy from the Englishman, John Poole. His play revealed shocking details of intrigue and plotting in the alliance of England's church and state.[16] This *cause celebre* was still shaking the continent, and Mrs. Royall, intending to use such an approach to shake the United States, still maintained her sense of humor in the midst of this new adversity.

Paul Pry came into being on December 3, 1931, just in time to note the machination with which Martin Van Buren hoped to achieve the vice presidency concurrent with Andrew Jackson's second bid for the presidency.

Mrs. Royall cut herself loose from Jacksonian politics with the first edition of *Paul Pry* with this terse announcement:

The welfare and happiness of our country are our politics. We shall expose all and every species of political evil, and religious fraud, without fear or affectation. We shall patronize merit of whatsoever country, sect or politics. We shall advocate liberty of the press, the liberty of speech, and the liberty of conscience. The enemies of our common safety, as they have shown none, shall receive no mercy at our hands![17]

These words from the redoubtable lady with her new steel pen meant exactly what she said. Martin Van Buren had eliminated the dedicated, selfless John Eaton from Andrew Jackson's side, but he had gained an implacable opponent to watch his every step.

Paul Pry kept vigilant watch on the Jackson administration. Martin Van Buren did place his friends where Jackson's once stood, and Mrs. Royall, in countless pages, documented the real history of her times, mounting a continuous crusade for Andrew Jackson's original promise and battling with his new advisors to keep the old man to his original perspective.

Mrs. Royall began her loyal opposition with her first pet peeve, the inordinate influence of Englishmen in American affairs, from bank board through publishing to the government offices. She stumped for the prerequisite of citizenship for service in government. It made no sense to her that a Joseph Nourse should sit in the United States Treasury for 50 years when he was not a citizen, and his son was the British naval captain who had assisted in the burning of Washington in the War of 1812.

Mrs. Royall was no jingoistic patriot, however. At the same time she excoriated English influence in government and business she still could approve of English commentary on American life if it rang true. She alone welcomed the Englishwoman, Mrs. Trollope, who, following in Mrs. Royall's own paths across the nation, demonstrated that Mrs. Royall was correct in most of her assumptions. Mrs. Trollope, like Mrs. Royall, had noted the tyranny of the priestly men over American women, and Mrs. Royall reprinted her writing for the American public to read. Mrs. Trollope had observed "the very satisfactory collections made by preachers for Bibles, tracts and other purposes" and she, like her predecessor, wondered what such collections had to do with the word of God.[18]

Mrs. Royall supported authors. Remembering her own experiences, she worked to publicize others. Dressing her paper with the latest in fiction and travel commentary, she kept her readers informed of the latest developments, including her close watch on Van Buren's "nobles" surrounding Andrew Jackson. It was a good thing she did; if she had not, she could have lost her original crusade against bank and blackcoat.

Martin Van Buren had to re-elect Andrew Jackson to move himself into place, but the New Yorker had a mania about opposition. He moved to dampen Jackson's crusade against the bank. To that end, rumors began that the President was favorable to giving up his original purpose and had softened his viewpoint about the bank and its activities. Martin Van Buren's friends worked overtime to trade opposition for position with Biddle as the election approached. The panic had quieted as the new Jackson banks took hold, and the new men about Jackson hid their overtures to Biddle in the assumption of public credit for the abatement of the financial squeeze. It appeared that Martin Van Buren and his pals would make their accommodation with Nicholas Biddle and his cohorts before the old Jacksonians knew what was happening.[19] Fate intervened once more, in the assertion of Biddle's own ego.

Nicholas Biddle was not a man to share power, not with Martin Van Buren, New York, or any other American group. He seized upon the sudden quiet and promoted it as the administration's weakness; he moved his own men into place in the Congress. Nicholas Biddle had decided to press the rechartering of his bank before Andrew Jackson was re-elected. Martin Van Buren had made promises, but Little Van's vows were not always kept. In a show of blatant money power, Nicholas Biddle sent his agents among the congressmen and openly bought that body in a well-publicized visitation of both bankmen and blackcoats upon the capital.[20] In so doing, he placed in Mrs. Royall's hands a club with which she could awaken Andrew Jackson from his five-month slumber, lulled by the false assurances of Edward Livingston, Colonel James Hamilton, and Martin Van Buren.

Life in Washington in 1831-1832 was far more simple than it is today. The President's house in that time was just another home, and people could drop in as they saw fit. It was unthinkable to deny a citizen the right to speak to the man who governed him, so those who wished to see Jackson generally did see him when the old man was up and around. If a person had the stature of Mrs. Royall, Andrew Jackson's door was open always. Nicholas Biddle's move on the Congress sent Mrs. Royall running to see Andrew Jackson.[21]

The President of the United States and his old friend had quite a talk. These two relics had a strange preoccupation with the American way. Both had lived through extraordinary times. The links of the bank and the Elyites were not imaginary events to either of them but dastardly cabals aimed at the nation. When these two got together, forgotten were the temperate arguments of the new thinkers and traders about them. Only Anne Royall could prompt Andrew Jackson to utter for posterity "You are a den of vipers and thieves. I have determined to rout you out! And by the Eternal, I will rout you out!"[22] This was said to a Philadelphia delegation of bankers and clergymen. "Den of vipers" indeed; these were the very words Mrs. Royall had written again and again to describe the strange alliance. The concept of conspiracy was ever on the minds of two people who had known many conspiracies, and the issues of the moment allowed no exception. If Andrew Jackson had lacked knowledge of Nicholas Biddle's latest actions before Mrs. Royall's visit, he did not afterward.

It was with great confidence that Mrs. Royall had announced to her subscribers that despite the public assurances of such as Edward Livingston, nothing would keep Andrew Jackson from vetoing any bank bill the "bought-and-paid-for Congress" would produce. If *Paul Pry* had lacked subscribers before, it did no longer. It was what the old Jacksonians wanted to hear, and both friend and foe read what Mrs. Royall had to say about the issue she had helped to originate. The woman who had started the bank war obviously knew the final disposition of it.

Andrew Jackson did not let his old friends down. He kept faith with his original followers despite his new advisors. When Andrew Jackson vetoed the bank, Mrs. Royall sat once again as the honored guest in the Senate chambers in the debates proceeding on the bank issue. Even such a pro-bank man as Henry Clay noted her presence. Thomas Hart Benton, complaining that the bank had stuffed the galleries with its supporters to howl down the bank opposition, drew this rejoinder from the man from Kentucky:

> The member ought not to be dissatisfied from the presence of those who are around them; for among them is a lady of great literary eminence.[23]

That lady was noted by the Senate recorder as "a noted female by name of Royall." Jackson's veto stood, and Martin Van Buren found himself tied to Mrs. Royall's bank position whether he and his friends liked it or not. He became Andrew Jackson's running mate, and the campaign was run on Mrs. Royall's issues of bank and blackcoat, confirmed by the emergence of the Anti-Masonic

Party with William Wirt as its standard bearer and Henry Clay's own spirited run for the old Federalists beginning to emerge as "new Republicans."[24] Andrew Jackson submerged them all. Wirt and Ellmaker and Clay and Sargeant went down to ignominious defeat before Jackson and Van Buren. The hickory poles had triumphed once again over the pulpits, the people over pious money. *Paul Pry* had scooped most of the nation's newspapers.

Mrs. Royall's role in this victory was enormous. The press of the nation was, in the main, against Jackson. It had been bought by Biddle with liberal loans. Mrs. Royall's old stalwarts in New York, Richmond, New Orleans, Cincinnati, and Pittsburgh had been wooed to open opposition to Jackson not only by Biddle's money, but by their fear of Martin Van Buren. Her small weekly, finding its way to the Masonic halls, the county seats, and the desks of state legislators and mayors carried the message that Jackson was still in control. When she proved correct, she was hailed for her feat, honored by it. Weekly newspapers sprang up in the countryside: *Anne Royall, Jr.* and *The Prying Eye* were sarcastic recreations to affront the Jackson opposition. Mrs. Royall was riding so high that the bankmen began to circulate rumors that she too had capitulated to them. If they couldn't have her one way, they would get her another, but Mrs. Royall put that record straight. "The United States Bank never had money enough to buy us up!"[25] Her steadfast position was in direct contrast to that of her good friend, Major Noah, who wailed in mortified defeat and sought her approval again:

We always looked to her as the source of our opinions — the individual who gave us the cue — the bugleman of the liberalists — the trumpeter of the anti-hypocrites.[26]

Major Noah didn't stop there:

In comparison with Mrs. Royall . . . Robert Walsh, Jr. was a mere school boy; Edward Everett, Domino Sampson; and Daniel Webster a mere country lawyer.[27]

It was fulsome praise from the man who led New York's newspaper fraternity. Edward Everett a "Domino Sampson"! That was Mrs. Royall's own jibe for a man who went whichever way he was pushed. Mrs. Royall had bested them all, and she accepted her friend's praise but never again did she shower applause upon him. Major Noah had sold out to Biddle, and that was inexcusable.

Mrs. Royall exulted as Jackson mounted his offensive against the bank. John Eaton was no longer in Washington directing, but his hand was still in the directives emanating from the old man. She watched the men congregating about Jackson, and as she did, she contributed more and more to the Jackson legend.

It was Mrs. Royall who, despairing at Jackson's constant bouts with Washington's swamp fever, suggested that if the government engineers did the work they were paid to do, filling in potholes and closing the festering canals, such fever would not attack the President and the other residents of Washington. That suggestion in print and arguments to the President himself resulted in action. The fetid pools of stagnant water were eliminated, and Mrs. Royall left her personal legacy in two words which forever characterize men who land government positions and do nothing, "no shows," and a concept which still finds it way to editorial pages: "laborers leaning on their shovels, not using them!"[28]

Mrs. Royall was the mistress of illustration. She could do with a few words what men could not do with a thousand high-flown phrases. The tariff question occasioned enormous debate in the Congress, but Mrs. Royall put all the issues in popular context with her own common sense. She introduced the picture of the housewife facing the problem of paying ever higher prices for necessities, a simple illumination for import taxes adopted forever afterward by the press. The public knew exactly where it stood when it read Mrs. Royall even when she championed the interests of American working men against foreign workers. She was a woman who knew how the ledger worked, and she used it well in propounding her views.

Mrs. Royall's greatest contribution was in the "nullification" crisis. As the threat to separate the South from the Union developed, Mrs. Royall recalled that it was a false issue raised up at the same time as the bank issue to confuse the nation. Resurrecting Richmond and the Virginia Constitutional Convention, Mrs. Royall reminded her subscribers that John Calhoun and his "nullification" was a red herring placed in the national stream to lead little black fish into a trap. The entire issue was the creation of "the manufacturing monopolist who, from a selfish desire of individual wealth, would see the United States sunk ten thousand fathoms under water provided he could heap up money," a strong allusion to the forces besetting Jackson. With these words, she characterized forever the Jacksonian Democrats' stance toward such threats.[29]

Andrew Jackson did not let Mrs. Royall down on any of the great issues. He handled the bank, the nullification crisis, and the Indian problem as she said he would. Martin Van Buren could not temper him one bit. Andrew Jackson expended himself completely in his second term carrying the burden more and more himself, but Mrs. Royall was there with phrase and encouragement. The nation accepted it, and Mrs. Royall's popularity rivaled Andrew Jackson's in their own time.

Andrew Jackson became the greatest American president to his generation, greater than the founding father, George Washington. The prominence of Jackson cannot be explained by the usual historical approach; it can be understood only when Mrs. Royall's premise about religion and bank, the strange alliance, and the dark shade both tried to bring down on the American spirit is accepted. Only through Mrs. Royall can the machinations of Nicholas Biddle, Martin Van Buren, John Calhoun, Henry Clay, William Wirt, Daniel Webster, John Quincy Adams, be divined. Posterity has to rely upon a woman writer to understand why and how the American people rallied to an old man, a general who became their idol.

Andrew Jackson was the darling of the nation not because he was an irascible old man, one with the people, but because he saved the United States from being engulfed by a medieval darkness which would have erased the American march towards enlightenment and development, a march which would take a whole world with it. There was in Mrs. Royall's time a conscious effort in the United States and abroad to hold Man in subjugation to a God who was all power and judgment, not love and compassion. There were religious and financial cliques that believed absolutely that Man should be a slave, held accountable for his beastly instincts, and not allowed an opportunity to develop Reason. There were men who wanted other men down on their knees, and those men were not southern slaveholders but men in black coats who played at being God, using his words to submerge their fellows. There was a church so brittle and so bombastic that it would justify any means to achieve civil authority, and that church was the Presbyterian Church as directed from Philadelphia. This institution was led by men who followed philosophies discarded by the country in which they had originated and now were bent on taking another country for their own. These men had been joined by aristocrats, men who despised democracy in any form and would pool their resources in one more valiant effort to promote their purpose. They had formed a potent compact: God and money. Their plan had been successful until exploded by one woman who made men who revered Reason listen.

The nation knew this in Mrs. Royall's time. A titanic battle had been mounted over the ideas put forth by the woman writer, but she had won. Mrs. Royall used men and Reason against her enemies and forced Americans to think for themselves. They too changed. The United States might have been submerged in the 1830s at the cost of all initiative, development, and invention. Like the other British colonies, it would have been held in total subjection. The likes of Ezra Stiles Ely, Lyman Beecher, Gardiner Springs, and Reverend Black not only wanted a nation, but they wanted women down on their knees serving men who had been cowed by their God and placed under the domination of their black cloth. It was poetic justice that such should be thwarted by a woman had been lifted from her knees by another kind of man, William Royall. The complicity of intelligent men like Nicholas Biddle, a man schooled in classic knowledge but interested only in extending his personal power, illustrated the continuing problem of the young nation. There were men who would appeal to the worst in other men, and Mrs. Royall was the reminder that at least one woman could reverse such evil.

Americans knew this in Mrs. Royall's days. Leading newspapers fought battles about her influence and her ability. She was a one-woman army, a promoter and recruiter for talent which she placed at the press's disposal. She introduced James Gordon Bennett, James G. Brooks, and Constans Daniel to national fame and Frank Blair to Washington. Mrs. Royall had found them all, touted their abilities to her friends, and visited them on American posterity. These men rode Mrs. Royall's pen to enlarge the journalism she had begun.

The Jackson administration, its policies, its issues, and even its confusion were its political reaction to the opinion presented by a woman with a forceful pen. Andrew Jackson recognized it, John Eaton used it, and Martin Van Buren rode it. If a history of the period would be true, it would have to be laid side by side with Mrs. Royall's writings, dated and crossdated, annotated with her places and people, and laced with her opinions and the Jacksonian reaction to them. There was a remarkable chain of cause and effect started by this woman and her travels, and what happened as Andrew Jackson sought to enlist the nation behind his policies. Only with Mrs. Royall can a historian record what happened in Andrew Jackson's times; then, and only then, can the corruption of events, the historical apology be erased. Andrew Jackson and the men about him are enigmas without Mrs. Royall.

Andrew Jackson is remembered as the darling of his people. Tales are told of how he bled for democracy and the underdog, but the proof of such an assessment is not recorded in history books. A deep silence obscures his first administration, and that shadow misinterprets his second. Mrs. Royall and her words can dispel all misconceptions; her religious history can reveal the true Andrew Jackson and why the nation still celebrates him.

Consider Andrew Jackson and his Indian position: the hero who expelled the first Americans from their lands, sent them forth to the uncharted wilderness. And Jackson's attitude in the Georgia Cherokee controversy, a mess sparked by Bible-toting missionaries spurring the Indian into raids against the nation. Those Bible-wielders were still leading the Indians when Jackson became president, not just in military raids but in raids on the U.S. Treasury. Who can understand Jackson's hard position against the Indians without Mrs. Royall in hand, her commentary about the blackcoats, their missionary influence and their strange affiliations? Andrew Jackson's policies were a general's reaction against a people used by enemies in a concealed but active war against the nation.

What about Jackson's war with the Bank of the United States, his deliberate promotion of crisis and panic? Was it a mistake from an untutored leader, or the reasonable strategy of a general destroying the supply lines of his enemy? Was it a personal vendetta between two men who would be king, as some have said, or the reaction of a patriot to a man who had sought to destroy the nation, to those who had announced they would dispense with the Constitution?

What about Andrew Jackson's infamous spoils system, his moves to replace office holders with his own men? Was it his desire to enjoy the spoils of victory at the expense of the nation, or the reasoned reaction of a military man removing the enemy from his general staff and the control of his supply lines from logistical position? Remember Joseph Nourse, George Watterston, poor Tobias Watkins, Mrs. Royall's complaints about the noncitizens who directed the nation's offices, the men allied to Biddle and Ely; remember Mrs. Royall's pen, not the malignant tongue of William Marcy, the errand boy for Martin Van Buren and New York bankers.[30]

What about Jackson's opposition to federal funds for public improvements, a large Navy, against a professional Army officer corps and West Point? Were these the policies of a man too preoccupied with paying off the national debt, or were they the beliefs of a man who knew where his enemies were, where the nation's enemies were? Remember Henry Clay and his plans for a Navy ignorant of defense and West Point brought to its knees. Recall federal funds spent not for the nation's good but for interest on bonds held by a bank which would exert pressure upon government to subvert the will of the people, and placed personnel in key positions to effect a takeover. In Jackson's time, the right of the people to direct their lives and elect their leaders was precious to men who had fought for that right, remembering when they had no such rights. Neither Andrew Jackson nor Mrs. Royall could suffer the elimination of those rights.

What about "nullification," that strange word which has so abused American history. What was it, what did it really mean? "Nullification" was not synonymous with state's rights, and Andrew Jackson knew it. Mrs. Royall tells us it meant nothing until read beside the Presbyterian credos promoted by Ely and his press and Biddle and his bank. John Calhoun cannot be understood until the Hartford Convention is remembered and the Sabbath controversy revealed again. Nullification was one more link in a chain which began with the closing down of a nation on Sunday in the midst of a war, in an explosion of divine rights against the rights of Man. What Connecticut and New England had threatened to do in 1812, John Calhoun and his South Carolinians promised to do in 1832: Divine right was to nullify the constitutional compact of free men in free states, and Andrew Jackson reacted to it as such. Jackson, shouting that he would hang John Calhoun "high as Hamen," has no real passion without Mrs. Royall on the Ely manifesto of July 4, 1827![31]

What about Jackson and slavery, the greatest of the new nation's troubles? Andrew Jackson did not recognize it as a question of free men versus slave; it was an issue promoted by British who had visited slavery upon North America, the Caribbean, and were now at it again. This time the blackcoats resurrected a dying institution to divide the nation, and it was known not just to Mrs. Royall. Andrew Jackson wrote to John Coffee on April 9, 1833:

> The nullifiers in the south intend to blow up a storm on the slavery question . . . be assured these men would do any act to destroy this union and form a southern confederacy.[32]

So Mrs. Royall had written in the Fall of 1829. Slavery could be no real issue to men and women who suffered some kind of bondage in 1830, and all suffered bondage then. Even as the North was in full cry against the South about it, Andrew Jackson could advise the new Republic of Texas:

Texas must claim California. The fishing interests of the North and East wish a harbor on the Pacific.[33]

Andrew Jackson knew what was at stake. Slavery in the South was no worse than seaman indenture in the North, and the real issue was control of the nation. The lash was applied equally to black and white backs, on farm and plantation, and at decks at sea. Mrs. Royall added that it was also for workers on looms and machines in New and Old England factories. In their times, there were always people down on their knees before masters; the problem was to get them on their feet.

And what about Andrew Jackson's religious beliefs, a source of great historical confusion? Andrew Jackson once had thought to be a minister in the Presbyterian Church but in later life refused to admit he held membership in it.[34] What was his passion? Andrew Jackson's sitting nine hours through the inquisition for heresy of Pastor Craighead, and sitting Sunday after Sunday with Peg Eaton in Rev. Campbell's church while he and she were vilified makes no sense without Mrs. Royall. Andrew Jackson's construction of a personal church for his wife and his pledge to "join the church," a promise made to her which he did not honor until he could wait no longer to do so, cannot be understood without Mrs. Royall. Andrew Jackson would not go down on his knees before a blackcoat.

What about Andrew Jackson and his friends, John and Peg Eaton, Major Lewis, Judge White, before and after his presidency? The woman writer makes sense where only nonsense has reigned so long.

The Age of Jackson was not only the work of a president and the men about him, but resulted from the determined actions of a strong-willed woman who found a truth and made men act upon it. It was her celebration in her own time and her obscurity in ours, for men hated to remember what she had made them do, and they had other men willing to pay them to express that hate.

The defeat of blackcoat and bank left a disillusioned army in disarray. God had not given them the United States, and one woman had taken all hope from them. Prayers were raised to the omnipotent to punish her, but while she lived, they could do nothing but appeal to their deity. Accordingly, as the real meaning of their loss engulfed them, anger was expressed against the men who had led them into debacle. Nicholas Biddle sat in his eagle's nest, insulated from them, and only one man was vulnerable to their passion. Ezra Stiles Ely was still on the pulpit but his exhortations were no longer attractive. Dr. Ely had led them astray, and for this he had to pay.

The religious fanatic is a deadly animal. Believing that God had made him and his kind all-powerful, he cannot admit of error or fault. When things go wrong, the fanatic disposes of all those associated with the failure, erases them from his record and his mind, lays the blame again on God, for the omnipotent punishes the wicked. This was to be the fate of Ezra Stiles Ely. He had acted to cause the destruction, and he was to be put away from them all. It was the beginning of a new blackcoat attack on posterity, for the man who had been involved with Mrs. Royall and Andrew Jackson, the one link to both, was to become an unknown, a man who had lived but whom no one remembered.

It was a carefully planned operation. By erasing Ely, all who knew him would be erased too. This man who had led the Presbyterian Church as moderator, who had established the Philadelphia headquarters of his sect, is not mentioned in any of his church's official histories.[35] That he did exist, they cannot deny, but he has been tucked away in rare book archives. Forgotten have been all the innovations and troubles he visited upon his people. No public mention is made of him except for a stained glass window in the Old Pine Street Church, which bears inexact years of his ministry, and a word still in our dictionaries— elyism, meaning great exhortation for money, preaching for profit. Just how Ely was kept from our view is fascinating.

The blackcoats did not do the deed themselves; they let a Biddle do it for them. A Biddle had given Ely to them and a Biddle could take him from them.36

Andrew Jackson did destroy Nicholas Biddle and his bank. The man lost everything, and bitterness flooded not only his soul, but everyone's about him. The wrath of such powerful men deposed is a great passion. A Biddle could not be made to pay, but Ely, the embarrassment, could; so the scheme was laid.

Biddle's laments to his family can be imagined. It was that fool Ely, his letters to Jackson, his prosecution of that heinous old woman, his concoction of the "common scold," his stupid revelation of the strange alliance they had enjoyed which had done them all in. Nicholas Biddle and his family had to have a scapegoat, and Ezra Stiles Ely was it.

A passion aroused was a passion inflamed. The Presbyterian leader had suffered nothing from the defeat of the Bank: he still held his pulpit, collected money, and went on preaching his coming dominion. The bank had failed, but he had not. The sight of Dr. Ely in the Old Pine Church was offensive to the Biddles. Ezra Stiles Ely had to go, be driven from Philadelphia, but how?

Dr. Ely had one great weakness. He loved power, and he whipped his congregation with it every Sunday as God's personal representative on earth. It was the key to his removal, and one Biddle, Nicholas' brother George, went to work to effect the family design.

The bank had one last great landholding, The Transylvania Company, a land speculation scheme on the western borders. A manager was needed to husband this great enterprise through its next period of development, which could be the beginning of a new nation on the American continent. The people on this land had been hand picked for their piety for two generations, were supported in Congress by Henry Clay and committed to his national aspirations, and all they lacked was a dynamic leader to take them to their destiny. Ezra Stiles Ely could be that leader. The good churchman had a new chance to lead forth a religious fraternity to power either as a new nation or as the support behind the man to be the next president of the United States. Andrew Jackson had refused Dr. Ely as his religious advisor; Henry Clay would welcome him. It was another challenge to American constitutional dominion, and Dr. Ely could not refuse it.

Transylvania became Ely's future and his promised kingdom. George Biddle laid the trap well. Millions of dollars in investments were involved, and Dr. Ely had to satisfy the business community with such a large financial position in the enterprise. The good churchman, despite his piety, would have to post a personal bond. Dr. Ely understood, but he did not have the cash required for the defeat of the bank had eliminated his control of funds. George Biddle reminded Ely that his own daughter, Harriet Ely, had a considerable estate from her maternal grandparents, and if Dr. Ely gave him the stewardship of that estate, he, George Biddle, would advance the money required to meet the bond. It would be a proper loan, and with Biddle administrating Harriet's estate, the security would be acceptable. Dr. Ely had nothing to fear; the Biddles were his very good friends.

Dr. Ely signed over the stewardship of his daughter's estate to George Biddle and, receiving his position with the Transylvania Company, began the long trek to Kentucky. Lingering along the way to visit with his fellow blackcoats,

George Duffield in Carlisle and Dr. Black in Pittsburgh, Dr. Ely was out of touch with Philadelphia. It was his mistake. One week after his departure, George Biddle sold out Harriet Ely's estate to meet the bond call from the man to whom he had sold Ely's loan paper. Dr. Ely did not learn of his misfortune until his arrival in Kentucky. Before he could do anything about it, the Transylvania Land Company was declared bankrupt, a result of legislation which deemed all such chartered land schemes null and void.

The confusion engendered by the bust of the Transylvania Company kept Ezra Stiles Ely in Kentucky and barely able to keep himself out of debtors' jail. It took a full year before he could raise enough personal money to get back to Philadelphia. Meanwhile, all his entreaties to the Biddles went unanswered and his personal troubles mounted with the death of his wife and the elopement of his daughter with a traveling salesman. At last, armed with the profits of back country preaching, Dr. Ely made it back to Philadelphia.

The City of Brotherly Love had precious little of it for Dr. Ely; so he camped on George Biddle's doorstep seeking an explanation of what had gone wrong. George Biddle had him arrested and charged with "common fame," the male equivalent of "common scold," the same infamous charge Dr. Ely had directed at Mrs. Royall. Ezra Stiles Ely stood ecclesiastical trial on this ancient curiosity and threw himself on the mercy of the sessions. Biddle then tossed him a bone. If he would behave himself, he could have the stewardship of the Old Swede's Church, a pulpit beset by Swedenborgian heresy. It was a precarious existence, but it was all Ely had left.

This is not the end of this curious tale. The man who invented the format for printed scandalmongering called "true story," and built his career on telling all about "fallen women" and his ministry for God to them, produced the greatest courtesan of her times. His daughter, Harriet, whose estate had been raided and eloped with the salesman, returned to Philadelphia as the infamous Mrs. Blackford, the woman who ran the fanciest bawdy house Philadelphia ever saw. She eventually took Europe as the illicit consort of the man designated to rule Russia but who never did because she ruined him.[37]

It took just five years for George Biddle to remove Ezra Stiles Ely from all public consideration. It was a masterful operation, and it set the means by which other men decided to remove Mrs. Royall from posterity.

Mrs. Royall was an established figure on the Washington scene. While Jackson was alive, she was unassailable. The great and the near great visited the woman writer constantly to make their presence and their aspirations known. Newcomers to the capital made her home their first stop. Men like Robert Owen, the great visionary, and the young Jefferson Davis, anyone with any pretension to national interest came to talk with the woman who was the public conscience of the country.[38] Mrs. Royall had contacts in every government office on the Hill, and any problem presented would bring forth immediate suggestion as to whom and how it could be processed for action. Mrs. Royall became more famous as the years passed.

The catalog of those who came and chatted with the writer covers most of the nineteenth century from the old boys who steered the nation through its first half to the new boys who would see it through its last half. For them all, Mrs. Royall had her lilting laughter, her wilting words, her quilled pen always tilting at the crooked windmills she saw on the horizon. Nothing escaped her, and she took a less partisan view than those who came to call. She had a constant stream of visitors for two decades, many of whom came with interesting propositions in hand for a woman whose fame they wanted to share.

The great showman, P.T. Barnum, was one who came to call.[39] As a young editor of the *Herald of Freedom*, a Connecticut weekly, he had begun correspondence with her in 1827. He, like Mrs. Royall and Andrew Jackson, hated the missionaries, for he knew the fanaticism of the blackcoats, had witnessed their Sabbatical activities against coastal defenses in 1812 to 1815, and had been prosecuted for attacking them in print.

The showman has left a personal reminiscence of his afternoon with Mrs. Royall. He wanted to sign her to a national lecture tour to discuss politics and history. Mrs. Royall would have none of it. She was done with traveling, and someone had to watch Washington while the rest of the nation played and worked. Young Barnum admitted that he supported Martin Van Buren, and Mrs. Royall hated Van Buren. That man would undo everything Andrew Jackson had done. She had a vague notion that "Matty" could well have a hand in Barnum's offer; it was too much like Biddle's from years before, and she would not leave the capital to such a man or for such a man. If she had thought about posterity, she might have accepted, but in January, 1836, Mrs. Royall had no interest in personal glory, only in opposition to men she had good reason to mistrust. P.T. Barnum was rebuffed by the writer, but he loved her still. Twenty years later, in his autobiography, he wrote about her with affection and wonder.

Mrs. Royall was enjoying a new kind of success when Barnum came to call. *Paul Pry* had been well received and was carrying her opinion and news into the nooks and crannies of the national mind, to the small newspapers and journals in every part of the nation. The bank war was behind her, the blackcoats had been forced to abandon their open assault on the Constitution, and even Congress had been reformed. Mrs. Royall's diatribes at the raunchy atmosphere of the private legislative club held on public property and the practice of selling congressional votes to the highest bidder had effected a congressional clean-up.[40] Mrs. Royall, cape flying, skirts rustling, lacing her arguments with her published words, had stirred constituents all over the nation to action. She had pioneered the elimination of debtors' prisons, the acceptance of the first labor unions to counter the capital pools of such as Biddle, was taking after the slavery of seamen, encouraging the beautification of Washington and other cities and countless other crusades. The nation was moving towards the total elimination of its problems, including the terrible issue of slavery.

The panic promoted by the bank in its dying struggle had abated. The double-dealers in the Jackson administration had been shoved aside by the obstinacy of Jackson himself. Mrs. Royall had weathered her own personal financial crisis, husbanded her few resources by living frugally and selling her books to her many visitors. Her editors had helped by paying her small sums for her sprightly comment from the nation's capital, and John Eaton and Daniel Carroll had presented her with her own home as a reward for her constancy to the masonic cause they both shared.[41] Sally Stackpool had joined her, and both enjoyed the small house and garden in the shadow of the Capitol dome. The Royall way was now the American way and *Paul Pry* kept a wary eye on Washington affairs, ever ready to mount another *exposé*.

One event continued to smolder. In March, 1833, just as Andrew Jackson had begun his final assault on the Bank of the United States, the United States Treasury building had burned to the ground, destroying the documents necessary to the planned investigation of the bank's affairs. The fire, at such an opportune time, punctuated a statement by Henry Clay that Biddle's bank was in fact the treasury of the United States and should be free from such examination.[42] It was a peculiar situation, and Mrs. Royall had her own ideas about it.

The Treasury fire was promoted by proponents of the bank as the reason for the Jackson administration to drag its heels on Jackson's own policy against the bank. This had incensed Mrs. Royall. Jackson had concluded an agreement with France which promised the repayment of long-standing reparations owed the

United States for French spoilations of American property and citizens on the high seas, payments which the President planned to use to relieve the financial crisis at home and abroad as he pressed his campaign against the bank. Seizing upon the Treasury's loss of its records by fire, the bank had encouraged the French government to withhold all payments to the United States to cover the bank's notes due French citizens. Then Biddle suspended payment on the dividends due the U.S. government itself from the bank stock it held as a public trust until the records had been "searched." The resulting uproar, this parading of the destruction of the Treasury records, had set back the Jackson attack for one full year. It was a topic for Mrs. Royall's pen.

Mrs. Royall pulled no punches. From the beginning she declared the fire was set and that Louis McLane had a hand in it, and when that gentleman was moved from the Treasury to the Department of State, Mrs. Royall was sure of it.[43] There was only one man left in the cabinet with whom Mrs. Royall could work. He was Postmaster General William Barry, and his chief clerk, Obadiah Brown, helped Mrs. Royall post her *Paul Prys* throughout the country.

Mrs. Royall's attack on Louis McLane and her inferences about the Treasury fire were unsettling to Martin Van Buren and his cohorts. William Barry's spirited defense of the writer and his support to Jackson to continue the bank war inflamed the cabinet, and the Treasury burning took an even more ominous direction. It was announced that post office contracts with mail carriers had been destroyed by the fire too. Martin Van Buren and his strange coterie spurred an army of contractors to take advantage of the situation, lodging claims against the post office which could not be checked. Postmaster Barry and his chief clerk, Parson Brown, held against these demands while Martin Van Buren and the rest of the cabinet demanded that they be met. The nation was treated to another Jackson cabinet controversy, this one more paralyzing than the Eaton affair. Mrs. Royall saw it for what it was:

> We said last year that from the conduct of the Secretary, Louis McLane, clerks and messengers, that the fire was no accident. It now turns out that copies of the Post Office contracts were burned up. There was a fireproof room in the department. Why were not all valuable papers kept in it?[44]

Mrs. Royall had put in print what the old Jacksonians had been thinking privately, and Martin Van Buren could tolerate her no longer, not with an election just a year away, not when he wished to succeed Jackson as president. The time had come to remove the power of this old woman, to rid the capital of her.

Martin Van Buren set out to take the Post Office Department from William Barry to solidify his control of the Jackson administration. Barry and his chief assistant, Obadiah Brown, were the last of the old Jacksonians with access to Andrew Jackson. The Van Burenites had formed an election unit among the other officeholders, and the Post Office was next to be organized for the Vice President and his designs. Accordingly, William Barry found himself assailed not by the anti-Jacksonians but by men he had thought to be his friends. Every cabinet meeting was an attack on him for not coping with the problems the Treasury fire had created. As the man tried to satisfy his cohorts, he was accused of allowing illegal payments to the very contractors presented to him by Martin Van Buren and associates. It was too much for a man to take, and William Barry did resign and was replaced immediately by Amos Kendall, now Martin Van Buren's chief lieutenant.[45]

Andrew Jackson was taken over by his new friends, who rewrote his policies to suit themselves. The President's annual message to Congress in 1834 incorporated a new idea, one which was repugnant to most of those who heard it. A "gag" was suggested against literature printed by abolitionists flooding the South with the intent to inflame the slave against his southern master.[46] The Post Office was the main distributor of any printed material in the nation and as such the mainstay of the blackcoat drive, even as it was for Mrs. Royall and her printed commentary. The religious presses had been turned loose to promote new division in the South, even as nullification was voided by Jackson's actions.

The blizzard of tracts and pamphlets attacking the South, were lurid and suggestive and not welcome in the slaveholding states. Complaints about the Post Office's distribution of these tracts poured in to the administration. Mrs. Royall echoed those complaints, but she favored an open attack on the licentiousness of the literature creating the problem, an open discussion of the facts, the kind of attack which had made her famous, but the new man with Jackson had other ideas. Martin Van Buren was politicking for his future and hiding behind Jackson's "words," he used the Congress to propose an unthinkable solution, then allowed the whole matter to drop. Amos Kendall, the new Postmaster General, was handed the problem.

The impetus for the proposed unconstitutional "gag" was to stop an antinational campaign before it disrupted the national unity with yet one more device. However, Amos Kendall did not use Van Buren's suggested "gag" against the abolitionist literature, he used his administrative power against Mrs. Royall and her *Paul Pry*. Henceforth, Mrs. Royall's weekly was not to be distributed by the Post Office. Beginning in July, 1835, through to Martin Van Buren's election in November, 1836, Mrs. Royall fought a running battle not with her old enemies but with Andrew Jackson's new friends and advisors.[47] As the Kendall "gag" cut deeply into her circulation, it also cut her effectiveness. Mrs. Royall found herself writing letters of explanation for the nondelivery of her publication to her friendly editors and subscribers, and even these letters did not reach their destination. It was too much for the old woman and she could not continue. Amos Kendall had killed *Paul Pry*, and she couldn't prove that he had raised his hand to do so. The mail contractors who had been used to depose William Barry were blamed again. She laid her *Paul Pry* to rest in her own characteristic way:

Always in the van of the editorial corps and attacking the enemies of the country in their strongholds, Paul Pry dragged them into the open day and pointed them out to the people. Paul Pry was the first to sound the alarm that there were traitors in the camp. It was the first to proclaim abandonment of Reform by General Jackson. It was the first to discover and challenge the organization of the officeholders as a party, at the 4th of July celebration in Pittsburgh and Brownsville in 1833. It was the first to discover and the first to challenge the Post Office frauds. It was the first that challenged the Indian Land frauds of the great land companies, and the perfidy of southern Jackson men in selling the country to Mr. Van Buren and his political intriguers, to conceal those frauds. Paul Pry was the first to put a stop to the enormous swindling of a knot of "god's people" as they impiously called themsevles. Millions of dollars were swallowed up by this concern . . . under the pretense of drawing money for corporation debts from Congress. Paul Pry was the first to trace these pious rogues to their den and drag them forth . . . to the light of day.
And it is to Paul Pry that the citizens of Washington are chiefly indebted for the last act of Congress in behalf of their Holland debt, by putting it out of the power of this pious B. to finger the cash. In return we are proud to acknowledge that the citizens of Washington have ever been the able, willing and untiring friends of Paul Pry. A thousand years of service of ten such papers rendered to such people could not nor would not repay them. The editress has only to say that if the people will do their

duty to themselves as faithfully as has been done by them all will yet be well. But let no man sleep at his post. Remember the office holders are desperate, wakeful and urgent![48]

This epitaph said it all. *Paul Pry* was buried forever on November 19, 1836. Two weeks later, on December 2, Mrs. Royall came back with her pen, and this time she called her new weekly *The Huntress*. The men about Jackson were no longer her friends, and she would hunt them out. If she could not use the U.S. mails, she would produce a "tip" sheet to tell the nation where its feet of clay were. Sally Stackpool joined her, and henceforth Mrs. Royall delivered her opinion with broadsides and handbills. Martin Van Buren and his associates could not stop her.

For 18 years, Mrs. Royall hunted down the facts and the wrongdoings, pressing them until they were rectified. Men came and went, and other women too, but still the old writer went on. Her spirit was tremendous, and as she was proved right again and again, people marveled at her determination and her perspicacity. Her pen was a sword to the very end. It made men and women sit up and take stock of what was happening. Her appearances in public always caused a stir, and her invasion of Congress's own premises was a signal for action to the very last. Mrs. Royall carried on in her Royall way until her eighty-fifth birthday and then quietly passed away. Congress memorialized her and her beloved Masons carried her in full regalia to the congressional cemetery. Her Episcopal friends read the service while her Catholic and Baptist friends garlanded her with flowers. Sally Stackpool closed *The Huntress* forever, the huntress being no longer.[49] Editors from every part of the nation noted that she had left them behind again, many with sincere grief and others with caustic glee. It was left to the important men in her life to celebrate her; men who had watched the nation respond to the challenges she had proposed, those who were the inheritors of her work. Not many of them did, for men do not celebrate women if they don't have to, and that is the most disturbing part of this history.

Mrs. Royall herself passed from sight, but her words and deeds went marching on. What if Mrs. Royall had not mounted her crusade against primitive religion, the blackcoats bent on national domination in 1829? What would the American future have been with Americans down on their knees before Ely's God? It was the important consideration in Mrs. Royall's day, for then science was beginning to shine its light to change the world. Mrs. Royall's successful fight against a vengeful God, her espousal of Reason and progress, placed her squarely with the proponents of the coming age—scientists!

Mrs. Royall had joined the New Age with her pleas to Congress to accept James Smithson's request to establish the Smithsonian Institution. As Mrs. Royall worked to achieve this national center for science, other scientists rallied to it, among them Arthur Vail and Henry Rogers. Robert Dale Owen had enlisted her in the crusade for this national pantheon to the inquiring mind, and, mindful of the crowded precincts of the patent office where the greatness of America's intelligence was allowed to gather dust unseen by American eyes, Mrs. Royall responded. This fight opened her eyes to invention and creation, the stuff of which the new world would be built.

Jedediah Morse, the clergyman turned geographer, was an old friend.[50] It was meet and correct that when his son, Samuel Finley Breese Morse came to Washington, he should call on Mrs. Royall. Liberalized by art but no scientist, he had an idea discovered in his travels. There was a strange force which seamen had discovered: wires wet with seawater would carry messages. Sam Morse had been experimenting with it, using the offices of his brother Sydney, editor of the *New York Observer*. He was ready to show it to the nation, but he needed funds from Congress to stretch the wire from Washington to Maryland for the ultimate test. Could Mrs. Royall help?

Young Morse was pious like his father, but redeemed by his genius. this was important to Mrs. Royall because Sydney, his brother, was a subservient employee of Colonel Stone, Mrs. Royall's long-time enemy. Perhaps she recalled how Jedediah Morse and his geography had been set aside by the blackcoats for an English import and wanted to insure that another Morse innovation should not be so treated.[51] In any event, she put aside her personal feelings to tramp the halls of Congress with Sam Morse, buttonholing her favorites, arguing for this new invention which could send news from Washington by electrical impulse in code.

It was a long promotion—seven years! Finally on May 24, 1844, in a small room in the Capitol, Morse's telegraph sat and Mrs. Royall stood by while he sent the first message from Washington to Baltimore: "What hath God wrought?" The crowd was entranced as the phrase was repeated and finally the answer came: "Mr. Rogers' respects to Mrs. Royall." Samuel Morse could thank God, but Henry Rogers knew who had done the footwork.[52]

"Respects to Mrs. Royall." It was a new image for the old writer. As the telegraph gained, so did another Royall campaign, this time for the Smithsonian. Robert Dale Owen got his bill into Congress with her help in 1845, and on May 1, 1847, Mrs. Royall attended the cornerstone laying of the great institution to promote science and progress in the United States. It was a thrilling moment for the woman who had promoted Reason all of her life. It was a turning point too.

"Respects to Mrs. Royall" had a new basis in fact. The old crusade against the blackcoats and the bank was over, and Mrs. Royall devoted her time to science and invention, art and literature. Her enemies mellowed. Finally in 1848, Mrs. Royall was voted the money she sought from Congress so long. An appreciative Washington, taking stock of the writer's contributions, finally forced the issue, and at 79 years of age, Mrs. Royall had arrived, respected by even some of her enemies. The Englishman, Edmund Burke, wrote of her: "No heroine in Billingsgate can go beyond the patriotic scolding of our Republican virago."[53] She would bask in the warmth of this acceptance until a new blackcoat crusade forced itself upon her.

It began with the publication of a series of new Bible tracts in Cincinnati, Ohio, written to inflame the nation by a member of a new generation of Bible spouters, Harriet Beecher Stowe, daughter of the blackcoat Lyman Beecher. These tales, from presses which had promoted Maria Monk and her lies about rape in the convents to spur anti-Catholicism to give birth to the Know Nothings, were lurid appeals directed against the South.[54] Mrs. Royall could remain silent no longer. She took on Mrs. Stowe and pegged her a latter-day tool of the Hartford Convention, an agent of her blackcoat father and brother, and of continuing the alien invasion and intrusion into American affairs. It was Mrs. Royall's last cause, and for two years she kept Mrs. Stowe and her blatant fiction where it belonged, in the churches sponsoring it, unable to promote it as "truth" to divide the nation once more.

It was Mrs. Royall who exposed that the Reverend Joel Parker, Presbyterian, had disavowed the letters which Mrs. Stowe claimed were the basis of her allegations in her articles published by the Bible tract groups. Newspapers followed Mrs. Royall's lead, and the *American Courier* attacked Mrs. Stowe "whose gross fabrications are now so widely abusing public confidence on this side of the Atlantic, and to a far greater extent on the other."[55] Mrs. Royall and her friends knew what the Beechers were up to; the old Sabbaticals, anti-constitutionalists, anti-Masons, and nullifiers were promoting lusty, lurid anti-Catholicism, and now abolition, all for the purpose of the destruction of the United

States and financed from London. It was a crusade to end all crusades, and Mrs. Royall intended to follow it despite her 80 years.

Harriet Beecher Stowe fled to London to escape the wrathful reason of old Mrs. Royall,56 but time ran out for America's conscience as she pursued this new fight. The woman who believed mightily in the great union of the American states, waging another valiant battle against the hatred pouring forth from the "God spouters" in one more attempt to destroy the United States of America, could not postpone death. As it came, she recognized it, and she wrote her own epitaph in a trembling hand for the last issue of her paper on July 2, 1854: "Our prayer is that the union of these states be eternal."57 As she wrote, she knew the forces of the blackness were massing to plunge the nation into a deliberate civil war, but she still believed in Reason.

Phineas T. Barnum clipped the notice of her obituary from a New York paper on October 5, 1854, and carried it with him thereafter as his own tribute to a woman he could not forget:

> Mrs. Anne Royall died at her residence in Washington on Sunday morning, October 1, 1854, at a very advanced age. She was the widow of a revolutionary officer, Colonel William Royall, and she published a newspaper in Washington for many years, first as "Paul Pry," which name was afterward changed to the "Huntress."58

Not a single mention of her books! But the *Washington Star* elaborated:

> Ever since the publication of the famous history of her peregrinations throughout the country, fighting the Presbyterians, she has made her residence here. For the last four or five years she has been out and about very little, owing to her increasing infirmities. When about however, her tongue went as before — always so as to attract a crowd of wonderers around her. Vehement and violent in her antipathies, and her expression of them, she was equally warm in her friendship of those she favored, through from her peculiar way of manifesting her likings, few, indeed, courted her affectionate regards. To the hour of her death she preserved all the peculiarities of thought, temper and manners which at one time rendered her so famous throughout the land.59

The obituary was read eagerly throughout the country, particularly by the Beechers and their new crew. The old woman was dead, and when the Civil War did come and the nation was split asunder, the new blackcoats took over the presses and the schools. When the South fell, all mention of Mrs. Royall and her crusades were systematically eliminated from any public consideration. Historians were funded to erase the years of her travail, and her name censored as a source. She was reduced to mention as "a writer of the period," or "a Washington paper," and as the new blackcoats celebrated the new British Victorian Age over the American Jacksonian Age and men's supremacy over women, Mrs. Royall was forgotten, conveniently stowed away in private collections.

Even her beloved Masons discarded her. After the crucible of their post-Civil War destruction at the hands of the blackcoats, they revived under strictures forced upon them. She was removed from their shelves too. History was rewritten to confuse the scholar, and what had been so plain and simple in Andrew Jackson's time became an enigma which made the man a mere shadow of what he had been. In Tennessee, Presbyterian ladies assisted by his own family moved into the Hermitage, and suddenly a new Jackson legend was created about the pious man who wore a black coat too. His letters and his papers were censored and edited until all mention of John and Peg Eaton and Mrs. Royall were deleted.[60] A total blackout occurred before the twentieth century.

Mystery has a way of presenting itself, even when it has been submerged. So it is with Mrs. Royall, she has returned to American history. As scholars assess the times in which she lived, precious relics of her writing surface to assail the conscience. Who was this woman who walked with so many greats, whose name once graced the pages of the nation's press? The answer comes in the remaining bits and pieces of discovered papers and journals. John Quincy Adams wrote these words in 1844:

> Mrs. Royall continues to make herself noxious to many persons, tolerated by some and feared by others, by her deportment and her books, treating all with a familiarity which often passes for impudence, insulting those who treat her with incivility, and then lampooning them in her books. Stripped of her sex's delicacy, but unable to forfeit its privilege of gentle treatment from the other, she goes about like a virago-errant in enchanted armor, and redeems herself from the cravings of indigence by the notoriety of her eccentricities and the forced currency they give to her publications.[61]

These words, from a man bested by the woman so described, would have made Mrs. Royall laugh, and we should too. Even as John Quincy Adams penned these notes in his diary, he had endorsed Mrs. Royall's petition for pension, her remuneration for assistance to the nation. To those exposed by Mrs. Royall, Adams's words give the perfect description of the art Mrs. Royall mastered and passed on to us—journalism.

Mrs. Royall disappeared from our national pantheon, our list of great contributors, in the aftermath of the religious crusade we call the Civil War. Her name put aside, her words went on marching. Bible belt, holy rollers, Elyism, moneygrubbers, and dens of vipers haunt those who pervert religion still, and the "Hoosier State" and "Jacksonian Democracy" ring at conventions yet. Even among her followers in the newsrooms, she is memorialized in anonymity, in the ribald "give them a royal screwing," an old newsroom direction which is a corruption of Mrs. Royall's promise to give the nation's enemies "a Royall skewering with my trusty steel pen." Her greatest memorial is her Washington imitators who still ride the Washington merry-go-round, even though they never use her name.

History is the art of redressing balances to expose truth and expunge lies. We have gained new perspectives about the Civil War, the reformation of our churches, and women in the American experiment, and we now wonder about banks and their role in our present economic crises. It is time to resurrect the woman who saw and told the truth, whose only crime was her ability to point us in those directions, and join with Henry Rogers in his reply to Samuel F.B. Morse. "What hath God wrought?"—"Respects to Mrs. Royall."

Chapter Notes

Chapter 1

1. A.N. Royall, *Sketches*, pp. 130-177; *Black Book III*, pp. 180, 217-218. Also W.B. Bryan, *History of National Capital II*, p. 63; from John Quincy Adams: "Everybody is a bird of passage from President down, and no one thinks of being at home there."
2. A.N. Royall, *Pennsylvania Travels II*, Appendix 1.
3. Ibid., pp. 21-24. Mrs. Royall states that Hannahstown was burnt in 1782. Also George D. Albert, *History of Westmoreland County*, 1882; John M. Boucher, same, 1906. Also *Pennsylvania Magazine of History and Biography*, 1877, p. 1-1. Also John F. Watson, *Annals of Philadelphia and Pennsylvania in the Olden Time*, 1850.
4. *World Almanac, 1973*. Official census—1830, p. 134.
5. Royall-Griffith, *Letters from Alabama*, pp. 18-19.
6. A.N. Royall, *Black Book I*, p. 223: "I am acquainted with seven nations of Indians. I was reared amongst them."
7. Marquis James, *Andrew Jackson*, pp. 488-489, 519-588.
8. Ibid., p. 861, footnote 46: "40 of Adams' eleventh-hour nominations were confirmed after Jackson's inauguration." Also L.D. White, *The Jacksonians*, pp. 15-25. Also John Quincy Adams' *Memoirs VIII*, p. 230, June 6, 1830. Also *Annals of America V*, p. 569; Thomas Cooper comments.
9. A.N. Royall, *Black Book III*, p. 183.
10. *The United States Telegraph* (Washington, D.C.), *The New York Inquirer*, *The Cincinnati Advertiser*, 1828.
11. Mrs. Royall lists over 100 editors by name and place with whom she maintained correspondence. *The National Intelligencer* (Washington, D.C.) January 19, 1829, acclaims Mrs. Royall for her correspondence with the nation's editors to establish the first nationwide distribution of activities in the capital. From this evidence, it appears that James Gordon Bennett appropriated to himself Mrs. Royall's innovation in his later memoirs.
12. Sarah Harvey Porter appends an incomplete list to her *Life and Times of Anne Royall*, 1909.
13. Note the frontispiece in every Royall work.
14. A.N. Royall, *Black Book III*, pp. 167-169.

Chapter 2

1. The Old Capitol, also known as the Brick Capital, served the Fourteenth and Fifteenth Congresses as a substitute meeting hall after the British burning of Washington in 1814. This building sat on land owned by the Carroll family. See full details in W.B. Bryan's *History of the National Capital II*.

2. *The Huntress*, December 16, 1843; *The New York Express*, March 4, 1843. Also A.N. Royall, *Black Book III*, p. 110.
3. Andrew Jackson left the Hermitage on January 18, 1829 (L.D. White, *The Jacksonians*), and planned to arrive in Washington on February 15, 1829 (Marquis James, *Andrew Jackson*, p. 487). He was met by John Eaton and escorted by his militia friends to Gadsby's, formerly O'Neal's.
4. The hatred of Rachel is part of the Jacksonian tale. Mrs. Royall noted it in her *Pennsylvania Travels II*, Appendix 19. Echoes can be found in Ezra Stiles Ely's *Discourse*, p. 31.
5. Mrs. Royall's successful attack on the blackcoats has been blunted by historical rewriters under the pseudonym "copperheads." Religious histories like Sydney E. Ahlstrom's *A Religious History of the American People* acknowledge it as "scattered explosions" with scattered exposition, but any reading of the journals and papers of the era substantiate Mrs. Royall's attacks in her *Black Books* and *Pennsylvania Travels*.
6. Holy roller was just one epithet Mrs. Royall tossed at the religious fanatics. See her fine rendition of a Tennessee revival in the *Annals of America V*.
7. Mrs. Royall was physically attacked by so-called "missionaries" many times in her career. This particular attack occurred on December 17, 1827, and she was unable to walk until June 1828. *Black Book I*, p. 247; Ibid., *III*, pp. 34-37.
8. A.N. Royall, *Black Book II*, p. 183.
9. A.N. Royall, *Pennsylvania Travels I*, p. 265.
10. A.N. Royall, *Black Book III*, pp. 121-157; *Pennsylvania Travels II*, Appendix 21.
11. Mrs. Royall acknowledges her debt to the Carrolls and Daniel and William Brent in all of her work.
12. A.N. Royall, *Pennsylvania Travels II*, Appendix 1.
13. A.P. Stokes, *Church and State in the United States*, II, p. 17.
14. Senator Johnson's speech, first reprinted in Mrs. Royall's *Black Book III*, pp. 230-34, is now included in such compendiums as Stokes above and *Annals of America V*, p. 284.
15. A.N. Royall, *Pennsylvania Travels II*, Appendix 2.
16. A.N. Royall, *Black Book III*, p. 203.
17. Ibid., p. 203.
18. Anglo-Saxon vulgarisms, including most of the four-letter words we hear today, were part of American speech in 1830. Until the advent of the blackcoats and their control of the presses of the nation and their later promotion of Noah Webster, Americans used pithy language. It is one reason why so much of early American reports about life have disappeared, burned under strict standards of religious morality, to shield past actions in American history.
19. A.N. Royall, *Pennsylvania Travels*, Appendix 1; *Black Books I, II, III*.
20. Mrs. Royall admired Thomas Benton. Even after *Black Book III*, p. 112, she heaped praise upon him.
21. Mrs. Royall hated Senator Chase, for he was one with those who had attacked her physically (*Black Book III*, p. 118).
22. Lewis Machen served as secretary to John Calhoun at this time (*Black Book III*, p. 120).

Chapter 3

1. Bessie R. James, *Anne Royall's USA*, p. 98. Also letter Royall/Matthew Carey, February 12, 1823.

2. Royall-Griffith, *Letters from Alabama*; "The date of her birth is accepted as 1769"; from Heber Blankenhorn in the *American Mercury*, Sept. 1927, p. 89: "June 11, 1769."

3. Mrs. Royall's own writing displays her humor, even in her recount of events through her trial. Critics used her levity against her later, citing her mockery as proof of her lack of ability. They claim she misused language citing *verbatim* reports of interviews. She reported in dialect, and compounded their bias by the usual devices used by those who seek to direct opinion against a subject.

4. A.N. Royall, *Sketches*, pp. 150-51, is favorable to the librarian, but by *Black Book II*, Mrs. Royall knows something is amiss, especially in note, p. 394. In *Black Book III*, she takes Watterston to task for everything (p. 217).

5. A.N. Royall, *Black Book II*, p. 394; *Pennsylvania Travels II*, p. 231. Also Watterston letter to Everett, January 26, 1829: "I have delivered to Mr. Coyle the Sunday School Books and as many Bibles and Testaments as he wanted agreeably to order of the Committee."

6. A.N. Royall, *Black Book III*, p. 210.

7. Ibid.

8. Ibid.

9. A.N. Royall, *Pennsylvania Travels*, p. 216, footnote.

10. Watterston letter to Everett, January 26, 1829. Everett, after recanting, is back in Mrs. R's graces: *Pennsylvania Travels II*, p. 136, footnote.

11. A.N. Royall, *Sketches*, pp. 200-201; *Pennsylvania Travels I*, p. 82: account of visit to William Duane. Ibid., p. 93, diatribe against British press control and booksellers aligned with it.

12. R.L. Wright, *Economic History of the United States*, p. 357. *Encyclopaedia Britannica*, "Printing."

13. A.N. Royall, *Black Book III*, p. 119; *Sketches*, pp. 264, 266, 383. See *Dictionary of American Biography* regarding each author. Also Ahlstrom, *A Religious History of the American People*, p. 598, and Warfel, H.R., *Noah Webster*; and Syndey Smith (Rev.), "Who Reads American Books?", 1820, reprinted in *Edinburgh Review*, January, 1830 (Boston), Vol. 23, pp. 78-80.

14. A.N. Royall, *Sketches*, pp. 20, 40; *Black Book I*, p. 251; *Letters to Alabama*, p. 33.

15. A.N. Royall, *Sketches*, pp. 20, 40.

Chapter 4

1. Bryan, *History of National Capital II*, pp. 77-78. One specific example of many cited throughout the book is that of William Lambert, English clerk in the Pension Office. In 1821 he was selected to determine the meridian of Washington, assisted by other Englishmen, clerks in government offices. This is a fact left out of all written exposition of Andrew Jackson's removals and needs historical investigation. How many American government offices were held by British citizens before and after the War of 1812?

2. A.N. Royall, *Black Book III*, p. 185. Machen, Senate clerk, cited as editor of the blackcoat paper, *The Chronicle*. Interesting fact: Bryan in *History of the National Capital* lists *The Chronicle* as the first Sunday publication, but puts it at the time of Lincoln's election and lists John W. Forney, secretary of the Senate as its owner. It appears this was a side occupation of the Senate clerks for some time to represent clerical opinion in the capital (pp. 463, 632).

Machen is referred to by Mrs. Royall as a "dishclout editor," referring to his influence with women rather than men, and in *Black Book III*, p. 197, she calls him "traitor." See also *Pennsylvania Travels II*, Appendix, and for Dunn, *Sketches*, p. 174.

3. *Cincinnati Advertiser*, October 11, 1828, reports receiving a certificate forwarded from Mr. Clarke, U.S. treasurer under J.Q. Adams, proving Adams to be a Presbyterian, said certificate signed by Thomas Handy, a clerk in Tobias Watkins' office. Just one month previous, the same paper, on September 13, 1828, ran an inquiry regarding Adams's adherence to Unitarianism. More to the point, one may read the *Encyclopaedia Britannica*, 11th ed., concerning Unitarianism and its strange relationship to Presbyterianism.

4. A.N. Royall, *Black Book III*, pp. 188-197; *Pennsylvania Travels II*, Appendix 22.

5. Ibid., pp. 120-121.

6. Bessie Rowland James in *Anne Royall's USA* has done the best tracking job on Mrs. Royall, Major Royall, and their antecedents. Also see *Virginia Magazine of History*, John Royall Harris's "The Colonial Royalls of Virginia," pp. XXXII and XXXIII.

7. B.R. James, *Anne Royall's USA*, pp. 116-117, also J.R. Harris, *Virginia Magazine of History*, XXXIII, p. 107; *Black Book III*, p. 215; *Letters from Alabama*, Appendix 118; *Pennsylvania Travels I*, p. 83. Letter from Lafayette to Duponceau (Desponso) of Philadelphia about Mrs. Royall (*Black Book I*, p. 150).

8. J.R. Harris, *Virginia Magazine of History*, XXXIII, p. 107; also Mrs. Royall's report of her travels to Camden, South Carolina, in *Southern Tour*.

9. B.R. James, *Anne Royall's USA*, p. 33.

10. Ibid., p. 33.

11. Ibid., p. 37. Pertinent certificates and claims in National Archives.

12. A.N. Royall, *Sketches*, pp. 168-69. Masons in full regalia were a regular feature of all celebrations and public events. Read papers of the period, including those of the inauguration of John Quincy Adams.

13. *A General History of Freemasonry*, edited by Rebold and Brennan, pp. 140-156. Masonic involvement with the evolution of the Age of Reason as the ruling doctrine for man began with the controversy between Jacques de Molai and Philip the Fair. Masons went underground with the overthrow of the Knights Templar, surfacing whenever Reason had a chance.

14. A.N. Royall, *Sketches*, p. 186. Marquis de Lafayette refused to stop at an inn called Waterloo.

15. A.N. Royall, *Black Book I*, pp. 312-13. Mrs. Royall attends a Masonic meeting. Important women have been closely allied to Masonic activity as in 1561, when Queen Elizabeth became Protectress of the Freemasons of her kingdom and confirmed Thomas Sackville as Grand Master (*General History of Freemasonry*, p. 241). Also J. Hugo Tarsch, *Transactions*, 1933, pp. I, 3: "Elizabeth Aldsworth received other ladies, masonic light in a lodge of masons" (p. 194). Also check Princess de Lamballe, Grandmistress of *La Maconnerie d'Adoption*, for information regarding a salon producing most of the women writers of the time, including Lady Morgan.

16. The renewal of papal admonition against Masonry in 1828, a clumsy attempt to dissuade the Irish from supporting Andrew Jackson, eventually led to the transfer of that Catholic Freemason, Father Mathews, to Philadelphia as bishop (*Pennsylvania Travels I*, pp. 63-64). The papal admonitions against the Masons began with Philip the Fair and allowed that French king to seize the properties of the Knights Templar from Jacques de Molai. Thereafter the Masons were allowed to rise and fall as the

church needed capital, a condition Charles Carroll and Mrs. Royall knew about.

17. A.N. Royall, *Pennsylvania Travels II*, p. 128; A.P. Stokes, *Church and States in the United States II*, pp. 20-25.

18. Augustus Buell, *History of Andrew Jackson II*, pp. 205-206. Also Stokes, *Church and States in the United States II*, p. 23.

19. A.N. Royall, *Sketches*, p. 174; "A man of light repute ran with such speed that the bushes took off the skirt of his coat" referred to Dunn in the Battle of Bladensburg. Also W.B. Bryan, *History of the National Capital*, p. 178: Dunn was involved with publishing unsuccessfully since 1816.

20. A.N. Royall, *Letters from Alabama*, January, 1818: Mrs. Royall renewed acquaintance with Jackson after anticipating his visit in three previous letters recounting his exploits.

21. B.R. James, *Anne Royall's USA*, pp. 58-60: Salt works. Also A.N. Royall, *Sketches*, p. 24; *Letters from Alabama*, pp. 44-47.

22. A.N. Royall, *Black Book III*, p. 126. Also R. Wright, *Anne Royall, Masonic Protagonist, Transactions*, 1933, pp. 1, 3.

23. A.N. Royall, *Black Book I*, pp. 78, 314: "Mr. Erskine aided me in my journey to the Atlantic states." *Pennsylvania Travels I*, p. 91: "True the Masons and the editors were my staunch friends."

24. A.N. Royall, *Letters from Alabama*, pp. 22-23. Also B.R. James, *Anne Royall's USA*, p. 39.

25. A.N. Royall, *Sketches*, p. 113; *Black Book I*, pp. 140-142. Ibid., *III*, p. 145.

26. A.N. Royall, *Letters from Alabama* were written to Matt Dunbar, lawyer-friend from Sweet Springs (*Pennsylvania Travels I*, p. 51).

27. Royall-Griffith, *Letters from Alabama*, p. 167. Lady Morgan is listed in the *Encyclopaedia Britannica*, 11th edition, as England's most prolific writer, friend to the French and Duke of Wellington, a close associate to important Masons of the period. Mrs. Royall salutes her in her letter of February 6, 1818.

28. Marchioness de Villette, confidante of Lady Morgan, was Voltaire's daughter (adopted), and together with Madame Denis, continued a literary salon promoted by a masonic group known as *La Maconnerie d'Adoption* (*General History of Freemasonry*, p. 241).

29. Royall-Griffith, *Letters from Alabama*, p. 167. *Seven Sermons* by Robert Russell was published in the 18th century, and Mrs. Royall was offered a 65th printing from a Philadelphia press (B.R. James, *Anne Royall's USA*, p. 87).

30. A.N. Royall, *Black Book I*, p. 141.

31. Matt Dunbar had the difficulty of cleaning up the legal problems left behind by Mrs. Royall, and he was fearful of possible new debts any new publishing venture might incur (B.R. James, *Anne Royall's USA*, p. 88).

32. A.N. Royall, *Black Book III*, p. 113: Mrs. Royall salutes Webster for his continued subscription. The great blackcoat knew whom to read to keep tabs on what was happening.

Chapter 5

1. Andrew Jackson's positions against the bank and federal money for internal improvements came with him to Washington, making him an inherent adversary to a Congress which was in favor of what he was against.

2. A.N. Royall, *Black Book III*, p. 120.

3. Ibid., p. 121, also *Sketches*, pp. 161-165. *Letters of Geo. Bancroft*, edited by M.A. Dewolfe Howe, pp. I, 197: "Talk of reform! The departments are full of the laziest clerks and men ever paid large salaries for neglecting the public business" (Dec. 27, 1831). This critic of the Jackson administration did not identify whose appointments are referred to but corroborates Mrs. Royall's complaints.

4. A.N. Royall, *Sketches*, p. 166.

5. Ibid., pp. 121-125.

6. Despite many historians' apologetic rewrites, there is damning evidence that H. Clay did design with J.Q. Adams (A. Buell, *A History of Andrew Jackson*, p. 177).

7. *Annals of America IV*. Introduction to #18 is an exposition of British Foreign Minister Canning's proposition to J.Q. Adams about joint action against intervention by the Holy Alliance in Western Hemisphere. The idea was for the U.S. to build a navy to relieve the British Navy of such responsibility. There are five pertinent selections in the *Annals of America IV*.

8. The Hartford Convention and the Essex Junto are covered well in "New England and the Union," *History of the Hartford Convention*, pp. 352-379. Mrs. Royall declares both are alive and well in the Presbyterian General Assembly (*Black Book I*, p. 228). Noah Webster served the Hartford Convention (*Pennsylvania Travels II*, p. 219).

9. A.N. Royall, *Sketches*, pp. 171-174. Clever recount of Battle of Bladensburg and the capital's reaction to it.

10. A.N. Royall, *Black Book III*, p. 138. Account of British anti-Jackson editors in Washington.

11. Ibid., p. 112. Favorable pen portrait of Daniel Webster. *Annals of America IV*, pp. 355-358. Webster frustrated defense in War of 1812, standing first against conscription (pp. 477-482), then representing the power of commitment to the King of England in the Dartmouth *vs* New Hampshire case.

12. A.N. Royall, *Sketches*, p. 240; *Black Book I*, p. 315; Ibid., *II*, pp. 126-131; Mrs. Royall defends the Adamses against charges of sour Puritans, Presbyterian bigots. Also Ibid., pp. *II*, 183: Mrs. Royall denies electioneering for Jackson.

13. A.N. Royall, *Black Book I*, p. 110; Ibid., *III*, p. 110: D. Brent gives Mrs. Royall lodging in the Bank house, formerly the Bell Tavern.

14. Colonel William Brent received his appointment as clerk of D.C. from J.Q. Adams; later became undersecretary of state under Jackson.

15. A.N. Royall, *Sketches*, pp. 169-170; pen portrait of Mrs. Adams. *Pennsylvania Travels I*, p. 90; relates circumstances of gift.

16. Jackson had first-hand knowledge of the Cherokee problem from his own encounters with them as one of 5,000 colonists in Tennessee against 20,000 Indians. A. Buell, *History of Andrew Jackson I*, p. 84.

17. A.N. Royall, *Sketches*, pp. 123, 163, 185. *Pennsylvania Travels II*, p. 146.

18. A.N. Royall, *Sketches*, p. 161; amusing footnote about Jackson and insolent treatment in government offices in his attempt to settle accounts after New Orleans.

19. A.N. Royall, *Black Book III*, p. 138; celebrates Congress for turning out Joseph Gale, Englishman, as its official printer. Also D.T. Lynch, *An Epoch and a Man*, pp. 330-331.

20. *Cincinnati Advertiser*, Sept. 6, 1829; letter from J.Q. Adams to Oliver Heartwell, Canandaigua, New York, April 19, 1828, in which Adams denies

masonic membership, side-by-side with copy of Henry Clay's 1822 address celebrating masonic fraternity of J.Q. Adams, Justice Marshall, and himself.

21. M. James, *Andrew Jackson*, p. 605. Also Rebold and Brennan, *General History of Freemasonry*, pp. 305, 332; on May 4, 1825, Jackson received Lafayette at the Grand Lodge at Nashville, Tennessee. Also, military lodges formed in Florida.

22. A.N. Royall, *Black Book III*, p. 194.

23. Ibid., *I*, p. 142; *II*, p. 11; Masons sponsored a theatre party for Mrs. Royall, netting her $400. Ibid., *II*, p. 111. Ibid., *III*, pp. 194-195. Also Ibid., *II*, p. 221: Charles Fox was Grand Master of Grand Lodge of Maine.

24. Ibid., *I*, pp. 35, 36, 44, 142-145, 148.

25. Ibid., *I*, pp. 312-314; ibid., *II*, p. 183.

26. A.N. Royall, *Sketches*, pp. 184-185.

27. *Sketches* was published in May, 1826 (B.R. James, *Anne Royall's USA*, p. 157).

28. *Sketches* debuted with anti-Masonry and went through three printings, launching Mrs. Royall on the national scene. This comprehensive American survey became so important that Mrs. Royall's enemies promoted imitations. Carey & Lea, her Philadelphia nemeses, in 1829 launched *Hall's Survey*, written by a British Navy officer.

Chapter 6

1. *Cincinnati Advertiser*, Aug. 2, 1828, reprints from *U.S. Telegraph*, announcement of *Farewell Supper*, a play by A. Royall.

2. A.N. Royall, *Black Book III*, p. 173.

3. A. Jackson ever after blamed H. Clay and J.Q. Adams for their dishonorable deal to frustrate American democracy.

4. J.Q. Adams, secretary of state to James Monroe, had full responsibility for Lafayette's *fete*.

5. J.Q. Adams's chief problems were the British blockage of American shipping in the Caribbean and damage claims against the French arising from depredations of Napoleon. M. James, *Andrew Jackson*, pp. 552, 681-683.

6. A.N. Royall, *Sketches*, pp. 175-178. *Black Book II*, pp. 344-345. *Pennsylvania Travels I*, p. 64, footnote.

7. W.E. Woodward, *Lafayette*, p. 426. W.B. Bryan, *History of the National Capital II*, p. 45 note, p. 60.

8. A. Levasseur, *Lafayette in America*, pp. 1, 173.

9. T.H. Benton, *Thirty Years in the U.S. Senate*, pp. 126-127.

10. C.F. Adams, *Memoirs of John Q. Adams VIII*, p. 546 (June 18, 1833), Adams called Jackson "a barbarian who could not write a sentence of grammar and hardly spell his own name," after Jackson had succeeded with Adams's failures.

11. A.N. Royall, *Pennsylvania Travels II*, p. 230.

12. A.N. Royall, *Black Book III*, pp. 176-177: Congress granted land to Lafayette which belonged to American Dr. E. Cooley which the famous Frenchman sold to an Englishman. Dr. Cooley, brother to Engineer Cooley of the famous Philadelphia Fairmount Waterworks, petitioned Congress for relief. Mrs. Royall despaired for him.

13. Ibid., *II*, p. 37: Liberal vs. orthodox missionaries. Also *Pennsylvania Travels I*, pp. 42-43; Ibid., *II*, pp. 150-163: Exposition on Pestolozzi Method.

14. A.N. Royall, *Black Book I*, pp. 240-243. Also *Annals of America IV*, p. 497: Robert Lee refers to Paper War.

15.   A.N. Royall, *Black Book I*, pp. 164, 210, 238. Ibid., *II*, p. 121: Lyman Beecher's congregation nothing but low-class women. Also *Pennsylvania Travels I*, p. 7.

16.   Mrs. Royall's opinions about the British-controlled press and booksellers find echo in an April 19, 1814 letter from Thomas Jefferson to N.G. Dufief of Philadelphia complaining about the censorship of books available. See *Annals of America IV*, p. 348. Also *Sketches*, pp. 199-200; *Black Book I*, p. 131; ibid., *II*, pp. 17-21; ibid., *III*, pp. 137-138, 172; *Pennsylvania Travels I*, pp. 6, 92-93. Also H.R. Warfel, *Noah Webster*, p. 386.

17.   A.N. Royall, *Black Book I*, p. 317; *Pennsylvania Travels I*, p. 82; ibid., *II*, p. 146 footnote.

18.   A.N. Royall, *Black Book I*, p. 317.

19.   Ibid., p. 317.

20.   Ibid., pp. 211-216. Also *Pennsylvania Travels I*: Congratulates Presbyterian Rev. Wilson and son "who abjure tracts and missionaries." Also ibid., *II*, pp, 83-87: American Tract Society document included.

21.   H. Blankenhorn, *Grandma of the Muckrakers*, American Mercury, Sept., 1927: "Bible Societies were blowing out of Scotland." Also E.C. Guillet, *The Great Migration*: "In 1822, 650,000 lbs (sterling) were raised to which Parliament had contributed 300,000 more to remove excess population to America" (*Pennsylvania Travels*, p. 238).

22.   *Encyclopaedia Britannica*, 11th edition. Also S.E. Ahlstrom, *Religious History of American People*, p. 92.

23.   E.C. Guillet, *The Great Migration*, p. 2: "In 1814 it was estimated that 10 persons emigrated to the U.S. for every one to the British Colonies." After the fall of Napoleon in 1824, Parliament made it legal for artisans to leave England.

Chapter 7

Heading for this chapter suggested by "She Was a Holy Terror," *Washington Post*, Feb. 22, 1891.

1.   A.N. Royall, *Black Book I*, p. 132.

2.   Andrew Jackson left a vitriolic testament to his resentment against his enemies Adams, Clay, and Calhoun in his letters and papers.

3.   H.O. Gibbons, *A History of Old Pine Street*.

4.   *Annals of America IV*, p. 288. Interesting comments on the Hartford Convention in the letter from Benjamin Watterhouse to J. Adams, July 8, 1811, discussing the northern confederation planned by Alexander Hamilton and George Cabot, leader of the Hartford Convention, to sever the New England States from the United States.

5.   A.N. Royall, *Pennsylvania Travels II*, pp. 85-88. Also J. Blau, "The Christian Party in Politics," *The Review of Religion*, p. 20. Also S. Ahlstrom, *Religious History of the American People*, p. 425: In 1814, New England Tract Society came into being with British financing. William Wilberforce, the man who was later to make slavery his life-long crusade, was the English contact for this group, which nine years later would become the American Tract Society.

6.   A.N. Royall, *Pennsylvania Travels I*, p. 89; *Black Book II*, p. 343: Mrs. Royall meets Hill and notes he heads Jackson party in his state.

7.   A.N. Royall, *Black Book I*; section on missionary organization begins p. 163. *Pennsylvania Travels I*, pp. 54-55. See eleventh edition, *Bible Society*, p. 907: First president of the American Society was Elias Boudinot, who figured so prominently in the Georgia-Cherokee affair.

8. A.N. Royall, *Black Book III*, p. 126; *Pennsylvania Travels I*, p. 79; *Pennsylvania Supreme Court Records*, Jan. 3, 1825, for Judge Ingersoll's opinion on cruel and inhuman punishment. Also L.D. White, *The Jacksonians*, p. 469 for Biddle letter of Feb. 11, 1832.
9. Sir E. Parry, *The Persecution of Mary Stewart*, pp. 27, 64-79. Also *Black Book I*, pp. 241-243.
10. B.R. James, *Anne Royall's USA*, p. 123.
11. James *vs* Commonwealth, Pa., Jan. 3, 1825, judgment reversed in favor of defendant found guilty Oct. 29, 1824. *Records: Pennsylvania Supreme Ct.*, Dec. 1824: Duponceau represented Mrs. James. "The error assigned was that this judgement is illegal." It is obvious that William Cranch had full knowledge of this when he was sitting in judgment on Mrs. Royall.
12. *Black Book I*, pp. 165, 210, 230 (Lyman Beecher). Also *Black Book I*, p. 226 and *Pennsylvania Travels I*, p. 59 (The Rev. Black—Pittsburgh); *Black Book I*, pp. 167, 214 (Col. Stone and Timothy Dwight); ibid., p. 240 (Rev. Spring).
13. B.R. James, *Anne Royall's USA*, p. 123. Also *Black Book I*, p. 177.
14. D.T. Lynch, *Epoch and the Man*, p. 315: Martin Van Buren utilized this fact.
15. A.N. Royall, *Black Book I*, pp. 155, 156, 158; ibid., *II*, p. 11. Also *Pennsylvania Travels I*, pp. 128, 229: "I suspect he had seen the hopes in the papers of my being Morgan in disguise." Ibid., *II*, p. 128.
16. Rebold & Brennan, *History of Freemasonry*, pp. 503-533. *Readers Encyclopedia*, Benet, 1948: "A good enough Morgan until after election," attributed to Thurlow Weed, p. 740.
17. A.N. Royall, *Black Book I*, p. 158; ibid., *II*, p. 12; *Pennsylvania Travels I*, pp. 144-145, footnote; A. Stokes, *Church and State in the United States II*, p. 23.
18. Ibid., p. 22.
19. A.N. Royall, *Black Book I*, pp. 12, 161.
20. A. Stokes, *Church and State in the United States II*, pp. 21-25.
21. A.N. Royall, *Black Book I*, pp. 229-234, 240-241; Ibid., *III*, p. 196: Ely sermon listed as published in the *Missionary Herald*. Also *Pennsylvania Travels I*, p. 89: Ely is attacked as traitor. Also Ely notes the attack in his *Discourse*, p. 6 (see below).
22. Ezra Stiles Ely, *The Duty of Christian Freemen to Elect Christian Rulers, A Discourse Delivered on the Fourth of July 1827*, p. 8.
23. Ibid., p. 11.
24. Ibid., p. 11.
25. Ibid., p. 11.

Chapter 8

1. A.N. Royall, *Black Book I*, p. 211; *Pennsylvania Travels II*, p. 237.
2. A.N. Royall, *Black Book I*, p. 163.
3. Ibid., p. 183.
4. Ibid., p. 132.
5. Ibid., p. 132.
6. Ibid., p. 163: Editor Stanbaugh led a continuing press crusade for Jackson. See J. Parton, *Life of Andrew Jackson*, pp. 300-302.
7. A.N. Royall, *Black Book I*, p. 164.
8. A.N. Royall, *Pennsylvania Travels II*, p. 133.
9. A.N. Royall, *Black Book I*, p. 238; Ibid., *III*, p. 103.

10. Ibid., p. 237.
11. Ibid., pp. 220-221.
12. Ibid., pp. 87, 135; ibid., *II*, pp. 27-29. Also L.D. White, *The Jacksonians*, p. 205.
13. A.N. Royall, *Black Book I*, p. 222. Also *Pennsylvania Travels I*, pp. 190-219.
14. A.N. Royall, *Black Book I*, pp. 163-247: Mrs. Royall's Pennsylvania Legislature appeal. Also, E.S. Ely, *Discourse*, p. 19.
15. A.N. Royall, *Black Book I*, p. 232; *Pennsylvania Travels*, p. 60: Senator Powell's stand against Ely. Also E.S. Ely, *Discourse*: "The following pages are respectfully inscribed to those members of the Senate of the State of Pennsylvania who in Feb. 1828, signalized themselves by refusing to grant an act of incorporation to The American Sunday School Union." Nicholas Biddle's name was on Ely's petition to the legislature.
16. A.N. Royall, *Black Book I*, p. 245.

Chapter 9

1. E.S. Ely, *Discourse*, p. 31: Ely admits Mrs. Jackson was reviled.
2. A. Stokes, *Church and State in the United States II*, pp. 22-23.
3. From Cromwell's time, the Irish, particularly the Catholics, had been subject to "extirpation" by Scotch Presbyterians.
4. A.N. Royall, *Pennsylvania Travels II*, pp. 245, 253, 257, 269.
5. Ibid., p. 245.
6. Ibid., *I*, p. 189; ibid., *II*, p. 268.
7. J. Parton, *Life of Andrew Jackson III*, p. 147; A. Buell, *History of Andrew Jackson II*, p. 184; M. James, *Andrew Jackson*, pp. 338-398. Also Gabriel Lowe, Jr., "J.H. Eaton, Jackson Campaign Manager," *Tennessee Historical Quarterly XI*, June 1952.
8. Richard Howell, governor of New Jersey 1792-1801, Federalist from *New Jersey Almanac*, 1964. *Dictionary of American Biography* states he was brother to Mrs. William O'Neal.
9. J. Parton, *Life of Andrew Jackson*, p. 184.
10. A. Buell, *History of Andrew Jackson*, pp. 225-232: "No other woman has ever exerted so great an influence on the political history . . . as Margaret Eaton."
11. M. James, *Andrew Jackson*, pp. 386-387.
12. A.S. Walker, "John H. Eaton—Apostate," *East Tennessee Historical Quarterly*: "In April 1828, near Smyrna, Greece, J.B. Timberlake died. The surgeon's report was 'pulmonary disease.' The Pursor's books showed a shortage of $20,000 but subsequent investigation by Amos Kendall revealed that the funds had been confused by Timberlake's successor" (p. 31). "Mr. Timberlake's account had been deprived through a series of shocking frauds of credits to the amount of $12,000 to $20,000 and that justly he was a creditor, not a debtor to the government" (p. 16). This tale of mutilated books, abstracts of accounts missing and inventory gone awry parallels the Watkins, Harris, Hamilton, and William Lawrence cases of the period. It appears the Bank of the United States was heavily involved in much of this chicanery. President Jackson thought so too, for he made mention of this in several messages to Congress.
13. M. James, *Andrew Jackson*, pp. 508-509; J. Parton, *The Life of Andrew Jackson III*, p. 185.
14. M. James, *Andrew Jackson*, pp. 432-433, and J. Parton, *The Life of An-*

drew Jackson III, p. 141; A. Buell, *History of Andrew Jackson*, p. 196; The first attack on Rachel Jackson began on her 1825 visit to the capital. "A grand debate ensued as to whether the ladies would visit her," from the letter of Mrs. Seaton quoted in A.H. Wharton's *Social Life in the Early Republic*, p. 199.

15. J. Parton, ibid., pp. 185-205; A. Buell, ibid., pp. 225-232; M. James, ibid., pp. 492, 516-519. The Eaton affair began with attacks on John Eaton.

16. M. Coit, *John C. Calhoun*, pp. 194, 200: Peg Eaton boasted that Floride Calhoun had called on her before Eaton's appointment, and she had Floride's card to prove it. M. James, *Andrew Jackson*, p. 495; inaugural ball saw all women in attendance without comment or friction.

17. Ibid., pp. 400-552; full exposition.

18. Ibid., p. 488.

19. L. Baker, *John Marshall*, pp. 650-651.

20. L. Durbin, *Inaugural Cavalcade*, p. 34.

21. Ibid., p. 34; M. James, op. cit., p. 493.

22. A. Buell, *History of Andrew Jackson II*, p. 207. Also J.D. Richardson, *Messages and Papers of the Presidents II*.

23. A. Schlesinger, *The Chief Executive*, p. 61.

24. Ibid., p. 62. T. Benton, *Thirty Years in the Senate*, I, p. 119. Historians chose to ignore Jackson's messages to Congress for some inexplicable reason.

25. Mrs. Samuel H. Smith, *Annals of America*, p. 288: Her account of the destruction of chairs of damask, gold spoons, etc., at the inauguration of Jackson. W.B. Bryan, *History of the National Capital II*, pp. 179-180: Tabulation of money expended by Adams for the White House, reports the congressional reluctance to appropriate more.

26. This is legend. Jackson ordered mainly American furnishings from Philadelphia or New Orleans but would tolerate French porcelain. See *The Magazine Antiques*, Sept. 1971 for story on Hermitage and furniture, pp. 413-417.

27. *Cincinnati Advertiser*, Sept. 8, 1827, reports on Adams's extravagances going back to his Russian mission expenses in 1808-1815. Also W.B. Bryan, *A History of the National Capital*, I, pp. 179-180.

28. L. Baker, *John Marshall*, p. 650.

29. J. Parton, *Life of Andrew Jackson III*, p. 167: Justice Story reflects on this.

30. Ibid., Mrs. S.H. Smith.

31. The refurnishing of the White House emphasized everything of American manufacture.

32. B.R. James, *Anne Royall's USA*, pp. 247-248.

33. A.N. Royall, *Black Book III*, pp. 114, 230-234, Appendix. See also *Annals of America IV* and *V*.

34. Ibid.

35. Ibid.

36. Ibid.

37. Ibid.; *Pennsylvania Travels I*, p. 85: Mrs. Royall quotes letter from Harrisburg, Pennsylvania declaring Richard Johnson's report to be equal to the Declaration of Independence.

Chapter 10

1. A.H. Wharton, *Social Life in the Early Republic*, pp. 240-241.

2. *Annals of America IV*, pp. 406-407: Alexander J. Dallas in a Dec. 24, 1815, letter to J.C. Calhoun, chairman of the committee on national currency, proposes the Second Bank of the United States. It became an actuality on April 10, 1816, and was the source of Calhoun's power.

3. President Andrew Jackson addressed himself to this problem and on December 8, 1829, in his first annual message said, "I consider it one of the most urgent of my duties to bring to your attention . . . that part of our constitution which relates to the election of the President and Vice-President . . . . to the people belongs the right of electing their chief magistrate: it was never designed that their choice should be defeated . . . . by the intervention of electoral colleges or by . . . . the House of Representatives." This call for reform was partially implemented.

4. John C. Calhoun represented the *status quo* while Jackson represented the people's demand for change. See M.L. Coit, *John C. Calhoun.*

5. A.N. Royall, *Black Book III*, pp. 111-112, pen portrait of Hugh White. James Parton, *Life of Andrew Jackson III*, pp. 176, 321: Jackson proposed Eaton first, but the friends of J.C. Calhoun made great efforts to prevent it (narrative of Major Lewis).

6. A.N. Royall, *Black Book III*, p. 160; *Pennsylvania Travels II*, p. 24: Colonel Towson, head of Christian Party in politics in the Army, under orders from Ely.

7. A. Schlesinger, *Age of Jackson*, p. 52.

8. J. Parton, *Life of Andrew Jackson*, pp. 178-179: William Barry supported Jackson in 1828 because he could not accept Clay's conduct in the presidential bargain in 1824.

9. A.N. Royall, *Southern Tour I*, pp. 35-38.

10. A.N. Royall, *Black Book II*, p. 394; *Pennsylvania Travels I*, p. 216.

11. A.N. Royall, *Sketches*, pp. 122-125; *Pennsylvania Travels I*, p. 80: Mrs. Royall visits Editor Binns. Ibid., p. 104, assesses Binns's role in election. Also M. James, *Andrew Jackson*, p. 468. A. Buell, *History of Andrew Jackson II*, p. 195: Footnote concerning Isaac Hill's counterattack.

12. Nicholas Biddle knew G. Watterson from earlier publishing association and had recommended him for appointment as the librarian to Congress.

13. J.T. Adams, *The March of Democracy*, p. 272. Also B.R. James, *Anne Royall's USA*, p. 305. Mrs. Royall gives the best exposition in her *Black Books*. Also Thomas Benton, *Thirty Years in the Senate I*, p. 198.

14. A.N. Royall, *Black Book I*, pp. 303-304.

15. Ibid.

16. J. Parton, *Life of Andrew Jackson III*, p. 321. Also M. James, *Andrew Jackson*, p. 491.

17. L.D. White, *The Jacksonians*, p. 191: Calhoun established the general staff. Also p. 199 (note); auditors given full control.

18. M. James, *Andrew Jackson*, pp. 144-150, 278-279; also J.D. Richardson, *Messages and Papers of the Presidents*, Vol. II, p. 439: Andrew Jackson replaced Adams's nominees for brevet rank in the Army with his own on March 11, 1829.

19. M. James, *Andrew Jackson*, pp. 278-279, 294, 297, 298, 301, 332.

20. L.D. White, *The Jacksonians*, pp. 189, 192.

21. Ibid.

22. A.N. Royall, *Sketches*, p. 375; *Black Book II*, p. 27. Also Thomas Benton's *Thirty Years in the Senate I*, all speeches and proceedings regarding West Point, the military academy.

23. B.R. James, *Anne Royall's USA*, p. 254.

24. M.L. Coit, *John Calhoun*, pp. 199-200: Tale of Jackson visit to Floride Calhoun concerning Peg Eaton.
25. Ibid., p. 23. *Pennsylvania Travels I*, p. 83.
26. A.N. Royall, *Black Book I*, pp. 99, 165-247.
27. M. James, *Andrew Jackson*; A. Buell, *History of Andrew Jackson*; and J. Parton, *Life of Andrew Jackson*.
28. *Dictionary of American Biography*.
29. A.N. Royall, *Pennsylvania Travels I*, p. 83; Ibid., *II*. Appendix 22.
30. M. James, *Andrew Jackson*, p. 513.
31. *Pennsylvania Travels*, Appendix 24.
32. B.R. James, *Anne Royall's USA*, p. 250. Also *Pennsylvania Travels I*, p. 216 footnote.
33. A.N. Royall, *Black Book III*, p. 134; *Letters from Alabama*, p. 190. George Kremer played a leading role in Jackson's presidential campaigns. See J. Parton and M. James.
34. A.N. Royall, *Black Book I*, p. 126: Pen portrait of John Eaton. *Black Book III*, p. 111 and *Letters from Alabama*, p. 190.
35. A. Buell, *History of Andrew Jackson*, p. 56: A. Jackson, March 15, 1767.
36. J. Parton, *Life of Andrew Jackson III*, pp. 135-136: Tale of Eaton's "corrupt" offer to Binns, but not one mention of Binns's association with coffin bills.
37. A.N. Royall, *Pennsylvania Travels I*, p. 239; ibid., *II*, pp. 191-192.

Chapter 11

1. Gabriel Lowe, Jr., "John H. Eaton, Jackson's Campaign Manager," *Tennessee Historical Quarterly*.
2. M.L. Coit, *John C. Calhoun*, pp. 69, 77, 81, 86.
3. Ibid., pp. 3-8.
4. *Annals of America IV*, pp. 406-407, 457-461: Exposition of Federalist stand.
5. Ibid.
6. M.L. Coit, *John C. Calhoun*, p. 6. Note: James Parton, *Life of Andrew Jackson I*, alludes to a possibility that A. Jackson as a child attended Waddell's Academy, and his fellow student was William Crawford.
7. M.L. Coit, *John C. Calhoun*, pp. 16-31. John Calhoun was taught by Timothy Dwight, father of the blackcoats.
8. Ibid., pp. 316-325.
9. J. Parton, *Life of Andrew Jackson III*, p. 288.
10. Eaton correspondence with A. Jackson Donelson.
11. W.E. Binkley, *American Political Parties*, pp. 120-151.
12. J. Parton, *Life of Andrew Jackson III*, pp. 185-186.
13. E.S. Ely, *Discourse*, pp. 31-32; A. Jackson's letters to E.S. Ely about Thomas Craighead and his heresy.
14. J. Parton, *Life of Andrew Jackson III*, p. 186.
15. M.L. Coit, *John C. Calhoun*, p. 199.
16. Ibid.
17. J. Parton, *Life of Andrew Jackson III*, p. 197. W.B. Bryan, *History of the National Capital II*, p. 183.
18. M. James, *Andrew Jackson*, p. 517.
19. Ibid., pp. 513-514.
20. A.N. Royall, *Sketches*, p. 166.
21. *Annals of America V*, p. 511. Moulton and Myers, *Against Appointing*

Chaplains to the Legislature. Calhoun supported chaplains for the national legislature.
22. A.N. Royall, *Black Book III*, p. 120.
23. Ibid., p. 121.

Chapter 12

1. A.N. Royall, *Black Book I*, p. 319; ibid., *II*, p. 141. Also T.H. Benton, *Thirty Years in the Senate*, p. 123. "Many of our finest ships were going to decay before they were finished, demanding repairs before they had sailed and costing millions for which there was no return."
2. L.D. White, *The Jacksonians*, pp. 215-250, 441; T.H. Benton, op. cit., p. 123; *Dictionary of American Biography*, Southard, p. 412: Navy increased on paper from 35 to 52 ships, but only 16 were on duty.
3. A.N. Royall, *Black Book III*, p. 215.
4. A.N. Royall, *Sketches*, p. 152: Pen portrait Tobias Watkins; *Black Book III*, pp. 164, 167; *Pennsylvania Travels II*, Appendix 8: "I foretold the swindling of Nourse and Watkins." Watkins came by his Washington position after serving as secretary to commissioners settling Spanish claims at Ghent.
5. M. James, *Andrew Jackson*, p. 501; Andrew Jackson letter to J.C. McLemore, April, 1829.
6. J. Parton, *Life of Andrew Jackson III*, pp. 168. Isaac Hill and Amos Kendall arrived in Washington in time for the inaugural.
7. W.B. Bryan, *History of the National Capitol I*, pp. 599-601.
8. L.D. White, *The Jacksonians*, pp. 307-310.
9. M. James, *Andrew Jackson*, p. 505.
10. Ibid., pp. 305-328, 518: Manuscript book contained correspondence between Ely and Jackson with reference to other comments.
11. J. Richardson, *Messages and Papers of the Presidents*, Vol. II, pp. 448-449, Dec. 8, 1829: position *vis-à-vis* corrupted and perverted in government service set forth strongly in Jackson's first annual message.
12. *Senate Document 73*, 21st Congress. Adams (J.Q.), *Memoirs, VIII*, p. 259 (Dec. 30, 1830).
13. *The Columbia Register* led the attack.
14. J. Parton, *Life of Andrew Jackson III*, pp. 183, 337: Jackson warned Francis Blair that his nephew, Andrew J. Donelson, was disloyal.
15. Hugh McGary was Jackson's cousin. From Irving Stone, *The President's Lady*, p. 105.
16. M. James, *Andrew Jackson*, p. 26; J. Parton, *The Life of Andrew Jackson I*, p. 89.
17. Royall-Griffith, *Letters from Alabama*, many references. *Sketches*, pp. 123-124.
18. *Black Book I*, p. 126: "Blackcoats" became the Jackson cry. See anecdote, M. James, *The Life of Andrew Jackson*, pp. 505-506. Also, by December, 1830, Andrew Jackson moved to end the pensions of Adams's Army holdovers. J.D. Richardson, *Messages, Vol. II*, p. 442.
19. Biddle Correspondence, pp. 53-54 (Sept. 22, 1828). It appears that the banker had a remarkable agreement about handling the bank's business with Asbury Dickens, chief clerk of the U.S. Treasury.
20. A. Schlesinger, *Age of Jackson*, p. 70.
21. A.N. Royall, *Black Book III*, pp. 164-169.
22. Ibid., p. 157.

23. Ibid., pp. 164-169.
24. Southard correspondence, *The American* (Baltimore), July 23, 31, 1829. Interesting plea to readers to contact "Mrs. T.H.W." *via* branch Bank of the United States, Washington, D.C.
25. A. Buell, *History of Andrew Jackson*, pp. 250-51; M. James, *Andrew Jackson*, p. 492.

Chapter 13

1. M. James, *Andrew Jackson*, p. 495.
2. *Dictionary of American Biography VIII*, p. 31. J.D. Richardson, *Messages and Papers of the Presidents, II*, p. 447. The exposition by Jackson in his first annual message should have aroused historical review about the Poinsett-Porter collaboration, particularly in the Watkins affair. Such mention does not make sense in any other context.
3. David Porter's involvement is mirrored in the attempt to assassinate him, and his later audience with Jackson, were reported in the papers of the day, including *The Chester (Pa.) Union* of May and August, 1829.
4. *Cincinnati Advertiser*, May 13, 1829: Announces Watkins's return to Philadelphia under arrest, by ship.
5. M. James, *The Life of Andrew Jackson*, p. 500: Watkins is a defaulter to the total of $7,000.
6. Mrs. Royall's work from the beginning of her *Black Books* through her *Southern Tour* is a condemnation of this alliance.
7. J. Parton, *Life of Andrew Jackson III*, p. 212.
8. L.B. White, *The Jacksonians*, pp. 441-479.
9. Ibid., p. 471.
10. M. James, *The Life of Andrew Jackson*, p. 562.
11. Ibid., p. 516; J. Parton, *Life of Andrew Jackson III*, pp. 192-193.
12. Andrew Jackson's correspondence: Letter to R.K. Call, May 18, 1829; to Francis Blair, Sept. 26, 1840.
13. A.N. Royall, *Black Book I*, p. 97; pen portrait.
14. B.R. James, *Anne Royall's USA*, p. 250.
15. Royall-Griffith, *Letters from Alabama*, pp. 182-224. Mrs. Royall refused a $2,000 bribe.

Chapter 14

1. The arrest and indictment of Hambleton in New York due to this.
2. It was not until the second administration of Andrew Jackson that the Federalists lost their control in the capital.
3. L.D. White, *The Jacksonians*, p. 433; Amos Kendall, *Autobiography*, p. 318-319.
4. J. Parton, *Life of Andrew Jackson III*, pp. 145, 150, 168, 182. A. Buell, *History of Andrew Jackson II*, pp. 208, 221.
5. A.N. Royall, *Black Book I*, p. 109: Mrs. Royall disliked Southard. *Black Book III*, p. 169. *American Dictionary of Biography* states Southard hated Andrew Jackson. Also letters in *The American* (Baltimore), July 23 and 31, 1829.
6. A.N. Royall, *Sketches*, p. 167. *Black Book I*, p. 109. R. Vexler, *Vice Presidents and Cabinet Members*: a full exposition of Southard's strange movements in and out of cabinet chairs. Each interim appointment al-

lowed Southard to juggle personnel and finances for the Bank of the United States.

7. J. Parton, *Life of Andrew Jackson III*, pp. 146, 260-61.
8. Ibid., pp. 221, 274-275. Also A. Buell, *History of Andrew Jackson II*, pp. 221-223.
9. J. Parton, *Life of Andrew Jackson III*, p. 182. Also A. Buell, ibid., pp. 210, 221-224: Hill fought these men and the Bank of the United States and when Webster, in his first big deal with Biddle, got the Portsmouth branch of the bank for his law partner, Jeremiah Mason, the Jackson stand against the Bank of the United States was set in concrete.
10. A.N. Royall, *Black Book II*, p. 348. Also A. Buell, *History of Andrew Jackson III*, p. 271: Hill referred in derision to his "missionary tour."
11. Richard Cutts was married to Anna Payne, sister to Dolly Madison. Old Dolly was not always the heroine, as is illustrated by the "John Gilpin" parody published after her flight from the White House in 1814:

> My sister Cutts and Cutts and I,
> And Cutts children three,
> Will fill the coach. So you must ride
> On horseback after we.

This is from F.T. Couper, *Rider's Washington*, p. 189. Nicholas Biddle's letter to Senator Levi Woodbury, cited by J. Parton, *Life of Andrew Jackson I*, p. 262, accused Cutts of defrauding the bank of upwards of $20,000, but Biddle allowed him to return to Washington as Auditor Lee's replacement (second controller of the treasury).

12. A.N. Royall, *Black Book III*, pp. 167-169. Mrs. Royall cites Cutts for having a den of missionaries.
13. J. Parton, *Life of Andrew Jackson*, pp. 56, 58, 260-261. Citizens and members of the New Hampshire legislature sent petitions to Washington alleging that small, safe loans to local businessmen were refused by the Bank of the United States while large, unsafe loans were made out of state.
14. Biddle spent one term in the Pennsylvania Legislature where his vote helped establish the bank's position. His previous service had been as secretary to ministers John Armstrong and James Monroe in Paris and London. Their main business was handling claims for and against the United States. This "service" earned him his appointment as head of the Bank of the United States.
15. J. Parton, *Life of Andrew Jackson*, pp. 260; ibid., *III*, p. 260.
16. Nicholas Biddle, letter to Alex Porter, June 14, 1834. M.L. Coit, *John C. Calhoun*, p. 261.
17. Ibid.
18. A.N. Royall, *Black Book III*, p. 134; pen portrait.
19. R.V. Remini, *Andrew Jackson and the Bank War*, p. 52; also J. Parton, *Life of Andrew Jackson III*, p. 175. Ingham was Calhoun's campaign manager in 1824 and in 1828.
20. J. Parton, ibid., p. 267.
21. M. James, *Andrew Jackson*, p. 498: Vice-President and President of the Senate Calhoun adjourned the august body on March 17, 1829, and Andrew Jackson was left with his interim men until December.
22. A. Buell, *History of Andrew Jackson*, p. 210.
23. J. Parton, *Life of Andrew Jackson III*, pp. 260-267.
24. Mrs. Ingham had marriageable daughters whom she wished to present to Washington society with the assistance of Floride Calhoun.
25. J. Parton, *Life of Andrew Jackson III*, p. 175.

26. Ibid., *III*, p. 303-309.
27. Ibid., *III*, p. 328.
28. N. Cousins, *In God We Trust*, p. 234: John Adams's letter to Thomas Jefferson, July 18, 1813, in which Adams recommends Ezra Stiles Ely's writing to his successor.
29. W.B. Bryan, *History of the National Capital II*, p. 181: J.Q. Adams not only joined the new Presbyterians but loaned money to build the new church.
30. John Quincy Adams stood for re-election to Congress after leaving the presidency to vote against Jackson's anti-bank legislation.

Chapter 15

1. Title registered March 9, 1829, with two volumes scheduled. Mrs. Royall registered her new work with the Library of Congress and visited George Watterston to do so.
2. A.N. Royall, *Pennsylvania Travels II*, Appendix, pp. 2-7.
3. A.N. Royall, *Black Book I*, pp. 241-242.
4. A.N. Royall, *Black Book III*, p. 183: account of the disorderly women who bothered Mrs. Royall and her visit to Magistrate Young. Also *Pennsylvania Travels II*, Appendix 5.
5. *Annals of America IV*, p. 49. Against the Alien and Sedition Act. Edward Livingston, ibid., p. 53.
6. Mrs. Royall portrays Webster in *Black Book II*, p. 327, ibid., *III*, p. 112; Wirt in *Sketches*, pp. 165-166; Southard in *Sketches*, p. 167 and *Black Book I*, p. 109. Ibid., *III*, p. 169. All three of these men served the Bank of the United States.
7. A.N. Royall, *Pennsylvania Travels II*, Appendix 7-8. Also *Memorial History of the City of Philadelphia*, 1895, p. 461: 40 percent of the stock of the Bank of the United States was held by religious and charitable organizations.
8. B.R. James, *Anne Royall's USA*, p. 123.

Chapter 16

1. J. Parton, *Life of Andrew Jackson III*, p. 293: from Major Lewis, "All through the summer and fall of 1829, General Jackson was in very feeble health and his friends were alarmed for his safety"; also p. 225, Jackson writes to John Donelson, "I have been ill since June 7, (1929)"; D.T. Lynch, *An Epoch and a Man*, p. 324, states that Jackson was ill from the end of March.
2. J. Parton, *Life of Andrew Jackson III*, p. 291. Van Buren knew the importance of the Eatons to Andrew Jackson.
3. "King" Jackson appeared in cartoons in Philadelphia in May, 1829, after the announcement of the capture of Tobias Watkins.
4. M. James, *Andrew Jackson*, p. 498: The kitchen cabinet was born when Calhoun adjourned the Senate, leaving Jackson with his appointees unconfirmed, suffering the *de facto* status of recess appointments only.
5. *Annals of America IV*, pp. 406-407, 457-461.
6. L.B. White, *The Jacksonians*, pp. 537-539. Calhoun, as secretary of war, established bureaus which became autonomous principalities.
7. Ibid., pp. 72-73: "Opposition to a Standing Army from Aurora," and pp.

112-113, "The Army and a Free Press." Also pp. 197-212, particularly p. 203 for Eaton's directives.

8. D.T. Lynch, *An Epoch and a Man*, pp. 331-335.
9. Unofficial protocol rules in this manner today in most capitals.
10. S. Ahlstrom, *A Religious History of the American People*, has a partial exposition concerning the Dutch East and West India companies and their total control of colonies, including New Amsterdam, later New York. Present-day holdings of the Dutch Reformed Church in America are intertwined with Crown properties.
11. *Encyclopaedia Britannica*, 11th edition, XIV.
12. D.T. Lynch, *An Epoch and a Man*, p. 335.
13. J. Parton, *Life of Andrew Jackson III*, p. 190; D.T. Lynch, *An Epoch and a Man*, p. 331.
14. D.T. Lynch, *An Epoch and a Man*, pp. 28, 158, 182.
15. Ibid., p. 344. This title came from Mordecai Noah, New York editor and publisher.
16. J. Parton, *Life of Andrew Jackson III*, p. 291; Thomas Benton, *Thirty Years in the U.S. Senate I*, pp. 128-130.
17. D.T. Lynch, *An Epoch and a Man*, pp. 333-335.
18. Ibid., p. 323.
19. Ibid., pp. 182-184, 247-249.
20. A.H. Wharton, *Social Life in the Early Republic*, p. 243. D.T. Lynch, *An Epoch and a Man*, pp. 332-333. Interesting fact: La Bellona was the name of a ship which occasioned the Supreme Court case, Gibbons *vs* Ogden, 1824.
21. The Dutch Reformed Church perforce maintains connections to Netherlands' royalty, and properties are still intermingled in tangled finances.
22. A.H. Wharton, *Social Life in the Early Republic*, p. 243; J. Parton, *Life of Andrew Jackson III*, p. 190; D.T. Lynch, *An Epoch and a Man*, p. 335.
23. J. Parton, *Life of Andrew Jackson III*, pp. 259-63 and others. Also W.B. Bryan, *History of National Capital II*, footnote p. 198: John S. Meehan appointed librarian May 29, 1829.
24. B.R. James, *Anne Royall's USA*, pp. 250, 252.
25. Ibid., p. 252.
26. *The National Intelligencer*, June 6, 1829.

Chapter 17

1. D.T. Lynch, *An Epoch and a Man*, pp. 327-329.
2. A.N. Royall, *Pennsylvania Travels II*, Appendix 6-8.
3. Ibid., Appendix 8-9.
4. A. Schlesinger, *Age of Jackson*, pp. 76-77, 80-82. Thomas Benton, *Thirty Years in the Senate I*, pp. 119 ff.
5. James *vs* The Commonwealth, Philadelphia, January 3, 1825. Compare page 229 of Pennsylvania Records to Cranch's written opinion. It is the same verbiage but not the same conclusion.
6. *Encyclopaedia Britannica*, 11th Edition, for exposition on John Knox and Thomas Cartwright and law.
7. Any dictionary will define scapegoat, and the definition fits Mrs. Royall's predicament.

Chapter 18

1. W.B. Bryan, *History of National Capital II*, p. 194. *Black Book III*, p. 171.

Harrison Smith succeeded Thomas Swann as Washington manager of the Bank of the United States.

2. A.N. Royall, *Black Book III*, p. 162: Mrs. Royall was favorable to Mc-Kinney here, she had not yet put two and two together but Towson and Calhoun against Eaton opened her eyes.

3. A.N. Royall, *Black Book I*, p. 62: Mrs. Royall castigates the missionaries for debauching Indians. Interesting fact is that Colonel Towson in his office with the War Department had charge of all government correspondence with and regarding Indians. Also J. Parton, *Life of Andrew Jackson I*, p. 623 and *III*, pp. 208, 315; L. Baker, *John Marshall*, p. 332: "missionaries and half-breeds had a direct financial interest in old Cherokee lands . . . alone prevented the mass of Indians from emigrating"; *Annals of America IV*: J.Q. Adams, December 2, 1828, Fourth Annual Message: ". . . and when we have had the rare good fortune of teaching them (Indians) the arts of civilization and the doctrine of Christianity, we have unexpectedly found them forming in the midst of ourselves communities claiming to be independent of ours and rivals of sovereignty within the territories of the members of our union." The Indian Bureau employed most of these missionaries.

4. A.N. Royall, *Black Book I*, pp. 184, 206. Mrs. Royall scores the missionaries for their Indian land grabs.

5. Ibid., *Black Book I*, p. 114; *Pennsylvania Travels II*, Appendix 12.

6. Indictment 118 is available from the National Archives, Record Group 21. Most writers on Mrs. Royall do not know that this previous indictment exists.

7. A.N. Royall, *Pennsylvania Travels II*, Appendix 8 and 11.

8. A.N. Royall, *Black Book I*, p. 127; J.K. Mahon, *War of 1812*, pp. 103-104.

9. A.N. Royall, *Pennsylvania Travels II*, Appendix 10.

10. Ibid., Appendix 5-6.

11. J. Parton, *Life of Andrew Jackson I*, pp. 265-294. A. Buell, *History of Andrew Jackson I*, p. 288 states that Swann inflamed Benton against Jackson, leading to that duel too.

12. J. Parton, *Life of Andrew Jackson I*, pp. 304-305.

13. A. Schlesinger, *Age of Jackson*, pp. 75-76. Biddle's letter to Swann (March 17, 1824) orders Swann to obey orders of the bank as against those of the government.

14. A.N. Royall, *Black Book III*, pp. 173-174.

15. Ibid., *I*, p. 108; ibid., *III*, pp. 154-155.

16. Ibid., *III*, p. 160.

17. J.Q. Adams, *Memoirs VIII*, p. 144 (April 25, 1829). L.D. White, *The Jacksonians*, p. 307.

18. A. Schlesinger, *Age of Jackson*, p. 147.

19. L.D. White, *The Jacksonians*, p. 19: Joseph Nourse removed by Jackson. The President promised to "soon clear out the Noursery" from A.H. Wharton, *Social Life in the Early Republic*, p. 106. Also, Jackson's first annual message, December 8, 1830.

20. A.N. Royall, *Black Book I*, p. 108.

21. A.N. Royall, *Pennsylvania Travels I*, p. 159: Mrs. Royall knows the workings of the pension office and offers to help someone else. L.D. White, *The Jacksonians*, pp. 535-536: clerks recommended those to receive pensions. This corroborates Mrs. Royall's attack on Nourse and the Pension Bureau.

22. A.N. Royall, *Black Book III*, p. 154.

23. Ibid., *III*, pp. 140, 154: Mrs. Royall levies charge of "treason." B.R.

James, *Anne Royall's USA*, pp. 499-500: defaulter for about $10,000.

24. W.B. Bryan, *History of National Capital II*, p. 76, says Nourse's public service began in 1779, and he was register of the treasury from 1789.
25. W. Lord, *By the Dawn's Early Light*, p. 53; J. Mahon, *War of 1812*, p. 291.
26. A.N. Royall, *Black Book I*, p. 108: attack on Lee; ibid., p. 109: takes after Southard and Henry Clay, his friend; ibid., *III*, pp. 140, 155, 159, 160.
27. B.R. James, *Anne Royall's USA*, p. 224. Mrs. Smith started the nasty stories about Mrs. Royall, who, however, did not return them in kind.
28. L.B. White, *The Jacksonians*, p. 92. Appointed by Madison in 1816. J. Parton, *Life of Andrew Jackson III*, gives McKinney's own narrative of his removal.
29. L.B. White, *The Jacksonians*, p. 92.
30. A. Stokes, *Church and State in the United States II*, pp. 22-23.
31. Attorney General William Wirt selected Swann for this "midnight" appointment by John Quincy Adams just as he had "recommended" him for the bank position.
32. William Cranch was a nephew to John Adams, first cousin to John Quincy Adams. A.H. Wharton, *Social Life in the Early Republic*, p. 69.
33. A.N. Royall, *Pennsylvania Travels II*, Appendix 9.
34. Sir Edward Parry, *The Persecution of Mary Stewart*, answers many enigmas here.
35. A.N. Royall, *Sketches*, pp. 179-181; *Black Book I*, pp. 113-116. There are many other references to Catholics throughout Mrs. Royall's work, all affirmative except for the Popes against masonry.
36. M.L. Coit, *John C. Calhoun*, p. 323: Floride Calhoun left Washington never to return "until it was free from the contaminations of Mrs. Eaton." She never returned.
37. J. Parton, *Life of Andrew Jackson III*, p. 196.
38. A.N. Royall, *Black Book III*, p. 144. Mrs. Royall called them gentlemen before their deal with the Bible societies. W.B. Bryan, *History of the National Capital I*, p. 517: description of the early printing office of Andrew and George Gideon; ibid., *II*, p. 214, Jacob Gideon.

Chapter 19

1. *The American*, Baltimore, July-Sept., 1829.
2. Dobbin, Murphy, and Bose were also publishers of the *Laws of the Union*, under their newspaper masthead.
3. *The American* (Baltimore) detailed the July 4 celebration despite the rain, and the parades were filled with masonic marchers. So did the *National Intelligencer* and *National Journal* as well as other papers of the period.
4. Historians have overlooked too long the financing involved in the Maysville Road project and what it meant to a good Jacksonian who didn't believe in the government guaranteeing such bonds for the Bank of the United States.
5. The Maysville Veto was a slap at the Bank of the United States. The Jackson position on selling off the public lands was also directed at the Bank of the United States since that institution had invested heavily in land companies holding millions of acres from public acquisition.
6. Publication of the Watkins case and the mention of the Southard correspondence flushed Southard from his New Jersey refuge, bringing him to Washington. *The American* (Baltimore), July 7, 1829.

283   *Chapter Notes—19, 20*

7. Public notice of contempt. *The American* reprinted this from the *Alexandria Gazette* since the *Baltimore Republican* was a competitor. It appears the *Republican* published first what Southard and Watkins said in their exchange of letters. The lapse in time for report, July 28, 1829, is understandable in this case.
8. A.N. Royall, *Black Book I*, p. 127; *Pennsylvania Travels II*, Appendix 11.
9. M. James, *Andrew Jackson*, p. 457.
10. H.O. Gibbons, *A History of Old Pine*; *The American* (Baltimore), July 11, 1829, also E.S. Ely, *Memoirs of His Own Life and Times*.
11. W. Lord, *The Dawn's Early Light*, pp. 27, 85, 86, 206.
12. A.N. Royall, *Black Book I*, pp. 184, 206.
13. Andrew Coyle was removed as chief post office clerk in July, 1829. Obadiah Brown was his replacement.
14. A. Stokes, *Church and State in the United States II*, p. 19. Amos Kendall, *Autobiography*, p. 288.
15. A.N. Royall, *Black Book III*, p. 214.
16. A.N. Royall, *Pennsylvania Travels II*, Appendix 11.
17. Ibid., *I*, p. 269.
18. Ibid.
19. Ibid.
20. Ibid.
21. Ibid.
22. Ibid.
23. Ibid.
24. A.N. Royall, *Pennsylvania Travels I*, pp. 265-269.

Chapter 20

1. *The American* (Baltimore), July 15, 1829, records Mrs. Royall's court appearance on Monday, July 13.
2. Ibid., July 13, 1829.
3. Ibid., July 13 and July 16, 1829: Purser Hambleton's N.Y. indictment set aside on grounds of statute of limitations.
4. A.N. Royall, *Pennsylvania Travels I*, pp. 190, 219; ibid., *II*, Appendix 7.
5. Ibid.
6. Ibid.
7. Ibid., Appendix 8.
8. Ibid., Appendix 22.
9. B.R. James, *Anne Royall's USA*, p. 255. A.N. Royall, *Pennsylvania Travels II*, Appendix 10.
10. Ibid.
11. English journals are given much acclaim but for real political results, a play, *Paul Pry* by John Poole, is still the bellwether for reform. Given its history and its intent, it is no wonder Mrs. Royall chose to use Poole's title as her masthead for her first newsletter.
12. *New York Commercial Advertiser*, July 6, 1829.
13. Ibid., July 31, 1829.
14. *National Intelligencer*, July 15, 1829.
15. Ibid.
16. Ibid.
17. Ibid., July 18, 1829.
18. *The American* (Baltimore), July 20, 1829.
19. Ibid., July 27, 1829, from the *Washington Telegraph* of Saturday, July 25, 1829.

20. *National Intelligencer*, July 28, 1829.
21. *The American* (Baltimore), July 20, 1829.
22. Ibid., August 26, 1829, reprinted from the *National Intelligencer* as a comment taking Mrs. Royall to task for spreading the fact of Jackson's illness.
23. A.N. Royall, *Pennsylvania Travels II*, Appendix 10. See comment on Cranch in William Carne, Columbia Historical Society Records, 1909, V, 299.
24. J.S. Voorhees, *Reports of Cases Civil & Criminal—District of Columbia*; W.B. Bryan, *History of National Capital II*, (223), John Coyle was Cranch's associate in Presbyterian Temperance Union. Also ibid., p. 217: Coyle with Southard in Howard Society an "aid" society for poor after 1829.
25. A.N. Royall, *Pennsylvania Travels II*, Appendix 10.
26. Ibid., Appendix 11.
27. Ibid.
28. Ibid.
29. Ibid., Appendix 12.
30. Ibid.
31. Ibid.
32. Ibid.
33. Ibid., Appendix 13.
34. Ibid.
35. Ibid., Appendix 14.
36. Ibid.
37. Ibid., Appendix 15.
38. Ibid.
39. Ibid.
40. Ibid., Appendix 16.
41. Ibid.
42. Ibid.
43. Ibid.
44. W.B. Bryan, *History of National Capital II*, pp. 436-437.
45. A.N. Royall, *Pennsylvania Travels II*, Appendix 17.
46. Ibid.
47. The fact that Mrs. Royall's first arrest was never publicized but her subsequent travail was proves her scapegoat position *vis-à-vis* the Watkins case.
48. A.N. Royall, *Pennsylvania Travels II*, Appendix 17: Mrs. Royall suggests that court reform is necessary. See echo in Andrew Jackson's first annual message during his complaint about the Hambleton case. (J.D. Richardson, *Messages II*, p. 454.) Also direct reference to Mrs. Royall's: "the peculiarities of many of the early laws of Maryland and Virginia remain in force, notwithstanding their repugnance . . . ."
49. A.N. Royall, *Pennsylvania Travels II*, Appendix 21.
50. A.N. Royall, *Sketches*, p. 172: Mrs. Royall says that Tingly "set fire to the Navy Yard himself, to save the British the trouble."

Chapter 21

1. L.D. White, *The Jacksonians*, pp. 215-250, 384. *Senate Documents*, 21st Congress, First Session, pp. 271-72, Nov. 30, 1829.
2. A.N. Royall, *Pennsylvania Travels II*, Appendix 10; also William Carne, *Life and Times of William Cranch*, p. 294. Thomas Jefferson confirmed this "midnight judge" appointment of John Adams. Interesting, since John Marshall was concerned because Cranch had ordered a libel suit

against the editor of a newspaper who had published a letter criticizing the federal courts (L. Baker, *John Marshall*, p. 373).

3. A.N. Royall, *Black Book III*, p. 214; M. James, *Andrew Jackson*, p. 498: McLean sought to protect "Adamsite" followers.

4. *National Intelligencer*, August 8, 1829.

5. A.N. Royall, *Pennsylvania Travels*, Appendix 10.

6. B.R. James, *Anne Royall's USA*, Introduction quotes John Hershey in the *New Yorker*. Also F.T. Cooper, *Rider's Washington*, p. 364.

7. M.L. Coit, *John C. Calhoun*, p. 23.

8. L. Baker, *John Marshall*, p. 80: enumerates huge quantities of land, title assumed by Marshall and his family and carefully skirts the "how."

9. A.N. Royall, *Pennsylvania Travels II*, Appendix 11; *The American* (Baltimore), Monday, July 27, 1829.

10. A.N. Royall, *Black Book III*, p. 171: Mrs. Royall gives pen portrait of Harrison Smith and likes his wife's novel; *Pennsylvania Travels II*, Appendix 11.

11. *Alexandria Gazette*, July 29, 1829.

12. *New York Commercial Advertiser*, Colonel Stone's paper, was against Mrs. Royall since 1827.

Chapter 22

1. See Washington newspapers of the time for letters of complaint about ruffians making merry with the crude copy of the Navy Yard contraption.

2. A.N. Royall, *Pennsylvania Travels II*, Appendix 21.

3. Ibid.; also District of Columbia *Court Records*, May Term 1829, Cranch.

4. A.N. Royall, *Pennsylvania Travels II*, Appendix 21.

5. D.C. *Court Records*, Cranch, p. 624.

6. Ibid.

7. Ibid.

8. Ibid., p. 625.

9. Ibid., p. 626.

10. Ibid.

11. Ibid.

12. Ibid., p. 627.

13. Ibid.

14. Ibid., p. 628; A.N. Royall, *Pennsylvania Travels II*, Appendix 20.

15. *National Intelligencer*, July 31, 1829.

16. A.N. Royall, *Pennsylvania Travels II*, Appendix 19.

17. Ibid., Appendix 20.

18. Ibid., Appendix 16-18, 20.

Chapter 23

1. *Annals of America IV*, pp. 53-61: Interesting section of Alien and Sedition Acts and Adams's opinions twenty years later.

2. A.N. Royall, *Pennsylvania Travels II*, Appendix 19.

3. Ibid., *I*, p. 218, footnote on p. 219; ibid., *II*, Appendix 22.

4. A.N. Royall, *Black Book III*, p. 119; H.R. Warfel, *Noah Webster*, p. 386: "Nothing now will be received or countenanced which is not British or sanctioned by British authority."

5. A.N. Royall, *Black Book II*, p. 119; H.R. Warfel, *Noah Webster*, p. 39:

"The growth of the British press (in America) pushed Webster's school books out of circulation and were continually attacked in print until he engaged Aaron Ely as his collaborator." Aaron Ely was Ezra Stiles Ely's brother.

6. A.N. Royall, *Black Book III*, p. 119. H.R. Warfel, *Noah Webster*, pp. 386-87: Webster admits his "sell-out" to British after his failure.
7. J. Parton, *Life of Andrew Jackson III*, pp. 180, 146: "Eaton, the circulating medium"; also Thomas Benton, *Thirty Years in the Senate*, pp. 128-129.
8. A.N. Royall, *Black Books I, II, III.*
9. A.N. Royall, *Black Book III*, p. 214: pen portrait.
10. A. Stokes, *Church and State in the United States*, p. 19: Obadiah Brown assisted Richard Johnson with the preparation of his famous message against the Sabbaticals with lines drawn from Mrs. Royall. It was he who arranged to "frank" her through on her travels.
11. M.L. Coit, *John C. Calhoun*, p. 184.
12. Ibid., p. 222-241.
13. Ibid., pp. 223-224: Joel Poinsett was the autocrat of Charleston's famed breakfast clubs.
14. A.N. Royall, *Black Book III*, 40.
15. There is much confusion about the several Brooks in New York publishing history, but Mordecai Noah hired Mrs. Royall's James Brooks. James Gordon Bennett got his editorship thanks to her too, but sought to deprecate her influence later on. Noah's praise of her gives the lie to Bennett.
16. A.N. Royall, *Black Book III*, p. 172.
17. *New York Commercial Advertiser*, July 6, 1829, and July 31, 1829.
18. B.R. James, *Anne Royall's USA*, p. 264; also J. Parton, *Life of Andrew Jackson III*.
19. B.R. James, *Anne Royall's USA*, p. 265.
20. Ibid.

Chapter 24

1. L. Baker, *John Marshall*, p. 767; B.R. James, *Anne Royall's USA*, pp. 265, 268; *Annals of America V*: Disestablishment was a campaign issue and went so far as to provoke outward warfare in Kentucky in 1827.
2. L. Baker, *John Marshall*, pp. 707-713. B.R. James, *Anne Royall's USA*, pp. 265-266.
3. B.R. James, *Anne Royall's USA*, p. 263; *Senate Document* 49, 23rd Congress, First Session: Tells of important persons given free transport by post office stage line contractors. January 22, 1834.
4. This was not only true in Richmond. There are many colonnaded "twins" in other cities too.
5. L. Baker, *John Marshall*, p. 707; B.R. James, *Anne Royall's USA*, pp. 265-269.
6. Ibid., pp. 266-67 (B.R. James).
7. Ibid., pp. 266-273.
8. *Virginia Historical Society Records*, 1854: "The Virginia Convention of 1829-1830."
9. L. Baker, *John Marshall*, p. 704.
10. Ibid., pp. 705, 714.
11. Ibid., p. 705.
12. Ibid., p. 705.

13. A.N. Royall, *Pennsylvania Travels II*, pp. 83-87. *The American* (Baltimore), July 8, 1829, recounts an interesting speech by James Barbour, American minister to London, castigating William Wilberforce for his misuse of statistics and his involvement in British Sunday schools in New England.

14. M.L. Coit, *John C. Calhoun*, pp. 308-309; Jackson denounced abolitionists as plotters of a civil war in a letter to Amos Kendall, August 9, 1835 (Jackson correspondence V, pp. 360-361).

15. L. Baker, *John Marshall*, p. 707: John Randolph on the Virginia Convention: "I go in mourning for the old constitution. I fear I have come to witness its death and burial." He didn't reckon on Mrs. Royall's appearance.

16. Ibid., p. 707.

17. A.N. Royall, *Southern Tour I*, p. 38.

18. Ibid.

19. Ibid.

20. Mrs. Royall had a particular interest in Chapman Johnson since he had been counsellor for the Roanes in the "legal" usurpation of her property and had taken her slaves as part of his fee. B.R. James, *Anne Royall's USA*, p. 70.

21. A.N. Royall, *Southern Tour I*, pp. 38-43.

22. Ibid.

23. Ibid.

24. John Calhoun did not return to Washington until just before the famous Jefferson Day dinner (April 13, 1830) when he went public with his conspiracy. The nullifiers were not disclosed by only the Webster-Haynes debate, but by the Virginia convention. The Civil War began here but was delayed by Andrew Jackson, with a major assist from Mrs. Royall.

25. *The American* (Baltimore), August 29, 1829.

26. J. Parton, *Life of Andrew Jackson III*, pp. 203-205.

Chapter 25

1. Thomas Benton, *Thirty Years in the Senate I*, pp. 121-124.

2. Ibid., p. 121.

3. M.L. Coit, *John C. Calhoun*, pp. 112-114.

4. Thomas Benton, *Thirty Years in the Senate I*, p. 122. Also J.D. Richardson, *Messages*.

5. Ibid.

6. Ibid., p. 123.

7. Ibid., p. 123.

8. Ibid., p. 123.

9. The pageantry of Masonic participation in all public events was a feature of all accounts at this period. As anti-Masonry grew, the brothers responded with more public display. Jackson, as a brother, became their leader while the backsliders deserted to Elyism.

10. B.R. James, *Anne Royall's USA*, pp. 294-308.

11. L.B. White, *The Jacksonians*, p. 468.

12. A.N. Royall, *Black Book I*, pp. 18-19: account of the Scioto Associates scandal; ibid., p. 324: Holland Land Co., part of Gennessee Lands, New York; *Pennsylvania Travels I*, p. 92: Mrs. Royall gives diatribe against Penn family and their land speculation.

13. M.L. Coit, *John C. Calhoun*, p. 262: "From August 1833 to January 1834, the Bank of the United States squeezed over $18,000,000 from a gasping public."

14. A.N. Royall, *Southern Tour I*, Appendix 10: "Crush the Monster."
15. M. James, *Andrew Jackson*, p. 602: Webster owed Biddle $20,000, took another $10,000. M.L. Coit, *John Marshall*, p. 261: over $110,000.
16. Schlesinger, *Age of Jackson*, p. 76 footnote: Letter from C.J. Ingersoll to Nicholas Biddle, February 2, 1832: Jackson "thinks there should be no currency but coin." Also Ingersoll's playing with Biddle caused a break in friendship with Mrs. Royall.
17. D.T. Lynch, *An Epoch and a Man*, pp. 336-345.
18. Wandell & Minnigerode, *Aaron Burr*, p. 306: Charles Biddle gave asylum to Burr after duel with Hamilton.
19. D.T. Lynch, *An Epoch and a Man*, pp. 313-330. Also numerous references in Parton and Coit.
20. J. Parton, *Life of Jackson III*, p. 322. D.T. Lynch, *John Marshall*, p. 336.
21. J. Parton, *Life of Jackson III*, pp. 324-330.
22. Thomas Benton, *Thirty Years in the Senate I*, pp. 130-131.
23. Ibid., pp. 121-734.
24. Ibid., pp. 131-143.
25. Ibid., pp. 131-143.
26. M.L. Coit, *John C. Calhoun*, p. 261: By Spring, 1841, Webster still owed Biddle $111,166. Letter from Nicholas Biddle to Alex Porter, June 14, 1834; also letters of Webster in New Hampshire Historical Society Collection.
27. M. James, *Andrew Jackson*, pp. 531, 540. The key here is Jackson's insertion of the word "federal."
28. Thomas Benton, *Thirty Years in the Senate*, p. 141.
29. A.N. Royall, *Southern Tour I*, Appendix 23-24.
30. Ibid.

Chapter 26

1. A.N. Royall, *Southern Tour I*, Appendix, pp. 58-77. B.R. James, *Anne Royall's USA*, pp. 270-271. Mrs. Royall, franked on Jackson's business, thought she took precedence over the Army.
2. A.N. Royall, *Southern Tour I*, pp. 86-92.
3. Ibid.
4. Ibid.
5. Ibid., pp. 116-118.
6. Ibid., pp. 120-121.
7. *Raleigh Star*, North Carolina, March 4, 1830.
8. A.N. Royall, *Southern Tour I*, pp. 223-225.
9. M.L. Coit, *John C. Calhoun*, p. 239.
10. B.R. James, *Anne Royall's USA*, p. 274.
11. Ibid., p. 275.
12. Ibid., p. 277; A.N. Royall, *Southern Tour I*, pp. 40-63.
13. *Camden Journal*, South Carolina, March 27, 1830.
14. A.N. Royall, *Sketches*, pp. 121-125: pen portrait of William Crawford. *Black Book I*, p. 236; *Southern Tour II*, pp. 58-78.
15. A.N. Royall, *Southern Tour II*, pp. 63-75.
16. *Augusta Chronicle and Advertiser* (Georgia), March 31, 1830.
17. B.R. James, *Anne Royall's USA*, p. 280.
18. The "pet" banks' new presidents and officers, and the men visited by Mrs. Royall are an insistent correlation calling out for a separate study.
19. A.N. Royall, *Southern Tour II*, p. 96.

20. B.R. James, *Anne Royall's USA*, p. 280.
21. Ibid., p. 281.
22. A.N. Royall, *Southern Tour III*, pp. 7-8, 47-48.
23. Ibid., pp. 57-73.
24. Ibid., pp. 47-48.
25. A. Buell, *History of Andrew Jackson II*, pp. 347-48: attributes White's apostasy to White's wife's abhorrence of Peg Eaton but White's son-in-law was the branch Bank of the United States manager sent to Jackson as an intermediary to try and temper his attitude. M. James, *Andrew Jackson*, pp. 677-694: says White first turned on Eaton and then accepted nomination against Van Buren.
26. A.N. Royall, *Southern Tour III*, pp. 130-136. *Dictionary of American Biography II*, p. 181.
27. A.N. Royall, *Southern Tour III*, pp. 130-136.
28. Ibid., p. 142: The similarity of Bible and gun boxes still infests our Western tales and novels.
29. L. Baker, *John Marshall*, pp. 731-746: Story (Joseph) and Boudinot again.
30. B.R. James, *Anne Royall's USA*, p. 292.
31. *Encyclopaedia Britannica*, 11th edition, Vol. III, p. 919: Nicholas Biddle prepared for the press from the explorers' own journals a history of the expedition under the command of Captains Lewis and Clark. He never finished the work, turning it over to another.
32. B.R. James, *Anne Royall's USA*, p. 292.
33. Ibid.
34. Ibid., p. 294.
35. Ezra S. Ely, *Discourse*, pp. 31-32: confirmation of the attack on Pastor Craighead. Thomas Benton, *Thirty Years in the Senate I*: Craighead's son joined White in opposing Jackson's bank policy; became an employee of the Bank of the United States.
36. B.R. James, *Anne Royall's USA*, p. 295.
37. A.N. Royall, *Southern Tour III*, p. 202.
38. Ibid., p. 203.
39. M. James, *The Life of Andrew Jackson*, pp. 565-566.
40. M.L. Coit, *John C. Calhoun*, pp. 336-341: Biddle's deal with Clay led to Calhoun's joining Van Buren against the Bank of the United States.
41. B.R. James, *Anne Royall's USA*, p. 296.
42. C.W. Wright, *Economic History of the United States*, p. 265: Huge blocks of land were held by the Ohio Company, the Scioto Company and the Symmes Company and attacked. Also *Encyclopedia Americana*, 16 (Kentucky), p. 369, exposition of Transylvania Company. Very interesting for further study since Clark has a connection to Biddle and Ely too.
43. Thomas Benton, *Thirty Years in the Senate*, pp. 129-130. Much confusion in poorly researched histories about Francis Blair. The Kentucky editor was recruited after Mrs. Royall's trip, and Obadiah Brown was the contact.
44. B.R. James, *Anne Royall's USA*, p. 298.
45. A.N. Royall, *Southern Tour III*, pp. 219-221, 236-237; B.R. James, *Anne Royall's USA*, p. 297.
46. A.N. Royall, *Southern Tour III*, pp. 230-235.
47. B.R. James, *Anne Royall's USA*, pp. 300-301.
48. Ibid.
49. Ibid., p. 297. Also A.N. Royall, *Southern Tour III*, pp. 223-225, 301.
50. A.N. Royall, *Southern Tour III*, p. 238.
51. Ibid., p. 240.
52. B.R. James, *Anne Royall's USA*, p. 305.

53. Ibid., p. 306; A.N. Royall, *Southern Tour III*, pp. 239-244.
54. A.N. Royall, *Pennsylvania Travels II*, pp. 125, 139-140; Holdship prints banknotes for the Bank of the United States. B.R. James, *Anne Royall's USA*, p. 307. A.N. Royall, *Southern Tour I*, Appendix 10.

Chapter 27

1. M.L. Coit, *John C. Calhoun*, p. 213; J. Parton, *Life of Andrew Jackson*, pp. 311-333: fascinating tale of skullduggery. Note that the "due time" for delivery of correspondence "covers" the trip of Mrs. Royall to William Crawford.
2. *The American* (Baltimore), July 31, 1829: The blackcoats have John Binns (coffin bills) giving a speech celebrating Catholics and the Emancipation of Ireland.
3. B.R. James, *Anne Royall's USA*, p. 311: James Watson Webb was an original supporter of Calhoun.
4. Ibid., pp. 341-345: ·Amusing account of the familiarity between James Gordon Bennett and Mrs. Royall. In her assessment of Mrs. Royall and journalism, Mrs. James relies too heavily on the latter-day Bennett.
5. William Van Ness was the connection between Livingston and Van Buren and Van Buren held a Damocles sword over Livingston: the misappropriation of $42,000 while mayor of New York which was not explained away until a much later date. D.T. Lynch, *An Epoch and a Man*, skims this.
6. New York City Records, New York Public Library.
7. Bank of the United States Records: Chevalier Huygens represented several foreign shareholders.
8. Chevalier Huygens was recalled July 1830. See State Department records.
9. A.N. Royall, *Black Book I*, pp. 11-12. Van Buren's bucktails had opposed Mrs. Royall because of her kind words for DeWitt Clinton in *Sketches*.
10. J. Parton, *Life of Andrew Jackson III*, p. 290.
11. Ibid., pp. 290-333.
12. Ibid., p. 303. On January 27, 1830, Richard Johnson called on Ingham at the U.S. Treasury; subject was Peg Eaton.
13. Ibid., p. 347: Eaton had agreed to help Van Buren; Jefferson Day dinner confrontation with Calhoun planned as of December, 1830. See John Eaton's letter.
14. Ibid., p. 346: Livingston's history begins a clean-up preparatory to taking over as secretary of state from Martin Van Buren. Van Buren's letter of resignation an artful masterpiece: his veiled references to Jackson's campaign pledge that no president would come from the cabinet can be misconstrued by blackcoat minds as his lack of countenance for the continuing Eaton affair. Many historians fell for this too.
15. B.R. James, *Mrs. Royall's USA*, pp. 252, 311.
16. S.H. Porter, *Life and Times of Anne Royall*: the inclusive dates of *Paul Pry* are December 3, 1831-November 19, 1836.
17. B.R. James, *Anne Royall's USA*, p. 314.
18. A.N. Royall, *Pennsylvania Travels II*, p. 174.
19. A.N. Royall, *Black Book I*, pp. 20, 42: Mrs. Royall notes that the bucktails are closely allied with the blackcoats.
20. M.L. Coit, *John C. Calhoun*, pp. 261-263.
21. Mrs. Royall was in the habit of calling on Andrew Jackson as evidenced in her many references in her correspondence with editors, particularly with Mordecai Noah. One pro-bank paper, the *Alexandria Phoenix*, states that

Mrs. Royall was a member and mentor of the kitchen cabinet. S.H. Porter, *Life and Times of Mrs. Royall*, Arno edition (1972), p. 165.

22. S.V. Henkels, Jr., *Andrew Jackson and the Bank of the United States*. A privately printed pamphlet in 1928 citing family records.

23. Thomas Benton, *Thirty Years in the U.S. Senate I*, p. 263: reporting on Henry Clay's remarks.

24. Martin Van Buren worked to transform Jacksonian Democracy into a new Federalism with New York financial circle's assistance. We suffer from it today.

25, 26. B.R. James, *Anne Royall's USA*, p. 316; A.H. Wharton, *Social Life in the Early Republic*, p. 290: "In 1836, when Mrs. Royall announced that *The Huntress* would be published every Saturday, she became the ancestress and forerunner in journalism of a long line of men and women who have since written of the sayings and doings of the people of their day."

27. B.R. James, *Anne Royall's USA*, pp. 318, 319: "The bank never had enough money to buy us up."

28. *Paul Pry*, February-December, 1832.

29. M.L. Coit, *John C. Calhoun*, p. 271; A.N. Royall, *Pennsylvania Travels II*, p. 186. W.B. Bryan, *History of the National Capital II*, pp. 82-86; L.B. White, *The Jacksonians*, p. 331. Adamsite friends were still trying to prevent court and law reform.

30. J. Parton, *Life of Andrew Jackson*, p. 220: Marcy's remarks have been misapplied to Jackson's removals by the usual blackcoat rewrite artists. Marcy spoke this phrase in defense of Van Buren's conduct, not Jackson's. (D.T. Lynch, *An Epoch and a Man*, p. 351.)

31. A.N. Royall, *Pennsylvania Travels I*, p. 83.

32. M. James, *The Life of Andrew Jackson*, pp. 603-604.

33. Ibid., p. 716.

34. E.S. Ely, *Discourse*, pp. 16, 17, 30, 32: prime examples of doublespeak.

35. There are few if any references to Ezra Stiles Ely in any public library, but the Presbyterian Historical Society, the child of his efforts, does maintain a rare book section where the scholar can meet the man face-to-face after a century and a half of neglect. It is located at 45 Lombard Street, Philadelphia, Pa.

36. B.R. James, *Anne Royall's USA*, p. 376, put Ely in exile in Missouri, but the records state that he went west for the Transylvania Company. He was marooned in that section for about two years, and there are references to his founding schools thereabouts. It is another field for investigation.

37. Kane and Leclerc, *The Scandalous Mrs. Blackford*. This book was found in the Presbyterian Historical Society.

38. B.R. James, *Anne Royall's USA*, pp. 365, 368: both excerpts from *The Huntress*, December 25, 1847.

39. *Barnum by Himself*, pp. 163-166.

40. *Paul Pry* and *The Huntress* initiated so many campaigns: from the removal of "toddy shops" in the Capitol's rotunda to the need for rules of deportment for members of our national legislature that a book should be written on those contributions alone.

41. After Mrs. Royall's death, the land where her gift house stood was deeded to the Congressional Library.

42. L.B. White, *The Jacksonians*, p. 546 and footnote; W.B. Bryan, *History of National Capital II*, p. 242. Also Andrew Jackson's fifth annual message.

43. B.R. James, *Anne Royall's USA*, p. 347.

44. *Paul Pry*, June 28, 1834; *The Huntress*, May 13, 1837, January 20 and November 3, 1838.

45. Thomas Benton, *Thirty Years in the Senate*, p. 181; B.R. James, *Anne Royall's USA*, pp. 326-327.
46. Andrew Jackson began the call for a halt to the blackcoat "incendiary" literature flooding the South calling the slaves to revolt in his message to the Twenty-Fourth (1835) Congress. Why historians have submerged this is one more avenue for study.
47. *The Huntress*, July, 1838: Mrs. Royall ran a running battle with her oppressor ever after this date.
48. B.R. James, *Anne Royall's USA*, p. 333.
49. Mrs. Royall did receive a recognition of sorts from the United States Congress. On her 80th birthday, she received her long-sought pension in a lump sum and before she could celebrate, her enemies were waiting. Royall's relatives claimed two-thirds of it for her "indebtedness." John Quincy Adams, the man who year after year "introduced" legislation for her, did not effect this; Abraham Lincoln, a little-known Congressman from Illinois, did. Sarah Harvey Porter wrote her history of Anne Royall in 1909 to raise funds for a proper marker for her grave in the congressional cemetery. It stands there now. It was erected in May, 1811. (W.B. Bryan, *A History of the U.S. Capital*, p. 233.)
50. A.N. Royall, *Sketches*, p. 118: Mrs. Royall takes Jedediah Morse to task for an error in "orthography," also pp. 120, 387-388.
51. *The Huntress*, January 11, 1845: Mrs. Royall continued to support Morse when the Bible societies dropped his geography for yet another British import. When his son could gain no hearing with Congress, she took on his crusade too.
52. *The Huntress*, February 22, 1845.
53. Burke's Correspondence, 1844.
54. A.N. Royall, *Black Book III*, p. 179: Mrs. Royall tagged the Beechers and kin as desirous of creating a civil war. She was no advocate of slavery (*Sketches*, p. 119), but she would not accept arguments from New England blackcoats who supported the total subjugation of seamen in foul ships and yet demanded "freedom for field hands" in the South.
55. R.L. Wright, *Forgotten Ladies*, pp. 129-186. Johanna Johnston, *Runaway to Heaven*; E. Wagenknecht, *Harriet Beecher Stowe*; Joseph C. Furnas, *Goodbye to Uncle Tom* do a good job on Mrs. Beecher's motives. Her own remarks in the Houghton-Mifflin Riverside Literature series, 1895, say it all. Mrs. Stowe's work is the Robert Russell *Sermons* of Mrs. Royall's day, with reprint after reprint selling lies as truth even now.
56. Ibid. All sources cited above.
57. *The Huntress*, July 24, 1854.
58. P.T. Barnum, *Barnum by Himself*, p. 166: "I cut the following slip from a New York paper on October 5, 1854." He wrote his book in 1855.
59. There were many obituaries, but they are yet to be collected.
60. Authors' opinion: The clumsy and fanciful rewrites of Jackson's last days appear in the same language and phrasing of all the blackcoat literature we read in the preparation of this book. Our research into the facts of Jackson's death have no beatific scenes from his deathbed. Andrew Jackson kept his vow to his wife and did rejoin the church, but even then he was not a constant churchgoer. The old general kept his character to the end.
61. John Quincy Adams, *Memoirs VII*, p. 321.

A Note on the *Black Books*

The *Black Books* could well have been a conscious design after the satire of Thomas Middleton, England, 1604. His was a prose satire on the vices and follies of his time. It was suggested by Nash's "Pierce Penniless." Mrs. Royall was a well-read woman thanks to Major Royall's extensive library. Her biographers to date have missed this fact.

Also, John Poore drew his "Paul Pry" from a living character, Thomas Hill, who was connected with the London press.

—Facts from the *Century Dictionary & Cyclopedia*, pp. 159, 787.

Bibliography

The following is a partial list of the documents, papers, and books read and perused to find Mrs. Royall in our nation's history. Here listed are those sources important to our story. The researcher who wishes to delve deeper is referred to the many bibliographies which attend any tome on the Jackson Era through the Civil War, which can be found in our great national libraries, particularly the Library of Congress and the New York Public Library.

Primary Sources (Mrs. Royall's own writings)

Sketches of History, Life and Manners in the United States. By a Traveller. 1826.
The Tennessean: A Novel Founded On Facts. 1827.
The Black Books: or Continuation of Travels in the United States, Volume One, 1828; *Volume Two,* 1828; *Volume Three,* 1829.
Mrs. Royall's Pennsylvania or Travels Continued in the United States, Volume One, 1829; *Volume Two,* 1829.
Letters From Alabama On Various Subjects: To Which Is Added, An Appendix, Containing Remarks on Sundry Members of Congress (20th and 21st) And Other High Characters At The Seat Of Government In One Volume. 1830.
Mrs. Royall's Southern Tour, Or Second Series Of The Black Book, In Three Or More Volumes. 1830-1831.
Various editions of *Paul Pry* and *The Huntress,* papers edited by Mrs. Royall.

Manuscript Sources

Freemasonry. State College Library, Pennsylvania.
Masonic Lodge Transactions. Madison, Bethesda, Helion #1, Huntsville, Alabama.
Revolutionary War Pensions (Applications). National Genealogical Society, Washington, D.C.
Sharpe correspondence. Archives of Maryland.
United States *vs.* Anne Royall, indictments and trial. National Archives Group 21, Washington, D.C.
Pamphlet: "An Interpretation of the Rev. Dr. E.S. Ely's Dream." Philadelphia, 1825.
Circuit Court of the U.S., Philadelphia. William Duane—Indictment for Sedition.
Pamphlet: "A Discourse Addressed to Religious People of All Denominations by a Pennsylvanian." Philadelphia, reprinted at Dover, Delaware, 1828. (J. Robertson)

Bennett, James Gordon. Papers, New York Public Library.
Noah, Mordecai. Biographical material not catalogued, New York Public Library.
Pennsylvania Legislative Records. February, 1828.
Presbyterian Patriots' Day: Historical Notes for Friends of Old Pine Street. Presbyterian Historical Society Library, Philadelphia.
Register of Debates, 21st and 23rd Congresses.
U.S. Senate Documents, 21st-26th. 1829-1834.
Watterston, George. Papers: 1815-35. Manuscript Division, Congressional Library.

Printed Sources

America: Great Crises in Our History Told by Its Makers. Veterans of Foreign Wars, 1925.
Annals of America. Encyclopaedia Britannica, 1968.
Dictionary of American Biography. Chas. Scribners, 1937.
Messages and Papers of the Presidents. Edited by James Richardson, Bureau of National Literature/Art, 1904.
Memorial History of the City of Philadelphia. New York Historical Co., 1895.
New Jersey Almanac. Trenton Times, 1963.
The Encyclopaedia Britannica, Encyclopedia Americana and *Harpers Encyclopedia.*

Periodicals and Newspapers

Alexandria Gazette, Virginia, 1829.
American and Commercial Advertiser (in text referred to as *American*), Baltimore, Maryland, 1829.
Augusta Chronicle and Advertiser, Georgia, 1830.
Boston Poste, Massachusetts, 1833.
Camden Journal, South Carolina, 1830.
Chester Union, Pennsylvania, 1829.
Cincinnati Advertiser, Ohio, 1828.
Columbia Register, Washington, D.C., 1829-30.
National Intelligencer, Washington, D.C., 1928-30.
New York Commercial Advertiser, 1829.
New York Enquirer, 1827-1829.
Niles Register, Washington, D.C., 1840.
Raleigh Star, North Carolina, 1830.
The Sun, Baltimore, Maryland, 1931.
Washington Post, D.C., 1891.
Washington Star, D.C. (evening), 1854.
Washington Telegraph, D.C., 1829.
Bulletin of the Essex Institute: Account of newspapers and other periodicals published in Salem, Massachusetts, 1856. (Massachusetts)
American Historical Magazine, Essex Inst., Mass.
American Magazine, Boston, Bewick Co., 1835.
American Mercury, 1927.
American Quarterly Review, 1832.
Columbia Historical Society, Records, 1902, 1907, 1919, Washington, D.C.

Edinburgh Review, Boston, 1830.
Freemason's Monthly, 1854.
New Age, 1911.
Masonic Mirror, Boston, 1931.
Pennsylvania Magazine of History and Biography, 1951.
The Magazine Antiques, Sept., 1971.
The Review of Religion, Columbia University, 1946.
Tennessee Historical Quarterly, 1952.
Transactions. American Lodge of Research, N.Y., 1933.
Virginia Magazine of History, 1901, 1924.
Western Pennsylvania Historical Magazine, 1962.

Books

Adams, John Quincy. *Memoirs.* Edited by C.F. Adams. 1877.
Adams, James Truslow. *The March of Democracy. The Adams Family.*
    1930.
Adams, Samuel Hopkins. *The Gorgeous Hussy.* 1934.
Ahlstrom, Sydney E. *A Religious History of the American People.* 1972.
Ammon, Harry. *James Monroe.* 1971.
Baker, Leonard. *John Marshall.* 1974.
Balcomb, Frank. *Masonry, Royal Arch, Salem and Vicinity.* 1867.
Barnum, Phineas T. *Life of P.T. Barnum Written by Himself.* 1855.
Barrows, John Henry. *The World's Parliament of Religions.* 1893.
Bassett, John Spencer. *Andrew Jackson: Correspondence.* 1926.
Bemis, Paul Flagg. *John Quincy Adams.* 1949.
Bennett, James Gordon. *Memoirs.* 1855.
Benson, Allan L. *Daniel Webster.* 1929.
Benton, Joel. *Life of Phineas T. Barnum.* 1891.
Benton, Thomas Hart. *Thirty Years in the United States Senate.* 1854.
Binkley, Wilfred E. *American Political Parties, Their Natural History.* 1944.
Botsford, Margaret. *The Reign of Reform or Yankee Doodle Court.* 1830.
Bradford, Alden. *History of the Federal Government for Fifty Years, 1789-
    1839.* 1840.
Bradsher, Earl L. *Matthew Carey.* 1912; reprinted 1933.
Brant, Irving. *The Fourth President, James Madison.* 1970.
Brennan, J. Fletcher. *A General History of Freemasonry.* 1871.
Bryan, Wilhemus Bogart. *A History of the National Capital.* 1916.
Buell, Augustus C. *History of Andrew Jackson.* 1904.
Burke, Edmund. *Correspondence.* 1844.
Burke, Pauline Wilcox. *Emily Donelson of Tennessee.*
Burr, Nelson R. *A Critical Bibliography of Religion in America.* 1961.
Burt, Nathaniel. *First Families.* 1970.
Carne, William F. *Life and Times of William Cranch.* 1869.
Clarke, Allen C. *Life and Letters of Dolly Madison.* 1914.
Cobbett, William. *Life of Andrew Jackson.* 1834.
Coit, Margaret L. *John C. Calhoun.* 1950.
Cousins, Norman. *In God We Trust.* 1958.
Craven, Avery O. *Letters—Andrew Jackson.* 1933.
Crawford, Mary. *Romantic Days in the Early Republic.* 1912.
Dexter, Franklin. *Biographical Sketches of the Graduates of Yale College.*
Donald & Donald. *The Adams Papers.* 1864.
Douglas, Emily Taft. *Remember the Ladies.* 1966.

Durbin, Louise. *Inaugural Cavalcade.* 1971.

Dwight, Henry Otis. *The Centennial History of the American Bible Society.* 1916.

Eaton, John Henry. *The Complete Memoirs of Andrew Jackson.* 1878.

Eaton, Margaret O'Neal. *Autobiography of Peggy Eaton.* 1932.

Ely, Ezra Stiles. *A Discourse: The Duty of Christian Freemen to Elect Christian Rulers, Delivered on the Fourth of July, 1827 in the Seventh Presbyterian Church in Philadelphia, with an Appendix Designed to Vindicate the Liberty of Christians and of the American Sunday School Union.* 1828.

Ely, Ezra Stiles. *Memoirs of His Own Life and Times.*

Ely, Ezra Stiles. *The Second Journal of the Stated Preacher to the Hospital and Almhouse in New York City.* 1813.

Forney, John W. *Anecdotes of Public Man.* 1881.

Fox, L.H. *New York City Newspapers, 1820-1850.*

Fuess, Claude M. *The Life of Caleb Cushing.*

Furnas, J.C. *Goodbye to Uncle Tom.* 1956.

Gibbons, Hughes Oliphant. *A History of Old Pine Street.* 1905.

Goldberg, Isaac. *Major Noah: The Life of Mordecai Noah.* 1936.

Goven, Thomas. *Nicholas Biddle.* 1959.

Griffith, Lucille. *Letters from Alabama.* 1969.

Griffin, Clifford S. *Their Brother's Keeper, Moral Stewardship in the United States, 1800-1865.* 1960.

Guillet, Edwin C. *The Great Migration.* 1937.

Hall, Margaret Esther. *The Hamilton Reader.* 1957.

Hamilton, Alexander. *His Works.*

Hamilton, Allan McLane. *The Intimate Life of Alexander Hamilton.* 1910.

Hart, Albert Bushnell. *American History Told by Contemporaries, 1783-1845.* 1901.

Heiskell, Samuel Gordon. *Andrew Jackson and Early Tennessee History.* 1901.

Henkels, Stan V., Jr. *Andrew Jackson and the Bank of the United States.* 1928.

Herring, Hubert. *A History of Latin America.* 1968.

Hitz, Ralph. *The House of Barine.* 1949.

Howe, M.D. *Life and Letters of George Bancroft.*

Jackson, Andrew IV. *Andrew Jackson, President of the United States.* 1925.

Jackson, George Stuyvessant. *The Uncommon Scold.* 1937.

James, Bessie Rowland. *Anne Royall's USA.* 1972.

James, James Boyer. *Notable American Women, 1607-1950.* 1971.

James, Marquis. *The Life of Andrew Jackson.* 1937.

Jenkins, John Stilwell. *Life of Andrew Jackson.* 1847.

Johnston, Joana. *Runaway to Heaven.* 1963.

Jones, K.V. *John Quincy Adams, Chronology, Documents and Bibliography.* 1970.

Kane, Harnett T. and Parry, Albert. *The Scandalous Mrs. Blackford.* 1951.

Kendall, Amos. *Autobiography.*

Lynch, Denis Tilden. *An Epoch and a Man.* 1929.

McAllister, J.T. *Virginia Militia in the Revolutionary War.* 1913.

MacDonald, William. *Jacksonian Democracy.* 1906.

Mahon, John K. *The War of 1812.* 1972.

Miller, William. *A New History of the United States.* 1958.

Nicolay, Helen. *Our Capital on the Potomac.* 1924.

Noah, Mordecai. *Gleanings from a Gathered Harvest.* 1845.

Parton, James. *Life of Andrew Jackson.* 1859.
Poore, Ben Perley. *Reminiscences.* 1886.
Porter, David Dixon. *David Porter 1780-1843.* 1929.
Pickering, David. *Address Delivered Before the Citizens of Providence in the Universalist Chapel on the Fiftieth Anniversary of the American Independence.* 1818.
Porter, Sarah Harvey. *The Life and Times of Anne Royall.* 1909.
Quincy, Josiah. *Figures of the Past.* 1883. *Memoir of the Life of John Quincy Adams.* 1859.
Rebold and Brennan. *A General History of Freemasonry.* 1871.
Remini, Robert V. *Andrew Jackson and the Bank War.* 1967.
Rider's Washington, edited by F.T. Cooper. 1924.
Royall, William L. *Andrew Jackson and the Bank of the United States.* 1880.
St. John de Crèvecoeur, J.H. *Letters from an American Farmer and Sketches of Eighteenth Century America.* 1963.
Scharf and Westcott. *History of Philadelphia.* 1884.
Schlesinger, Arthur M., Jr. *The Age of Jackson.* 1945. *The Chief Executive.* 1965.
Shimmell, L.S. *A History of Pennsylvania.* 1900.
Singleton, Esther. *The Story of the White House.* 1907.
Smith, Margaret Bayard. *The First Forty Years on Washington Society.* 1908.
Smith, Walter B. *Economic Aspects of the Second Bank of the United States.* 1953.
Stillson and Hughan. *History of the Ancient and Honroable Fraternity of Free and Accepted Masons.* 1906.
Stokes, Anson Phelps. *Church and State in the United States.* 1950.
Stone, Irving. *The President's Lady* (novel). 1951.
Tocqueville, Alexis de. *Democracy in America.*
Tyler, Alice F. *Freedom's Fremont.* 1944.
Van Duesen, Glyndon Q. *The Jacksonian Era.* 1959.
Vexler, Robert. *Vice Presidents and Cabinet Members.* 1975.
Voorhees, J.S. *Reports of Cases Civil and Criminal, District of Columbia Courts, 1801-1841, 1852-1853.*
Wagenknecht, Edward. *Harriet Beecher Stowe.* 1965.
Walker, Peter. *Punishment.* 1973.
Wandell, Samuel H. and Minnigerode, Meade. *Aaron Burr.* 1927.
Warfel, Harry R. *Noah Webster.* 1936.
Wharton, Anne Hollingsworth. *Social Life in the Early Republic.* 1902.
White, Leonard D. *The Jacksonians.* 1954.
Wilburn, Jean Alexander. *Biddle's Bank: The Crucial Years.* 1967.
Wilson, Rufus Rockwell. *Washington, The Capital City.* 1902.
Wolf, C.S. *Mordecai Noah.* 1897.
Woodward, Helen Beal. *The Bold Women.* 1953.
Wright, Chester W. *Economic History of the United States.* 1941.
Wright, Richardson. *Forgotten Ladies.* 1928.

Index